DANGEROUS
ILLUSIONS

Vitaly Malkin

Dangerous Illusions

Translated and adapted from Russian

Arcadia Books Ltd
www.arcadiabooks.co.uk

First published in the United Kingdom 2018
Copyright © Vitaly Malkin 2018

Vitaly Malkin has asserted his moral right to be
identified as the author of this work in accordance with
the Copyright, Designs and Patents Act, 1988.

A catalogue record for this book is available from the British Library.

ISBN 978-1-911350-28-6

Foreword

My editor says that this is not a regular book like he is used to publishing, but a battle cry or a call to arms (*combat et cri de guerre*). Generally speaking, I agree with this assessment of the main message of the book: today the chimeras are back; they have invaded our lives and we cannot survive without a war against them. Chimeras are all the ideologies, traditions and customs that do not come from our consciousness or individual experiences. They are all that interfere with our nature, mind, freedom and earthly happiness. The amazing thing is that, over the last 10 to 20 years, our civilisation and our minds have made phenomenal progress; we have powerful social networks, artificial intelligence and forthcoming flights to Mars. At the same time, it has become difficult and dangerous for a person to live on earth without his mind regressing under the onslaught of dark forces – chimeras that pull us back into barbarism and savagery.

I blew the horn and went to war with the chimeras, although I understand well that I will not become a commander; there are so many chimeras around and they are so strong that in order to win, it would take an entire army of politicians, philosophers, historians and, simply, volunteers – an army I do not have. All I can do is to call things by their proper names and encourage people to do everything possible to protect themselves from the influence of chimeras. Although I do lead, albeit in my small but personal war; my charitable foundation Espoir ('Hope') quite successfully fights with extreme forms of female circumcision in Ethiopia, in the Somali and Afar regions, under the auspices of UNICEF. Ten years ago, I happened upon this criminal infamy, still thriving on our planet, and I cannot escape from the shock it has brought upon me, as if a part of my brain was infected with some form of leprosy and died off. It was from then on that I began to seriously reflect on the essence of man, and the influence of pagan beliefs on cultural traditions and religions within human civilisation.

In a more general context, I perceive this book as 'stolen air' – an expression I am borrowing from Osip Mandelstam. This outstanding Russian poet witnessed terrible famine and cannibalism from 1923 in Crimea, an area primarily populated by Tatars at that time. In 1933, he wrote a poem about Stalin that became one of the most famous poems of the twentieth century: 'We are living, but can't feel the land where we stay.' It was Mandelstam who said that free self-expression in a non-free country reminds one of 'stolen air' (which I breathed enough in the 'free' Soviet Union). He paid for all he wrote and said with his life, dying in the Gulag in 1938. The burning, uncontrollable desire to write the book came to me only when I felt that there was no air to breathe. I felt that if I did not do something, I would lose my inner balance and start hating not the chimeras, but myself. And then, I would definitely 'blow up'.

Today, after five years of living in Europe, I increasingly feel that this notorious 'stolen air' moved here with me, and I have developed an interest in understanding how people breathe it here. Or do they prefer not to breathe this air, but rather hide in an ivory tower? Look around. Do you really not see how the situation in our world has radically changed and become lethal for us all?

The powerful light of the Enlightenment turned into a barely glowing one, indicating the withering of the secular world and the radical strengthening of the religious world. The main provision of the French *laïcité* of 1905 is 'The Republic doesn't recognize any cult'. If this is the case, then soon they will forget about this law at all. Religious obscurantism is back and, if we do nothing, it will gladly destroy not only our present, but also the future of our children.

Our civil society is bent before the chimeras, weakened and split, and with each day the split deepens and expands. We are being divided into separate tribes, each of which is formed around its own One God. The policy of multiculturalism failed miserably, and the best culture in the world faded away in meaningless debates. When you read these debates, you begin to doubt the common sense not only of their participants, but also of yourself.

Totalitarian political correctness killed the beloved child of the great French Revolution – a magnificent critical tradition of free-thinking. Freedom of thought and speech shrank to the size of a flowerpot on the balcony, and disgusting hypocrisy destroyed our existence from top to bottom. And yet, instead of crying 'Crush the infamy', society calls for conformism and boundless respect for religious ideals that are alien to us.

Was it possible to imagine something like this only a couple of decades ago? How could I resist trying to protect my mind? I could not resist. I stopped doing anything else and devoted a few years of my life to this book, which at first glance has nothing to do with my previous occupation as a banker and senator

*
* *

No serious book in humanities can bypass the religion that moulded our culture and continues to actively influence our civilisation. I was always fascinated by the fact that mankind has spent trillions of hours, hundreds of millions of lives, and a huge amount of resources on various religious cults. Such a giant mountain of emotions and hopes, this peak of senselessness and a feat of worship, should not go unnoticed, and so my goal was to assess what mankind found in these cults and whether such an enormous waste of resources was justified. Therefore, I contrast two systems of values.

One of them takes the world as it is and defends the primacy of human values over all others. This means that only man himself is able to create a practical morality, and to separate what is allowed from what is forbidden in his personal and social life. Hedonism, resting on natural human features – corporality, sensuality and enjoyment – is considered in this system as indispensable for achieving social progress and has only one limit: respect for the interests of another person.

The other does not recognise the natural human values. Instead it rests on ideals and revelations that lie outside of man, denounces hedonism as the worst enemy of a religious community, and brings the artificial rules of life based on divine commandments into the world, corresponding to them the absolute notions of Good and Evil.

I'm not going to try to prove to you who is right and why; such an attempt would be doomed to failure before it even began, but it was important for me to understand which one of these two systems makes a person stronger and happier and which one people should follow in their life. Such a goal was not possible to achieve within the framework of one discipline, even such a respected one as philosophy. What we need is a symbiosis of all human sciences, which is what the discipline called 'general culture' (*la culture générale*) does. It does not divide the world into subsections and does not rely on separate 'foundational ideas,' since there are too many ideas in the world around us and all of them are mixed up together. For this reason, I did not want to artificially link the chapters of the book with a rigid causal link while discussing different variations of the same thesis. The book did not suffer from this in any way, because its main task is to consistently expose some of the most common chimeras – parasites that have been torturing humanity for thousands of years. The rest of them I will explore in the following books.

An honest analysis of monotheism should begin with a simple and obvious question: what does it give us and what does it take from us? I am ready to recognise monotheism as a rallying social force that forms moral guidelines. I do not deny the intensity of feelings and emotions that some people experience from the idea of the existence of the Supreme Being – the Protector, who is able to fill one with 'spirituality,' bring comfort in difficult life situations, help to endure extreme suffering, prepare for the most difficult event – one's own death – and bring one into the eternal Bright Kingdom. Religion certainly plays the role of a soothing and analgesic remedy for a huge mass of humanity, something like a very strong painkiller. Who wants to part with this obsession and accept that everything will inevitably end with worms? I would first publicly burn this book and rush into the nearby church to put my tent there if the existence of the Kingdom of God and eternal life would be guaranteed by fifty per cent, even only 5 per cent.

But the faith in the One God, like all other things and concepts, has its dark side, which while being bigger than the bright side, is not socially acceptable to talk about. All religious preachers enthusiastically tell us about the gifts of the One God, but none of them talk about what people have to pay for these gifts. There is nothing free of charge, neither in material life, nor in spiritual life; we have to pay for everything, especially for such a thing as hope for an eternal afterlife. Not for the afterlife itself, but for the hope of it. Alas, the promised joys are fictitious (we can also recall the promises of passionate love and fidelity to the grave). Worms are feasible, but the promise of an afterlife is not.

This chimerical tale costs a lot. For the sake of its maintenance, religion has made man – a perfect biological machine and incomparable mind – an imperfect puppet. Man is divided into two irreconcilable halves – the soul and the body – which destroys the natural harmony with oneself and the environment. Religion forced humans to give up natural morality and many pleasures, and replaced them with a senseless waste of precious time for daily worship of God and strict observance of His commandments. And most importantly, humans were instilled with panic and fear of the possibility of not being 'saved' and receiving an after-punishment instead of 'resurrection' in accordance with the concepts of good and evil described in holy books, which radically differ from the concepts given to man by his nature. The human, in fact, is pushed into the abyss; religion asks us to exchange human life for the illusion of life after the grave.

In earthly life, a person does not receive any reward from religion, either. Spiritual life as an act of creation is impossible in the religions of the Revelation. When all the values have already been created and are eternally set in the Holy Books, where is the space for creative potential? It is also impossible to use a religious base to build an idea of absolute morality, which, at the same time, all religions of the Revelation are so proud of. Each of them rests on its own One God, is intolerant to other opinions, divides believers into 'us' and 'strangers' and opposes groups of people to others. Otherwise, why did they fight each other for millennia and continue to fight today? There is only one thing that unites them: the doctrine of the fundamental insignificance of man in the face of God, who has the last word in all affairs of human existence, and the burning desire to break free from the personal sphere of the individual believing person, which is their rightful place, and to penetrate into the public sphere of the whole state.

Such a situation is quite understandable; the ideal is unattainable in principle and it was this principled unattainability that became the source of all possible illusions and the driving force of all atrocities committed in human history. The unattainable and inhuman set sky-high goals and always violently destroy the truly human around themselves, suppressing the healthy human desire to live a natural life and gradually improve the world around.

In my childhood and many years after, I remained indifferent to religion; my family did not have God, and I did not like the gods of other people. But in the process of writing this book I felt the existence of a God-Creator that was common for all people, who came to us beforehand in different pagan beliefs and radically differs from the One God of the Abrahamic religions. God the Creator is only the Creator, but not the Ruler and certainly not the Elder Brother-Dictator, who is 'sold' to us by the Abrahamic religions. My God-Creator never dictated any divine Revelations to anyone, did not claim to have created a man out of nothing in His image and likeness (in fact, what's so terrible about being different from Him?); nor did He insist on our human insignificance, and He always respected the human mind. His existence does not exert any influence on the life of the person (created by Him); He cannot see us, He cannot hear us, He cannot read our thoughts, and He has not promised us eternal life; and, most importantly, He is useless to pray to. He will not help and will not change anything in a human life. My God-Creator is God-the-beacon, the centre of heat and light, and fire. A person can come to Him to be inspired and get warm. A person might choose not to go and no one will punish him for it; never has there existed Paradise or Hell.

My convictions do not please me at all; if the all-powerful, all-seeing and all-knowing One God existed, He would certainly actively interfere in earthly affairs and we would live much better lives. But He is not around us and for this reason we have to blame only man for the existence of evil.

■ The Story of this Book ■

This book began with an accident. Many important and unimportant events begin with an accident that clears the way for the inevitable.

Accidentally, because of the rain, I saw a Hollywood film about family love. I have a great respect for love – there is no feeling more natural and valuable – and I have always admired its ability to survive despite all the difficulties of a long-term marriage. However, this film was filled with so many nauseating lies, and so aggressively imposed sugary and dreamlike family values on the viewer that I left the theatre with a sharp feeling, as if I could not breathe; all the diversity and richness of a romantic relationship was reduced to a vulgar and hypocritical romantic ideal. I purposely use the word 'vulgar'; the primitive idealisation of human life depreciates natural values and discourages any desire to strive for them. Almost immediately, I felt an irresistible desire to understand how other people live and breathe in similar situations. What do they think about each other and how do they live together – in truth or in lies?

In the lives of three-dozen married couples I know, I have not witnessed much lightness in their relationships or happy family values. It is possible that I simply could not see these things behind a pile of problems and mutual irritation. All I could see was a striking disparity between reality and the ideals imposed on us. The tale of loyalty until death, which is so sweet to believe at the church altar, inexorably turned into a hateful reality of soul-eating hypocrisy, betrayal at every opportunity, and exhausting quarrels.

And, the strangest and most surprising thing is that no one in particular is to blame for this – something is wrong in the kingdom of marriage itself. Taken by a desire to help newlyweds to find true Hollywood happiness, I have decided to look at the institution of marriage with an impartial gaze of an alien looking for the origins of human monogamy. Pure science: without looking back to the past, without limitations of traditions, piety and emotions. Is this not how a real scientist should behave, while watching the process of reproduction of unicellular organisms under a microscope?

After getting acquainted with basic research on the topic of marriage, I reached the conclusion that all of it satisfies me in much the same way as does sexual life after thirty years of marriage. My enthusiasm for studying it was only enough for the first few months, after which I realised that my idea failed. Recognised scientists did not study marital problems, not because of an oversight, but because of a clear understanding that marriage itself is not an independent discipline; all of its problems are inevitable and, while being vital for each individual, are completely insignificant for the human population as a whole. It is quite possible that this explains why ancient philosophers almost completely ignored the important topic. The great Socrates, as he almost always did, said it best. When asked if one should marry or not, he gave a quick and brilliant answer: both options are equivalent in their consequences, since in any case one will have to regret it.

As a result, the importance of the problem of marriage finally faded in my eyes, from a high-priority research topic into something secondary. It became clear to me that the basis of the institution of marriage is not the couple, but the individual, and we need to start from other topics: human loneliness, secular and religious community, social norms and universal morality. In order to have the right to talk about the institution of marriage, it is necessary to involve the research of liberal arts and social sciences. And if one really wants to research this topic, then there is more than enough of material for a few human lives and dozens of doctoral dissertations. The volume and complexity of the task has increased enormously, and the familial-marital problems it contains are not the most important or the largest part.

For a long time, I did almost nothing, trying to decide whether I wanted to continue writing this book and if I had enough strength and patience for such a large amount of work. Could I see the world not through the perspective of great ideas, but with my own eyes? Would it be possible for me to clearly and succinctly talk about fundamental philosophical, historical, religious and social phenomena without losing all the wealth of their content along the way? Or was it better to forget this unrealisable idea and just enjoy the beach every day, especially since I live quite close to it?

Still, the ineradicable obstinacy that has been living in me since early childhood has not allowed me to retreat. If it worked out for others, then why would I not be able to do it? I began to slowly accumulate materials on different and, at first glance, incompatible topics related to each other only by my constantly changing interests, intuition and even caprices. I worked without any specific plan or clarity on where I would go next, what my book would be about, or whether it would be written at all. And then came the moment when the chaotic ideas surrounding me suddenly began to dissipate and I was seized with a clear, almost physiological sensation that my book as a whole was over and the one thing that remained was to write it. I was not deceived by that feeling: I wrote it.

But there was one more complication; even a superficial, brief statement of all collected materials would not fit into one book, and I could not for a long time agree to remove some of the content from it – it felt like cutting off my own hand. Such a book would be difficult to carry out of a bookstore. The only advantage would be that the book would protect from a bullet on occasion. I realised, reluctantly, that it was necessary to divide it into three separate books, the first of which you hold in your hands. I was especially worried about the choice of the name – since it is the beginning of everything, that initial will, the first knocking of wheels when a long-distance train departs. Pythagoras believed that the beginning is half the work, but Aristotle disagreed with him and believed that the beginning is even more than half. No wonder any professional publisher shouts himself hoarse when arguing with the author about the title, seeing in it half of the success or three quarters of the failure. In fact, the name reflects best the style of thinking of an author or, as happens quite often, the absence of both. Some of the names are so successful that they stand on an equal level with the rest of the content.

Gabriel Garcia Marquez called his famous novella *No One Writes to the Colonel*, and this title expressed the author's main idea so brilliantly that one could award him the Nobel Prize without any subsequent text. Eighteen-year-old Françoise Sagan titled her first novel *Hello, Sadness* (*Bonjour Tristesse*) and almost instantly turned from an unknown girl into a respected literary author.

I do not possess such bright talent and, therefore, after a long and painful search for a suitable title, I resorted to plagiarism and wanted to use as the title of the book the popular Spanish proverb '*El sueño de la razón produce monstruos*' (The sleep of reason produces monsters), which inspired Francisco Goya to create his most famous etching. I love the laconic imagery of Spanish proverbs and you will find a few more of them in epigraphs to the main chapters. It seemed to me that this proverb accurately reflects the main idea of this book: the sleep of the mind, that is, the refusal to perceive the world around as it is, costs a very high price to a man – he tries to find the omnipotent and all-knowing Teacher outside himself, to rely on something illusory, but finds only monsters – chimeras, devouring his life from the inside and out. Only the mind that never parts with its faithful friend and squire, common sense, is able to assess the surrounding reality and help us to find happiness in it. But then I felt ashamed of the plagiarism – a sure sign of lack of talent – and I came up with my own name for the book – *Dangerous Illusions*.

At first, I decided to publish the book under a pseudonym – John Doe – the traditional choice in cases when one wants to preserve the anonymity of a person who conveys important information or takes part in public discussions on sensitive issues. Anonymity, in my opinion, has major advantages for both the author and the reader. It allows the author to remain a ghost, who might be living anywhere in the world, and belong to any people, ethnicity, social group, or religion. The anonymous author does not need to tell the reader where he comes from, what languages he speaks, what he has done earlier, how he lived and what he believed in. With anonymity, it is difficult to blame such an author's prejudices and to reject all their arguments from the beginning without spending any effort to understand the essence of the matter, and, therefore, it is much easier for the author to address people directly.

It is good for the reader as well – they get rid of idle curiosity about the author's personality and do not get distracted from the book's content: information about the author is not only completely useless for understanding the ideas of the book, but also devalues these ideas. It tempts the reader to explain their appearance not by the objective reality and common sense of the author, but by his origin and way of life, which in my case has absolutely nothing to do with what I wanted to say and what I finally said. So then (in the case of anonymity) the reader has to deal with 'orphan' ideas, which, theoretically, induce in him an interest in reading and reflecting impartially on what has been read.

But then I rejected anonymity – would I really not be able to wake a reader's interest in reading and thinking by using my own name?

At the time of writing this book, I repeatedly asked myself the same question: Do I have the right, without having received any formal education in humanities, to engage in the most complex topics where the spheres of philosophy, history, anthropology and sociology intertwine? In the end, I still found an excuse for my literary impudence: my strong interest in the humanities that started in my early childhood, and the many thousands of books, articles and electronic publications that I read over seven years of work on this book. Of all these sources, I selected about eight thousand pages of material on specific topics, analysed them and used them to write this book. The bibliography included only a small fraction of all that I read.

Nevertheless, I decided to abandon any claims to the academic discourse, while retaining the main features of my scientific approach: an objective perception of reality, careful analysis of material, and strict systematisation of results. How else could it be done? To reveal the wide variety of all covered topics with due academic completeness would have been impossible for me – there would not be enough life or paper, but I have to convince the reader that I am familiar with the basic views of the greats and that I can defend my point of view. Taming my own ambitions allowed me to implement simple creative principles, quite natural for any book that does not have claims for academic excellence.

Firstly, I gave up on debates with other authors and references to them, which was very difficult for me, as it marked a radical departure from the scientific and publicistic canon. I felt that I was heretical, uttering my first blasphemy on the porch of the cathedral, then a freedom fighter, shouting a fiery appeal in the central square of a totalitarian state. However, I have no doubt about the admissibility and validity of my approach to presenting the material: the number of publications has grown so much that one can easily and quickly find one hundred convincing opinions 'for' and one hundred equally convincing opinions 'against' regarding any issue. (I myself can play the role of the Devil's advocate and bring as many objections as possible to my own arguments.)

Such a state of affairs turns into a problem for the reader: While stuck between the ideas of great thinkers taken out of context and contradicting each other, one cannot understand with whom and about what one should argue, and as a result the reader renounces his own opinion in favour of someone else's – capitulation before emptiness. In my case, it is different. I am perfectly aware of the diversity of existing opinions on all the topics touched in this book and, while I am not inclined to simplify the issues, I am tired of endless statements of 'on the one hand' and 'on the other hand' and I choose not to hide behind the opinions of others.

One should not think that the rejection of discussions with other authors made it easier for me to write. Rather, I lost a thick protective layer of other people's opinions and took upon myself a personal responsibility for the content of my texts. In short, I remain naked in the face of my clever reader.

Secondly, I did everything possible to avoid repetition, and usage of pseudoscientific words. But I do use a lot of sarcasm.

I'll start with my stance on repeating.

The main reason for repetition is a lack of organisation of the author, who quickly forgets what he wrote earlier. Or he does not believe in what he wrote and tries to convince himself and his reader by constant repetition of controversial thoughts (this is especially noticeable in religious texts and catechisms of totalitarian ideologies). We also can not exclude that the author considers his reader an idiot incapable of remembering and, in order to be understood, repeats the same thought many times, just as he did with himself at school. All these reasons have nothing to do with me: I am well-organised, believe in what I have written, and appreciate the intellectual abilities of my reader. So, if you see a repetition in the book, do not believe your eyes.

Regarding verbosity: I was always unpleasantly surprised by the presence of definitions for definitions sake and long complex sentences even in great philosophical texts, not to mention journalism. In the exact sciences, it is not customary to write like this – you will be ridiculed. This does not mean at all that I deliberately resorted to simplifying the material: there is a heavy responsibility for preserving the intellectual baggage accumulated by previous generations on my shoulders. But why not explain this baggage briefly and clearly? In ancient Rome, this style of presentation was called lapidary and was used to inscribe the facades of public buildings and monuments. The authors of the inscriptions had to answer to the people for every word: you can not erase anything off the stone. The remarkable tradition of saving thoughts and words was almost completely lost by the time of the invention of printing; the Romans did not share their skills with modern authors and editors. The verbosity of both is quite understandable; they are paid on the basis of the number of printed pages. No one pays anything to me for the amount written and I did not have any incentive in inflating the text – I inflated it on my own.

Regarding pseudoscientific words: many authors use them to demonstrate their intellectual superiority, persistently developing in the reader a sense of their lack of education and inferiority. Other authors themselves do not understand what they want to say and hide their misunderstanding and their inability to present the material simply and clearly behind a screen of words which are not used in everyday life, the exact meaning of which is difficult to find even in the most respected dictionaries. I am sure that any intellectual concept in the humanities can be clearly and fully explained by ordinary words, widely used in everyday life and understandable to any high school graduate. I began the crusade against inappropriate scientism with myself. At first, I pulled the essence and the basis of the 'quintessence' and then I locked the annoying 'sublimation' in the closet, which thanks to the classics of psychoanalysis almost completely buried healthy sexuality.

Regarding sarcasm: for me there are no 'untouchable topics', for, as the great Russian writer Dostoevsky said, 'if there is no God, then everything is allowed.' A free person has every right to openly discuss any topic and express his opinion in the way he wants. Otherwise, all the values of liberalism and democracy are worthless, even though we all paid dearly for them. Sarcasm reveals the essence of the issue better than any other technique, clearly expresses the speaker's position and is pleasant to literary taste. It was very widely used in the political life of Antiquity and was the hallmark of the best orators and thinkers of all time: Demosthenes and Cicero used it, Voltaire and Rabelais used it in their struggle against theology and her beloved daughter – scholasticism – and the great Einstein said: 'Two things are infinite: the universe and human stupidity; and I'm not sure about the universe!' So, in terms of sarcasm, I'm just a grateful student. In this book you will meet a lot of sarcasm in relation to the widespread dogma, ideals and customs. I understand that such a style can cause irritation and even accusations of libel, but I am ready to accept any justified challenge. My sarcasm does not aim to mock and destruct, but to purify and create; by challenging the reader, I help him to strengthen his ideals and his faith, that is, to better understand what he believes in, and also what he needs this faith for and what he can expect from it.

While I was writing this book, I desperately tried to bring everything to common sense – I did not see anything else that I could rely on. I often bring my statements to extreme conclusions, but I'm not at all ashamed of subjective exaggerations. All books in the world, including the sacred ones, are absolutely subjective and rely on some sort of ideology or religion. It is possible that somewhere I lost the logic of the presentation, and somewhere else I missed something or did not think it through. And the reader has the right to make judgements about the validity of my thesis and criticise me. I offer the reader my own clear and unequivocal opinion, invite him to argue with me, and will accept any of his assessments from admiration to hatred with gratitude. It would even be upsetting for me if such criticism was absent – that would be a sure sign of total indifference to the text. Nevertheless, I would like the criticism to be substantive and substantiated, which is impossible without reading first at least a small part of the sources mentioned in the bibliography or any other books on critically discussed topics, in order to avoid the situation that Sigmund Freud described: 'The weakness of my position does not imply a strengthening of yours.'

I believe that this book will be useful to you. Most importantly, it will save your valuable time, because almost every one of us insistently searches for the meaning of our short earthly existence or irrefutable proof of its senselessness, taking time off from our favorite pursuits. I spent several years of my life reading thousands of sources, developing a cohesive concept and writing it on paper. You will only need a few days to read it, so you would be exchanging several days for several years. It may also happen that after reading the book you will come to the conclusion that it is superficial and filled with untenable arguments, obvious delusions and slander of the holy.

CHAPTER I

Reason
or Chimeras

Cría cuervos, y te sacarán los ojos.
Feed crows, and they'll peck your eyes out.
Spanish proverb

What is a chimera? The word 'chimera' comes from Ancient Greek, and in ancient mythology was a monster. Chimera is first described by Homer in the eighth century BC as a fire-breathing creature with a lion's head, goat's body, and serpent's tail. The philosopher Hesiod describes the leonine part of Chimera's torso at the front as being the size of a horse, and the back part as having a goat's head in the middle, with a snake in place of a tail completing the image. All three heads breathe fire. Likewise, the fourth-century poet Virgil had no doubt that Chimera was an ungainly, aggressive monster with three heads on a single body. Chimera was an object of terror and disgust for the Ancients because it embodied entirely incompatible elements, denoting a return to the primordial chaos, and symbolising the destruction of natural harmony and the cessation of rational thought – all objectionable states in the ancient value system. Ancient reason had every confidence in itself and so defined a 'chimera' as anything that was not reasonable. This chapter deals with chimeras, our book's target. Those chimeras that, though they poison our lives, we continue to feed and nurture – until it is too late, and they pick out our eyes. Ever since we were children and until we die, we can be attacked by these chimeras.

In principle, this affinity is unsurprising, not to say expected; first and last, things are connected by an invisible but nevertheless secure thread. Every birth carries in itself the inevitability of death. It's the same sort of thing as the advice given to children by parents and insurance companies; we are urged to think about our pensions and death while still in our childhood, to make a provision for our old age and save for our own funerals.

Chimera of Arezzo, 15th century, bronze.

18

■ Meet the Chimeras ■

A few years ago, I spent a fortnight travelling around Morocco, accompanied by my son and his girlfriend. The start was inauspicious; some know-it-all advised us to begin in Tangier: it's the Moroccan gateway to Europe and a stone's thrown from Spain and Gibraltar. The advice turned out to be useless. We found ourselves in a noisy, confusing and filthy city. Morocco, however, turned out to be a fascinating place with much to stimulate the normally sluggish tourist brain. The most remarkable feature was the way Islam was wondrously combined with a European-style freedom of manners. The peaceful coexistence of women clad in their niqabs and the brightly dressed, mini-skirt-wearing girls with loose hair surprised us at first, but we grew used to it. It reminded us of those un-combinable elements from our chemistry lessons. We went from the extraordinarily beautiful Fez, a focal point of early Islamic culture untouched by time, to the modern hubs of business life that are Rabat and Casablanca, to Marrakech, with its justly famous gardens and royal hotels, and to the resort city of Agadir. We spent our last two nights in a tiny hotel made of four tents in the Sahara desert.

On the final day of our trip, our Bedouin driver, burned by the unforgiving sun, was driving us to the airport in his jeep. The journey was a long one – over two and a half hours right through the desert. There were no roads there in the usual understanding of the word, or, more accurately, there was a multitude of them, as with no rain in the area everyone just crosses the desert where they please.

Our Bedouin turned out to be rather uncommunicative, while we chatted merrily amongst ourselves and recalled our simple Moroccan adventures. Suddenly, he stretched his hand forward and said, 'Look!' The splashing sea was right in front of me, a few hundred metres away, and what a sea.

This sea was indistinguishable from a real one; it was a deep azure in colour, with a well-defined sandy bank and even a rippled surface. It was reluctant to make our acquaintance, floating lazily away from our gradual approach and keeping us at a safe distance.

We'd all read about such optical illusions and knew perfectly well that there was no sea in this heart of the desert, nor could there ever be one. Nevertheless, dismissing this mirage was incredibly difficult. All five of us were seeing the same thing and this conferred unprecedented authenticity on our 'common' sea. (Later my son confessed to looking for seagulls above the water; after all, what kind of sea is it without seagulls?) Nevertheless, for some time my reason deserted me; I was ready to believe in anything at all – ghosts, demons, or aliens.

The mirage didn't last long; fifteen minutes later, by the side of the village, the path became firm and the sand dunes vanished into the hot dry air of the Moroccan desert, taking the azure sea with them. This was my first encounter with a mirage, the simplest, friendliest and least dangerous to the human mind of all chimeras. One can only imagine how hard it would have been for a simple nomad to deal with a similar illusion many millennia ago, and consequently how easy it would have been for him to believe in the existence of miracles and gods.

This, my first encounter with a chimera, proved highly significant for my life, for it was this that first moved me to contemplate the fragility of the human mind. I began searching for information pertaining to human reason that same evening.

■ Reason or Faith? ■

With some condescension, various encyclopaedias and dictionaries of philosophy make it clear to us that we learn about the world by our reason alone. Reason enables man to navigate through abstract notions, to think critically, to establish logical connections between phenomena and concepts, and then use these connections to formulate general laws, worldview principles and ethical positions that guide his own conduct in life.

If reason represents our highest level of knowledge, then why is it so fragile and vulnerable and easily lost? Why is it that even the tiniest and briefest mirage is able to rob us of our critical facilities by which we analyse the world around us?

In order to answer this question, I have to ask another: What is the opposite of reason? The first thing that springs to mind is that reason is opposed by foolishness, but this would be a wrong answer because foolishness is the opposite of wisdom, not reason.

The opposite of reason is faith. I haven't just made a mistake and will happily repeat myself: Faith is the antithesis of reason. Reason and faith live together as close neighbours but exist in a sort of anti-phase – the moment reason weakens, faith immediately becomes stronger and rears its head and vice versa.

Faith is a particular psychological state that is characterised by a readiness to accept any idea at face value. Sometimes it is even worse than that, and an idea that is a priori un-provable is accepted as true. Faith doesn't want to be encumbered by the burden of proof. Usually, faith doesn't just accept an entirely unfounded thesis as true, but actually sees the absence of evidence as valuable in itself.

> Religious faith is the strongest of all faiths. It asserts the existence of supernatural things that cannot be explained by reason alone. Religious faith denies all common sense and the sum of human experience, which are replaced by the illusion of the existence of a Higher Being, the embodiment of absolute truth, trustworthiness, and the only reference for debates on the nature of good and evil. Today, a vast multitude of people prefers to live in accordance with this gigantic illusion rather than in the tangible and visible reality that surrounds them. Gustave Le Bon has this say on the matter: Of all the factors in the development of civilizations, illusions are perhaps the most powerful. It was an illusion that built up the pyramids and covered Egypt for five thousand years with colossal stone monuments. It was an illusion that, in the Middle Ages, raised our gigantic cathedrals and induced the Western world to dispute the possession of a tomb with the East. It is the pursuit of illusions that has founded the religions which exert their influence on half of humanity and founded or destroyed the vastest empires. It is not in the pursuit of truth, but in that of error that humanity has expended the most efforts.

Le Bon's contemporary, Sigmund Freud, claimed that humans exert themselves most in the defense of their religious illusions because otherwise their whole world would collapse around them and they would be forced to question everything.

So it's hardly surprising that I decided to look at the unfamiliar world of illusion more closely; I've wondered for a long time what sustains it and I wanted to check my resistance to it at the same time. I'll begin with reason. Without a clear understanding of reason, defining chimeras is impossible.

■ In the Ancient World, ■ Reason was a Superstar

Man is the measure of all things: of the existence of the things that are and the non-existence of the things that are not.
Protagoras

Antique civilisation could justifiably be called a civilisation since the human mind had a cult status. The cult of reason was the main source of pride to the Ancient World, with rationality in everything as its basic principle of daily existence. Even today, a large proportion of humanity, reared on a diet of chimeras from childhood, is no more rational than the Ancient Greek civilisation. This is true notwithstanding all the attractions of our modern civilisation: aeroplanes, cars, social networks, and mobile phones.

Reason was responsible for the creation of a civilisation so sophisticated that its fruits are still enjoyed by us even to this day. Its most significant achievement was the emergence of the truly great ancient philosophy which succeeded in producing general laws dealing with the material world and developed a system of proof to support them.

The celebration of reason seen in the culture of Antiquity was the logical extension of its anthropocentric approach. After all, reason is Man's one distinguishing feature, the thing which makes Man human and allows him to learn about the world.

It's important to acknowledge the direct correlation of this cult of reason with the weak influence that religion exerted on Man's life in the Ancient World. In the 800 years of existence of the highly developed Graeco-Roman civilisation, the concept of the One God never took hold. Yet, nobody could say that this ancient civilisation was populated by idiots; even if they hadn't thought of this by themselves, they could have easily borrowed this astonishing concept either from Jews or, later, from Christians.

However, they did have the cult of reason. The great Epicurus writes in his *Letter to Menoeceus*: that 'wisdom is a more precious thing even than philosophy; from it spring all the other virtues'. And the equally important Roman philosopher Seneca, alive in the early Christian era, states firmly that 'if you would have all things under your control, put yourself under the control of reason; if reason becomes your ruler, you will become the ruler of many'. A century and a half later, the emperor-philosopher Marcus Aurelius concurred: 'every man's intelligence is a god'.

An absence of God in their lives didn't hinder the ancient philosophers at all. Anaximander of Miletus, for example, anticipated the main concepts of a whole range of disciplines as far back as the sixth century BC: cosmology that stated that the universe is born, matures, and dies; physics that developed the law of conservation of matter; philosophy that proposed a theory of movement whereby any state moves to its exact opposite, which is essentially dialectics and a starting point on the road to the 'unity and struggle of opposites'.

The pagan worldview really did operate according to the principles of dialectics, viewing the state as a union of two opposing tendencies – order and chaos. The healthy balance between the two was thought to underpin the normal cycle of life.

We shouldn't think that the Ancient Greeks exalted reason just on a whim, 'for the sake of art'. On the contrary, they did so for understandable and selfish reasons, common to all normal people: They firmly believed that human survival and personal happiness were found in reason alone. Happiness is the result of a reasonable view of the world.

I don't need to prove to my reader that everything happens for a reason, but how did reason in the Ancient World achieve its superstar status?

The answer is important not only in order to understand the way the ancient mind functioned, but also for the later comparisons with the principles behind monotheistic cultures, especially Christian ones. From a contemporary point of view, the points outlined below are hardly original or in need of any commentary or explanation, but back then they would have appeared revolutionary and were entirely repudiated by the Christian civilisation that followed:

1. Irrationality reigned supreme in the Ancient World; events and phenomena occurred not according to objective or logical laws, but in obedience to the will of both a multitude of mythological deities and Man himself. A good harvest, an effective hunt, or even a death were all predetermined by the fulfilment of certain rituals, or else the occurrence of unforeseen events such as the breaking of a pot or the dropping of a piece of bread butter-side down. The French ethnologist Levy-Bruhl called this approach 'the principle of participation'.

In only four or five centuries (from 800-700 to 400-300 BC) the Greek civilisation completed a tremendous journey, moving to an objectively rational thought process away from the irrational and mythologised thinking that was quick to ascribe all world events to the will of the gods.

2. The ancient mind's particular efficacy can be explained by the lack of constraints imposed on it by religious dogma or eternal immutable divine truths. Ancient philosophy sought to find a rational explanation for different phenomena without resorting to religion, and thus it sought to identify a purely human morality. It was reason, autonomous and self-sufficient reason, rather than faith that was the main arbiter in pronouncing judgement. The main academic discipline of the Age of Antiquity was not theology, as became the case in subsequent years, but philosophy. And it is well known that philosophy's preferred method is to start at ground zero and question everything.

3. The vast majority of trends in ancient philosophy endowed reason alone with the ability to impart knowledge to men and to provide a practical guide to a successful and happy earthly existence. Knowledge was limited by the material world around Man and was considered the highest authority in settling all questions pertaining to human life, being commensurable with the body; the body and mind are indivisible and die at the same time. Reason emanates from the body, which is why a mind never struggles against the body and its instincts and needs.

4. The flourishing of ancient culture in general, and in philosophy in particular, can be explained by the complete tolerance people then showed towards anything novel or different – new concepts about the creation of the world, new religions, gods, or simply alternative points of view. The ancient philosophers regarded individual human consciousness as the seat of higher reason, the basis of all judgements, and the criterion for establishing the truth. For this reason it was believed to be important to allow individuals complete freedom of thought and expression. In Plato's *Theaetetus*, Protagoras says that 'there are two opposing judgements to every question' and 'as each thing appears to me, so it is for me, and as it appears to you, so it is to you'. I must note for the sake of fairness that such relativist sophistry wasn't appreciated by all educated Greeks and that the Sophists themselves were frequently criticised for their lack of principles and their ability to prove anything they liked.

5. Ancient culture was competitive, but the Olympic Games were not the only arena for contest. Above all there was lively competition between philosophical concepts

relating to ontology and the cosmos as a whole. New ideas critiqued the old, presenting an updated view of the world, and rather than seeing this criticism as a threat to society's foundations, it was considered an absolutely essential tool for its development.

6. In Antiquity, reason was placed higher than ethics and was itself a source of ethical standards. Reason fulfilled the role of Man's personal 'higher judge' and helped him to create an individual scale of values and morality. I must disappoint those of you who now shut your eyes in horror, imagining the streets of Ancient Rome and Athens awash with orgiastic crime; in fact these societies were distinguished by being highly ordered and having a particularly low level of crime. Socrates was wont to place morality in the sphere of human experience and considered it subject to rational examination. The choice between different kinds of pleasure or between pleasure and suffering is based on reason alone, and therefore morality is subject to reason. To be wise is the same as to be moral; a choice justified by morality will concur with a decision based on reason.

Seneca adopts an altogether harsher position in this matter; by placing a particular emphasis on individual reason, he anticipates future debates between the Pagans and Christians.

> Reason, however, is surely the governing element in such a matter as this; as reason has made the decision concerning the happy life, and concerning virtue and honour also, so she has made the decision with regard to good and evil.
>
> But we shall be healed, provided only that we separate ourselves from the vulgar.

Thus did the Ancients place reason as highest on the scale of human values. The basis of any moral code is in human values and deducing what this basis should be is a matter for reason. All things – morality included – have to account for themselves before reason.

One can confidently say that the unfettered thought of the Graeco-Roman philosophers cultivated the intellect of all civilisation. By relying on nothing but reason they managed to develop the human intellect. The evolution of the prosimian *Homo superstitiosus* into a creature capable of superlative thought, the man of reason that is *Homo sapiens*, was thus complete. Thereafter, beyond the Age of Antiquity, there began an unstoppable downward movement which lasted for centuries. Pythagoras, my favourite since school days, once said that 'a place without numbers or rational measures is the dwelling place of chaos and chimeras'. I too reject chimeras from my system of values. When chimeras take hold of Man he is thrown back into the primitive thought processes of a savage and he begins to torment his mind. The best and the most vivid illustration of this is the chimera of religious belief. I've coined the term 'religiosus' precisely to describe such a person. In the next section I attempt to examine the process by which the reasonable man of Antiquity, intent on creating things of value, turned into a religious man intent on creating chimeras. How and why did *Homo sapiens* become *Homo religiosus*?

■ Homo Religiosus's Ascension, ■
or, a Brief History of the Depreciation of Reason

Homo religiosus, a religious man, first came into being and became established as a feature of Judaism, but it was only later, within Christianity and Islam, that it assumed its full power and might.

At first glance, the idea of the One God appears altogether positive, progressive, and useful. In place of the perpetually squabbling pantheon of amoral deities, the believer was offered God-as-an-Idea, personified as an exclusive abstract order and a unity of all being. It also offered exclusively absolutist morality and law, capable of uniting humanity in the name of common earthly values and a bright future beyond the grave.

However, when you dig a bit deeper, it appears a lot less attractive. It is, unfortunately, a fact that the vast majority of progressive, positive, and useful human endeavours have a tendency to come to a bad end – the road to hell is paved with good intentions.

Against all expectations, the noble and exalted idea of the One God resulted not in the blooming of reason but in its general impoverishment. There was one entirely obvious reason for this; once the metaphysical origins of Revelation are accepted, the belief in the One God and the belief in reason become incompatible.

To understand this better, let's look at the relationship between faith and reason in the age of monotheism. In the 'Reason in the Ancient World' section earlier in this chapter I asked myself: 'How did reason in the Ancient World achieve its superstar status?' Now I pose another question: 'How did it happen that reason lost its superstar status in the age of monotheism?' Because not only did it lose this status, it did so only thanks to itself.

The path travelled by Greek philosophy led from irrational, mythologised thinking to an entirely rational thought process. Monotheism made the same journey in reverse, finding itself back at the irrational mythological starting point. Ancient philosophy is now supplanted by the grim and universal Written Law. All world events are now explained by the irrational will of God, and this becomes monotheism's main distinguishing feature compared to ancient mythological thought where decisions were made in accordance with human nature and individual desires.

Since the tenets of the faith are above reason, the laws of rational thinking are not applicable to faith. Thus, the irrational is placed higher than the rational and religious spirituality higher than secular materialism. As faith is higher than reason, it refuses, in principle, to attempt to prove its main propositions, and instead bases its claims on the authority of tradition and miracles. The Ancients' well-developed rational mind struggled in the company of Revelation, tradition, and miracle. After sojourning for many centuries alongside the exacting and demanding Logos, it was then being asked to embrace the notion of metaphysical events which contradicted the all familiar logic-based order. As a result, reason became gravely ill and quickly lost its strength. No cure was attempted; monotheism, which succeeded Antiquity, didn't attach much value to human reason, having no real use for it. Reason's increasing weakness was also due to the fact that monotheistic religions are inclined to favour ascetic practices; reasonable thought is impossible without a healthy body and the harmonious co-existence of body and soul found in Antiquity. By tormenting the body, we also torment the mind. The obvious success enjoyed by reason in the Ancient World could be explained by the complete freedom it also enjoyed in selecting its areas for research. The advent of faith in One God and in Revelation sounded the death knell for the freedom of thought. The stronger the religion, the less willing it is to allow individual thought. Faith itself exists within well-defined boundaries: God is the one and only centre of all and the source of all power. There is only one unalterable sacred text and only one worldview. Man has ceased to be the law-maker and the source of reason in the world; henceforth God is the only centre of the world, the universal source of all reason and the acknowledged authority for everything. This makes religion's endeavours to undermine the Ancients' tradition of independence of thought logical from religion's point of view.

The weakening of reason in these conditions is par for the course; an acceptance of premises formed by the workings of one mind invariably undermines one's own.

Unfortunately, it hasn't been possible to destroy reason completely, so the only solution was to limit the areas where it could be used. Reason became corralled off within certain boundaries and as a result it lost its zest for life. The service of God, with its purpose of attaining a more exalted spiritual state, became reason's only worthwhile purpose of existence. Thus, the summit of intellectual development was seen to be possible only through the most exhaustive study and the most profound understanding and detailed interpretation of the Revealed Truth.

In the Ancient World, reason used the consequent knowledge to improve everyone's quality of life and create a system of values. Reason was naturally attuned to the real world; it was inclined towards independent critical analysis. It demanded objective proof for everything and was ontologically opposed to mystical experiences, murky traditions and miracles. Unlike reason, religion is guided not by the world as it really is, but by the blind faith in truths dictated by the Sacred Scripture. This kind of faith is most easily embraced by the grey, nameless masses enticed by promises of personal immortality and scared of punishments for sin. From a religious point of view, Man is unable to understand the material world, let alone comprehend God's purpose with the aid of reason alone; all our logical conclusions about the world depend entirely upon the will of God. The tremendous success enjoyed by reason in the Ancient World is explained by the fact that it was based on individual consciousness and for that reason possessed absolute tolerance of all metaphysical constructs and religious beliefs, and was simply an alternative point of view.

Monotheism swiftly put an end to tolerance; the Holy Book contains absolutely everything one needs – it describes the past, lays down the rules of life for the present, and predicts the future. Within the constraints of a religious worldview, theology replaces philosophy as the most respected discipline of the Ancient World. All other disciplines suffered a complete collapse.

Theology's chosen subject is the study of the belief in God. By its very nature, theology is as authoritarian as its object of study; it denies reason any autonomous purpose on the basis that reason is also the product of God's creation. It is fundamentally inclined to irrational and subjective thinking based on the miraculous and the absurd.

Theologians claimed that once Man has been shown absolute and universal divine truth through Revelation, commandments, and dogma, he has no need to waste time on further enquiries into philosophy and science. All truths have been discovered already and further searches simply detract Man from God. divine truth must be accepted without any discussion or investigation. If I had been a theologian, I would have adopted an even firmer stance against reason. All that reason stands for is diametrically opposed to religion's purpose, which makes all attacks on reason justified from religion's point of view. Reason is a significant threat to religion. As in the struggle over Man's influence, it is religion's main rival. Let's not forget about culture either. The existence of the one dominant book has rendered all other books superfluous. Who needs them? You can't argue with dogma; it guides the direction of Man's worthless and weak mind and forms his conclusions. All statements found in religious literature must be accepted by faith, and we must disregard any internal logical contradictions, obvious inconsistencies, and even copying errors.

A true believer should be perfectly content without empty secular education and unnecessary information about the world around him. At best, it's superfluous. At worst, dangerous and undesirable. An absence of education was frequently a source of pride, and for many centuries all that remained of great ancient philosophy was scholasticism. It's still the case today. Professional believers waste all their time in studying the divine Law for the whole of their lives. They have no interest in acquiring purely human, secular knowledge and do everything they can to avoid discussing matters which their faith doesn't recognise. A 'wrong' question causes them torment and makes them lose their cool, which is why their answers never address the matter in hand but rather skirt around the issue, postulating hackneyed doctrines, and quoting their proponents.

Through developments within culture, Antiquity was facilitated by the passionate but peaceful struggle of ideas, seeking out new concepts in the understanding of the world and the principles behind human existence. A critical attitude to old ideas was very much welcomed in the world of knowledge.

The acceptance of the eternally fossilised Written Law changed this situation once and for all. Deprived of competition or criticism, reason lost all impetus for development. Henceforth, criticism was not just unwelcome, but strictly proscribed. All people capable of critical thinking were also 'proscribed'; understandable as these were the kind of people who had particular difficulties with placing their whole faith into the Revealed 'truths'.

This was especially true when it came to questioning Revelation's principal propositions, the kind of heresies deemed highly dangerous for the stability of the ruling religion. Asking questions such as 'What if He doesn't exist?' was considered equal to treason and punishable with the whole strength of the law, usually resulting in death. The Fathers of the Church understood very well the personal dangers inherent in any impartial doctrinal criticism: Revelation could not withstand any rational analysis as it simply would fall apart. The unknowable mystery of the doctrine had to be guarded and remain inaccessible for the purposes of verification.

There didn't appear to be many volunteers willing to take this risk and the unwillingness to assume personal responsibility for one's opinions slowly destroyed the ancient tradition of individual authorship. Names, personalities, and individual standpoints moved to the background – any author merely became the mouthpiece of the divine truth, no more than that.

The ancient thinkers prioritised reason over ethics and were convinced that, aided by reason, Man is capable of creating his own morality. After all, everything – morality included – needs a rational basis.

Through the mouths of its theologians, monotheism declared the human mind to be secondary; because of its innate inability to discern moral good independently, reason alone can't make the right moral choice. The source of true morality is to be found outside of Man and can only be realised with the help of religious faith.

Should people, by some miracle, begin to have an ardent faith in the One God again, mankind would be immediately freed from the injustice of social inequality, offences against human beings, and wars. Once again, I must return to the fate of all good ideas. The idea that religious people are somehow endowed with a higher moral sense is not supported by facts – indeed, quite the opposite. This would be the logical conclusion of any dispassionate observer; paganism, the period immediately preceding monotheism, didn't place faith at the top end of the scale of human values and this is precisely the reason why religious wars were unknown in paganism. With the advent of monotheism, faith became everyone's main occupation in life and, as a result, religious conflicts cut short the lives of tens of millions of people who perished in defense of the most nebulous ideas, completely removed from their daily lives.

Ancient philosophy supposed that the outside world could be comprehended by reason alone and it was this knowledge that was the key to Man's happiness.

From a monotheistic point of view, reason is unable to bring happiness, as it's unable to rise above its earthly existence, which is by definition nothing but a vale of tears, suffering, and a temporary place of preparation for the eternal life. It is only through faith that he is given the opportunity to know God, to approach Him, 'to see His face', and to gain hope. In this way, happiness flees life on earth for life after death.

The principles of abstract thought were first formed in ancient philosophy and science, and we continue to use these principles to this day.

Monotheism claimed that that the origins of abstract thinking lay with itself and not with Antiquity. Abstract concepts, devoid of any factual basis, were used directly in relation to objects from the material world, calling into question all previous ideas about Man's existence and purpose. In relation to this, Nietzsche said that religious faith presumes the existence of hypostatic objects – that is, objects which do not belong to the material world and exist outside of time and space, such as God, angels, and devils. It also presumes an 'ability to communicate with these objects, accepting the existence of mythological events as a reality symbolised by religious action and the supernatural power of authorised persons (ministers of the cult, teachers, saints, prophets etc.).'

It is not the findings of enquiring reason that theology advances as its main argument to prove the veracity of Revelation, but rather an appeal to the past. No amount of progress or the latest scientific discoveries can be equal in value to the 'eternal truths' of the past. The truth of Revelation is not just based on God's word but is also sustained by tradition and authority. The source of both these concepts is in the past, which is also their exclusive point of reference. The ideas and opinions of contemporary believers, however well-educated and authoritative, are considerably less valuable than the opinions of authoritative believers from the past, despite being uneducated and living many millennia ago. In other words, a thing is believed to be true only because our ancestors said so. It is clear even to children that this approach does not make any sense. Freud spoke admirably about it in *The Future of Illusion*:

> Religious ideas are teachings and assertions about facts and conditions of external (or internal) reality which tell one something one has not discovered for oneself and which lay claim to one's belief. Since they give us information about what is most important and interesting to us in life, they are particularly highly prized [...] When we ask on what their claim to be believed is founded, we are met with three answers, which harmonize remarkably badly with one another. Firstly, these teachings deserve to be believed because they were already believed by our primal ancestors; secondly, we possess proofs which have been handed down to us from those same primeval times; and thirdly, it is forbidden to raise the question of their authentication at all. In former days, anything so presumptuous was visited with the severest penalties, and even today society looks askance at any attempt to raise the question again.

In general, religion considers the past much more valuable than both the present and the future. It's hardly coincidental that the most important religious miracles took place way back in the past. The further removed a given miracle is, the more readily one is meant to believe in it. It's fair to say, however, that miracles are rather rare nowadays – God's probably very disappointed and doesn't love us any more.

It's not surprising that all views based on the same unchanging premise are as similar to each other as identical twins. The original authors of sacred texts were the only ones displaying any degree of individuality of expression; all their successors were allowed to do was to repeat.

As a result, religious science closed in on itself; a commentary on the Book became the beginning, middle, and end of all its investigations. These were invariably followed by 'commentaries on the commentaries' (the Talmud being an excellent example of this) and so on ad infinitum, thus blocking the way to any new knowledge. A crowd of religious experts flapped around Revelation, like moths around a flame; their expert opinions served to strengthen tradition and attained a sacred status themselves. (Of course, civilisation's progress was consequently slower, but it couldn't stop entirely and sooner or later new

Duccio di Buoninsegna, Jesus Opens the Eyes of a Man Born Blind, 1308-1311.

ideas forced their way through. This, however, only happened because their proponents didn't believe as fervently as they ought to have done.) I don't want to lay the blame for the unfortunate fate suffered by reason in the Ancient World entirely at monotheism's door. It'd be as unreasonable as blaming a lion for being hungry and devouring an antelope. What happened to reason was inevitable – no 'monofaith' is compatible with reason. Faith is a cage for reason. Confined to this cage, reason ceased functioning as reason and was quickly transformed into a simple interpreter of Holy Scripture. Reason became weak and atrophied, much like muscles which have wasted away without physical activity. Your arms grow spindly, your six-pack gets covered up with a layer of fat, and your glutes become soft and flabby. Anyone looking in the mirror would spot this deterioration of his body straightaway, yet the mirror unfortunately can't show him his mind's sad deterioration.

The time has come to draw some conclusions. We were taught both in school and university that in order to conduct an unbiased investigation, we must not only question everyone's position, but also play Devil's advocate against ourselves. I've decided to do just that.

Does an ordinary person even need reason? Does it make life easier? Developing and maintaining reason requires self-sacrifice and a great deal of work, commensurable with the effort required in the world of professional sport, high finance, or glittering artistic success.

Wouldn't it be easier and more logical to forego reasoning altogether and instead to live out your life steeped in religious faith in the hope of eternal life after death? Isn't this artless life worthwhile and even enviable?

No, you can't call this life worthwhile, still less enviable. On the contrary, it's unworthy.

In the first place, whatever anyone says about free will, for practical purposes any truly believing person is deprived of his right to make an autonomous and considered moral choice. In any case, his need for morality is in order to ensure a more successful religious life and to extract the advantages that follow it, namely a guaranteed place in heaven. If, by way of experiment, you could imagine this person suddenly learning that there is neither God nor heaven, you would see his whole earthly existence collapse forthwith. Deprived of the ability to make up his own moral code, the believer stops growing intellectually and his natural creative potential begins a slow but inextricable decline. So,

Socrates and Moses.

instead of a creative life in the company of other people as befits a free individual, the believer ends up with an almost vegetable existence. Is this really what we all dreamed of in our childhood?

Secondly, being a creature of God robs the believer of his freedom and a person that isn't free is not capable of creating values for himself or others. His contribution is confined to creating chimeras. This isn't because he is lacking in natural talent, but because adding anything to dogma is, by definition, impossible. The denigration of the culture of the mind and the inability to form one's own values lead to a catastrophic decline in quality of life. Instead, participating in a world of plurality of people and opinions, the believer has to content himself with living by himself with only the Book for company.

Thirdly, deprived of the ability to create his own moral code and value system, Man's multifaceted and three-dimensional nature, common to all human beings, becomes flat. *Homo religiosus* is a one-dimensional fellow; with dogma for a backdrop, nothing is allowed to stand out and shine.

So it's no wonder that he thinks of himself as a complete cypher rather than the master of the universe. There he stands – a single weedy stem in a field of religious similitude, a speck of dust, a lowly creature; a thin, fragile line on a single page of a colossal Book of Genesis.

■ Why do we Need Reason if we Have the Torah? ■

Seek not out the things that are too hard for thee,
and into the things that are hidden from thee inquire thou not.
In what is permitted to thee instruct thyself;
thou must not discuss secret things.
Jerusalem Talmud, Hagiga 2, 2; B'reshith Rabbah 8

Reason first came under attack under Judaism, the first monotheistic religion. The Revelation purported to come from God imprisoned reason within an intellectual cage and confined its activity to the 'permitted' areas only. God has plenty of reason to impose such limitations. He knows the thoughts of men, and that they have no value whatsoever: 'He catches the wise in their own craftiness, and the counsel of the cunning is brought to a quick end.' (*Job 5: 13*)

Judaism spares no effort in criticising Greek philosophy, so influential amongst the young educated Jews of the Hellenistic period, and explains that a philosophy seeking to find answers in a material rather than a spiritual reality will always be unable to rise to the true understanding of His Being. Indeed, analysing the reality is a heinous crime itself.

None of this means that Judaism denies the value of human reason altogether.

But reason in Judaism is intended to comment upon and disclose the meaning of the Revelation. It is only a means of knowing about God and drawing closer to Him. Judaism emphasises that God is unknowable by reason alone and even forbids any attempt to prove His existence by this means.

The first person to question this was the famous first-century Jewish philosopher, Philo of Alexandria. For him, reason (or the intellect) is a substance that is analogous to the soul.

> The intellect naturally appears to be the only thing in us which is imperishable, for that is the only quality in us which the Father, who created us, thought deserving of freedom; and, untying the bonds of necessity, He let it go unrestrained, bestowing on it that most admirable gift closely connected with himself – the power of spontaneous will. For while the mind is in a state of enthusiastic inspiration, and while it is no longer mistress of itself, but is agitated and drawn into a frenzy by heavenly love, and drawn upwards to that object, truth removing all impediments out of its way, and making everything before it plain, it may advance by a level and easy road, its destiny to become an inheritor of the things of God.

At first glance, this has a fine and noble ring to it, but looking closer, it's obvious that reason in this system – very much like the soul – is presented in diametric opposition to the material world, and together they conspire to torture the body: 'For when the mind busies itself with sublime contemplations and becomes initiated into the mysteries of the Lord, it judges the body to be a wicked and hostile thing.'

Saadia Gaon, a Jewish philosopher and a Talmudic scholar living on the cusp of the ninth and tenth centuries, had much to say on the interrelationship between faith and reason. Saadia had a milder attitude towards reason than Philo and claimed that there are two fundamental approaches to the study of the world.

The first is a scientific and philosophical approach, which consists of observing and analysing the phenomenological world.

The second, a religious approach, is based on the interpretation of the Revelation from above.

Saadia believed that these two approaches were equally valid, that is to say, a correctly formulated philosophical proposition will always be identical to the correctly interpreted Revelation. And here Saadia makes a very interesting statement: the knowledge presented by Revelation is a 'ready truth', intended for the obtuse, uneducated, and ignorant masses who are expected to have simple, artless and unconditional faith. The elite, on the other hand, are able to approach Revelation through philosophy, which they can access thanks to their superior education and trained minds.

In the twelfth century, Moses Maimonides, one of the most influential philosophers in the history of Judaism, followed Philo is his definition of reason as the soul's form. This approach suits Judaism as everything is subjugated to a religious worldview: reason becomes an immortal entity and at the same time remains obedient to the faith.

The problems of how to reconcile reason and faith so they can peacefully coexist becomes the central theme of Maimonides' teaching. He declares in his seminal work *Moreh Nevuchim* (*A Guide to the Perplexed*), that there is no inherent contradiction between faith and reason. Only fools accept scriptural allegories as literal descriptions of events and then point out the way they contradict the laws of nature. These apparent 'contradictions' must be viewed allegorically, as metaphors.

Just like Saadia, Maimonides is full of respect and aglow with an ardent love for the simple Jewish folk:

> You must know that the words of the sages are interpreted differently by three groups of people. The first group is the largest one. I have observed them, read their books, and heard about them. They accept the teachings of the sages in their simple literal sense and do not think that these teachings contain any hidden meaning at all. They believe that all sorts of impossible things must be... They possess no perfection which would rouse them to insight from within, nor have they found anyone else to stimulate them to profounder understanding. They therefore believe that the sages intended no more in their carefully emphatic and straightforward utterances than they themselves are able to understand with inadequate knowledge. They understand the teachings of the sages only in their literal sense, in spite of the fact that some of their teachings, when taken literally, seem so fantastic and irrational that if one were to repeat them literally, even to the uneducated, let alone sophisticated scholars, their amazement would prompt them to ask how anyone in the world could believe such things as true, not to mention edifying. The members of this group are poor in knowledge. One can only regret their folly. Their very effort to honour and to exalt the sages in accordance with their own meagre understanding actually humiliates them. As God lives, this group destroys the glory of the Torah of God and they say the opposite of what it intended.

I do, however, have to give Maimonides some credit. He was one of the few Jewish scholars who wrote about the necessity of studying secular disciplines and philosophy; he believed that one couldn't receive the 'revealed truth' without some appreciation of the way of the world.

Another major Jewish scholar and philosopher of the fifteenth-sixteenth centuries, Levi ben Gershom (also known as Ralbag), followed Maimonides in his view that the study of the world is a necessary 'preamble' to the study of Revelation for, 'by acquainting ourselves with the nature of the world, we learn of the wisdom of the Almighty as far as we are able so to do.'

Still, it's no use pretending that this favourable view of knowledge was shared by all Jewish philosophers. A negative attitude to secular learning and culture was far more common in Judaism, in which religion opposed all worldly knowledge.

Yehudah Halevi, an outstanding poet and philosopher of the eleventh and twelfth centuries, is vehement in his attack on any idea of a 'rational knowledge' of God and Revelation. For him, Revelation and philosophy are always in opposition; they are as far removed from us as the followers of a religion from a philosopher. The former seek God not only for the sake of knowing Him, but also for other great benefits which they derive from Him. The philosopher, however, only seeks Him that he may be able to describe Him accurately in detail.

If I had believed in God even a little bit, I would never have agreed with Saadi, Maimonides and Ralbag's opinions of reason, but instead assumed Halevi's stance. Science, particularly the science of philosophy, poses a great threat to religion because its aim is the acquisition of knowledge rather than drawing ever closer to God. Halevi was fearful that heat from the light of knowledge would melt any faith: 'That which thou dost express is religion based on speculation and system, the research of thought, but open to many doubts.'

Medieval Judaism actively opposed reason as a proper means of learning about the world; many of the famous Jewish sages were categorically against the study of any philosophy except that pertaining to Judaism and the natural sciences. Isaac bar Sheshet, a well-known rabbi from the end of the fourteenth century, wrote:

> The famous books on physics are thus not of God's Providence. It is appropriate to refrain from them in that they attempt to uproot the principles of our Holy Torah, especially the two fundamental pillars on which it rests, creation *ex nihilo* [...] They also maintain that God's Providence does not extend to anything below the sphere of the moon. They also wrote in their books that perfect knowledge is attainable only through investigation, not through tradition. But we have received the truth that our Torah, which came to us at Sinai from the mouth of God, through the intermediation of the master of all the prophets, is perfect. It is superior to everything and all their investigations are null and void compared to it. [...] It is thus forbidden to believe them and even to read them.

The most notable element here is not the praise of the Torah and the denigration of science – there is nothing new in this – but the assertion that 'they maintain that God's Providence does not extend to anything below the sphere of the moon'. For a religious mindset this represents a clear threat; the moment believers understand that they are not watched by God every second of their existence and that He is not the omnipotent and omniscient Big Brother they believed Him to be, religion as an institution will come to a speedy end. For this reason, the only proper occupation for a faithful Jew is the study of the Torah, which conveys only the truth – even regarding such miracles as the crossing of the sea on foot or the turning of rivers into blood.

The Talmud is prolific and eloquent on the dangers of secular learning: Ben Damah, the son of R. Ishmael's sister, once asked R. Ishmael, 'May one such as I who has studied the whole of the Torah learn Greek wisdom?' He thereupon read to him the following verse:

> This book of the law shall not depart out of thy mouth, but thou shalt meditate therein day and night. *(Joshua 1:8).* Go then and find a time that is neither day nor night and learn then Greek wisdom'. (Menachoth 99b)

But the best thought dealing with the place of reason came from the eighteenth-century Rabbi Nachman, grandson of the founder of Hasidism: 'Where there is knowledge, there is no need for faith.'

Contemporary Orthodox Judaism has not moved very far from its co-religionists living two thousand years ago. Compared to Christianity, it is much more suspicious of secular sciences and arts and tends to limit the number of subjects studied in religious schools, lest they introduce students to ideas contrary to Revelation. Even a cursory acquaintance with these subjects is deemed undesirable; a pious person has no need of them and education is only valued to the extent that it fosters a more rigorous observance of religious traditions and strengthens the faith of the community.

Children brought up in religious households have it bad too. As a rule, corrupting influences such as the TV and the internet aren't allowed. Why distract the youth from serving God?

If truth be told, science and secular culture really are a threat to the religious mindset. These disciplines, especially secular philosophy, are based on rationally proven natural laws that have no use for the unproven precepts of God, and thus lose any point of contact with Him. But I have to be fair in my treatment of Judaism. Although I believe that studying the same religious texts for many years is a waste of one's intellectual and physical resources, I have to acknowledge that, when compared to the other Abrahamic religions, Judaism's attitude to intellect is by all means not the worst. Abstract thinking and a critical approach are essential for the understanding of both the Torah and especially the Talmud. That's why Yeshiva students are taught effective abstract thinking and how to construct logical arguments.

■ Reason will not Bring you to Paradise ■

Credo quia absurdum est.
I believe because it is absurd.
Tertullian

Christianity had a much longer battle with reason than the two other Abrahamic religions. It is not a purely monotheistic religion; it got stuck somewhere between pagan polytheism and monotheism. It is only in Christianity that the abstract and notional God of Judaism descends on earth and becomes a God-Man. It is only Christianity that refused to acknowledge that depictions of God and His mother (in icons and statues) are the same as the ones of the idols, the symbols of paganism, though there is really no difference. It was only the Christian religion that developed such a powerful cult of a miracle-making God, His Apostles and ordinary saints all able to make miracles. From the very beginning, Christian theology has always asserted that, along with everything else Man possesses, human reason belongs to God and that the wisdom of men and the wisdom of God exist in direct opposition to each other. Reason has three fundamental failings:

One: its inability to embrace 'moral goodness'; that is to say, it has no inherent connection to religious ethics. What's more, it is forever attempting to construct its own moral system and a mode of behaviour independent from God.

Two: it's adversely affected by Man's inherent passions, which in turn cause Man to make mistakes leading to sin – Christianity's main enemy.

Three, and perhaps its greatest failing: its inability to help Man reach salvation, which can only be effected through faith. And so, reason is useless for an assured entry into paradise.

This kind of backward and unspiritual reason must be converted with all due haste into a predicate of the divine soul. It must sever all connections to the body or, better still, must engage in its own battle against human nature.

Thus Christianity's first crusade was not against the heathen, but against reason. It all began with Paul the Apostle, who said that the wisdom of the world is defective if only because it regarded the commandments of Christ as folly. From God's point of view, Man has nothing to boast about since 'the wisdom of this world is foolishness'. And again, 'The Lord knows that the thoughts of the wise are futile.' (1 Corinthians 3:20)

Paul is quite convinced that taking pride in one's intellect is a sure sign of haughtiness and false self-reliance; one must adopt a subservient position by acknowledging one's foolishness in order to be able to learn from God. Reason is inclined to look critically at Revelation – its way of transmission, its line of argument, and its content.

Paul also sees problems with reason's propensity to regard itself as definitive. Reason adopts a 'superior position' in relation to all other agencies, is intolerant of alternative points of view, and lacks the humility to be able to learn from others or simply 'to sit in quiet admiration' of its opponents. Adulation of worldly wisdom and, more generally, the arguments advanced by reason, sow disputes amongst Christ's brethren, destroy 'God's castle', and hinder the operation of the Holy Spirit.

I think that everything said here by Paul can be also successfully applied to religion. It would seem as though he is unwilling to notice the log in his own eye.

In agreeing with Paul's view, Christianity applies the basic principle of juxtaposing the divine soul and the unworthy body with the interrelationship between faith and reason. Henceforth, there are two ways to acquire knowledge – by faith or through the rational mind. It goes without saying that, as God can't be known by reason, faith must first and foremost be one's guide. 'The mind must be lodged in the heart,' as the ascetic Fathers declared.

The early Christian martyr, Justin the Philosopher, wrote that the Revealed Word 'disdains to fall under any skilful argument, or to endure the logical scrutiny of its hearers. But it would be believed for its own nobility, and for the confidence due to Him who sends it.'

His disciple Tatian, one of the founders of the ascetic Encratite (self-controlled) sect, was highly disdainful of the human intellect. For the Encratites, extreme asceticism was a prerequisite for salvation; they abstained from all meat and wine, not to mention sex. Tatian would later declare that, 'Obeying the commands of God, and following the law of the Father of immortality, we reject everything which rests upon human opinion.'

So you see, Tertullian's famous saying – 'I believe because it is absurd' – that proud hymn to irrationality, which I chose as this chapter's epigraph, didn't just appear out of nowhere. All Christians would do well to call this statement to mind frequently, just to remind themselves what their faith is based on. He places faith unequivocally higher than reason and makes another remarkable statement to this effect: 'and the Son of God died; it is by all means to be believed because it is absurd. And He was buried, and rose again; the fact is certain, because it is impossible.'

Tertullian was categorically opposed to the allegorical interpretation of the Scripture and regarded all debates about the hidden meaning of the biblical texts as fruitless ponderings which 'upset the stomach' and frequently lead to heresy. If a certain text appears absurd to our mind, this is only an indication that it contains some divine truth. The more absurd, unfathomable, and implausible the text, the more reason for us to place all our faith in its divine origins and meaning.

'But, after all, you will not be "wise unless you become a fool to the world by believing the foolish things of God".'

> 'There is one, and therefore definite, thing taught by Christ, which the nations are by all means bound to believe.'
>
> 'We want no curious disputation after possessing Jesus Christ, no inquisition after enjoying the Gospel! With our faith, we desire no further belief.'

Now, that's what I call taking pride in one's religion. Something for our contemporary fanatics to envy. All of this is not to say that Tertullian forgot about philosophy. The truth was revealed by God and is therefore entirely free from sin. By contrast, philosophy is a product of the human mind, which is affected by the Original Sin along with the rest of the human body. Philosophy is thought to give rise to heresy, whereas the soul, having no part in popular culture, perseveres in Christian virtue. Philosophy must confine itself strictly to the interpretation of the Holy Scripture. After many years of studying pagan

Benozzo Gozzoli, Saint Peter and Simon Magus, 1461-1462.
Saint Peter prevented Simon the Sorcerer from flying by invoking the name of Christ.

(ancient) philosophy, Tertullian's contemporary Clement of Alexandria concluded that no philosophy by itself is capable of understanding the world. Only Revelation has a direct and complete access to truth, bypassing any need for proof.

Arnobius, the acknowledged critic of paganism, seconds Paul and declares all educational instruction futile. What's the use of knowing grammar, rhetoric, and especially how to 'decline nouns according to cases and tenses'? Gregory of Nyssa, the philosopher-bishop of the fourth century, describes the situation thus:

> And let no one interrupt me and say that what we confess should be confirmed by constructive reasoning. It suffices for the proof of our statement that we have a tradition coming down to us from the Fathers, an inheritance as it were, by succession from the Apostles through the saints who came after them.

> Man has no further need for scientific knowledge. What's the use when the believer who belongs to Christ already rules the whole universe? Faith has no need for proof; the witness of the past is entirely sufficient.

Augustine supposed that Man's happiness consists of knowing God, and since Man's God-given soul already possesses all knowledge, rational truth can be comprehended by a simple act of faith. Faith, most commonly the possession of the least educated people, becomes higher than any philosophical truth: 'Let us therefore believe if we cannot understand.'

John Chrysostom, true to his reputation as a master preacher, used to console those less skilled thus: 'If your soul is chaste, you will lose nothing from being a stranger to eloquence', and he generally warned against relying too much on reason: 'There is nothing worse than Man measuring and judging divine things by human reasoning. For thus he will fall from that rock a vast distance and be deprived of the light.'

Indeed, why would anyone need the evidence of reason if there is a miracle? God is omnipotent and can alter natural laws whenever he wishes: he can part the sea in order to save his people, make old men and women fertile again, and young people conceive innocently; he can walk on water, heal the incurable and resurrect the dead. Christianity is way better off with miracles than any other Abrahamic religion.

Thanks to Christianity, the ghost of miracles is still out there, allowing the reasonable part of humanity to make acrimonious commentaries about it. Christopher Hitchens writes in *God is Not Great*:

> However, there has not been a claimed resurrection for some time and no shaman who purports to do it has ever agreed to reproduce his trick in such a way as to stand a challenge. But according to the New Testament, the thing could be done in an almost commonplace way. Jesus managed it twice in other people's cases, by raising both Lazarus and the daughter of Jairus, and nobody seems to have thought it worthwhile to interview either survivor to ask about their extraordinary experiences. Nor does anyone seem to have kept a record of whether or not, or how, these two individuals "died" again.

I am quite convinced that simple, believing folk have always rather liked this negative view of reason and knowledge; education has long been seen as an identifying feature of the aristocratic oppressor. The best way to avoid having to engage in 'fruitless ponderings' was to receive no education whatsoever. There is a good reason why the Rule of the Franciscan Orders states clearly that 'if they do not know of letters, take no trouble to teach them'.

It was therefore entirely natural that the Ancients' regard for reason went into a steep decline at practically the same moment that Christianity became universally established.

It began to recover almost a thousand years later, at the time of the Renaissance, but even that recovery was far from complete. Scientists, philosophers, and apostate theologians (Giordano Bruno) were still being happily burnt at the stake or poisoned (Picodella Mirandola) at the beginning of the seventeenth century.

In the Middle Ages, attitudes to reason didn't improve – quite the reverse. They became much more intolerant, and seemingly innocent areas like art became governed by strict canon. Art was to be used only for depicting religious themes, a kind of Bible for the illiterate. For many centuries, the Holy Scripture became the dominant theme in the prevailing Christian culture.

When Peter Damian, a cardinal and Catholic saint of the eleventh century, made his famous statement – 'Philosophy should serve theology as a handmaid serves her mistress' – he expressed the view that reason has nothing to say, not just on the questions of faith but on all spiritual and vitally important matters too. There can be only one true guide on the quest to know God and to attain salvation, only one intermediary between God and Man – the 'lament of prayer'.

His contemporary, archbishop Anselm of Canterbury, also placed reason after faith: 'For I do not seek to understand in order to believe, but I believe in order to understand. For I believe this: unless I believe, I will not understand.'

Bernard of Clairvaux, a most authoritative theologian and mystic, suggested the dedication of oneself wholly to the study of religion. 'To be sure, all knowledge is good in itself, provided it be founded on the truth. But you, who hasten to work out your salvation with fear and trembling because of the brevity of time, should take care to know more that what you feel is closely bound up with your happiness.'

The renowned church authority, Thomas Aquinas, is in agreement with them:

> This science can in a sense depend upon the philosophical sciences, not as though it stood in need of them, but only in order to make its teaching clearer. For it accepts its principles not from other sciences, but immediately from God, by revelation. Therefore it does not depend upon other sciences as upon higher authority, but makes use of them as of the lesser, and as handmaidens.

Gregory Palamas, the Byzantine mystical theologian, considers a recognition of one's intellectual frailty an important prerequisite of salvation:

> Moreover, for our intellect to know its infirmity and to seek healing for it, it is incomparably greater than to know and search out the magnitude of the stars, the principles of nature, the generation of terrestrial things, and the circuits of celestial bodies, their solstices and risings stations, retrogressions, separations, conjunctions and, in short, all the multiform relationships which arise from the many different motions of the heavens.

What a wonderful use of scientific heritage of Antiquity. If society had blindly followed this opinion, we would still have only the bow and arrow to protect us.

I have no way of knowing what sort of mystical 'light of knowledge' Palamas is talking about, but the inability to challenge the 'truth of Revelation' has caused a profound decline in the study of science. From the time of the establishment of Christianity as the state religion of the Roman Empire until the end of the eighteenth century, Europe existed on a diet of the same 'divine truths' and developing 'proofs' for the existence of God. The absence of any logical proofs inspired Ignatius of Loyola to call for the intellect to be sacrificed to God. This call, alien and unacceptable though it is to the rational intellect, is easily embraced by a religious mindset. Something which looks like healthy intellectual curiosity to a rational mind is regarded within the religious value system as a form of 'lasciviousness of the eyes'.

By the same token, the brilliant preacher Martin Luther declared reason to be religion's greatest enemy and issued many warnings as to the dangers it poses:

> Reason is the greatest enemy that faith has; it never comes to the aid of spiritual things, but more frequently than not struggles against the divine Word, treating with contempt all that emanates from God…Reason should be destroyed in all Christians. Whoever wants to be a Christian should tear the eyes out of his reason. Reason is the Devil's harlot, who can do nought but slander and harm whatever God says and does.

The intellect, which is a priori incapable of abandoning its imperative subjection of everything and everyone to analysis, conceals itself in the darkest corner of our ego, ever ready to introduce doubts into the God-bound soul. In order for true spiritual progress to be achieved, one must lock away one's physical sentiments, muffle the imagination, and renounce all forms of intellectual enquiry. In other words, one must empty oneself entirely, ready for the coming of the Holy Spirit, who will help to purge any lingering sin and evil inclinations.

It would be wrong to omit to mention the views of Pascal: 'He who knows Jesus, knows the reason of all things,' and, 'It is the heart which is conscious of God, not reason.' Pascal believed that, following Revelation, Man lost his title as the 'crown of creation' and 'the king of nature', becoming as insignificant as 'an atom' and his life a 'shadow which endures only for an instant and returns no more'.

I have to disagree with Pascal on this; humanity had its geniuses both before and after the advent of Revelation. As for Pascal himself, his initial life of research and many brilliant scientific discoveries in the fields of mechanics, mathematics, physics, and philosophy lost all of their creative impact after he abandoned science for religion. His life became subsumed in religious monotony and indeed became a 'shadow which endures only for an instant'.

However, by no means did all of the great minds of the Middle Ages agree that faith was more important than reason. As the Age of Enlightenment advanced, proponents of the Christian worldview began to shrink exponentially. The English philosopher and scientist Thomas Hobbes (1588-1679) became the first defender of reason, a view he expounded in his famous 'natural law': 'A law of nature (*lex naturalis*) is a command or general rule, discovered by reason, which forbids a man to do anything that is destructive to his life or takes away his means for preserving his life.'

Spinoza was convinced that the Holy Scripture wasn't God's Revelation beyond the limitations of the human mind. It contains no proofs for the existence of God as a supernatural being and, unlike reason, is of little value for learning the truth. This is the conclusion he reached after a thorough critical analysis of the texts of the Scripture: discovering a mass of contradictions and absurdities. Adam was not the first man; Moses could not have written the Pentateuch; various holy books weren't written by their supposed authors but by a collective of writers working many years afterwards (it's true that the Gospel writers' accounts diverge greatly in their description of various mythical details; each presents different versions of the Sermon on the Mount, the anointing of Jesus, the betrayal by Judas, and Peter's 'denial').

All this leads Spinoza to make the following conclusion: No wonder there's nothing left but credulity and prejudices. And what prejudices. They turn men from rational beings into beasts because they won't let anyone use his free judgement to distinguish the true from the false, and seem deliberately designed to put out the light of the intellect entirely.

Neither the Early nor the Late Modern periods brought much change. Not much could change anyway; the irrational nature of religion remained the same and wasn't going anywhere.

Søren Kierkegaard didn't shy away from the absurd in religion. In his opinion, Christian faith begins at the point where rational thinking ceases. To illustrate this point, he expounds the story of Abraham and Isaac.

Wishing to test Abraham, God orders him to sacrifice his one and only son Isaac, whom Abraham 'begat' at the age of seventy after many years of trying. Despite the fact that this order is both cruel and senseless, Abraham abandons the realm of rational and ethical thinking and makes a 'leap of faith'; he entrusts himself to God in spite of all reasonable human conventions. The moral here is quite simple: the more absurd the call of faith, the greater the determination needed to follow it.

According to Kierkegaard, this kind of desperate 'leap of faith' is only possible if one believes in a Higher Being who exists beyond human comprehension. The divine truth cannot be understood by any other means.

The Russian religious philosopher and existentialist Nikolai Berdyaev wrote that Christianity's main achievement was liberating mankind from the power of the Greek Cosmos and from the false impression that Man is able to comprehend and exist in the world autonomously. I wonder where we all would have been now if we had all recognised the 'main achievement' of Christianity? In the monastery rooms?

Roger Mehl, the well-known French Calvinist and sociologist, suggested that the existence of reason cannot be understood only in a positive light since what is commonly known as the 'light of knowledge' carries the marks of the Original Sin. Paul's 'renewal of the mind', which he connects with the faith in the Saviour, is a far better proposition. It alone opens to us new paths of knowledge, which were hitherto concealed from our mind.

In other words, we began with Paul and to Paul we returned.

John Hick, a famous British theologian and philosopher of religion, explains the process whereby Man receives his knowledge about God and the way faith differs from other forms of knowledge. I very much appreciated reading this from *Who or What is God?*:

> God can and does perform miracles, in the sense of making things happen which would not otherwise have happened, and preventing things from happening which otherwise would have happened. These interventions are either manifest or – much more often – discernible only to the eyes of faith. But it is believed that God does sometimes intervene in answer to prayer. Otherwise, what is the point of those prayers?

This is one of those far-from-rare cases when one attempts to prove one thing and ends up proving something quite different. If God's miracles are seen only by believers, then He is useless to unbelievers. What's more, if you follow Hick, it transpires that God is of little use even to the believer; He reveals Himself on earth only 'sometimes', and only 'sometimes' does He respond to the prayers addressed to Him. I agree with Hick that prayer is meaningless.

C.S. Lewis had the same ideas about miracles: If God were good, He would wish to make His creatures perfectly happy, and if God were almighty He would be able to do what He wished. But the creatures are not happy. Therefore God lacks either goodness, or power, or both.

This aforementioned 'part of Christian faith' would undoubtedly be bigger and stronger if the 'miracles' occurred more regularly. I don't know about you, but I certainly wouldn't mind seeing a real resurrection from the dead for myself – or at least a man walking on water.

The negative attitude exhibited by Christianity towards reason is easy to understand. If the world could be 'saved' by reason alone, no advent of Christ would have been needed. Thus, as far as religion is concerned, all of these eminent human disciplines (philosophy, history, anthropology, sociology, and psychology) achieved precisely nothing since they entirely failed to 'save' humanity from sin.

And then down came religion with its higher knowledge and saved everyone. Never mind that the very question of Man's need for salvation effectively finished him off as a rational being. He becomes a cipher, because all irrational propositions undermining the fundamental principles of human thought are anti-human by their very nature. The intellectual revival of the Western world, that is, the very civilisation that I like living in so much, was stimulated by a general trend, rejecting religion in favour of reason and the acquisition of knowledge. So you see, our 'salvation' originated not from God, but from reason.

I would like to end my tale of struggle between reason and faith with this wonderful piece of reasoning by Nietzsche from *The Antichrist*:

Rembrandt, The Sacrifice of Abraham, 1635.
Abraham takes the 'leap of faith'.

Under Christianity neither morality nor religion has any point of contact with actuality. It offers purely imaginary causes ["God", "soul", "ego", "spirit", "free will" – or even "unfree"], and purely imaginary effects ["sin", "salvation", "grace", "punishment", "forgiveness of sins"]. Intercourse between imaginary beings ["God", "spirits", "souls"]; an imaginary natural history [anthropocentric; a total denial of the concept of natural causes]; an imaginary psychology [misunderstandings of self, misinterpretations of agreeable or disagreeable general feelings, for example of the states of the *nervus sympathicus* with the help of the sign-language of religio-ethical balderdash, "repentance", "pangs of conscience", "temptation by the devil", "the presence of God"]; an imaginary teleology [the "kingdom of God", "the last judgment", "eternal life"]…the whole of that fictitious world finds its sources in the hatred of the natural…

■ The Quran Cannot be Understood by Reason ■

A man of reason is the one who submits to God.
Abu Hamid al-Ghazali, *Revival of the Religious Sciences*

In common with the other Abrahamic religions, Islam distrusts reason and seeks to limit its use as much as possible.

Reason is understood in exclusively religious terms by Islam; the intellect is a gift of God and so its function is governed only by divine principles. If the whole of Man is created by God, then the mind is also His creation. Reason can't embrace the divine and the mystical; all it can do is make insolent demands for proofs and engage the believer in endless philosophical discussions. Yet divine teaching has no need for any discussion; the commandments of God are simply to be accepted without any discussion or questions. That's why reason's main function is to be found not in its capacity for free analytical thought, but rather in its ability to heed God, to obey Him, and to inspire Man to constant prayer. Also, reason is not intended to be used for making free choices in a secular society; its use is confined to making choices between good and evil within Islam's well-defined boundaries. Its sole use to the believer is the help it gives him in scaling moral heights, a process which, in itself, exposes his soul to divine intervention.

The intellect becomes an object of great interest to the Islamic mystics (the Sufis) of the ninth to the eleventh centuries, the 'golden age' of Islam. This period saw a great deal of Islamic rehashing of Ancient Greek philosophy heritage, particularly the ethical parts of the philosophy of Aristotle.

One of the first Islamic followers of Aristotle was ninth-century philosopher Al-Farabi. Al-Farabi preached that reason was a tool for choosing between good and bad actions: 'In everyday language, "an intelligent man means a man of reliable judgment who knows what he has to do as right and what he has to avoid as wrong".'

Understood in this light, reason becomes removed from the process of interpreting the real world outside and instead is directed towards studying religious precepts and expounding moral arguments. His follower Ibn Sina (Avicenna), a renowned tenth-century Persian thinker, was also of the opinion that reason's sphere of influence should be highly restricted. Nevertheless, his teaching allowed the unworthy intellect the consolation of one light – albeit a very small one – at the end of that particular tunnel; although connected to the body, reason nevertheless remains an attribute of the soul, and at the death of the body, it is joined to the World Soul.

All Sufis believed that it is this sentiment, not reason, that is the main agent of understanding. Even such intellectual giants as the eleventh-century philosopher Ibn Arabi thought that: 'True knowledge is the understanding of the heart. What is unknowable by the mind, is open to the heart.'

Al-Ghazali, Ibn Sina's contemporary, and one of the acknowledged founders of Sufism, was the first to develop the concept of a proper Islamic attitude towards knowledge and reason. In his work, *The Revival of Religious Sciences*, he claimed that Muhammad himself said that 'striving for knowledge is a duty of every Muslim'. The Islam of the 'Golden Age' had high regard for erudition and empirical knowledge of the world (especially in medicine and chemistry/alchemy). It considered that rational Hellenic philosophy and religion were compatible with each other.

Nevertheless, Al-Ghazali believed that no amount of philosophy or knowledge can lead one to the truth, that true understanding is only possible through Revelation (most Muslims believe the same thing to this day). The ability to make reasoned choices is not a privilege but a burden: 'The man who possesses the most mature mind among you is he who fears God most, fulfilling best what He enjoined and desisting from what He has forbidden, although that man may be the least willing to obey.'

Reason's only major defender from the Islamic tradition was Ibn Arabi's friend Ibn Rushd (Averroes). He proposed the existence of two types of reason – the mortal, material kind, and the immortal, spiritual one. The former is attached to the human body and dies with it – 'The material reason is mortal learning.' The latter cannot die as it is connected to the immortal soul and morality.

Averroes was an avid reader and translator of Aristotle, who first proposed the 'duality of truth'. The essence of this theory is that religious truth and reason exist in mutual independence from each other. The truth expressed metaphorically by the Quran could be interpreted just as successfully by a philosophical discourse. Averroes not only defended the rational approach to knowledge but he even considered philosophy as being higher than theology. (There is no reason to fear for religious truths; any rational explanation would always concur with Revelation.) Moreover, Aristotle's dialectics easily overcome any contradiction as it allows the philosopher to argue simultaneously for two diametrically opposing theses. It's notable that Averroes' years of life coincided almost entirely with the lifespan of the great Maimonides, with whom he also shared the view that religious and scientific claims cannot exist in contradiction to each other.

Averroes had no particular respect for common believers either. He was in the habit of dividing people into three categories. The first group was the uneducated masses, the second was the theologians, and the third the philosophers. In the end, the philosophers turned out to be cooler than everyone else, even the theologians.

These rationalist ideas did not meet with much approval in the Islamic world, however, and were quickly forgotten, returning theology to its rightful starting position. Many years later, an Egyptian mufti, Muḥammad Abduh, concurred that 'Allah did not create His book (the Quran) in order to expound facts and natural phenomena in it'.

It's appropriate to mention here the fact that Islam also allows for miracles, although on a much smaller scale than Christianity. Prophet Muhammad transported himself from the Sacred Mosque in Mecca to Jerusalem's Al-Aqsa Mosque in a single moment; He miraculously filled vessels with water, and comforted a tree-trunk that was weeping after being parted from Him.

Thus, Islam's attitude to reason is varied. There are strands within it that have a very positive view of reason and science, extolling cultural progress within the guidelines laid down by the Quran. God never acts against His own natural law, within which all people have a free will and are bound to use their God-given intellect for the improvement of their own lives as well as for the advancement of a more ethical society. This type of Islam is responsible for building excellent roads, constructing the world's tallest buildings, and developing nuclear weapons.

The other Islam has an extremely negative attitude towards the secular logic of reason. Wahhabism, for example, is adamant that a recognition of human ability and of natural laws of cause and effect is a form of blasphemy as it limits the power of the Almighty God. It is said that one of the walls of the Ministry of Justice building, at the time of the Taliban, was adorned with an enormous placard which said, 'Throw reason to the dogs – it stinks of moral corruption.' The fundamentalist form of Islam, which is becoming increasingly popular, attempts to limit the non-religious deployment of the intellect even today. To this end, it forbids one thing after another: secular science and culture, music, women's education and representational art.

I end my story of the difficult interaction between reason and Abrahamic religions with the description of the biggest and most voracious Chimera.

■ How One 'Can See the Face of God' ■

You cannot see My face;
for no man shall see Me, and live.
Exodus 33:20

This expression 'to see the face of God', which at first glance seems rather strange, features here for a reason. I first encountered it when I read some books on circumcision and it made such an impression on me that I simply couldn't let it go till I'd written this section. There is a reason for according such honour to this expression – it has a long religious pedigree. It elucidated for us the true, inner meaning behind the ritual of circumcision. Isaac ben Judah Abarbanel, the famous Talmud scholar of the thirteenth century, explained that a decreased sexual desire effected by circumcision is of vital religious significance: an uncircumcised man is tormented by his flesh and is therefore unable to 'see the light of the Lord's face because his eyes and mind are intoxicated by women'. This was my first encounter with the idea that the ability to 'see the face of God' goes hand in hand with the compulsory suppression of sexual feelings. Abarbanel did not say anything about the circumcision of reason. Most probably, his own reason had been so violently circumcised during his pluri-annual studies in a *yechiva* that he had no more connection to our world. His reason did not have any more worldly interests since faith had swallowed all of his desires and ideas. He then had only celestial desires. The strongest desire amid them was the desire to 'see the face of God'.

The meaning behind the expression 'to see the face of God' extends beyond the bounds of Abarbanel's own work and even Judaism as a whole. It is of fundamental importance not only to each individual but to the whole of our civilisation. This remarkable idea so full of love for humanity initially attracted me to the principles of monotheism and became a fundamental feature of this book. But I realised that suppressing one's sexuality would not be sufficient to achieve these higher ideals; one is called upon to renounce all other human pleasures too. I have now accepted this notion of renouncing all human pleasures as universal advice to be given to anyone who, for whatever reason, desires to 'see the face of God'. My own desire to 'see the face of God' and explore the idea here was strengthened after I had read Pope Benedict XVI's address of 16 January 2013, in which he claimed that the desire truly to know God, that is to 'see His face', is fundamental to all human beings, even atheists.

This assertion from the ultimate Catholic authority on earth helped me to overcome my own primitive atheism and decide to 'seek His face' for myself. To start with, I wanted to understand who would be capable of such an achievement, what one would be required to do, and how much it would all cost (because, of course, none of this would be given away for free). It seems that this kind of pleasure is within the reach of only very few people and would cost a great deal.

The idea of 'seeing the face of God' is as old as the world itself, or at any rate, as old as human vanity, just as prevalent in the Stone Age as it is in our own.

Gazing on the faces of gods was not so popular in ancient civilisations; there was neither much interest in it, nor a particular need for it. These gods were anthropomorphic, that is, rather similar to people, and were in any case all around, gazing at people from the porticoes of numerous temples. Pagan religions never required Man to dedicate himself wholly to his deity. Moreover, it was unclear to which deity one should have dedicated his life to, since there were so many gods that even remembering their names was a real problem.

The problem of the 'face of God' coincided with the appearance of Judaism on the universal stage of humanity, the world's first comprehensive monotheistic religion, and migrated later into Christianity and Islam. These religions placed God simultaneously at the centre and on the edge of existence; He became both the meaning and the essence of all that is, the universal Creator, and the righteous Judge.

Perfection is impossible without God and Man's life only gains meaning by searching for unity with Him. Nothing is too much in pursuit of this unity; one is happy to sacrifice anything. It's obvious that the shorter the distance between you and the object of your search, the stronger your bond will be. Out of this grew the notion of approaching God so closely as to be able to 'see His face'.

Strictly speaking, no adherent of an Abrahamic faith is allowed to 'see the face of God', at least during his or her lifetime. This prohibition is rooted in the very essence of monotheism, and relates to the care taken to preserve its purity and to avoid any form of idolatry. One is not permitted to depict God; any depiction of Him is also an idol. Moreover, the very desire to see and to depict God is seen as a challenge, an attempt to become like – and equal to – Him.

These prohibitions form a part of the fundamental difference between monotheism and paganism.

The God of monotheism is all-pervasive and, by definition, can't become incarnate. The God of monotheism is infinite, elusive, has no form, and exists outside of space or time, although He is also a part of every human event, even the very air we breathe. Spinoza asserted that God is everywhere and in everything ('*en tout et partout*'). How can you depict a God like that? The good old Old Testament commandment is very clear on this score:

> You shall not make for yourself a graven image, or any likeness of anything that is in heaven above, or that is in the earth beneath, or that is in the water under the earth; you shall not bow down to them or serve them; for I the Lord your God am a jealous God, visiting the iniquity of the fathers upon the children to the third and the fourth generation of those who hate me, but showing steadfast love to thousands of those who love me and keep my commandments. (Exodus 20:4-6)

One is not given to seeing God, nor is it allowed anyway. All the same, one wants to very much, if only because the fact of seeing God means that one is now in heaven. This is the reason why the longing to see Him has existed in all three Abrahamic religions from their very beginning. And this is what I want to tell you about. In looking at this question, I have decided to amalgamate Judaism and Islam because both of these two religions have managed to preserve the purity of monotheism. Both are equally and vehemently opposed to a pictorial depiction of God, and deny as a matter of principle the possibility of God becoming a man.

In the Old Testament there are more than a hundred instances of the expression 'the face of God', both in the context of refuting the possibility of seeing God within one's lifetime and of affirming the same. God's words of warning to Moses are deemed to be the most authoritative statement on the subject; to encounter God is to place yourself in mortal danger: '...you cannot see My face; for man shall not see Me and live.' (Exodus 33:20)

There is such a chasm between God's holiness and Man's worthlessness that a mere attempt to see Him would cause Man to die instantly. (Lev. 16:2, Num. 4:20) Even God's favourite – Moses – was no exception. When he asked God to show Himself (he obviously had certain doubts), God passed by Moses, who was standing in the cleft of a rock concealing him with His divine hand. All Moses could see were God's palm, rough from the work of creation, and His back. The meaning of this is clear: a direct encounter with God in this life is not possible.

There are countless paintings of Moses holding the tablets of the law given to him by God, but none depicting this seminal encounter. The depiction of God the Father is in any case a fairly rare occurrence in the history of world art. The only possible explanation for this artistic restraint is artists' unaccountable fear of the Judaic God. With good reason too – the God of Judaism is the God of divine wrath and human fear.

In the first place, He often 'hides His face' (Deuteronomy 31:17-18), i.e. keeps silent and leaves Man to his own devices. I will surely hide my face on that day on account of all the evil which they have done, because they have turned to other gods.

I have to agree with God on this one – there is no crime more heinous than turning to other gods. This is even worse than turning to other women.

Kabbalists go even further and maintain that God created Man's body while His face 'was hidden', whereas everything spiritual was created in the 'light of His face'. This is the reason why the body is dark, coarse, and defective by its very nature, whereas the soul is eternal and pure. If Man opposes the divine word and allows his body to rule over the soul, the Creator God will hide His face from him. After acquainting myself with the Kabbalah, I was left in no doubt; I personally didn't have a hope in hell of seeing God's face.

On the other hand, there is an alternative position in the Old Testament that asserts that Man's highest calling lies precisely in his ability to gaze upon God. For example, take these beautiful words of Jacob: 'I have seen God face to face, and yet my life is preserved.' (Genesis 32: 30) Or Job's dream: 'I shall see God, whom I shall see on my side, and my eyes shall behold, and not another.' *(Job 19:27)* 'I had heard of thee by the hearing of the ear, but now my eye sees thee.' (Job 42:5) David, who was given to pathos, also concurred: 'Thou hast said, "Seek ye My face. My heart says to Thee, Thy face, Lord, do I seek".' (Psalm 27:8)

In contrast to poetic Judaism, Islam is as ever concise and unambiguous. One cannot see Allah during one's lifetime because He is 'not to be seen through sight'. When asked whether he had seen the great and mighty Allah during his lifetime, the Prophet Muhammad replied:

> There was light, how could I see Him? The human eye is not able to gaze on much of creation's light; if one looks directly at the sun for a continuous period of time, one's sight would deteriorate. So, if the great and mighty Allah created the human eye in such a way as to make it impossible for it to gaze at the sun, so much more is Man during his lifetime unable to gaze at the great Allah.

In the life to come, the righteous will be able to see Allah without any limitation, both day and night.

> "O Messenger of Allah, will we see our Lord on the Day of Resurrection?" The Messenger of Allah said, "Do you doubt that you see the sun and the moon when there is no cloud?" They said, "No, O Messenger of Allah". He said, "You will see Him likewise". *(Hadith by Abu Said and Abu Hurayrah)*

> The only Muslims who believed in the possibility of seeing Allah during one's lifetime were the self-assured Sufis. Some Sufi thinkers of the ninth and tenth centuries claimed that the whole purpose of a journey to God is not just to be able 'to see' Him, but to be subsumed by Him and remain in Him.

Christianity initially began with promoting the same line of argument as Judaism with regard to the ability to see God. It called upon believers to know and love God, whom no one can see in this life, although this chance will come after one's death in the life to come. Moreover, the very expression 'to see God' meant a complete union with Him. There are many witnesses to this – from apostles John, Paul and Philip to the acknowledged theological authority, Thomas Aquinas: 'No one has ever seen God.' (John 1:18) 'Beloved, we are God's children now; it does not yet appear what we shall be, but we know that when He appears we shall be like Him, for we shall see Him as He is.' (1 John 3:2) 'And they shall see His face, and His name shall be on their foreheads. And night shall be no more; they need no light of lamp or sun, for the Lord God will be their light, and they shall reign for ever and ever.' (Revelation 22:4-5)

Still, in dealing with the question of seeing God, Christianity comes much closer to paganism than true monotheism. It proved unable to resist the temptation of God-gazing and quickly began to allow the possibility of seeing God in one's lifetime. This departure on the part of Christianity from the concept of God as an abstract idea is impossible to deny. First of all, Christ himself allowed this possibility. When the apostle Philip expressed his desire – natural to any believer – to see God, he received a definite answer; Jesus said to him, 'Have I been with you so long, and yet you do not know me, Philip? He who has seen me has seen the Father; how can you say, "Show us the Father?"' (John 14:9)

To those who, unlike the tiny band of apostles, did not get to interact with Christ, but who nevertheless proved their worthiness by the piety of their lives, Christ offers a brilliant opportunity to see God even before death: 'Blessed are the pure of heart, for they shall see God.'(Mt. 5:8)

One of the most ardent proponents of the possibility of seeing God already in one's lifetime was the tenth-century Hesychast monk, Symeon the New Theologian. His teaching formed the basis of subsequent Christian mysticism and the Orthodox ascetic practice. Symeon continued the tradition of the hermit saints of the third century but decided to withdraw, not to the desert but straight to the cemetery. Basing his assertion on his personal experience, Symeon claimed that God became visible to any man who repeated the prayer, 'O Lord, Jesus Christ, Son of God, have mercy on me, a sinner.' Symeon himself saw God many times in the form of a gleaming cloud (if he were my contemporary, he would have undoubtedly headed the World UFO Council).

Christian theologians see a new departure in the understanding of seeing God, as shown in the New Testament. No one had seen God until He came down on earth in the form of God the Son and revealed His face. Henceforth, God could be seen in the person of Jesus Christ. As for me, I discern clear elements of idolatry here, seeing that Christ has assumed the role of the incarnation of the Almighty God, that is, the role of an idol.

Moreover, according to Christian doctrine, even ordinary people, with a lot of effort on their part, can see the reflection of 'God's face' in those around them. The emphasis here is on 'a lot of effort'. In this way, one idol becomes many.

Also noteworthy is the place of icons in the religious cult, namely man-made depictions of God, which represent a compromise with paganism and an obvious backward step in relation to the concept of God as an idea. This view was shared by both opponents of Christianity and some of its proponents. Christian iconoclasts regarded all sacred depictions as idolatrous and the cult of icon veneration as idol-worship. This view didn't prevent them from acknowledging the positive role that icons played both in decorating churches and in maintaining piety among the faithful (visual aids are much better received than abstract ones). Also, icons were a sure help in attracting pagans to Christianity; all they had to do in order to convert was to substitute icons for their old idols. Does it even matter what you worship?

Generally speaking, no amount of justification or embellishment could hide the fact that we have moved very far away from the pure monotheistic concept of God as an elusive and formless Abstract. The most important point, however, is that in Christianity the ability to 'see the face of God' forms a watershed, separating the few righteous people from the sinful majority. The ability to 'see the face of God' is a privilege available only to the chosen few.

'When you shall have put off the mortal, and put on incorruption, then shall you see God worthily. For God will raise your flesh immortal with your soul; and then, having become immortal, you shall see the Immortal, if now you believe in Him'. (Theophilus of Antioch)

Christianity claims that all people are born spiritually blind and with nature marred by Original Sin – in other words, they are born defective. This natural defect sends people to their 'spiritual prison' and prevents them from 'seeing the face of God' and the light emanating from Him (the poetically disposed Orthodox even say that an ordinary human being is a damaged icon). It can't be helped; we must all live with this defectiveness and sinfulness. For God is seen by those who are enabled to see Him when they have the eyes of their soul opened: for all have eyes, but in some they are overspread and do not see the light of the sun. The appearance of God is ineffable and indescribable, and cannot be seen by eyes of flesh.

If a believer truly desires to see 'the face of God', he must turn the focus of his being onto God, that is, renounce his flesh and dedicate his whole life to Him. In following Christ, the believer first catches a glimpse of His back, just as Moses once saw the back of God the Father. Then, when Christ sees the believer's religious zeal, He turns around and the believer is thus able to 'see His face' also. In other words, in order to see the face of God – that symbol of heavenly holiness – during your lifetime, you will have to become holy yourself. This privilege would cost him dearly. It is impossible to 'see the face of God' without first losing one's own human one.

For an ordinary believer, the kind that can only dream of holiness, the desire, however ardent, to see the face of God is practically unrealisable. In order to achieve this, the person would need to make fundamental changes in his defective and imperfect human nature: to be cleansed from sin by means of a relentless struggle with himself and many personal sacrifices. This is unbelievably difficult; it is much easier simply to die all the sooner.

Let's draw some conclusions. Chimeras are dangerous illusions, because they are imposed on people by ethical standards that are contrary to common sense and biological nature. When one tries to live by these standards the results are internal neuroses and poorly controlled aggression; departing from them creates a sense of guilt in the face of society in general. As a result, the person is permanently unhappy because, on the one hand, he can't fulfil his basic needs, and on the other he falls short of the ideals proclaimed by the chimera in question. This situation often ends with a crime being committed against other people or an internalised disorder. The similarity of chimeras to psychiatric disorders leads us to the thought that their behaviour and method of reproduction greatly resembles another human affliction, in particular that most terrifying of human illnesses, the malignant tumour, whereby the natural multiplicity of benign cells is replaced with the uniformity of aggressively mutating ones. The similarity is borne out in linguistic analyses, starting with the word 'malignant'.

This comes from *malignus*, meaning 'evil' or 'envious' in Latin, the native tongue of medicine – what is there to be envious of, our good health? – and at this point has no affinity with the devil *diabolus*. However, in later languages, which evolved in the age of chimeras, the French word *malin* and the corresponding Spanish *maligno*, both denoting malignancy, are cognates with the names given to the Devil (*le malin, el maligno*). It would seem that in the Ancient World, chimeras had not yet infiltrated human lives to the extent that people were as routinely scared by the dangerous leader of the dark forces, who became the embodiment of all evil.

The parallels between the main features of malignant tumours and chimeras are really quite impressive:

Healthy cells normally undergo fifty divisions and then activate the process of self-destruction. Malignant cells are immortal as they can divide indefinitely for as long as the host organism is alive. They die together.

Chimeras always insist both on their own immortality within the body of humanity and on the immortality of their doctrines/commandments. The chimeras' life cycle is really very similar to that of cancer cells: they are born, grow exponentially, and rapidly gain strength. When they are actively opposed, they weaken, become wasted, but practically never die altogether, coming back to life from time to time to poison their hosts' earthly lives (or the lives of their descendants).

Healthy cells of different provenance co-exist peacefully and fulfil their allotted functions in a complementary way. Cancer cells always release toxins in order to kill off the host cells and replace them with their own kind.

Chimeras always mould all previous beliefs, ideologies, and social structures according to their own pattern, or do away with them altogether. Those who disagree are expelled or destroyed. One need only remember the persecutions unleashed within religious and totalitarian societies on even marginally different forms of religious doctrine, alternative opinions, or perceived heresies.

Healthy cells are unable to move spontaneously around the body and cause metastases.

Cancer cells begin to metastasise to other parts of the body when the tumour reaches a certain developmental stage, and these parts are destroyed in the same way as is the site of the initial tumour.

Chimeras infiltrate all aspects of human existence; they traverse society, moving from one group to another, and easily breach boundaries between different areas and countries. In connection to this, I would like to mention both the former and the present-day proselytism of religion as well as the rampant spread of social utopias in the twentieth century.

Healthy cells can exist and replicate only in certain temperatures and with the availability of certain chemicals that regulate cell division – the so-called growth factors – as well as in the presence of oxygen. Cancer cells are very hardy and can duplicate in almost any conditions.

Chimeras are also very unfussy and require neither intellectual achievements nor cultural diversity in order to thrive. In any case, science and the arts are not their growth factors. Moreover, the lower the level of Man's development and the worse his living conditions, the better the chimera feels and the easier it grows within him. The uneducated and oppressed masses were the breeding ground and nursery for the most numerous and successful chimeras.

A healthy body is made up of a large number of different forms of tissue, each one fulfilling a vital role unique to itself. Cancerous tumours are different from the tissue they originate from, but are very similar to tumours formed in other types of tissue.

The religious and social utopia chimeras are very similar to each other wherever they are found and irrespective of any previous characteristics of their new dwelling place. They adapt easily to any social structure and rapidly turn its healthy variety of life into a homogenous mass, similar to a single faith and/or a single purpose.

Cancer cells require nutrition in order to reproduce. This is extracted from the body's healthy cells, or rather from whatever is left of them.

Chimeras don't inhabit some parallel, disembodied world. They live alongside us, within us and without, and they also require food for sustenance. For them, this food is made up of natural human values and emotions.

So, you see, chimeras are nothing like childish fairy tales and fantasy; they are an aggressive destructive force in human lives. A person under the guidance of chimeras ceases to be the measure of things and the main player in his own life; he loses his natural integrity and feels unfulfilled. He can no longer judge his true needs and let go of autonomy.

Loyalty to chimeras is never an innocent or a harmless undertaking; a person maintaining fantastical notions about the future can't place much value in his own life today. Life is neglected in favour of future hopes in a nonexistent ideal world.

But most important of all, this person loses the ability to be happy. A person like this is easy prey for religious extremism and social utopias and is ready to dedicate his whole life to anything, to any kind of chimera, to anyone but himself. The more you love someone or something, the less you love yourself.

In astronomy, there is an apt and elegant notion called the black hole. This is an area of space-time with such a strong gravitational pull as to prevent any material object and even light from leaving it. As soon as an object approaches within a specified minimal distance, the black hole sucks it in like a giant cosmic vacuum cleaner. There is no possibility of ever returning back or even sending a distress signal.

Chimeras are black holes too. Every year, they consume vast amounts of your energy. That same energy could have been put to use in creating something of value for yourself and others. In the end, they will have gradually and insidiously consumed your ardour, your efforts, your faith in miracles, and your hopes for the future, and not once will they have returned your calls or offered any encouragement, reward or help. Your entire life will have fallen down one of those holes and there'll be nothing left.

There are too many chimeras around us, too many. The majority of people don't know how to separate the wheat from the chaff, real values from chimeras, and they spend their lives hoping for a better future or for a fair Last Judgement. Brought up this way, they bring their children up the same. It begins with the quite innocent vow to love another person till death us do part (the majority of us repeat this promise to a number of people) and finishes with the highly dangerous ardent romantic desire to build a heaven on earth in a particular country.

However, one should not despair. There is no certainty that children will follow the path of their parents. It is likely that our descendants will not see any sense in our chimeras, will have no desire to rely on them for their future, and so will create a different life for themselves. Ideals, like everything else in this world, are mortal: the indestructible, 'thousand-year long' German Reich lasted twelve years; the unshakable bastion of the bright future that was the Soviet Union – seventy-four years; the peasant kingdom of Democratic Kampuchea – four years; even the good old mythological gods left nothing behind except a pile of academic theses and a picture book.

Perhaps one day everyone becomes independent and will not need any Big Brothers. Here I would like to paraphrase an amazing diatribe of the British philosopher Bertrand Russell, 'Why I am not a Christian', in which he pronounced in 1927:

> What really moves people to believe in God is not any intellectual argument at all. Most people believe in God because they have been taught from early infancy to do it, and that is the main reason. Then I think that the next most powerful reason is the wish for safety, a sort of feeling that there is a big brother who will look after you.

It's quite possible that the modern chimeras will also one day be reduced to mere ruins, like the Ancient Greek and Roman temples.

One thing is certain; we shall all die and nothing will remain of our bodies and our splendid sensitive minds. In the words of Charles Bodler in his poem 'The Corpse':

> Yet you'll resemble this infection too
> One day, and stink and sprawl in such a fashion…

I don't know how old you are, dear reader, but from the bottom of my heart, I wish you the longest life possible. However, we have to be realistic; in any case, our 'longest' can't last more than a few decades. Wouldn't it be wiser to spend every minute, every moment, not on chimeras but on our own lives?

■ What I Want to Say to You ■

I stand against an idealistic interpretation of reality and do not accept any monotheistic doctrine. I hold with neither Gods nor any other Big Brother authority figures. The gods and authorities who my parents and society taught me to respect in my childhood gradually lost their lustre for me when I reached adulthood and saw how they were irrelevant or tainted. I wasn't attracted by any other gods or superior beings and they didn't have anything to offer me. So, with respect to other people's opinions, the opinion I respect most is my own. My position isn't based on a blind adherence to an ideology, as is often the case. I think that monotheism has done everything it could do to destroy reason and a rational approach to reality. Calls to test religious propositions (and especially the idea of the divine presence) by empirical means have been silent for many millennia. This kind of position has no place in my value system, where reason occupies the first – and every other place – in the list of priorities. My estrangement from monotheism is motivated by my conviction that its appearance heralded a radically new and harmful stage within human history. The adoption of monotheistic doctrines significantly slowed down the progress of human civilisation and, despite trying it out for many centuries, people didn't become any happier. Quite the opposite, in fact.

Likewise, I don't accept the view that human society was positively influenced by religious consciousness. Those brief periods when religious culture tolerated reasoned enquiry were immediately succeeded by much lengthier periods of time in which it was obliterated.

Without a doubt, somebody will say to this that today's monotheistic religions are different from each other and will produce masses of arguments in their favour. I know all the arguments and I am happy that they are there; I even support the freedom of religion, although I personally have much more sympathy for the freedom *not* to believe.

I accuse no one, and don't expect anyone to do anything in particular. Likewise, I don't judge people according to their religious allegiances but according to their personal qualities; after all, in real life, there isn't just a single type of human being.

Reasonable and highly rational people knock on wood three times to avoid bad luck, just like everyone else. They also cross the road when they see a black cat, often say 'God willing', and even put their heads round the door of the church sometimes.

At the same time, religious people engage in forbidden sex on forbidden days with forbidden partners. They are very fearful of death and, when they fall seriously ill, rush off not to pray in church, but to see the doctor.

So you see, this division of people into pagans and those who believe in the One God serves only one purpose – to describe the eternal struggle between reason and the chimera and to find our own place within it.

It is now possible to give a more or less accurate description of the contents of this book. It is a kind of manual containing the methodology for 'cleansing' people from their sin, as religion understands it, and avoiding the temptation that leads to such sin in the future. If you follow the advice contained in it, you should be able to distinguish an exalted spiritual life from a sinful materialistic one. You will learn to appreciate the advantages of the ascetic life. That is to say, the voluntary renunciation of natural desires and their associated pleasures, in particular masturbation and sex, and thereby see the most direct route to holiness.

Or, if I am being serious, this book is about the way people mutilate themselves both physically and spiritually for the sake of a chimera.

I have never really appreciated this situation but I have tolerated it for a very long time, almost for my whole adult life. Until on one fine day – I do not even remember when exactly – I did not have any more patience and I was practically obliged to start to meticulously denounce the chimeras surrounding me. One after another.

The connoisseurs of the art of war, especially of artillery, would immediately recognise in this approach a literary analogue of a very efficient practice of target shooting: in each chapter I attack only one chimera; there is only one target. My reader has a momentous choice: either he can shoot with us, hiding his backside, or he can try to protect his beloved chimera with his own body.

The Sovereign of Evil

Is a God who cannot protect us from Evil really worth worshipping? The existence of evil is an undeniable fact; no one would attempt to deny that for some, life is an ocean of evil with a few islands of goodness scattered here and there. This ocean begins with petty instances of evil, usually something quite insignificant and forgivable – a grazed knee, an unexpected bout of flu, a reprimand from the boss – and finishes with evil that is universal and lethally dangerous – world wars, genocide, religious purges, and political terrorism. If one were to cast a cold and disinterested look at all this evil, one might easily conclude that if there is a God, He doesn't much like us and shows this in every possible way. Let me first explain what the One God is for the believers.

The un-circumscribed, almighty One God the Father is the cause of absolutely everything. He is the primary and pre-eternal Being, the Creator and Source of all that is material and non-material, the absolute Truth and Goodness, and consequently the Supreme Lawgiver, Master, and ultimate Judge.

The One God is actively involved in all our daily activities; He knows the fate of each individual person and anticipates both their actions in the nearest future and their consequences. God is able to alter everything, correct all mistakes, end all injustice, and compensate for any loss.

This wonderful tale about the One God has a single weak spot: how is the existence of the almighty and omniscient God compatible with the existence of Evil? If we consider God to be almighty and omniscient, Evil cannot simply exist.

I know perfectly well that the majority of believers require no additional arguments justifying the existence of God. They think of religion in the context of their upbringing, ancestral ties and cultural traditions, and have never seriously considered the relationship between God and Evil. There is nothing more important to them than God since they have been brought up thinking that their purpose in this life is to serve and worship this God.

The very thought that God could be the source of evil is so unacceptable to them that they are ready to defend God with all their might and at any cost, without recourse to any facts, logic, or common sense. It's as if they are defending some sweet childhood dream; their god, just like their parents and family, is obviously kinder that all other gods and by definition can't have anything to do with evil. He has everything to do with goodness, but certainly not evil.

They have another ready character to fulfil that role – the Devil – who is responsible for evil and generally everything that's bad. In consequence, the Devil's existence is inseparable from God's. In his 'Last Philosophical Testament', Bertrand Russell can't 'see that from what mystics tell us you can get any argument for God which is not equally an argument for Satan'.

Moreover, the Devil is necessary to God's survival. If he didn't exist, God would have to assume the responsibility for Evil. I strongly doubt that he'd have any supporters after this.

So I really couldn't continue this chapter without saying a few words about the myth-ological figure known alternatively as the Devil, Satan, Lucifer, and Iblis. He is the chief slanderer, the tempter, the master of hell, the supreme spirit of evil who sows divisions among us, ruins us, and then causes our final perdition.

■ The Prince of this World ■

Better to reign in Hell, than serve in Heav'n.
John Milton, *Paradise Lost*

The Devil has a history no shorter or less illustrious than his antithesis, God. Theologians paid so much attention to the Devil and devoted so much of their time to writing about him that it would be difficult or even impossible to summarise all the material here. Nevertheless, I decided to systematise the existing material on the Devil and present the main ideas concisely. Historically, the problem with the Devil can be divided into five main propositions.

First proposition
The Devil doesn't exist at all; instead there is a multitude of different gods. This doesn't mean there is no evil in the world; its existence was obvious even to primitive savages. To put it simply, any of the gods could cause both good and evil.

All the gods had capricious, unpredictable personalities and were ready to dispense random gifts or undeserved punishments; the two-faced Janus is an embodiment of this very prototype. The multiplicity of gods that these nations possessed didn't change a thing; each one of them could exhibit positive as well as negative qualities and every believer was free to choose not just a favourite deity but a favourite 'face' too.

The notion that there is a separation between good and evil forces in the world arose relatively late in religion and started with classifying gods into benign ones who exem-plified good, and malevolent ones personifying evil (we don't need to remind you that the highly developed civilisations of Ancient Greece and Rome didn't take to this idea).

The benign gods were later conflated into the One Great God, the only source of universal good, and the malevolent ones produced our image of the Devil.

Second proposition

The Devil exists, but God is much more powerful than him. This view of the Devil arrived on the back of monotheism. In the theology of monotheism, good and evil are not equal. God is the Good. Evil is personified by the Devil, the destructive force in the universe, the master of hell, and the embodiment of Man's sinful nature and passions, but whatever he thinks of himself, he is no match for God.

The Devil's origins are given as follows. God created virtuous and decent Angels to dwell in paradise but the excessively proud among them eschewed goodness and demanded equality with God. In other words, they became His fiercest enemies (for who wants to share power?). The rebellious angels headed by the Devil, Lucifer, were expelled from paradise and sent to oversee hell. Nevertheless, God allowed them some very limited freedom of action in order to test His believers.

Judaism, which had absorbed many of the near Eastern and Anatolian pagan gods, portrayed the Devil variously, as God's adversary or else the accusing angel in His service, and endowed him with a variety of names.

The Book of Job portrays him as the people's tormentor who had been given autonomy by God to test their free will – a free will biased towards God, of course.

Christianity usually names the Devil Satan, the father of all evil and lies, and he is identified with the serpent in the Garden of Eden who brought death to the whole world. It was he who tempted the unfortunate Adam and Eve, and thereby started the chain reaction of momentous events – the expulsion of Man from paradise, the loss of immortality, the appearance of Original Sin, and the necessity of the advent of Jesus Christ for its expiation. All of the Devil's actions are directed towards Man's destruction, and therefore Man can only earn his place in paradise by repudiating the wiles of the Devil.

Certain Christian writers even claimed that the Devil appeared on earth exclusively in order to have unclean sexual relations with its fallen women. This is the reason why the Devil is most commonly symbolised by a phallus.

As Christianity spread both within the enormous Roman Empire and beyond its borders, the image of Satan became conflated with local pagan deities as well as with certain heretical and schismatic Christians, the Gnostics, Manicheans, Bogomils and Cathars. It's notable that every religious confession is quick to call a rival confession demonic. For example, Luther, the father of Protestantism, was convinced that the Pope of Rome was the Devil.

Beginning with the Enlightenment, the fear of the Devil began to lessen somewhat and he came to personify the religious aspects of human emotional excesses. Even the entire French Revolution was seen in this context by the conservative philosopher, Joseph de Maistre.

In Islam, the Devil is represented by the fallen angel Iblis. He is the father of evil spirits, the genies, and personifies a lack of faith in God. He is forever stealthily inciting the believer to sin.

Third proposition

Both God and the Devil exist independently and their powers are roughly equal.

This was the view of those teachings within Christianity that inclined towards dualism, the juxtaposition between the spiritual and the material, and that are generally classified as Gnostic.

I believe that the dualism espoused by the Gnostics had a most logical basis – a concern for God's image. The Gnostics believed (with good reason) that the material world is imperfect, sunk as it is in the mire of sin and evil.

There is no way that the perfect God, the source of absolute goodness, could have created such a world. One possible solution to this dilemma was to suppose that our world was created by an 'evil force', the imperfect Demiurge or Devil, whom the Gnostics identified as Yahweh (clearly the Old Testament wasn't their favourite book).

The higher spiritual world, the kingdom of the future life with God, of absolute goodness and light, is on the other side. The master here is the eternal God the Redeemer, who exists outside of time and space. He has no interest in our material world whatsoever; He hasn't created it, doesn't rule over it, and bears no responsibility for it.

Both these worlds have always been there but never mixed. They are engaged in a constant battle between themselves; their powers are equally matched so that Goodness can never vanquish Evil, which is indestructible and therefore invincible.

Only on one occasion did the light and darkness mix. Man was the result of this fusion and immediately faced an agonisingly difficult situation. Since his immortal soul was made from light and his mortal body from darkness, he himself became the battlefield of the eternal struggle between good and evil. Worse than that, human souls became locked in the prison of the material world, which was ruled over by the Devil.

Naturally, every believer wants to free his soul from the constraints of the darkness of the material world and help it along to the place appointed for it – the Kingdom of Light. In order to achieve this, Man must possess true spiritual knowledge about God and the aeons that surround Him, which can be imparted through supernatural Revelation.

Now for some good news. Since the believer can't receive Revelation by his own efforts, the Redeemer God comes to his aid and resolves this sad state of affairs. Because of His great love and limitless compassion for Man, God sent His messenger Jesus Christ who, through His teaching and Gospels, taught Man how to escape from the power of the Demiurge/Devil.

Fourth proposition

There is God, but the Devil is stronger. This idea is called 'Religious Satanism' and its history is even older than that of monotheistic religions. The practice of venerating particularly gloomy and cruel deities can be observed in the most ancient civilisations. In monotheistic times, Satanist numbers even increased because they were swelled by the adherents of the ancient pagan religions who had survived persecution and had not recanted.

Religious Satanism exists to this day and continues to worship fallen angels and their leader, Satan. His followers believe that Satan has much more to offer to humanity than the so-called benevolent forces, which exhort, admonish, promise, but deliver nothing at all. At the end of the day, Satan is also a god and has a god's power, freedom, and knowledge.

I also believe that the power of the Devil as a concept is definitely underestimated and a greater use of his image could be highly beneficial to many people. If we take evil works as proof of the Devil, we have all we need. God's existence, on the contrary – a mere hypothesis – cannot be proven by reason or senses.

The Devil requires no justification or defence, which makes his designation as the source of all the world's evil most convenient.

The Devil's power is at least equal to that of God and he uses it freely. If you are not convinced, just look around and watch the news on the television.

In contrast to God, the Devil is good at keeping his promises; far from waning, evil is actually on the increase.

The Devil has been by God's side from the very beginning and has conclusively proved his loyalty and dependability by his actions. If this were not so, God would not have entrusted the all-important task of punishing sinners after their death to the Devil.

The most attractive of all is the ability to blame the Devil for all of our personal failings without feeling any guilt for it ourselves. Being able to trace our sinful sexual desire to the Devil's wiles is particularly satisfying. Who can better prove to our wives that it was not our fault?

Also, all true believers will be glad to know that Christ's opinion of the Devil as 'the prince of this world' (John 12:31) has been confirmed.

Fifth proposition

There is neither God nor the Devil, only Man. If this is the case, then should we include this proposition in this list of positions on the nature of the Devil?

The answer is very simple. Modern philosophy acknowledges a movement known as 'modern-day Satanism'. This movement arose as a reaction against a religious chimera: in the course of many millennia, monotheistic religions have indoctrinated people into a zombie-like acceptance and worship of the mythological God and a hatred of the similarly mythological Satan.

Modern Satanism is a philosophy of atheism par excellence, which uses the myths of the Devil/Satan to enable Man to find his own place in the world and to strengthen him as a personality. Satan's image in this philosophy is used symbolically to represent the Cosmos (in the ancient understanding of the word), the force of nature, the freedom of the individual, his pride, and a healthy egotism and belief in the self.

In the Abrahamic religious tradition it was the rebellious Satan alone who dared to challenge the Almighty God. For this he was deposed and endured extreme loneliness, nevertheless remaining proud and truly free. It's not for nothing that this fact was noted by many great writers and poets, especially those already inclined to romanticism.

There are as many varieties and subsets of Satanism as there are branches of Christianity, but the acknowledged best exponent of the teaching is found in the works of Anton LaVey. His ideas are so attractive that if we were employed by a ministry of education in some Western nation, we would make his texts compulsory reading in high schools and lycées (if only as part of the study of world religions). I have always upheld democratic principles in education, especially as far as resisting chimeras and upholding humane ideas are concerned.

The main ideas of modern Satanism represented by Anton LaVey can be explained as follows:

Reason. Our life must be based only on reason, logic, and the information imparted to us by our sensuous organs. This concerns everything: our values, convictions, aims, desires, and actions. In connection to it, we must renounce all forms of mysticism and the so-called 'supernatural' knowledge.

Flesh. A human being is first and foremost an animal, albeit a higher functioning one. You can't torment his nature without dire consequences; this denigration doesn't ennoble the soul, as monotheistic religions assert, but destroys it. Man's carnal instincts are sacred. This is especially true of the sexual instinct, which doesn't tolerate any limitations or artificial constraints. Any human being is equally free to remain faithful to a single partner or to satisfy his or her sexual needs with a number of people, according to his or her individual choice.

Religion. God did not create Man; instead it was people who invented God. This makes any form of self-torment for His sake foolish. Religion espouses a herd mentality and, being an entirely irrational phenomenon, cannot bring happiness to people. On the other hand, it's very successful in quashing all human individuality and with it the human ability to develop and create.

The notion of the death of God advanced by some philosophers is rather positive; when Man has lost any hope in divine Providence, he turns away from suffering and begins to savour his earthly existence.

Morality. A person can attain moral perfection without any external help. That's why he should live his own life and refuse to believe any moral dogma thrust on him because of its supposed 'divine origins'. Religious moral codes are as much a product of human hands as pagan idols are.

Society. Governments try to 'sell' to us the idea that all people are equal in value. This 'white lie' is far from reality – equality is against the laws of nature. This is true both in relation to the body and to the mind. Strong, intelligent people should co-operate with weak and stupid ones, but only up to a point. They shouldn't waste excessive amounts of time on them; weak 'vampires' demand enormous attention and care, which they never reciprocate.

Despite all of the above, it would be wrong to say that modern day Satanism has no sacred aspect. It contains rather a lot of sacred qualities. This is a different sort of sacredness from the one preached about in churches.

Modern Satanism believes that religion should point not outwards towards a mythical God, as happens in monotheism, but inwards towards Man himself. A human being is the only thing we have of ultimate value; he is also a god and there are no other gods beside him.

Offering one's veneration and sacrifice – no matter who you are offering them to – demeans Man and has an adverse effect on his psychological make-up. If you are going to venerate someone and take part in rituals, it's far better to direct them yourself. Better still is to worship no one; prayer consumes a lot of time and effort which can be put to a better, more creative use.

When you look at the matter in hand like this, it all becomes crystal clear. Man's most important feast is his own birthday and his greatest loss, his own death.

There is nothing new, but this philosophy is still very refreshing. And the last. Isn't this Satanism and its Man-Devil worthy of interest and respect? What's not to like here?

▪ Theodicy: God is not Evil ▪

The co-existence of God and the Devil must be given the right interpretation lest it cast a shadow on the Creator's power and wisdom, and prove a hindrance in recruiting more of the faithful in need of a Protector God.

In fact, it is easy to ascribe all Good to God, but who is then responsible for Evil? Why are there natural cataclysms, destructive wars, and fearful epidemics in the God-created ideal world? Why do children die? Why does He, the Supreme Creator and wise Ruler, allow the existence of evil and suffering? How can anything take place outside of God's will?

Theodicy, meaning literally 'the justification of God', was created as a separate religious doctrine precisely in order to resolve these issues and to answer these fundamental questions. The main purpose of theodicy was to combine the uncombinable – the idealised world of the divine with the real world of evil. What was required was to offer decisive and irrefutable proof that the existence of evil in no way contradicts the religious definition of God as almighty and good. Otherwise, faith would lose all meaning, because the fundamental idea of all monotheistic religions is the belief that Faith, Hope, and Goodness will be victorious; Evil will be punished and Goodness rewarded.

Theodicy had another important task, namely to detract the believer's attention from evil and to direct it towards God, to divert the attention from daily life on earth to the one further down the line in heaven.

It is an old trick. Politicians have done the same for centuries, attempting to divert people's attention from internal problems at home by highlighting a potential external enemy. This is quite logical: the more we worship God, the less readily we notice the evil around us. Ideally, we wouldn't notice it at all, or if we do we explain it away with improbable theories. Best of all, we need only repeat Tertullian, 'I believe, because it is absurd.'

Theodicy was quick to identify the source of all the evil in the world, namely Man. This premise, fully in accordance with the basic precepts of monotheism, demonstrated Man's fundamental worthlessness, at the same time placing God beyond his reach and knowledge and thus making Him bulletproof to Man's criticism and discharging him from any responsibility for human suffering. Theodicy is not a science, but a religious doctrine, a means of strengthening the ideal. The true goal of this doctrine lies neither in the justification of God, nor in the impartial search for some incontrovertible evidence or rational explanation for the possibility of the co-existence of God and Evil. The objective truth is that the world is imperfect and full of suffering and injustice, but from a religious standpoint the world is perfect and full of goodness.

The point of theodicy is altogether different – to convince the world by all possible means of the existence of the One God despite the total absence of His mark upon the material world. Without theodicy, monotheism would not have developed so successfully and survived to today. Theodicy provided justification for the occurrence of Evil, citing divine Providence and Man's sin as reasons for its existence. In this way, through theodicy, the death of paganism and the enthronement of the One God were irrevocably established. The best theological minds, the most educated people of their time, spared no effort in trying to explain something which is fundamentally inexplicable. The Fathers of the Church announced the advent of God and declared solemnly that faith is fundamentally irrational and requires no intellectually valid proofs. Why then do they seek to justify God? Why do they need theodicy?

I think the answer is simple. The vast amount of unexplained evil in the world was, for the Fathers themselves, a cause of doubt in the Almighty's existence and goodness. Maybe a worm of doubt was stirring within: is there a God at all? What if there is no God and we have wasted our entire life – itself devoid of pleasure and utterly consumed by being at His service? They deployed theodicy not in order to justify God, but in order to protect themselves from their own doubts (even if they failed to realise this). It became a sort of invisible bullet-proof vest, guarding minds and souls. No person capable of critical thinking can find long discussions on theodicy very interesting. In order to take theodicy seriously, one must believe in God very fervently and nowadays this is a great rarity in the Christian world.

The classic theory of theodicy (that developed in the period from the earliest Christian writers until the middle of the twentieth century) doesn't recognise the existence of evil at all, or it regards it as a trial sent to the world by God. The theory explains the world's imperfection by Man's free will, by the consequences of the fall from grace, or by the special providence of God which leads the believer to salvation. God is either not responsible for the appearance of evil or not guilty of the same.

Despite there being a whole variety of different theological theories, theodicy can be reduced to a set of general ideas.

Evil is the result of Man's God-given freedom and a punishment for his sins. God gave people the possibility of choosing between good and evil and they used it to commit evil and sinful deeds. Humanity marred with its sin the perfect world created by God, and therefore the existence of evil in the world can't be blamed on Him. But this concept of free will is incompatible with God's omnipresence and omnipotence. If He knows everything ahead of time, including Man's choice, then there is no freedom by definition.

Moreover, if God created every soul, why did He endow it with the ability to sin? What was He thinking of? So, why doesn't He interfere to prevent evil and sin? Is He in fact to be blamed for evil? Or does he enjoy the role of a powerful manipulator?

Also – if evil originated from Man, how can you explain the existence of natural disasters? Those do not depend on Man. Does it mean that God is entirely responsible for them?

Or probably the One God profits from the existence of evil in the world. Natural suffering, disease, old age, and inevitable death – all of these rob Man of his self-assurance and pride. It is important that Man is humbled by being shown the temporary nature of his existence and the futility of his hopes. Only then can he give up his foremost sin – his love for this unworthy world – and thus be easy to manipulate.

Nothing will change if God doesn't exist and it was the Church which invented Him and his Laws in order to manipulate the believers. The Church benefits from making this illusory God innocent because it helps it to humiliate Man and make him insignificant and dependent.

Evil is God's agent intended for Man's improvement and moral perfection. Without free will and evil, it is impossible to make a right moral choice, to place any value in goodness, to avoid sin and acquire virtue. God allows evil inasmuch as it serves to improve Man's moral formation. What appears as evil to an imperfect and limited mind is actually goodness. God's whole purpose is just; only God knows what is good and what is evil. But why hasn't the Almighty God found another method of explaining the difference between good and evil? Why hasn't He created a kind of man who would not need free will and always chose good over evil? I have always been convinced that free will is very dangerous because it usually leads to sin and suffering. If God punished evil-doing immediately, people would be quick to realise that behaving well was in their own interests.

The idea that virtue cannot exist without sin reminds me of my mother-in-law, with whom I had a very tense relationship. She didn't like me because I could always find a way to please everyone, deal with everybody, and I earned extra money outside my job as a university professor. Her own husband was also a university professor but never earned any extra money.

So, during a calm evening at home, when everyone was reading and no one said a word for at least one hour, she suddenly raised her head and solemnly pronounced: 'During twenty-five years of impeccable service I was never engaged in any sort of corruption and I was never bribed. I would never take a bribe.'

At that time, I was about thirty years old and surprised by what she said. I answered her: 'But in order to know whether you'd accept a bribe or not, you must be in the position to be bribed. And if nobody ever tried to bribe you, you can't make any conclusion whether you would accept a bribe.' I was moved by the best motives and only wanted to express the idea that it was unreasonable to talk about virtue if there was no place for sin. That I was motivated by moral concerns didn't help me. The next morning I had to take my wife and son and move from their spacious house to a rented flat. I have never spoken to my mother-in-law again.

Evil is a part of divine providence and people are not given to understand it fully. God created the best possible world for our use, where evil is relative to and occupies only a small part of the Absolute Good. Unfortunately, the human mind is so weak and limited in relation to the mind of God that it is unable to discern divine providence and thus comprehend the meaning of evil and suffering. The mind of God is beyond human understanding, as are His plans, and we therefore have no right to judge Him. But there's no reason to despair: the final answer to the problem of the existence of evil will be given in the day of the Last Judgement. God Himself will explain everything to you, wherever you happen to be, in heaven or in hell.

I am not offended that God is more intelligent than I am and that He doesn't plan on telling me his plans. This is why He is God. However, I don't really want to suffer during my life on earth just so that one can explain to me one day why exactly I suffered. Even if there is a huge recompense for it. So I prefer to live without suffering and evil right away. I can pass now to the history of theodicy and its main heroes. Theodicy is so expansive as to render virtually impossible any systematic account of it, particularly within a single section of a chapter. While the author has a chance of living long enough to finish writing it, the readers are most likely to turn to flight before getting even halfway through.

This is the reason why I decided that my stop on this planet would be brief, as would be my account of what we have seen there. For some reason I keep thinking of the American first moon-landing, which lasted only two and a half hours. But what an impact it had.

▪ How Job Doubled his Assets ▪

With faith, there are no questions; without faith there are no answers.
Israel Meir Kagan

Although the term theodicy was only coined by Leibniz in 1710, the notion of God-justification has a much longer history, stretching back no fewer than 2,500 years. The problem of the co-existence of evil with God was first stated by Greek philosophers. First Socrates and then Epicurus posed the question of the co-existence of evil and the Higher Power, by which they understood both a multiplicity of gods and a single abstract God.

There are only four possible solutions to the problem. The Higher Power or God:
– is willing to free the world from disaster, but is unable to do so, or
– is able to do so but is not willing, or
– is both unable and unwilling, or
– is both willing and able, in which case, why does evil still exist in the world?

The first three options are inconsistent with our understanding of God. The third one is particularly bad; this kind of God is lacking in both power and morals.

The absence of any visible result in the fourth option also puts the whole necessity of God's existence and veneration into doubt. Plato was the first to identify evil as a fundamental problem for theology; the One and Good God is the First Cause of all that is, and the existence of evil challenges His very being. The problem is this: if there is evil in the world, then the world is ruled by someone other than God, which in turn means that God is either not Good or not One. At this point Plato came to a stop and did not defend God any further.

There is nothing to add to this dry and devastating conclusion and the best solution would have been to close the subject of theodicy forever. But it was not closed; fruitless discussions on the matter continued until our own days.

I am convinced that ancient philosophers developed this question for one reason only, which is curiosity. They didn't worship the One God, and gods and the divine in general didn't have any special place in ancient philosophy. All efforts were concentrated on Man.

The problem of co-existence of God and Evil became a key topic for all monotheistic religions, and particularly for Christianity, being a faith of a God who is Love and the Universal Good. However, we must start with the first monotheistic religion, Judaism.

Theodicy is not a particularly relevant subject for Judaism; Yahweh needs no justification. The God Yahweh never declared that he was kind. Yahweh is the God of Vengeance, the tyrannical and jealous God who is equally responsible for good and evil: 'I form the light and create darkness, I make peace and create calamity; I, the Lord, do all these things.' (Isaiah 45)

On a whim He destroys whole nations, threatens the pharaoh to kill his son if he doesn't set the people of Israel free, and for no reason kills anyone not to His liking.

In other words, Yahweh is nothing like the God of Love. Even when there were valid reasons for Yahweh's wrath, such as people's disobedience, as in the case of Adam and Eve, or failing to fulfil His commandments, as happened with the shepherd Onan, the punishment doled out was usually far too severe in relation to the initial offence.

Did Adam and Eve really deserve the punishment of being exiled from paradise and losing their immortality? Was the unfortunate Onan really guilty of death for indulging in our beloved masturbation?

The only thing I am not sure about is whether Yahweh would accept his responsibility for the Holocaust and make some necessary changes to the Old Testament. I will deal with this question later.

Richard Dawkins gave what seems in my opinion the best description of the dark side of the Judaic God:

> The God of the Old Testament is arguably the most unpleasant character in all fiction: jealous and proud of it; a petty, unjust, unforgiving control-freak; a vindictive, bloodthirsty ethnic cleanser; a misogynistic, homophobic, racist, infanticidal, genocidal, filicidal, pestilential, megalomaniacal, sadomasochistic, capriciously malevolent bully. Using today's legal definitions, the Old Testament is engaged in inciting hatred and violence on the grounds of religion, race, and nationality. It's not entirely clear why Judaism, which is so proud of its unfathomable God and its Tanakh (Old Testament), should be so concerned with theodicy.

All the same, Judaism is concerned with it. The Book of Job contains the first practical exposition of theodicy in human history. Its exposition of the ideas and arguments around the justification of God were so comprehensive that practically nothing remained that could be fashioned into a subsequent Christian doctrine of theodicy.

The story didn't raise any questions about the existence of God or offer an explanation of the nature of evil; it was dedicated entirely to the essence of divine morality. Can the Almighty God possess a moral sense, and is He obliged to be not just a supreme, but also a *moral* being?

This classical story of Judaism, which is a part of the Writings section of the Jewish Bible, is in our opinion one of the most exciting, contradictory, not to say provocative stories of the Old Testament. Some Jewish exegete even insisted that Job never existed and the whole account is nothing but a didactic allegory. Most probably they didn't like the fact that the Book of Job could be interpreted as a challenge to the faith, seeing that it portrayed God as not only allowing the possibility of evil, but as its actual source.

This naive approach is hardly justifiable; Job's historical existence is as likely as it is unlikely since it concerns all the other biblical prophets. It is impossible to believe in one part of a miracle but not another. Many people (myself included) believe that God never existed either, but this doesn't mean that this is reason enough to stop worshipping Him, still less to stop learning His divine Law.

The story of Job goes as follows. A righteous man named Job was a very wealthy man and possessed a large and united family – his faithful wife and their 10 children:

> There was a man in the land of Uz whose name was Job; and that man was blameless and upright, and one who feared God and shunned evil. And seven sons and three daughters were born to him. Also, his possessions were seven thousand sheep, three thousand camels, five hundred yoke of oxen, five hundred female donkeys, and a very large household, so that this man was the greatest of all the people of the East.

God drew his partner Satan's attention to Job:

> "Have you considered My servant Job, that there is none like him on the earth, a blameless and upright man, one who fears God and shuns evil?" So Satan answered the Lord and said, "Does Job fear God for nothing? Have You not made a hedge around him, around his house-hold, and around all that he has on every side? You have blessed the work of his hands, and his possessions have increased in the land. But now, stretch out Your hand and touch all that he has, and he will surely curse You to Your face!"

Job's extraordinary fidelity to God made Satan jealous and the latter persuaded God to put Job's faith to the test; perhaps the righteous man only serves God because of the untroubled and happy life with which God blessed him.

Satan's idea clearly appealed to God; after all, what absolute ruler wouldn't want to test his subject's loyalty? He therefore allowed Satan to do anything he wished to Job, except deprive him of his life. Through Satan's efforts, Job loses all his property and his children, but remains firm in his faith in God. Then Job arose, and tore his robe, and shaved his head, and fell upon the ground, and worshipped. And he said, 'Naked I came from my mother's womb, and naked shall I return; the Lord gave, and the Lord has taken away; blessed be the name of the Lord.' *(Job 1:20-22)* God tells Satan that

Job 'still holds fast his integrity, although you incited me against him to destroy him without reason.' Satan is not satisfied with his answer:

> "Skin for skin! All that a man has he will give for his life. But stretch out your hand and touch his bone and his flesh, and he will curse you to your face." And the Lord said to Satan, "Behold, he is in your hand; only spare his life."
>
> So Satan went out from the presence of the Lord and struck Job with loathsome sores from the sole of his foot to the crown of his head. And he took a piece of broken pottery with which to scrape himself while he sat in the ashes.
>
> Then his wife said to him, "Do you still hold fast your integrity? Curse God and die." But he said to her, "You speak as one of the foolish women would speak. Shall we receive good from God, and shall we not receive evil?"

Job's faithfulness is even more extraordinary if you consider the fact that at the time the book was written, the concept of a blessed life after death had not yet been formed. Thus Job had no expectation of a just reward from God beyond the grave; rewards had to be received only during one's lifetime. Man's fate after death resembled the one outlined by Homer in the *Iliad*. The dead, or rather their shadows, pass on to the perpetually dark underworld kingdom of the dead, where they live a shadowy life devoid of either the blessings of heaven or the torments of hell.

The only way to achieve at least a semblance of immortality was through the offspring left behind, but Job was deprived even of that; his children perished and with them 'all the memory of him'. Job knew that his death would end everything – all joy, grief, and hope.

Although blameless and subjected to severe trials, Job still did not waver in his faith. The case of Job moved the Jewish philosophers to conclude that Man is not given to understand the real meaning of suffering. Job's grief was exacerbated by the fact that he did not get 'to see the face of God'. God ignored Job's questions about the place of justice in the world full of injustice and wicked people. Job never doubted God's almighty power (especially after losing all his property and children in a single moment); he simply wanted to be sure of God's moral stance and the existence of divine justice. His despair led him to abandon his faith in the justice of God. God's answer took the form of a long and eloquent list of all His achievements in creating a perfect world and a demonstration of the signs of His might.

'Can you draw out Leviathan with a hook, or snare his tongue with a line which you lower? Can you put a reed through his nose, or pierce his jaw with a hook? Will he make many supplications to you? Will he speak softly to you? Will he make a covenant with you? Will you take him as a servant forever'? (Job 41:1-8)

There was nothing left for Job but to accept this answer and this God: 'Then Job answered the Lord and said: "'Behold, I am vile; what shall I answer You? I lay my hand over my mouth."' (Job 40:3-4)

After receiving this answer from Job, God was so impressed by the strength of his faith that He restored all his former wealth, granted him 10 new children, and 140 years of life.

It turned out to be quite a profitable business for Job after all; in a very short time, he managed to double his assets (all except the children).

Such is the value of a strong and sincerely held faith. However, some ancient Talmudic scholars were highly doubtful of Job's sincerity and humility, and claimed in agreement with Satan that after recovering from leprosy, Job continued to serve God only out of fear rather than love. Although God gave Job twice as many cattle as before (and this is no small matter), He did not simply restore Job's perished children but caused new ones to be born to replace them. You can imagine that Job could have had some favourite children among the 'old' set whom he would still miss, and be angry with God because of this.

I can't help but note that other faithful Jews fared rather less well. Yahweh didn't express any desire to talk to them, to alleviate their suffering, or help in any way. There was no recovery for the terminally ill, nor was there a way out of the ovens for the six million Holocaust victims murdered during the Second World War.

The story of Job is a solemn hymn which glorifies dogma, according to which God is almighty, beneficent, and rules over His world with wisdom. God always rewards goodness and punishes evil. The fact that Satan, the originator of evil, remained unpunished, leads one to the unhappy thought that for God, Satan was always more of a colleague rather than His opponent.

It goes without saying that the Judaic sages who'd dedicated their whole lives to the minute examination of every word (not to mention every sentence) of the Old Testament paid particular attention to the story of Job, from which they drew definitive conclusions. Given this fact, it's a little unclear why Christian theologians wasted so much of their time and effort on developing the following theories of theodicy:

> God never punishes anyone without due cause; God cannot be accused of injustice. Just because Job never acknowledged his guilt in the course of his suffering doesn't mean there wasn't any. No one can consider himself altogether blameless in the sight of God because sin is an inseparable part of human nature. The cause of human suffering is to be found *within* Man, not *without:* "For affliction does not come from the dust, nor does trouble spring from the ground. Yet Man is born to trouble, as the sparks fly upward." (Job 5:6-7)

As suffering is not an absolute evil, but is used by the Creator for the good of humanity, it must be received with gratitude, not hatred. Nor is suffering necessarily a punishment for sin already committed; suffering can be sent by God as a warning to a person who has just entered or is about to enter a path of sin. Frequently, he is unaware of this and considers himself to be innocent and righteous – a prideful attitude which deserves punishment in itself. Yet, no amount of suffering gives Man the right to examine God's justice, still less to criticise the Creator.

God's motives and design can't be judged by human criteria or comprehended by the limited human mind. Protesting God is senseless; in its depth and breadth, God's wisdom exceeds all human reason.

■ Theodicy in Christianity: ■
We Live in the Best of All Worlds

Judaism's presentation of Job's story would not be as interesting to the modern, Western reader as its Christian interpretation. This independent-minded and enquiring Old Testament character who sought after the higher truth became changed into yet another martyr. This is particularly obvious in John Chrysostom's famous sermon. Chrysostom promises 'great rewards for suffering – no less than one receives for good deeds, and often even more for the latter than the former'.

Chrysostom turned the measured biblical account into an accomplished but nightmarish morality tale in praise of human suffering. The Marquis de Sade himself could not have derived so much pleasure from suffering as did Chrysostom here.

The book of Job says: 'So Satan went forth from the presence of the Lord, and afflicted Job with loathsome sores from the sole of his foot to the crown of his head. And he took a potsherd with which to scrape himself, and sat among the ashes.' (Job 2:7-8)

And Chrysostom relates it as follows in his 'Commentary of the Book of Job':

> Now why did he not scrape with his hands or fingers? To prevent the attention providing a greater source of revulsion [...] He was his own executioner, not wringing his withers but scraping out his oozing sore.
>
> The loss of his children was a heavy burden, but an even greater calamity followed thereafter giving him no respite. What followed were the maggots, the streams of pus, the sitting on the dunghill, and the stench of the wounds, which caused a new kind of pain because they made partaking of food impossible and caused pain worse than hunger. All this lasted not two, or ten, or a hundred days, but many months. The example of Job was a ready comfort to those who grieve, for the wounds of the righteous man and his dunghill are more glorious than the king's throne.

Christian theodicy is a huge philosophical planet hostile to true science and welcoming to infertile scholasticism.

> The apple doesn't fall far from the tree and Christ was, and remained, a loyal Son of His fierce Dad, Yahweh, "inflicting vengeance upon those who do not know God and upon those who do not obey the gospel of our Lord Jesus. They shall suffer the punishment of eternal destruction and exclusion from the presence of the Lord and from the glory of His might." (2 Thessalonians 1:8-9)

On the other hand, Jesus Christ is a God of Love, and one day Good will vanquish Evil. The last book of the New Testament, the Revelation of John the Theologian (or the Apocalypse), promises: God will wipe away every tear from their eyes, and death shall be no more, neither shall there be mourning nor crying nor pain any more, for the former things have passed away. (Revelation 21:4)

Thus, evil is everything that opposes the nature or the will of God.

A tacit proscription to doubt the existence and benevolence of the Loving God was established as far back as the fourth to fifth centuries AD, a period which coincided with the final overthrow of paganism. In the sixth to seventh centuries, holding to any form

Léon Bonnat, Job, 1880.

of doubt became hazardous to one's life, as the fate of tens of thousands of heretics and pagans shows.

Theodicy became a by-product of this proscription, nothing more than a sort of warning for those tempted by criminal thought.

The proscription lasted for more than twelve centuries. It subjugated philosophy to theology and directed all its efforts towards proving fundamental religious tenets (the existence of God and the infallibility of Scripture) and discussing Church dogmas. Even the greatest minds of the time, such as Blessed Augustine, Thomas Aquinas, Irenaeus of Lyon, and John Chrysostom could hardly be described as philosophers in the classical Greek meaning of the term. They are no Aristotle. The main direction of their work consisted of figuring out the rationale behind religious doctrine rather than attempting to penetrate the mysteries of the reality around them. Where is their philosophical heritage today? One of the first Fathers of the Church, the untiring warrior against Gnosticism and a pioneer of theodicy, was Irenaeus of Lyon. He claimed that God had created the best of all possible worlds.

This idea of 'the best of all possible worlds' became a cornerstone of Christian theodicy and it remains so until now. There is nothing surprising about it – how can God do anything bad?

Irenaeus explains his theory as follows. The problem is that people are born imperfect and morally underdeveloped; in order to attain maturity they are given a free will and the necessity of making moral choices, both of which require experience of evil and suffering. Death and suffering only appear evil; without them we have never been able to comprehend God.

Irenaeus' God is responsible for evil without being guilty of it since the experience of evil shapes the soul and brings a person closer to the imitation of God. Naturally God never leaves Man to his own devices and He monitors his spiritual progress constantly.

However, if God is responsible for evil, why shouldn't we ask him to take back not only evil but also death?

In his *Three Homilies on the Devil*, Chrysostom illustrates Irenaeus's views:

> For the physician is not to be commended only when he leads forth the patient into gardens and meadows, nor even into baths and pools of water, nor yet when he sets before him a well-furnished table, but also when he orders him to remain without food, when he oppresses him with hunger and lays him low with thirst, confines him to his bed, both making his house a prison, and depriving him of the very light, and shadowing his room on all sides with curtains, and when he cuts, and when he cauterises, and when he brings his bitter medicines, he is equally a physician.

No one can take away from Chrysostom his profound knowledge of human nature and talent as a writer. If he lived today, he would probably become a leader of a big left-wing political party (Chrysostom doesn't like rich people), or even a president of some country. The religious philosopher Origen of Alexandria agreed with Irenaeus' ideas. Origen was a romantic: he emphasised God's love and goodwill, and believed that at the end of time all evil would be vanquished. Every soul, even the most wicked ones, would be saved and returned to God. Even the Devil would be saved. Heaven would be a dull place without the Devil.

Augustine the Blessed agreed with Irenaeus that God created the best of possible worlds and supported the view that free will gives rise to evil but is necessary. He diverges from Irenaeus on the question of God's responsibility for Evil. Augustine's main idea is contained in the assertion that evil has no reality of its own; it exists only as it a lack, an absence of goodness, rather like illness is an absence of health.

There cannot be any evil in God since he never created it. Natural evil (ecological cataclysms and disasters) is the work of the fallen angels but all other forms of evil enter the world through Man. This is a just punishment for original sin.

It is interesting to note Augustine's certainty that without God, people would inevitably choose evil (a rather exalted view of people).

After Augustine's death, the subject of theodicy did not arise for another eight centuries. Just try to imagine such a long period of time – cars appeared one century ago and planes even later. It would appear that no one had any doubts about the existence of God, goodness, and love; evil had run away somewhere and one was free to pray in peace without any worries. In the thirteenth century, theodicy revived. Nearly a millennium later Thomas Aquinas' views of theodicy fused those put forward by Irenaeus and Augustine, diverging in insignificant details only.

Thomas didn't believe that evil could exist on its own; rather, for him, evil was a corruption of grace and an abuse of free will. People are responsible for their own sins and they cause evil to appear in the world. Although God doesn't wish for evil, He nevertheless has a moral basis for allowing it to exist as without it the universe would be less complete. Suffering has a positive value because it reminds people of the evil in the world and highlights the contrast between Heaven and Earth.

This approach is quite comprehensible. Why should a sinless man go to church? When it comes to the difference between Heaven and Earth, Thomas had probably taken a business trip to Heaven to know for sure.

The arrival of the Renaissance, which many define as nostalgia for classical Antiquity, changed nothing of substance for theodicy. God remained as He was: untouchable and altogether removed from evil. The power of evil was either artificially played down or blamed on the sinner himself.

This position of the Church is understandable; admitting the possibility that religion could have internal problems which could be critiqued is inconceivable – that way lie heresy and atheism. Never mind seeking to understand the origins of monotheism or blasphemously doubting the existence of the One God. No one, absolutely no one, could say that 'there is no God; He doesn't exist'. People endured long prison sentences and were executed for lesser transgressions against the Church.

Pico della Mirandola proclaimed himself a fan of the Christian God, but was at the same time a supporter of ancient philosophy, the Kabbalah, and pantheism. For this reason he was declared a heretic and poisoned under mysterious circumstances. Giordano Bruno was unlikely to have doubted the existence of God (he considered himself a martyr for the faith and hoped to be admitted to paradise), but was nevertheless imprisoned for eight years on the charge of denying key dogmas of the Catholic Church and then burnt at the stake. It's telling that the Catholic hierarchy confirmed the legitimacy of the sentence both in 1942 and again in 2000; Bruno offended the Holy Church and was justly punished. Lucilio Vanini, a slightly obscurer but for all that no less brilliant philosopher, physicist, and pantheist, had no doubts as to the existence of God either. But he had the misfortune to be the first man to declare that the universe was governed by natural laws and that Man had descended from apes. The Catholic Church treated him with more clemency than Giordano Bruno; rather than being burnt alive in the soul-purifying flames, he first had his tongue torn out, then was strangled and burnt at the stake when already a corpse.

Confronted with these salutary examples of justice, most people feared the Catholic Church to such an extent that they didn't even think of doubting its dogma. It was far easier just to pretend that evil didn't exist or forget its very existence for real.

However, there have always been some divergences on the origin of evil and God's responsibility for it. They got stronger during the Reformation. Indeed, the Protestants were there to protest Catholics.

John Calvin and Martin Luther left Man his sins, but took away his free will. Although evil is a consequence of sin, it is unavoidable since everything is predetermined; all events and all people's fortunes have been decided by God well in advance.

> It stands fixed, even by your own testimony, therefore, that we do all things by necessity, and nothing by free will; so long as the power of the free will is nothing, and neither does nor can do good, in the absence of grace. *(On the Bondage of the Will)*

So far, so doctrinally Christian. However, the next turn of events left me in complete bewilderment. I had naively supposed that the diseases and death I was subject to were a penalty for the original sin of human disobedience, but it turned out that we weren't to blame for anything from the start.

The fall of Man is a part of the divine plan. The original sin was provoked by God deliberately in order to justify any punishment He wanted to mete out. God is responsible for all evil, but you can't blame Him for it (is there anything you can blame Him for?).

In this way, the God of Goodness and Love was transformed into a malevolent conspirator. You have to be thankful that they at least left Him with power and omniscience.

I can't understand what we can blame God for. The idea is perfectly expressed in George Orwell's immortal novel *Nineteen Eighty-Four*. All must be guilty; otherwise ruling over the masses becomes absolutely impossible.

The question of the existence of God began to be asked again only in the Modern era, when Benedict Spinoza advanced his own concept of God: eternal, infinite, and quite odd. He is not omnipotent, has neither consciousness nor a divine plan, and is unable to wish for anything – either good or bad. In fact, He doesn't even think in these categories. For Spinoza, God permeates the whole of the material world leaving nothing outside of Him. For this reason, nothing can depend on this God, so praying to Him is an absurd waste of time. Man would do just as well to pray to himself because Man is also a part of God.

Spinoza was the first thinker after Aquinas (four centuries later) who became preoccupied with theodicy as a subject, particularly in his *Letters on Evil*. He denies the concept of free will. The only one who is truly free is the one who understands that there is no free will and everyone acts according to the only available option dictated by his nature. It all goes without saying that where there is no free will there is no evil either. Evil does not exist, it is 'merely an illusion', a product of our ignorance because evil is God too.

Man is incapable of understanding the reasons behind God's actions and regards them as evil, whereas in reality our world is perfect and the best of all possible worlds. In other words, we must accept evil and suffering without tormenting ourselves about the reasons for them. 'Voir le mal, c'est mal voir!' ('Seeing bad is seeing badly' = 'To the pure all is pure').

Ever since I took a philosophy class I have liked Spinoza's understanding of the divine. He was given the title 'prince of philosophy' by no accident. It is a very honourable title indeed; there was only one prince of the world, the Devil.

Famine in South Sudan.
Spinoza maintained that to see Evil was to see badly.

Just take a look at Spinoza's revolutionary mix: refusal of the divine origin of the Holy Scripture, of God's existence, of the Ascension, of the salvation after death and free will. Even his idea that it is useless to pray to God is revolutionary. The only thing I disagree with Spinoza about is the denial of evil's existence. While I was studying Spinoza, my neighbour's three-year-old son died of cancer.

However, not all thinkers of the time were as radical as Spinoza. Many became deists (after creating the world, God takes no further part in its fate) and continued to cling to religion, if only to prove that humanity's existence is not an absurd and senseless chaos, but has a noble and meaningful purpose. This process turned the One God from God-the-Big-Brother who could read everyone's minds into a philosophical God-the-Creator who created the world and imparted a moral code to us, but is now absent from our universe.

One of the committed deists was Gottfried Leibniz, who had coined the term 'theodicy' in 1710. His theodicy was very similar to that of Spinoza. This eternally absent God managed to create a perfect, harmonious world. Our world is the best because it is a balance of all possible benefits it could potentially contain (not all are possible or logically compatible) and thus achieves the greatest conceivable variety.

And what about evil? Without evil, there would not be such variety; only a world containing evil could be part of God's plan. God is just and permits evil for the greater good, or rather that which we, in our ignorance, consider evil. Without evil the world would

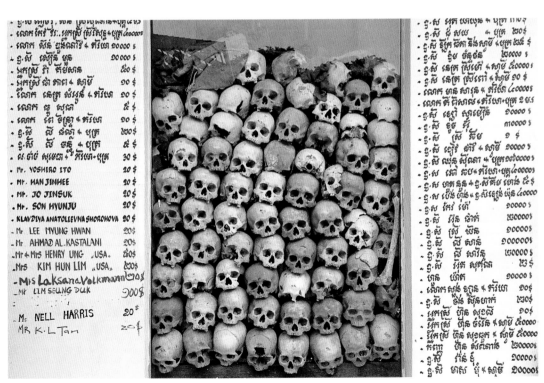

Democratic Kampuchea under the Marxist regime of Pol Pot.
According to Spinoza, Evil does not exist and is only an illusion.

be less perfect, and it is only in this world that we can hope to attain the most goodness: 'When God permits evil, it is virtue.' God has a reason for everything and earthquakes, the plague, and blindness from birth are all just the means of achieving divine purpose, a punishment for sin, and an opportunity to prevent greater evil.

The theodicies of both Spinoza and Leibniz do not suit me at all. Firstly, I am sure that evil does exist and I prefer to be happy, not virtuous. Secondly, I am not interested to know whether our world is perfect or not, I just want it to be comfortable and pleasant to live in. Thirdly, I see a big ethical problem in these theodicies: if there really is no evil, then morality has no meaning since goodness has no particular advantage over evil. However, I can accept this statement. For many years I have doubted the existence of universal morality and every dead body I see broadcasted on TV proves me right.

During the Enlightenment the world began a gradual retreat from religion towards secularism, at which point the paths of faith and public life diverged. Some philosophers of the Enlightenment made a point of repudiating the Holy Scripture, criticising the dogma of the Church, and declaring religious faith a dangerous superstition. Some sought arguments in support of the existence of God which would allow them to reconcile reason with faith. During the Enlightenment, Christian faith considerably weakened as a political entity, lost its attractiveness for educated classes and never managed to restore its lost power.

Earthquake in Nepal.
Leibniz believed that God created the best of all worlds.

Voltaire ridiculed the theodicy of Leibniz, saying that if God had created the best of all possible worlds, it follows that we must love the executioner leading us to the gallows and the disease poised to kill us. 'If this is the best of all possible worlds, what are the others like?'

The Lisbon earthquake of 1775 seemed to him a particularly vivid example of the world's lack of perfection and a proof of 'God's cruelty'. I don't quite agree with this conclusion and propose that God can be forgiven for the mere 80-90,000 fatalities. I propose to persecute him instead for the tens of millions he massacred during the twentieth century. Even if lots of people had been like Voltaire, the situation wouldn't have changed drastically. People were intoxicated with the idea of God to such an extent that all social and political concepts up to and including the time of the French Revolution were informed by religious theories. One can hardly blame them for wanting to do this, just as one doesn't blame humanity for its blindness in supposing that the earth was flat for many millennia. Even the mightiest of minds had to wrestle with the fear of losing on a personal level: what if He really does exist and in giving up on faith, we lose our eternal life? However, as soon as the Church's influence over people's minds waned and the danger to suffer for your beliefs became considerably smaller, people soon sobered up.

Classical German philosophy (eighteenth to nineteenth centuries) finally did away with God as Big Brother. Some philosophers turned God into an abstract philosophical Absolute, while others rejected Him as a concept. Great minds and the Holy Scriptures were found to be on opposite sides of the barricade.

Kant says that all previous theodicies have failed. By theodicy he understood 'the defence of the highest wisdom of the creator against the charge which reason brings against it for whatever is counter-purposive in the world.' This statement can be interpreted in two ways, much like the glass some see as being half empty and others half full. The proponents of the full glass theory emphasise the 'highest wisdom of the creator', and the empty glass brigade stress the 'charge which reason brings against it for whatever is counter-purposive in the world'.

Kant proposed three possible arguments in defence of God:

– God's laws are sacred; we see evil as evil only according to our human laws (curiously enough, we've always thought we lived according to His laws), but looking from a higher standpoint isn't evil at all. God never wanted evil and has not brought it about. All evil originates from people because of the limitations of human nature, especially intelligence, and God simply allows it to exist.

– God's rule is good – there is more good in the world than evil. We suffer for the sake of a future life of blessedness, which will bring about even more good.

– God's judgements are just, a fact we will appreciate later since the end of earthly life is not the end of life as a whole.

There is nothing particularly new in any of these three points; the same arguments have been rehashed for the last 1,500 years. As for Kant himself, he remains a sceptical theist and acknowledges that none of these arguments are sufficient to defend the wisdom of

God in the face of evil. There is no such thing as definitive theodicy and the problems it addresses can only be resolved by blind faith.

Fyodor Dostoyevsky also made his own contribution to theodicy. He believed that true love could not be expressed through suffering; there was already too much suffering in the world, which ordinarily did not lead to moral perfection. He was particularly opposed to the suffering of young children.

I am not quite sure on what grounds he separated children from adults. As soon as we admit humanity's fundamental sinfulness, it immediately embraces absolutely everyone; no one is immune from original sin; it encompasses all ages, from the smallest to the greatest.

At the end of the nineteenth and the beginning of the twentieth centuries, God sat particularly awkwardly among the intellectual elite, who were either estranged from Him, or considered Him a purely cultural and historical phenomenon. So we shouldn't have any illusions that the best minds shared in the religious faith of the majority.

Nietzsche, for instance, was vehement in repudiating the central tenet of theodicy, namely that although Man is unable to comprehend the ways of God because of the limitations of his nature, he is nevertheless obliged to revere Him. In response to this glaring contradiction, he proposed an ingenious idea – if humanity is unable to comprehend the motives of God, it may well be that it worships not God but the Devil. Nietzsche recommended substituting a faith in God with a faith in Man.

Before passing to contemporary theodicy, I would like to say a few words about Islam. Anyway, it is not possible to do more – theodicy is a completely unpopular concept in Islam. Man has no right even to think of justifying Allah, who makes absolutely all decisions himself and distributes good and evil as he sees fit. Evil has no essence in itself but is rather an absence of goodness, a bit like darkness being an absence of light. It comes about through Man's will that refuses to submit to the will of Allah, in other words to wait patiently and hope for his mercy.

■ Theodicy Today: How to Save God ■

By the beginning of the twentieth century it became clear that classical theodicy, that is, the theodicy of Irenaeus, Augustine, Spinoza, Leibnitz, and Kant had failed. It is impossible to justify the all-powerful, the all-knowing, and the all-good God by relying on it.

This was, most likely, the sad conclusion that the modern authors of theodicy arrived at. They realised that the main aim of theodicy had radically changed: now they had not to justify God but to prove that he exists and explain why we need him. These credulous, romantic thinkers introduced a new theodicy into the world. This type of theodicy insists on the reality of God, but at the same time acknowledges His – at least partial – responsibility for the evil in the world, as well as His inability to manage it.

The new theodicy has an extremely difficult task – to combine things which are hardly compatible, to handle reality objectively, while keeping the idea of God unsullied and intact.

Auschwitz.
Leibniz was convinced that to allow for Evil, as God does, is a manifestation of the greatest kindness.

Contemporary religious philosophers have set out a multitude of propositions, some serious and some not particularly so. This multiplicity is not surprising; the impossibility of knowing God or getting a response from Him has created a fertile field for human imagination.

This modern theodicy appeals to me more than the classical kind, if only because its healthy parts do not attempt to present wishful thinking as reality, but prefer to look truth in the eyes. This theodicy has every right to exist, even in our sceptical times. Before I explain the main tenets of the proponents of modern theodicy, I will state one provison.

The authors of modern theodicy must be divided into two unequal groups. The minority is represented by those world thinkers who have made a significant contribution to the development of academic disciplines in general and philosophical thought in particular. These writers are philosophers first and theologians only second. I count among them Alfred North Whitehead, his successor Charles Hartshorne, and John Cobb. They were responsible for developing process philosophy, out of which process theology naturally followed, which in turn became a new paradigm for understanding God and His relationship with humanity. In my opinion, only this type of theology was successful in reconciling the contradictions inherent in the idea of the Almighty God and the existence of evil, in reconciling critical thinking and religion. This was a kind of philosophical revolution. It provided a mechanism for creating new values rather than just stressing the importance of historical facts and traditional 'divine' commandments.

The majority of the authors of modern theodicy includes those modern philosophical theologians who became known specifically for their work on theodicy; we have every reason to suspect that if they weren't dealing specifically with this pertinent topic of God-justification which appealed to mass audiences, their names would never have reached the general public at all.

Everyone has heard about the bestsellers *The Da Vinci Code* by Dan Brown and *Fifty Shades of Grey* by Erica James, which had publication runs of many tens of millions. Despite their wild popularity, everyone knows that these books are not high literature. This is obvious to anyone who's read even a single classic. It's likely that the authors of *Code* and *Shades* themselves don't aspire to being considered figures of world literature, but are nevertheless perfectly content with their multi-million dollar royalties.

I wouldn't want to say that the writers of these modern theodicies are neither scholars nor philosophers, but we have to remember that they are faithful Christians first and philosophers only second. And because Christianity has for many centuries ceased to be the predominant standpoint of Western philosophical thought, its thinkers can no longer claim a star position for themselves. In any case, not the position of such stars as Popper, Sartre, Baudrillard, and Derrida. Their debate is confined to their own narrow circle, a kind of charming and intimate intellectual rally. And whereas secular philosophers usually do not shy away from posing fundamental questions as to the possibility of God's existence and avail themselves of the whole arsenal of propositions available to modern philosophical thought and science, religious philosophers persist in restating universal principles justifying God's existence using arguments drawn heavily from Holy Scripture.

I shall begin with the minority group I've referred to – those engaged in process theology. The basic idea introduced by Alfred Whitehead almost a hundred years ago and later developed by Charles Hartshorne was that the reality around us is not a collection of disparate, independent material objects, but interconnecting processes with concomitant substances. Man is apart from these processes; he is endowed with free will to act according to his own judgement, but all his actions have a bearing on the world around him. (So that's where modern ecology has sprung from.) Then the idea of interconnecting processes was extended to God and thus the theology of process was born.

The theology of process became the foundation of the new understanding of God and his relation with Man. Whitehead rejected categorically the traditional monotheistic view of God as an absolutely changeless, infinite, and all-powerful Supreme Being existing outside the world and bending it according to His will.

God does not exist outside the world and is not excluded from the general laws of the universe. On the contrary, He is an example of the action of metaphysical principles when the individual entity exists in process and is also the highest actual entity. He exists only because a transcendent source of order is needed to do battle with chaos. This transcendent source is able to give value to all the other actual entities and co-operate with them dynamically, endowing them with a certain 'primary purpose', inherent values, and setting 'limits for freedom'. Although there is a fundamental difference between God and us, namely His eternity, God is not a stranger to mutability, mortality, weakness, and emotion, which remain attributes of other material entities and humans.

This idea pleased me very much. I have always felt that there was an inconsistency between the dogma of God's omnipotence and the veneration of Christ's humility and meekness.

Whitehead even claimed that the assertion that the world was created by God was no more correct than the assertion that God was created by the world.

Another fundamental idea of the theology of process was advanced by Hartshorne. He described God as having a di-polar nature – an abstract pole presenting eternal and unchanging qualities such as wisdom and goodness, and a concrete one which God had acquired in the process of His involvement with the world and humanity. The life of every creature unfolds in this process of co-operation with God; in other words it's not just that God influences Man, but Man can be said to influence God. Everything that happens in the world, all human decisions, moral or immoral actions, reflect back on God who is changed by them. In this sense, our co-operation with God is like a two-way street: although God is transcendent in relation to the world, He remains a 'living entity', able to feel, suffer, and 'grow spiritually' together with the world, that is, with you and me. Hurray. We are all God's teachers.

God's constant process of change does not imply His imperfection. On the contrary, the process helps Him to understand humanity better and participate in its experiences of joy, happiness, grief, and suffering, thereby increasing His influence in the world. This God is much closer to the God of the New Testament who struggled against the sins of humanity and Himself underwent suffering and a painful death.

However, there is (as is always the case) the other side of the coin. The God of process theology is palpably weak. Unlike the traditional God – the Big Brother figure – this God is not omnipotent or omniscient; He is not able to exercise total control over all the world's events or to predetermine people's future actions. Jean-Paul Sartre satirically advanced a rather original explanation of God's incapability to fight evil. According to him, God doesn't fight evil only because he is scared to make things much worse.

God exists, but He is not all-powerful, or all-knowing, or (in many instances) all-good. Henceforth, God's power is limited by His personal co-operation with each specific believer.

He can no longer compel, judge, and punish; all He can do is influence the free will of each person by the power of His authority, suggest alternative models for moral conduct, and persuade by His divine Love. Process theologians claim that persuasion is a more significant and effective tool than compulsion. The God who possesses a superior power of persuasion and is able to awaken us to goodness is worthy of veneration much more than the perfect, terrible, implacable God-the-Warder. People don't need an almighty ruler endowed with superpowers who remains alien to the joys and sorrows of His faithful; they need a God who is a friend.

Those are golden words. Modern teaching methodology is in agreement. Everyone knows that it is much more effective to convince a child with love than to beat or scold him. All main ideas of contemporary theodicy come from theology of process.

God truly is the God of Love and His presence in the world is a supreme good, but He is not omnipotent. Although he has influence over all of life's processes, He is not able to rescue humanity from evil or ensure its prosperity. In any case, God is doing everything He can, but not everything that happens in the world is the result of His will. The only thing that is definitely in God's power is to love each of us, despite the terrible crimes we've committed.

God is unable to act in any way that contradicts the laws of nature; He won't manage either to send a flood or an earthquake, or prevent the same. It follows then that it's unreasonable to demand the impossible of Him.

God is incapable of stopping the world of evil, oppression, and suffering either now or at any point in the future. However, rest assured that He sympathises and co-suffers with you. (Feel free to pity Him.)

On the other hand, evil can't only be blamed on God. Although God has a say in everything that happens, He is not able to stop people from making free choices and acting on them. A man is easily capable of behaving in a way that has never been a part of God's purpose. God can persuade, cajole, entice, beg, attempt to inspire more goodness, but He cannot compel. However much He might want to, He is not able to prevent any evil at all, even the most heinous. (I instantly thought of the Holocaust.)

Process theology received a great deal of response both in scientific as well as religious circles; but opinions were sharply divided.

Some believed that theology, previously characterised by a mass of irrational commandments and miracles, was finally being endowed with metaphysical meaning. Metaphysics is a useful tool for describing the more general principles of creation, and God, as the most prominent embodiment of these principles, was allowed to have self-awareness, self-reflection, emotions, and even social responsibility.

The theology of process managed to inspire new life in the routine of religious rites. Personally, I liked process theology so much that for a short while I even believed in the existence of the Christian God and started dreaming that he would console me.

Many subjected process theology to sharp criticism; here was a theology that undermined the power of God and made Him unworthy of veneration. Some even went as far as to say that this theology did away with God altogether.

Now let's return to the Dan Browns of contemporary theology. I didn't find anything original in their ideas: a simple rehash of classical theodicy's ideas from Irenaeus to Kant with a couple of points borrowed from the theology of process. And a lot of absurdities and blind faith.

Alvin Plantinga is the pride of American Christian thought and one of the leaders of the evangelical intelligentsia movement (which until now I had no idea existed). For him, God's existence does not form a logical contradiction to the existence of evil, although the existence of God requires no further proofs because the idea is in any case embedded in our consciousness. In reality, this assertion means that the vast majority of the acknowledged great thinkers of both the last few centuries and the present, as well as the hundreds of millions of Soviet people, have never had nor will never have any consciousness.

Plantinga continues with Augustine's argument that Man must have free will to enable him to attain perfection. God could not create a world in which moral good existed without its evil counterpart. However, the world has another source of evil; it is connected with the work of the evil powers, or demons. This is a truly astonishing argument, both in its impact and relevance, especially for people living in the twenty-first century. God is not all-powerful and that's the reason the demons have multiplied like mice while the cat's been away. Plantinga doesn't explain why we need this God, who cannot fight petty demons.

Plantinga is also convinced that the absence of proofs of God's existence is no reason to be an atheist. We must stop searching for these proofs and turn our efforts towards recognising the fact that the crucifixion of Christ was the culmination of God's love and, as such, the Supreme Good.

What we'd like to know is this: how many more millions must sacrifice their lives for the sake of this one crucifixion and this divine love?

Peter van Inwagen, another pride of American Christian thought, is the president of the Society of Christian Philosophers (where he is Plantinga's superior). A Christian apologist *à l'extrême*, he considers it his duty to 'deflect philosophical attacks on the Christian faith' and in doing so he uses terms such as 'heretics' and 'enemies of the Church' – charming expressions mostly forgotten since the days of the Holy Inquisition.

Inwagen disagrees with the proposition that the existence of evil is incompatible with the almighty power and goodness of God. He dismisses it if only for the simple reason that this proposition is a purely philosophical argument and the majority of such arguments are untenable and pale into insignificance when placed next to pure faith. Indeed, who would doubt it? We must thank God for not being burnt on the stake.

Inwagen's arguments are familiar – it's another rehash of Leibnitz. God can do anything except that which is logically impossible. God Himself has created this world with its natural laws, which encompass everything, including the limitations on His own power.

> That God is omnipotent means that he can do anything that doesn't involve an intrinsic impossibility. Thus, God, if he exists, can change water into wine since there is no intrinsic impossibility in the elementary particles that constitute the water in a cup being rearranged so as to constitute wine. But even God can't draw a round square or cause it both to rain and not to rain at the same place at the same time or change the past because these things are intrinsically impossible.

I didn't really get the opposition between rearranging water into wine and a round square. Now, according to modern science this isn't quite true. If non-Euclidean geometry allows two parallel lines to intersect at one point, why shouldn't you be able to make a square out of a circle? It is much more absurd, even if it could be a real deal, to try to transform water into wine. The past, as we know well from history, has been re-written before, is being re-written even now, and no doubt will be re-written in the future.

We are powerless to discern God's plan in every individual case. What we see as an expression of evil may well be a part of His plan leading to the greater good; God's plan must be underpinned by Man's right moral choice: 'To say that God is morally perfect is to say that He never does anything morally wrong – that He could not possibly do anything morally wrong.'

It's quite possible that God has not done it and isn't capable of doing it, if only because His existence has never been proven. On the other hand, so much immorality is committed in His name, both in the course of history and today before our eyes, that a regular human brain is simply incapable of containing it.

John Hick has dedicated his entire life to eschatology (religious theories of the end of the world and life after death). This British theologian continues along the Irenaean line in maintaining that the process of soul-making is not yet complete and that the free world in which we live is the best of all worlds for our moral development and the acquisition of faith through the world of evil. As far as extreme cases are concerned – deaths of random innocent babies and the like – the answer is traditionally the same: we can't understand God's motives and His plan for us.

Most probably this answer would be of immediate comfort to the parents of these babies who met their untimely end. Best known for his works of fiction, especially *The Screwtape Letters* and *The Chronicles of Narnia,* C. S. Lewis was also an internationally renowned Christian theologian acclaimed for his works *Mere Christianity, Miracles,* and *The Problem of Pain*. He tried to refute the main accusation levelled against the Christian God, 'Why does our God of love allow the existence of so much evil, suffering, and pain in the world?' He therefore formulates the main problem of theodicy in terms of the difficulty of reconciling God's wish to turn evil into good on the one hand and the immutability of the laws of nature that rule the world of free men on the other:

> If God were good, He would wish to make His creatures perfectly happy, and if God were almighty He would be able to do what He wished. But the creatures are not happy. Therefore, God lacks either goodness, or power, or both.

Still, we shouldn't delude ourselves into thinking that such a through-and-through theologian as Lewis would deny the almighty power and goodness of God. Not at all; his task is to smooth over the blatant contradictions between the teaching of the church and reality at large by correcting the 'erroneous interpretation' of these notions. Alas, his arguments differ little from those of Irenaeus, Augustine, and Thomas Aquinas, which, considering his 'world' status, makes for a sad state of affairs. The original sin was Man's first instance of choosing evil over good, which resulted in the first instance of deserved suffering. Of course, the Almighty God could have prevented the consequences of the original sin, but if God did indeed interfere in everything to prevent us from abusing our free will and experiencing consequent suffering, He would have had to remove our free choice. In this case, Man would have been immediately returned back to his worthless, unspiritual existence:

> We can, perhaps, conceive of a world in which God corrected the results of this abuse of free will by His creatures at every moment: so that a wooden beam became soft as grass when it was used as a weapon, and the air refused to obey me if I attempted to set up in it the sound-waves that carry lies or insults. But such a world would be one in which wrong actions were impossible, and in which, therefore, freedom of the will would be void; nay, if the principle were carried out to its logical conclusion, evil thoughts would be impossible, for the cerebral matter which we use in thinking would refuse its task when we attempted to frame them.

What a strange idea. Formal logic tells me that if God had forgiven Man his disobedience and allowed him to remain in paradise, it would have been the ideal place for spiritual growth. After all, in paradise, the first people lived in close proximity to God and could 'see His face' every God-given day. In this case, we would not need either earthly life or free will.

Nor had Lewis forgotten natural disasters, that favourite subject of Leibnitz's. Lewis restates Leibnitz's idea that all natural disasters are a means for God to enact His unfathomable divine purpose, which punishes the sinful, disobedient, and excessively curious.

Peter Kreeft is probably the most successful and popular Christian philosopher in the US and has written over fifty books. One of his earliest books was dedicated to the themes of evil and suffering, entitled in familiar Christian style, *Making Sense Out of Suffering*. Kreeft describes the Scriptures as a history of the love for God – the same love which is the answer to all our problems and the key to the fulfilment of all our desires. He is not very interested in other forms of love, because the love for God alone is stronger than evil, suffering, and death.

I hate even to think about the kind of universal evil that could arise (and already has) as a result of such passionate love devoid of fairness and justice. I shall talk about this later on in this book.

Marylin McCord Adams is a phenomenal woman. She is a relatively well-known American academic philosopher and theologian, as well as a pastor of the Episcopalian Church. This combination has made her contribution highly original, setting her apart from partisans of either traditional or contemporary theodicy.

On one hand, she refutes the traditional argument that the ability to sin and exercise a free will is conducive to spiritual growth.

On the other hand, Adams disagrees with those who claim God to be far from omnipotent or to lack the will, patience, and resources needed to fight evil and correct the sins of every person. She believes that absolutely all people, including those far from sainthood, will be saved sooner or later. As I have already mentioned, Origen even believed that the Devil himself would be saved. I wish I knew Adams' opinion on this.

In *Christ and Horrors*, Adams states that theodicy isn't needed at all: 'My own view is that talk of theodicy – of *justifying* the ways of God to humankind – is misleading, because God has no obligations to creatures and hence no need to *justify* divine actions to us.'

I agree with her conclusion that we don't need theodicy. Why bother defending God if he doesn't have any obligations towards us?

With this in mind, every believer is advised to adopt his own, personal theodicy which will allow him a glimpse of goodness in every instance of personal experience of evil. At this point, evil ceases to be evil and becomes a means of mystical union between God and Man. Besides, if evil and suffering is a path bringing us closer to God, do we really want to strive for this closeness?

Practically speaking, this means that everyone is supposed to have his or her own rose-tinted spectacles, all the better to see the chimera.

■ Accusing God ■

What do today's ordinary believers think about theodicy and the problem of evil? Indeed, it has only been a century since the last important theodicy – the theodicy of process – was established, but nobody remembers what millions of ordinary believers thought of it. They didn't leave any trace in history. So goes the world: a genius or a dictator decides humanity's fate. My democratic principles demanded that I ascertain the views of ordinary people. I immediately threw myself into phoning all the believers I knew, and even those unbelievers who might have believing friends or relatives. After that, I immersed myself in every type of Christian website, forum, or blog. I gleaned no new information from this exercise. All that I confirmed once more was that the vast majority of ordinary Christians ask no questions at all. This can be attributed both to naivety and gullibility (Church ministers, especially the hierarchs, know best), and also to a complete lack of any critical thinking – and doubt, its bastard offspring. On the other hand, I saw with my own eyes the fruits of the excellent work by professional believers, priests, and preachers.

I collected about 300 different views on God's responsibility for evil. I was particularly interested in Dostoevsky's question about prematurely dead children. If I give here all 300, my book would break your shelf. Fortunately for me all these views looked like identical twins, so I can reproduce just the three most popular ones.

– You shouldn't question God's responsibility for evil because it's a temptation from the Devil designed to instil doubt.

– The love of God is altogether different from human love, so that the things that appear cruel and unacceptable to us are normal and acceptable to God.

– There is no need to torment yourself over the deaths of innocent children. If a child dies, it's a cause for rejoicing because he or she is saved and is already in paradise. A Christian shouldn't worry when confronted by the suffering of small children because God's wisdom and love are found there too. Usually, God uses the suffering of children to correct their parents, force them to turn away from sin, and repent. If somebody's evil action remains unavenged, it will be answered by his ancestors.

I read some extreme nonsense, too. Some religious parents whose children suddenly died one after another confessed that they understood quite quickly that these unexpected deaths were nothing but God's tenderness. They immediately stopped mourning. They had no doubt that their dead infants would meet them in paradise.

So, what conclusion did I reach after talking to ordinary Christian people? Just this: the results of the intense work of the world's best minds for the last 500 years have passed them by completely and taught them nothing. More's the pity.

The time has come for me to declare my own position. You don't need to be especially insightful to work out from the examples in my chapter that my attitude to classical theodicy is, to put it mildly, sceptical.

My opinion of theodicy is in line with what we generally think about examples of a prolonged and fruitless philosophical enquiry on the part of humanity. Fruitless scholasticism helped to launch the science of logic and futile alchemy led to the development of chemistry.

What theodicy gave to humanity is hard to say. I find the whole question of theodicy senseless; rather than fighting the evil in the world, it consumes enormous resources in presenting arguments exonerating God from any blame for it.

I see no reason to justify God in the face of the evil in the world. I have always thought that this task is beyond anyone; how can a weak man, whose ability to think is highly limited, justify God? Is God really unable to justify Himself? To give us some sort of sign?

Besides, any God who needs our justification and defence doesn't merit being called God – this is no God at all. I leave this justification to those who desire to believe in the supernatural.

My sceptical attitude towards both modern and contemporary theodicies is easy to justify.

Irenaeus and Augustine were taken in by an illusion and made a gross error of judgement; Man has no a priori 'free will'. All believers know well that their hands are tied – they are obliged to choose good that has been sanctioned by God in order to save their souls. Given that's the case, the only person responsible for evil is not the believer, but God Himself.

According to formal logic, the existence of evil is not compatible with God. An all-knowing God would have known about the evil to come and foreseen it; an all-good God would have done everything possible to prevent it; and an all-powerful God would have certainly destroyed it.

After thousands of years of Christian belief, it's simply impossible to carry on believing this nonsense – that all problems and suffering in adults can be explained by their accumu-

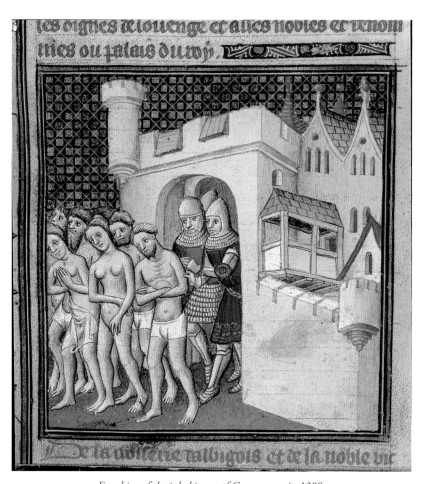

Expulsion of the inhabitants of Carcassonne in 1209.
"Kill them all, God will recognise His own". This sentence is attributed to Arnaud
Amalric, papal legate and one of the most active participants in the Albigensian Crusade
of 1209-1229 against the Christian Cathars who called themselves 'Good Men'.

lated sins, and that the incurable illnesses and deaths of innocent babies are a consequence of the lack of faith by their parents, and represent an opportunity for spiritual growth.

Traditional theodicy can offer only a couple of adequate explanations to the acts of God: Although God is really all-powerful and all-knowing, He is not, alas, all-good. Love is not God. Instead of helping us in our struggle against evil, He toys with us like a cat with a mouse, or, even worse, like a child with a butterfly he's just trapped. In case your childhood days are long behind you, let us remind you that children usually tear those butterfly wings right off.

After creating the world, God departed from it forever. He has placed us inside a moving car with no brakes or ignition key and we now bump along all the potholes of life without any direction or purpose. Without God, the world has quickly deteriorated into chaos and moral turpitude, which are sure signs of the great evil.

Or else, He is still here but we don't interest him in the slightest because He has more important things to attend to. Whatever the reason, human beings have not been able to find any trace of Him, however sincere their attempts. Quite unlike the trace of evil, which is impossible not to notice.

There is no God at all. Perhaps, he has never existed, or maybe He existed at first but then died. Many philosophers talked about the death of God. Whatever really happened, we will have to deal with evil on our own.

People have chosen the One God as their Defender and have discarded all the other gods without a second glance. Considering Man's imperfections and irresponsibility, shouldn't God accept the lion's share of the blame for evil? What more important business could have detained Him and what other is he responsible for? Why do we even need this 'Protector'? The answer is pretty obvious to me.

The situation is not much better with contemporary theodicy. It tries to justify God by stressing his weaknesses. Even if God loves us, he is not all-mighty and cannot defend us from Evil. This God doesn't deserve our veneration and is as useless as his religion. Both cases give me the criminal thought that either God simply doesn't exist or we considerably exaggerate his significance. We live alongside an ignorant, immoral, and powerless God. Placing your hope in such a God is useless; it's impossible to build any practical moral code on His commandments and for this reason you would do better to become a committed atheist and rely on yourself and on others like yourself.

From the point of pure practical logic, it would be simpler to let go of the God hypothesis. Rather than waste one's energy in trying to defend God, it would obviously be far more worthwhile to attempt to protect Man from evil. When you let go of God, you also let go of His goodness, and make the evil in the world more acceptable. Instead of seeming like a wicked aberration of the divine order, evil is seen as an ordinary daily occurrence, an unavoidable presence in the life blessed by the gentle sun, good health, and career success – the way, in fact, it has always been regarded in paganism.

However, the general debate on theodicy leaves a place even for me. Any fair court proceedings should include two sides – the prosecution and the defence. Theodicy had no problem with its defence: God's acquittal is guaranteed every time. But where is the primary, normally the most important side; where are the prosecutors laying out the charges against God? They are absent altogether; all we can see are His many defenders. This leaves us no alternative but to take up on our far-from-mighty shoulders the heavy burden of being the prosecutors of God. If you like, you can think of us not so much as God's accusers but the Devil's advocates.

In my case it really would be more correct to call me an advocate rather than prosecutor because my main task lies not in accusing God but in defending Man from Him. I want to enumerate his actions calmly and objectively without hiding or exaggerating anything.

I assert that believers can't exonerate God from being responsible for the evil in the world. God has shown conclusively that He is the source of all evil and suffering and He should therefore answer for the harm caused to humanity in His name. Good intentions don't count. Or, as Milan Kundera expressed in *The Unbearable Lightness of Being*, 'The criminal regimes were made not by criminals but by enthusiasts convinced they had discovered the only road to paradise.'

Following the bright road to paradise resulted in the destruction of a great ancient culture, history's first and still-ongoing mass genocide of one's own people, also known as the killing of one's 'heretical' co-religionists, a major 'contribution' to the destruction of the indigenous peoples of Latin America, and millions of deaths during crusades and religious wars. Let's not forget such trifles as many hundreds of thousands of 'witches' having been burnt at the stake, Rwanda's genocide and 9/11. The Marquis de Sade was right: 'Human losses from wars and religious massacres number almost fifty million people. But is there a single religion which is worth so much as a drop of blood from an innocent bird?'

Is it possible that this evil and this suffering were necessary? It is not worth taking into account the arguments that these terrible acts have nothing to do with 'true faith'. What else do they have to do with?

I would like to finish this chapter with a description of Absolute Evil. It's a sort of evil which casts a shadow over Yahweh and other monotheistic gods' existence. As you have already understood, I am talking about the Holocaust.

■ God has Burnt in Auschwitz ■

The term 'holocaust' doesn't appear first in the twentieth century and can be traced back to ancient Greece and to ancient Judaism. This term referred to an animal sacrifice, offered to a god, in which the whole animal is burnt. Later on, it denoted expiatory suffering in general. In the nineteenth century this term started to be used in European literature to refer to massacres of big population groups based on social, ethnic or religious criteria, as, for example, the massacres of Jews during a famine or a plague.

During the Second World War the Nazis massacred more than 10 million people, including six million Jews. At the end of the war everyone knew what 'holocaust' meant.

Human history knows of no analogy to such evil and no amount of pain and suffering that befell Christians in the course of their religion's 2,000-year-old history that could be compared to even a small part of that suffered by the Jews in just one decade of the twentieth century. Judaism should not be addressing the problems of theodicy quietly, from the pages of learned books aimed at particularly committed believers, as happens in Christianity. Instead, it should be yelling its arguments loudly enough to burst the eardrums of every Jew in the world. In all fairness, theodicy post-Holocaust should cease to be a pertinent subject for Christianity, while for Judaism it should be picked out with the brightest of lights.

After this tragedy, every Jew had to finally ask himself the inevitable question: 'How could God – that God whom we worshipped for the past 3,000 years, whom we prayed to unceasingly, whose sacred texts we persisted in studying, and whose Law we followed assiduously – how could God have allowed such evil to befall His "chosen" people?' What reasons did Jews find to justify their belief? Has this experience changed Judaism's perception of Yahweh? Do they think there is still place for faith for the mystical power of God? Do Jews still believe in their God and did the number of believers change after the Holocaust?

Do believers still want to approach God and to 'see His face'? And if so, did they not glimpse in His face the imprint of the millions who had been shot and burned in gas ovens?

How did Judaism's attitude towards the value of human suffering change?

To try to find the answers, I started to research the Holocaust. I was absolutely sure that I would read about accusations against Yahweh and his religion, about the profound deception of their religion. But I saw nothing of the kind. Instead, I got the impression that faithful Jews are much less concerned with theodicy than are Christians; in any case they discuss and write about the subject infrequently. You can even say that they are ignoring the subject altogether; no one is questioning Yahweh about the Holocaust, and He seems to have got away with it rather lightly. As if millions of murdered Jews just vanished or went directly to paradise.

Moreover, certain post-Holocaust rabbinical publications display such surprising statements on the subject that I am at a loss as to how to interpret them. Are they a product of brains addled by God or an example of foolishness?

To prove it, I want you to read some of the most popular explanations of the Holocaust accompanied with my brief comments, which, despite their sarcasm, are full of bitterness.

Nothing special happened. The Holocaust was perhaps the most extensive of all previous Jewish catastrophes, but it doesn't mean that it is somehow different from other suffering that Jewish people endured. Jews were killed and discriminated long before it. Indeed, let's not deny that the Holocaust was bigger than any other tragedy of Jewish people before that but this fact has no theological significance. It doesn't matter whether it was one Jew or six million who are dead. That is the reason why the Holocaust has changed nothing in the relationship between Jews and their God and the faith hasn't lost its sacred meaning.

American rabbi Jacob Neusner explained in 'The Implications of the Holocaust' and 'The Holocaust in the Context of Judaism':

> What then are the implications of the Holocaust? In one sense, I claim there is no implication – none for Judaic theology, none for Jewish community life ... Judaic theologians ill-serve the faithful when they claim Auschwitz marks a "turning" ... In fact, Judaic piety has all along known how to respond to disaster.

He also said that the Holocaust 'revealed the awesome power of faith that could not be murdered by the most systematic assault on it ever undertaken... The fact that after Auschwitz the Jewish people still live and can still affirm its faith is the most powerful testimony that God still lives.'

Theologian and philosopher Michael Wyschogrod boasts that in his religion 'the Prophets speak more loudly than did Hitler': If there is hope after the Holocaust, it is because, to those who believe, the Prophets speak more loudly than did Hitler, and because the divine promise sweeps over the crematoria and silences the voice of Auschwitz.

In general, one doesn't need any particular explanations. It is a de facto omission of the events: the tragedy has nothing to do with sacred principles of the religion. Of course, families of millions of innocent people who were massacred or burnt can mourn them, but they should not forget their main duty – to pray and to go to the synagogue.

The Holocaust was necessary to the spiritual development of Jews. We have gone over this idea that evil is good because it helps us to morally develop, grow in virtue and know

Warsaw Insurrection. Photograph taken from the report of Jürgen Stroop for Heinrich Himmler, May 1943.

God, which can be traced back to the father of the Christian theodicy, Irenaeus. A huge number of religious commentators expressed the same idea, stating that the impossibility of rational explanation for Jewish people's horrible suffering shows that this suffering was not in vain and that it made them closer to understanding God's plan.

Some say that it is precisely faith in God which helps many to overcome the horrors of the Holocaust. Some commentators uttered obvious absurdities, suggesting that in choosing Judaism Jewish people had declined a happy life for themselves and for their descendants. Ezriel Tauber writes in his *Darkness Before Dawn*: Jewish suffering is a by-product of choosiness, so much so in fact that, as strange as it may sound, the forefathers of the Jewish people chose suffering for their descendants.

We shouldn't lie to ourselves and to others. The horrible suffering of Jewish people was in vain. The only possibility it created was to fully understand the absence of God and his plan, to deny the tale of a 'chosen people' and to feel the solitude. In fact, if Jewish suffering must be considered 'the other side of the coin' of their status as God's chosen ones, isn't it a call to genocide?

Jews are responsible for the Holocaust. The Holocaust is a just punishment for the lack of faith and disobedience on the part of the Jewish people. The Torah and the faith ceased to offer protection to the Jews because instead of using their God-given freedom for piety, they used it to gain power over others and for sin and debauchery. In this way, they incurred God's wrath upon themselves, as in fact it was foretold and aptly described in the fifth Book of the Torah:

> But if you will not obey the voice of the Lord your God or be careful to do all his commandments and his statutes which I command you this day, then all these curses shall come upon you and overtake you. Cursed shall you be in the city, and cursed shall you be in the field. Cursed shall be your basket and your kneading-trough. Cursed shall be the fruit of your body, and the fruit of your ground, the increase of your cattle, and the young of your flock. Cursed shall you be when you come in, and cursed shall you be when you go out. The Lord will send upon you curses, confusion, and frustration, in all that you undertake to do, until you are destroyed and perish quickly, on account of the evil of your doings, because you have forsaken me. The Lord will make the pestilence cleave to you until he has consumed you off the land which you are entering to take possession of it. (Deuteronomy 28:15-22)

The idea that the Holocaust was God's punishment of Jews who lost their faith was first advanced by the rabbinical chief justice of Vilnius, Chaim Ozer Grodzinski:

> The whole Jewish People drowns in rivers of blood and seas of tears. In the Western countries, the Reform Movement has struck at the roots, and from there [i.e. Germany] the evil has gone forth now, to pursue them with wrath, to destroy them and expunge them. They [i.e. the non-Orthodox] have caused the poison of hatred against our people to spread to other lands as well.

In 1941, days before he was executed, a Lithuanian Talmudist and rabbi called Elchonon Wasserman said that the Holocaust was a sacrifice Jews had to make because of those who lost their faith: 'We are being asked to atone with our bodies for the sins of Israel.'

After the end of the Second World War, some ultra-orthodox rabbis maintained that at some point Jewish people had committed so many sins that God was obliged to punish them with the Holocaust so that they could atone and repent (what a nice way to repent – by sacrificing six million people). This idea, full of praise of 'compassionate and merciful' God, was advanced by one of the founders of the Israeli ultra-orthodox political party Shas, in an orthodox newspaper *Yated Neeman*: 'God forbid one must not think that God is cruel, after all He is a merciful and compassionate king.'

> What has God done to us? Did this happen for no reason? Does a wild human being like Hitler have the power to annihilate six million Jews? If we think this is true then we are lacking in our faith in divine providence in the creator of the World and his creations... It is clear that the answer is very obvious. God kept count of each and every sin, in a running count over hundreds of years, until the count amounted to six million Jews, and that is how the Holocaust occurred. So must a Jew believe, and if a Jew does not completely believe this, he is a heretic, and if we do not accept this as a punishment, then it is as if we don't believe in the Holy One, blessed be He. After exterminating the six million, He began counting again... Now things are quiet and good for us because the new count has not reached its conclusion, however when it does then there will be a new period of judgement.

There are two interesting ideas in this citation. Firstly, it is nice to see that the word 'heretic' still exists and secondly, it announces a wonderful perspective: if the Jews don't learn from this lesson, God will send another Holocaust.

Let me quote another ultra-orthodox rabbi, Avigdor HaKohen Miller:

> Hitler was not only sent by Heaven, but was sent as a kindness from Heaven... Because assimilation and intermarriage are worse than death ... and the German Jews and others ignored the Torah-teachers and refused to desist from their mad race into assimilation, the Nazis were sent to prevent them and rescue them before they were swallowed up by the nations.

I have only one thing to say. If this God is really 'merciful and compassionate' and Hitler was sent by Heaven, Eliezer Shah and Avigdor Miller are both crazy.

They are not alone in their madness. There have always been rabbis who thought that preservation of the religion was more important than believers' lives. Maimonides maintained that one had to thank God that not all the Jews were massacred. And one shouldn't fall into despair about millions of innocent victims, because this sacrifice pleases God. From a teleological standpoint of presenting God's final purpose, all punishment, however tragic it may seem, is an expression of God's love for His people, a means of attaining a higher degree of spiritual perfection, of returning to God, and of the ultimate salvation to come.

Why has God chosen to reveal His purpose through the Holocaust? This is something which a believer is not given to understand. God has His own secret purpose and Man must be equally thankful for everything – good as well as evil.

Jews are not responsible for the Holocaust. The Holocaust was the result of the struggle against the One God, the morality of monotheism and Israel's spiritual message to humanity. If we really think the Holocaust was the result of a struggle, then we would have to say that the One God, the morality of monotheism and the spiritual message are clear and indisputable losers. The Holocaust was a brilliant proof of the Jewish God's incapacity; Hitler clearly proved to be far more powerful. It wasn't God who destroyed Hitler, but the Allies. Without their determination and enormous sacrifices, Hitler would have been quite capable of conquering the whole world and murdering all of its Jews, every single one of them. The Jewish God can take no credit for the fact that this, fortunately, did not happen.

God was absent during the Holocaust. In the human history there are periods of God's absence, when He is hiding his face (Esther Panim). At this time, he is not in charge of history and thus not responsible for the tragedies. We cannot understand the reasons for his absence. It is precisely during such a period that the Holocaust occurred. Why not? From time to time, we also leave our family, to go to the restroom for example, but we always come back.

The idea of the absence of God during the Holocaust was advanced by the rabbi and theologian Eliezer Berkovits:

> Such is God. He is a God who hides himself. Man may seek him and he will not be found; man may call to him and he may not answer. God's hiding his face in this case is not a response to man, but a quality of being assumed by God on his own initiative...

American theologian and writer Arthur Allen Cohen maintains the same idea and writes about it in *The Tremendum: A Theological Interpretation of the Holocaust.* He suggests that Man cannot understand God's actions during the Holocaust. It cannot be explained by any theodicy. Man can love God, but cannot ask him to interfere, especially in such an extraordinary event, which doesn't correspond to any notions we have. One should regard God as one doesn't know anything about him: 'Without addressing He Who Spoke and Created the Universe as though he were new to us, as though everything that had been thought about him was now demonstrably implausible or morally inadequate.'

Even if we cannot understand God's absence, we can still guess the cause:

First, God gave to men freedom and free will, but some of them chose evil. God was upset and abandoned his people for some time. For some reason, he only returned after the Holocaust, once the Allies vanquished Hitler.

Second, not very different from the first. God turned away from the sinners. In this case, we go back to the ultra-orthodox rabbis' conception of the Holocaust as a punishment for the sins. The idea of God's absence during the Holocaust strikes me as bad, because it takes away our last hope for divine help. Jews hoped for such help in 1939, but what they got was six million dead bodies. On the other hand, maybe this is precisely the kind of situation in which it would be more expedient to absent oneself from than to be accused of criminal inactivity in the face of the massacre of one's people. Yahweh's absence in this critical situation is not unique and He is not alone in acting this way. Christ did not help the Christians in Rwanda, and the Buddha did nothing to save one third of the population of the Democratic Kampuchea slaughtered by Pol Pot and his mates.

So isn't it better to think that He left forever before the war and will never come back? In this case, if there is a danger, we won't rely on anyone but ourselves.

God never left the Jewish people. Philosopher and reform rabbi Emile Fackenheim is convinced that Jews shouldn't renounce God because of the Holocaust, because that would mean that Hitler had won. Fackenheim maintains that God never left his people. He was with Jews even in Auschwitz, in the gas chambers: 'We are forbidden, finally, to despair of the world as the place which is to become the kingdom of God, lest we help make it a meaningless place in which God is dead or irrelevant and everything is permitted.'

There is nothing new in the words of this respectable rabbi. Other rabbis have also maintained that God the Creator suffered in the ghettos and concentration camps with them.

It is hard to imagine God in the gas chambers, but if he were really there, this phrase needs to be continued with 'and died along with them'. His death was as terrible as Christ's death on the cross and he redeemed Jews from all sins. It is well known that Hitler didn't really care whether Jews believed in their God or not. His accomplices killed Jews who had converted to other religions with just as much pleasure.

The Holocaust was sent by God to enable the creation of the State of Israel. In this way, the rise of Hitler was a part of the divine plan and it was impossible to prevent it.

This is the point of view of the liberal theologian Ignaz Maybaum, author of *The Face of God after Auschwitz*. Such catastrophes often have a positive influence on the history of humanity, as they finish the old era and start the new one. When Nebuchadnezzar destroyed the first Temple of Solomon, the Jewish diaspora was created. It led to the propagation of Judaism and the Torah. The destruction of the second Temple led to the creation of the synagogue. Following this logic, the destruction of the majority of European Jews helped to establish the national home for all Jews, the State of Israel:

> We, too, must regard the years 1933-1945, the years of tribulation, persecution and martyrdom as "a small moment" [Isaiah, 54:7]. We, too, must see God, as does the prophet, as the merciful God, in spite of Hitler, in spite of the concentration camps, in spite of the six million Jewish martyrs. We must see our churban as the prophet sees the first one: as "a little wrath" ... measured against the eternal love which God showers on His people. After every churban, the Jewish people made a decisive progress and the mankind progressed with us.

I cannot leave such an amazing example of religious paranoia alone. This rabbi affirms that despite the fact that 60 per cent of the Jewish population of Europe perished during the Holocaust, this catastrophe is nothing but a 'little wrath' of God who turned away from his people for a small moment. It is nothing compared to his eternal and merciful love for his people and to the progress that humanity accomplished thanks to it. I wonder if Hitler won and massacred not 60 per cent but 99.9 per cent of Jews, would a handful of survived rabbis call this tragedy a 'big wrath'? Or would it remain a 'little wrath' and a sign of God's merciful love?

Following this logic, the Turkish people contributed to humanity's progress by massacring one-and-a-half million Armenians during the First World War. The Armenians should thank Jesus Christ for it.

And one more thing. Imagine what people like Ignaz Maybaum could do if they ever got any political power. In the critical moment they would gladly sacrifice not only foreign nations but also their own just not to offend their 'merciful' God.

Religious Zionist and rabbi Zvi Yehouda Kook says that Jews who were unfaithful to the idea of the Land of Israel merited the collective punishment: God sent them the Holocaust and Hitler.

> When the end comes and Israel fails to recognize it, there comes a cruel divine operation that removes [the Jewish people] from its exile... because of the reality [expressed in the verse] "they rejected the desirable land and put no faith in His promise." (Psalm 106: 24)

In fact, you can find an explanation for everything in the Torah. Hassidic rabbi and anti-Zionist Joel Teitelbaum doesn't agree with this point of view. According to him, the Holocaust was a punishment for Zionism. Jews didn't wait until the Messiah came and decided to establish Israel by themselves:

> No one takes note of the fact that six million Jews were killed because of these [Zionist] groups, who drew the hearts of the nation [to their cause] and violated the oath of hastening the end by claiming sovereignty and freedom before the time... [From] the very beginning of their establishment for many years they informed terribly on the Jews to the nations, and spoke of them badly to the authorities, as though [the Jews] were highly dangerous to the nations and they had to be expelled from their countries, [which the Zionists did] thinking that it would thereby be easier for them to carry out their scheme to come to the land of Israel and to organise a government there.

I shall pass over this theory – Hitler as God's messenger, His Messiah – without comment. It's just as well I don't know its originators in person and haven't met them face to face. I might not have been able to restrain myself. It would have ended badly for me – a long stay in prison. The only good thing is that I would have never regretted what I would have done to these thinkers.

Are you satisfied with these rabbis' explanations of the Holocaust? I was not. Yahweh's complete inaction during the Holocaust has proved that he is either immoral or weak or simply doesn't exist. What more proof do you need?

It would be much better to use time wasted on these explanations for commemorating the victims or for reinforcing the military spirit of the Jewish nation.

However, what else could we expect from people who lost their reason after many years of religious studies? To tell you the truth, these 'explanations' for the Holocaust are predictable, simplistic, and mostly uninteresting. Their conclusions are at best ludicrously weak, and at best obviously absurd. The only response any rational person can give to them is pity and disgust.

Fortunately, there were a few intelligent and honest people among devout Jews (first and foremost the rabbis) whose brains refused to accept this explanation for the Holocaust and who demanded better answers from God and His religion. In so doing, they only went halfway, failing to deny God's actual existence.

An Orthodox rabbi, Irving Greenberg, concludes that God is to blame for the fact that His covenant with the Jewish people has been permanently broken. God has failed to honour the Ten Commandments and to respond to prayer and thereby lost any moral claim to leadership. In retrospect, it is now clear that the divine assignment to the Jews was untenable. After the Holocaust, it is obvious that this role opened the Jews to a fury from which there was no escape. Morally speaking then, God can have no claims on the Jews by dint of the covenant. Greenberg says that Jews can freely accept new obligations and develops an idea of a new covenant. I, on the other hand, believe that the covenant was broken for the simple reason that it never existed in the first place. Or, if it did, it brought the Jews no benefit whatsoever. So why try again and assume new obligations? Everyone knows what happened because of the first covenant.

An American writer, Rabbi Rubenstein, writes in *After Auschwitz* that the only honest response to the Holocaust is to accept that the God of the Bible, the God who loves his creature, is dead. If this God was alive, he wouldn't have let the Holocaust occur. However, not only did he let it happen, but he also used Hitler as his special agent, a tool of death.

> How can Jews believe in an omnipotent, beneficent God after Auschwitz? Traditional Jewish theology maintains that God is the ultimate, omnipotent actor in historical drama. It has interpreted every major catastrophe in Jewish history as God's punishment of a sinful Israel. I fail to see how this position can be maintained without regarding Hitler and the SS as instruments of God's will... I am compelled to say that we live in the time of the "death of God...the thread uniting God and man, heaven and earth, has been broken. We stand in a cold, silent, unfeeling cosmos, unaided by any purposeful power beyond our own resources."

After the Holocaust, it is no longer possible to talk about the existence of any divine plan, or to discern God's will and care for the world. It is also inconceivable that the Jews are God's chosen people. It is time to stop focusing on God and turn to Man. If God doesn't rule history, humanity is solely responsible for the creation of its values. Jews should focus on their culture and their community and find in it the new meaning of their existence.

Rubenstein writes in *Job and Auschwitz* that one shouldn't seek to explain the Holocaust – there is no sense in it – or compare this tragedy to the story of Job, which is a Jewish theodicy's traditional method. Those who died in the gas chambers are not Job, but his children who died forever.

> The agony of European Jewry cannot be likened to the testing of Job. To see any purpose in the death camps, the traditional believer is forced to regard the most demonic, anti-human explosion of all history as a meaningful expression of God's purposes. The idea is simply too obscene for me to accept.

Elie Wiesel, a Nobel Laureate and former prisoner of Auschwitz and Buchenwald, had shared the same point of view. In his autobiographical *Night* and *All Rivers Run to the Sea*, Wiesel writes that:

> Nothing justifies Auschwitz. Were the Lord Himself to offer me a justification, I think I would reject it. Treblinka erases all justifications and all answers. The barbed-wire kingdom will forever remain an immense question mark on the scale of both humanity and its Creator. Faced with the unprecedented suffering and agony, He should have intervened, or at least expressed Himself. Which side was He on? Isn't he the Father of us all?

Nothing can justify the death of children. Besides, if in the biblical story Job received an answer from God, the prisoners of the Holocaust didn't. That is why, without renouncing to his personal faith, Wiesel compares himself to Job: 'Job never understood his own tragedy which, after all, was only that of an individual betrayed by God…' Wiesel accuses God of the Holocaust: 'This day I had ceased to plead. I was no longer capable of lamentation. On the contrary, I felt strong. I was the accuser, God the accused.'

He is absolutely right. Even in the story of Job, God restored everything except a mere trifle – Job's 10 children murdered by the Devil were not restored, but God allowed Job to have 10 more. To be fair, the situation with the Holocaust is a bit more complicated. No one restored the six million murdered Jews (or is ever likely to) and giving birth to six million more requires the time and effort of many future generations.

Other reasonable rabbis claimed the Holocaust made it abundantly clear that not only is God not all-powerful, He is also downright weak and quite immoral. He over-exerted Himself by creating us and has grown weak. There is nothing new in it: the Torah gives us a wonderful example in Job who, while not doubting God's existence and power, nevertheless had severe doubts as to His moral code and sense of justice.

The theodicy project is over, once and for all, for Judaism. It is immaterial for the Jews to know whether or not God was present during the Holocaust. For the sake of their own well-being, the Jews should let go of the dream of their (extraordinary) 'special relationship with God'. This relationship is over; it was burned in the ovens of the camp crematoria.

It is impossible and useless to justify God: he is not of use to anyone in this state. All that remains for people to do is to lead a good life, and try to build up a good world by their own efforts. One can still believe in God and help Him regain His former strength through offering Him our prayers.

What phenomenal loyalty to a God no one knows what they need Him for. I wish I had such a friend.

And the last thing. All my efforts to find out how many people left Judaism after the Holocaust were unsuccessful. I understand perfectly well why there are no official statistics dealing with Jews who have rejected God, or why none could be collected in the future. This is a particularly painful subject, so it is not addressed, nor has it ever been or likely to be in the future. One simply understands that some religious Jews lost their faith, but their places were then taken up by others who were not religious before. Thus, Jews have no fears either for the survival of their beloved religion or for the synagogue attendance records.

It is however surprising that there are still any believers after such evil. On the other hand, I understand how difficult it must be to separate oneself from the God your people have been worshipping for 2,500 years. That is why nobody accused Yahweh for this absolute evil and he got away with it. Any pagan god wouldn't emerge unscathed from making people suffer so much.

I did everything I could to tell you about the reaction of the Jewish theodicy to the evil of the Holocaust and to explain to you my own point of view. But when I started to read what I had written, I realised that I hadn't said anything important, and I hadn't succeeded in doing it. However deep and far-reaching, no historical or philosophical analysis could truly explain these events.

Moreover, I had a feeling that I was going crazy. I felt the same acute pain that permeated my entire being when I was writing this chapter. Then I was blinded by anger and couldn't work for more than three weeks.

It became clear to me that I had to stop for a moment and express this anger that was torturing me from inside. I won't be able to continue writing without it. My eyes don't see and my hands tremble.

TO JUSTIFY GOD AFTER THE HOLOCAUST IS A BLASPHEMY AND A BETRAYAL OF YOUR OWN PEOPLE. IT IS AN OBVIOUS INSULT TO THE MEMORY OF MILLIONS OF VICTIMS.

The Holocaust is an example of the evil which is not compatible with God's existence. After the Holocaust it is impossible to justify Yahweh. The Holocaust has carved a wide and infinitely deep crevice between Jewish religious doctrine and practical life, over which one could never leap or build a bridge. The Holocaust is entirely different from the suffering of Job, both in the scale of its evil and its consequences. After all, God restored all his cattle to Job and allowed him to have more children and live till he was 140 years old, whereas six million Jewish lives perished forever.

So why not bring this whole project to an end – not just the question of theodicy but the whole God question too? Why not return God to the place whence He came – the place of non-being?

I can understand why people are so afraid even to raise the question of God's existence. Most, probably, are worried that they would end up feeling as naked as did the emperor in Hans Christian Andersen's fairy tale. The One God has always been viewed as the Supreme Lawgiver and Judge who, while existing outside our empirical life, gives it meaning, historical context, and a final purpose. The idea that this God can be dead is hardly new; it was made popular by Friedrich Nietzsche, referring to the Christian God.

Judaism's relationship with its One God, Yahweh, is somewhat different. He has always occupied a special place in Jewish life – one can even say that He is in fact the point of this life. While there has never been a Jewish philosopher who could have proclaimed His death, the Holocaust happened and presented an incontrovertible proof that Yahweh is dead. Even if He had existed once, He too perished in the gas chambers.

Indeed, Yahweh, the God of Judaism, became the Holocaust's first ever victim, and perhaps the most important victim, and died once and for all. But lamenting Him is useless. Man is weakened by every instance of regret and by all suffering. It would be far more prudent to forget the past, and to attempt to enter into a covenant, not with God – old or new – but with the people around us. It will be possible to focus entirely on building a bright Jewish future of secular virtue.

What would the Jews lose if they were to renounce God? The worst has already happened. Is it possible that Jews do not have other values to believe and to defend except for God? There are so many businesses to launch, so many books to write, so many discoveries to make and so many Nobel Prizes to win. And the State of Israel is not in perfect shape yet.

I understand quite well why my idea to renounce Yahweh might encounter severe criticism not only from irrelevant theologians, but also from psychologists and psychiatrists. They might say that believers in God have an easier life. The believers can convince themselves of anything in order not to see evil, just as war horses didn't recognise danger. They'd do anything to discharge their responsibility.

I want an easy life too, but can't quite manage it. The best we can do is to calm down and attempt to prevent theodicy being put out with the rubbish. So let's not attack theodicy – it contains much that is positive, much like tranquilisers for the anxious and strong painkillers for the terminally ill. If you want to learn the art of self-delusion.

Only theodicy could convince you that, even though the three most pious members of your family have died in terrible pain, even though your young and healthy wife was killed by a passing train and your little nephew took three years to die from leukaemia, you are still obliged to love God, trust Him, and thank Him for all the blessings He has bestowed on you and your family. Whatever happens, you must remain firm in your belief

Survivors from the Ebensee concentration camp.
If Yahweh exists and loves His people, how could He allow this tragedy to happen?

that God created the best of all possible worlds in which we now happily find ourselves. However, if you see the world differently and ubiquitous evil is before your eyes all the time, don't despair. Just don some rose-tinted spectacles and see only good. Or close your eyes altogether.

I would like to finish this chapter on a positive note. Without any sarcasm, I assure you that in this hard situation theodicy still has some hope. It can become a respectable and important part of the religious doctrine once again on one condition. It must admit that the Gnostics were right: our world of Universal Evil has always been governed by a mighty Devil rather than the Almighty God of the Bible. In any case, following the Holocaust, our belief in the Devil should have been given a tremendous boost. And not only among Jews.

It is enough to start worshipping the Devil instead of God for everything to come together. In fact, the Devil is a much better companion to theodicy and the faithful than God. There is no need to justify him for the existence of evil – you can simply praise him.

CHAPTER III

Hello Death,
Our First Step
Towards Heaven

A burro muerto, la cebada al rabo.
(Feeding a dead donkey is a waste of oats.)
Spanish proverb

I have always been fascinated by the fact that monotheistic religions managed the impossible and convinced their believers not only not to regret their inevitable death, but also to desire it with joy. By adoring God they overcome the powerful instinct for survival, in which every cell of one's body clings to life, the only tangible symbol of individual existence.

I first encountered the idea that death can be a joyful thing when my son's friend Sergey told us a story about his grandmother. At the age of 10 he went for a summer vacation to his grandmother's farm. Before that, death filled him with consternation, its image firmly associated with the corpse of a stray dog he stumbled upon when playing Cowboys and Indians. The remains of the dog smelled gross, and was caked with a thick layer of green-blue cadaver flies enjoying their unexpected happiness.

The grandmother was a Russian Old Believer, a 'true' Orthodox Christian who did not accept the Church reforms of the mid-seventeenth century. In the view of these Christians, this reform, the aim of which was the reunion of the Russian and Greek Orthodox Churches, was a threat to a feeling of identity and spirituality, and led to inevitable secularisation.

They can be easily recognised, even at a great distance: Orthodox Christians look exactly the same as they did in the seventeenth century – women still in headscarves and long skirts, and men with beards. Old Believers are hard-nosed and even somewhat unique, characterised by their deep religiousness. They believe that only the followers of their faith can be saved. They have a passionate love for peasant labour, a blind adherence to the old precepts and traditions, and a lukewarm attitude to education.

The grandmother could talk about faith for hours, including how the Russian spelling of Jesus' name, Iisus, was to be written with just one 'i' – Isus – and that you should cross yourself with two fingers. She also spoke of numerous religious holidays, the most important of them being Holy Easter. The grandmother saw the gospel story of Christ's resurrection as something personal, and from an early age she wanted to die on Easter Sunday. She believed that if she died on the first day of Easter she would go straight to paradise. On this blessed day the grandmother was prepared to die not only from illness or old age, but in perfect health at any age, even when she was young and flourishing. And every time she woke up the next morning in good health she was disappointed by another failure.

But miracles exist. In the end the passionate prayers of the grandmother were heard and she was handsomely rewarded – she died on the first day of Easter. Although it took a while: she was eighty-seven years old. Most likely only her venerable age has prevented her from sending us news of her safe arrival in paradise.

I am convinced that it is more reasonable to worship life instead of death. This is the reason why I chose my epigraph for this chapter. Neither I nor Spanish people doubt a dead donkey could be helped in any way. It wouldn't have another life and even the best oats would be wasted on it.

■ Death is the End of Everything ■

Dying is a universal concept. Death touches everything that exists around us: all forms of matter change over time and lose their properties, transforming into something else. Death is irreversible and can be seen as the process of erasing the differences between material objects. Physicists call this 'increasing entropy'.

This is true for both living and non-living matter. Nothing is eternal, even the things with a lifespan, which make all forms of organic life; even thousand-year-old trees seem fleeting. Black holes evaporate, stars and planets disappear, mountains subside, rocks scatter, and plastic decomposes (to the joy of environmentalists). Social life is no exception: seemingly immutable mighty empires break up, huge political parties fade away, and cultural stereotypes and lifestyles crumble.

Great philosophers saw in death the fundamental question of human existence, since it is impossible to understand the meaning of life without death. It is death that sets up temporal boundaries and reunites us, so different, in one big human tribe. Yang Chu, the fifth-century Chinese philosopher, is simply incredible in the *Lieh-tzu*:

> The myriad creatures are different in life but the same in death. In life they might be worthy or stupid, honourable or humble. This is where they differ. In death they all stink, rot, disintegrate, and disappear. This is where they are the same. However, being worthy, stupid, honourable or humble is beyond their power, and to stink, rot, disintegrate, and disappear is

also beyond their power. Thus life, death, worthiness, stupidity, honour, and humble station are not of their own making. All creatures are equal in these [that is, they all return to nature]. The one who lives for ten years dies. The one who lives for a hundred years also dies. The man of virtue and the sage both die; the wicked and the stupid also die. In life they were [sage-emperors] Yao and Shun; in death they were rotten bones. Thus they all became rotten bones just the same. Who knows their difference? Let us hasten to enjoy our present life. Why bother about what comes after death?

Death is a much more important frontier than birth. At birth a person is empty, a tabula rasa, whereas a person has left an actual mark by the time they die. Or they don't: all achievements and failures of the deceased become final and obvious.

The situation is compounded by the fact that death is always another's death: a person can't experience their own. A normal person isn't only afraid of their own death, but also pushes away all thoughts of it.

This is what Jean-Jacques Rousseau says about it in *Julie*, or *The New Heloise*:

> The one who pretends to be able to look without fear in the face of death, is lying. The man is afraid of death, and this is the great law for terrestrial creatures; without it, the end of everything mortal would come quickly.

And I was particularly delighted to learn from Kant that it doesn't probably hurt to die:

> No human being can experience his own *death* [for to constitute an experience requires life], he can only observe it in others. Whether it is painful cannot be judged from the death rattle or convulsions of the dying person; it seems much more to be a purely mechanical reaction of the vital force, and perhaps a gentle sensation of the gradual release from all pain.

The philosophy and literature of the nineteenth century were concerned with death. Nietzsche writes in his *Gay Science*:

> How even now everyone's shadow stands behind him, as his dark fellow traveller!... Yet death and deathly silence are the only things certain and common to all in this future! How strange that this sole certainty and commonality barely makes an impression on people and that they are *farthest* removed from feeling like a brotherhood of death!

The painful fixation on the disgusting image of decay and half-decayed remains of what was once a living and beautiful creature, inherent to medieval thinking, never died off in European culture and organically 'jumped' into the nineteenth century, as in this most famous verse of Baudelaire's 'Carcass':

> And yet you will be like this corruption,
> Like this horrible infection,
> Star of my eyes, sunlight of my being,
> You, my angel and my passion!
> Yes! thus will you be, queen of the Graces,
> After the last sacraments,
> When you go beneath grass and luxuriant flowers,
> To moulder among the bones of the dead.

107

It is not optimistic but at least true and useful for the next generations' education.

Some contemporary philosophers also claimed that death was not meaningless – it was the hope of Man, as it gave his life depth and revealed its ultimate meaning. Martin Heidegger in particular emphasised that Man was the only living being that could perceive life as finite. It is this consciousness that makes us human.

Although this idea is not new, it again reminds me that in this aspect Man is not lucky. Such consciousness did not lead to a carefree existence. Sometimes I think that it would be better to be born as an animal, preferably as a pet – you have fewer problems and always enough to eat.

Jacques Derrida noted that although no one can resolve this conflict and come to terms with the idea of one's own death, it is only in this that a person finally finds himself. In this sense death is a gift, the only situation in human existence where a particular individual becomes irreplaceable, when he fully identifies with himself in the sense that he cannot pass on his death to someone else. In this situation, Man is first left alone with himself, free from everything, and his subjectivity and individuality manifest themselves to the fullest.

With all due respect to Derrida, I would have gladly refused the gift, together with subjectivity and individuality.

Jean-Paul Sartre said that we should not fall into the illusion that we have full control of our lives. Our life is a total coincidence and has no clear goals defined for us by other people or a deity. Our freedom to choose goals and how we set about achieving them nevertheless do not help us to avoid the same inevitable end – death. What immediately comes to mind is the well-known expression 'All roads lead to Rome', only in this case all these roads lead nowhere; everywhere it's the same impasse. It fills a person's life with constant fear; one might even say that Man does not exist, but is constantly in a state of death.

We don't know where, when, and how we fall: Man's days are like diving into the void and for this reason it is equivalent not even to conflict with oneself, but with oblivion. However, we should voluntarily accept nothingness and be responsible for our freedom. This will allow us to rise above ourselves and gain satisfaction from the fact that they were able to give our existence some meaning.

I like Sartre's ideas most of all. He helped me not to fear anything and write this book without taking into consideration other people and their gods' demands. None of the philosophers I have just referred to talks about an immortal soul which will go to heaven after death. Scientists and philosophers are confident that consciousness dies with the person. Listen to Camus in *The Myth of Sisyphus*:

> From this inert body on which a slap makes no mark the soul has disappeared… Under the fatal lighting of that destiny, its uselessness becomes evident. No code of ethics and no effort are justifiable *a priori* in the face of the cruel mathematics that command our condition.

This belief is shared by modern secular humanism, which refuses the possibility of an immortal soul's existence. Humanists, who do not like that 'cities of the dead jostle the cities of the living', emphasise that suffering for the dead is pointless; and they insist on embracing cremation as the most economical use of space for the living. According to Corliss Lamont, 'We cannot feel sorry for the deceased person because they do not exist and cannot know sorrow or joy.' The different funeral rites hold only therapeutic value for humanists, with the goal being to comfort the relatives and friends of the deceased.

The views of humanists reminded me of the views of my father, which horrified all his relatives and friends. He had an older sister whom he loved very much and of whom he took daily care, as if he were her older sibling. But after she died he never visited her grave and he was not able to comprehend the bewilderment of my mother. He did not understand why he needed to go there since she was no longer with us.

■ In Search of Immortality ■

Death has always been terrifying. It had to be avoided at all costs, or at least post-poned. Mircea Eliade says that Man has a paradoxical desire 'to be fully immersed in life and at the same time involved in immortality, which comes from a passionate desire to exist simultaneously in time and in eternity.' It would be strange for human beings not to crave the longest life possible. Sentient beings have a much stronger survival instinct than animals, and the desire to survive at any cost is primary.

This search for ways to go on living was one of the main driving forces of human development: a source of philosophical doctrines, morality, the inspiration for religion and science, the impetus for the development of art. It hasn't ceased during the history of humanity, but it is another mere chimera. But a chimera, at least, that is less dangerous and more humane: it doesn't pretend to attain the impossible – eternal life after death – and limits itself to life on earth.

The means of acquiring immortality, which humanity has developed throughout history, are so widely popular that they seem trite.

I will therefore only mention the most famous, the elixir of immortality. Work in this direction has been conducted for almost the entire history of culture, and in all societies. The mixture would necessarily contain gold – indeed, how can one manage without gold, the object of everyone's desire? How else could one justify its value and all the blood shed for it? There is a recipe made by the personal physician of Pope Boniface VIII: 'You should mix in crushed gold, pearls, sapphires, emeralds, rubies, topazes, white and red coral, ivory, sandalwood, heart of deer, root of aloe, musk and ambergris.' In other words, one should put everything valuable together. I don't know the result, but I hope that good sense will keep readers from too hastily mixing this recipe.

An Oriental book suggested a recipe as complicated as the previous one: 'You need to take a toad, who lived 10,000 years, and the bat who lived 1,000 years, dry them in the shade, crush into powder and consume.'

An ancient Persian text was even more original: 'It is necessary to take a person, red-haired and freckled, and feed him with fruits up to thirty years, then place him in a stone vessel with honey and other substances, place this vessel in hoops and hermetically seal. After 120 years his body will turn into a mummy.' The contents of the vessel, including what became of the mummy, were to be taken as curative and life-prolonging.

Everyone was doing it: sorcerers, shamans, frivolous alchemists, serious scholars, and even kings. They crushed rocks, plants, and trees into dust, burned and boiled insects and the organs of animals, transfused themselves with the blood of boys and girls, drank urine and the menstrual flow of virgins. They even made thick reference books with recipes.

In the twentieth century the idea of freezing a dead person and reviving them in the distant future when science will reach unprecedented heights became popular. To reduce space, you can store only the brain and then later find it another body. Medicine, genetics, biological engineering, microbiology, and especially nanotechnology all work on attaining immortality. The proposals for the preservation of DNA (cloning) and the construction of cyborgs, hybrids of machine and Man, stand out especially. And there is the idea that we could enter all the data about a person (appearance, thoughts, psyche) into a computer and keep them there forever. That is, leave the 'biological shell' and go to live in a 'digital archive'.

All these approaches, seemingly different, have one thing in common: they are all fruitless. There is no doubt that the project entitled 'immortality' has failed. Science has nothing much to say: despite the evident achievements of medical science, it hasn't managed to considerably extend human life.

So humanity really has only three symbolic and traditional ways of overcoming its fear of death and achieving at least a 'surrogate' immortality.

The first method is to perpetuate themselves through their children or through dissolution of their personality in the collective fate of the clan, tribe, nation, or ethnic group. Do not be surprised: your desire to have children is also a part of the race for immortality.

This method is obvious and simple, but not devoid of disadvantages: the presence of adult offspring enhances feelings about one's own mortality (we personally have seen it among our friends); the offspring will also die, and the memory of the biological ancestors is erased fairly quickly.

The second method is an attempt to perpetuate oneself in the memory of others, to leave a mark in history by creating human values. Such values are immortal by definition: the death of an individual destroys the human body but cannot destroy human achievements, which live their own life. This method is successfully implemented by great kings and conquerors, major political figures, brilliant scientists, artists, and athletes – all the people whom you learned about in school or from the internet. Awareness of the transience of life is what forced these people to appreciate every moment of life and gave them the mighty impetus to develop and accomplish. I cannot prevent myself from quoting Rousseau on this occasion, from *On Education*:

People think only of preserving their child's life; this is not enough, he must be taught to preserve his own life when he is a man, to bear the buffets of fortune, to brave wealth and poverty, to live at need among the snows of Iceland or on the scorching rocks of Malta. In vain you guard against death; he must needs to die; and even if you do not kill him with your precautions, they are mistaken. Teach him to live rather than to avoid death: life is not breath, but action, the use of our senses, our mind, our faculties, every part of ourselves which makes us conscious of our being. Life consists less in length of days than in the keen sense of living. A man may be buried at a hundred and may never have lived at all. He would have fared better had he died young.

Whether we like to admit it or not, also immortalised in human history are the perpetrators of atrocities. Scandalous personalities like Herostratus, famous criminals like Bonnie and Clyde, and mass murderers like Stalin, Hitler, Pol Pot, and Osama bin Laden.

The third and last method is to transform your fear of death into the concept of life after death. It is quite advantageous, especially to couch potatoes. Indeed, if you believe in life after death, you don't need to cherish every moment any more and try to do anything with your life. You can just stay on the couch and dream. This method is offered by all monotheistic religions and I will talk about it later. And now I propose to study death in its historical aspect.

■ The Taboo of Death ■

Death was considered by ancient people as the moment of separating the dead from the living. The ancient pagans drew a clear boundary between the world of the living and the world of the dead, and the living wanted nothing to do with the dead.

The attitude to dead bodies was twofold. On the one hand there was a natural fear of death: the body was a source of foul-smelling decay and dangerous infections, and the best idea was to stay away from it. Primitive tribes were convinced that death was contagious in every sense.

This position is evident in funeral rituals: the bodies of the dead are usually carried out before sunrise, so as not to defile the sun with a view of the corpse. In addition, the dead were to forget how to return and in no way to appear as ghosts among the living.

Many of these fears and rituals, especially the idea of the uncleanness of a dead body, were later adopted into Judaism and Islam, as I will explain later. I want to quote a wonderful passage from *Our Attitude Towards Death* by Sigmund Freud, who believed that 'the attitude of our unconscious towards death…is almost like that of primitive Man… The man of prehistoric times lives on, unchanged, in our conscious.' Besides being a psychoanalyst, Freud shows his genius in anthropology. *Totem and Taboo*, was written long before the era of political correctness. The descriptions offer wonderfully vivid and accurate images of attitudes towards death. I am going to quote at length.

> Among most primitive people the taboo of the dead displays...a peculiar virulence. It manifests itself in the first place, in the consequences which result from contact with the dead, and in the treatment of the mourners for the dead. Among the Maori any one who had touched a corpse or who had taken part in its interment became extremely unclean and was almost cut off from intercourse with his fellow beings; he was, as we say, boycotted. He could not enter a house, or approach persons or objects without infecting them with the same properties. He could not even touch his food with his own hands, which were now unclean and therefore quite useless to him. His food was put on the ground and he had no alternative except to seize it as best he could, with his lips and teeth, while he held his hands behind on his back.
>
> Calling a dead person by name can also be traced back to contact with him, so that we can turn our attention to the more inclusive problem of why this contact is visited with such a severe taboo. The nearest explanation would point to the natural horror which a corpse inspires, especially in view of the changes so soon noticeable after death.
>
> The hypothesis that those whom we love best turn into demons after death obviously allows us to put a further question. What prompted primitive races to ascribe such a change of sentiment to the beloved dead? Why did they make demons out of them? According to Westermarck this question is easily answered. As death is usually considered the worst calamity that can overtake Man, it is believed that the deceased are very dissatisfied with their lot. Primitive races believe that death comes only through being slain, whether by violence or by magic, and this is considered already sufficient reason for the soul to be vindictive and irritable. The soul presumably envies the living and longs for the company of its former kin; we can therefore understand that the soul should seek to kill with them diseases in order to be re-united with them…

Despite this fear of dead bodies, the corpse is nevertheless the body of an ancestor, so it should be kept within the community. The most reasonable solution is to isolate the dead by allocating specific spaces within reach, for example outside the city, but certainly not in the residential zone.

In Ancient Egyptian civilisation, human earthly existence was seen as preparation for the afterlife. Pharaohs, from the beginning of their reign, paid special attention to the construction of their pyramids and their future tombs. Rich and noble Egyptians spent their whole lives concerned with the ceremony of their burial and even ordinary people studied the rules of conduct in the Kingdom of Osiris. In those faraway times people referred to death as a friend and they were not scared of in vivo preparations for their burial.

Don't miss the fundamental difference: Egyptians understood the inevitability of death as well as Christians did, but, unlike the latter, they did not see any spiritual significance therein. Their religion focused not on the moral side of death, but the cult: apparel, funeral rituals, the decoration of the tomb. It was not about the cult of death as such, but about the preparation for the afterlife. And if you believe in it, why not prepare and take with you your most loyal servants and sexiest concubines? Once in heaven you will probably be even more horny.

So, adherents of almost all pagan religions were sure that death was a natural part of the life cycle. For Mesopotamians, Hittites and others, the dead were mere shadows, helpless and miserable.

Now, I propose to turn to Greek Antiquity. Like in many other pagan cultures, back then people held beliefs about the afterlife, but they were entirely focused on life on earth.

All the myths were abstract and their content depended entirely on the personality of a narrator, so they didn't impose any moral standards. Every reasonable person (there is no reason to doubt the reason of the ancient Greeks) understands that death is the end of life, the end of everything. No way back, no way forward.

Ancient (classical Greek) philosophy, tending to look for answers to all questions besides God, generally proposed that the only important thing in the problem of death was to accept death as an inevitable law of nature and to accept the complete disappearance of the individual and of oneself. Before death a person is trapped in an endless search of himself; in death, this search ends and he reunites with the Cosmos. Greek philosophy also did everything possible to calm a person filled with fear of their finite nature and taught them to adopt an intelligent and courageous attitude towards death.

The best exponent of this attitude was probably Socrates. After he received a death sentence, the brilliant philosopher explained to the court that he did not fear death for two fundamental reasons:

Gustave Doré, Styx, 1861.
The Ancient Greeks expected nothing good to come from death.

'If we accept the hypothesis of immortality of the soul and consciousness, then he will inevitably end up in the place where the souls of other great people, heroes and thinkers are, and will happily continue his philosophical debates.'

If the death of the body entails the death of the soul and a loss of consciousness, and therefore complete oblivion, he also has no fear because in this case he will be free from bitter feelings and sufferings. His disciple Plato was probably the only one of the Greek philosophers to accept the possibility of the existence of the immortal soul. This predisposition made him respected among Christian theologians, even though Plato didn't have any coherent conception of an afterlife. He simply said that because of the limitations of our judgement we cannot reach a world we imagine, a world of ideas, and remain chained to the material world in which we live. The soul eventually separates from the body and finally understands the full meaning of its existence.

Epicurus echoes Socrates, saying Man is not destined to meet his death:

> Accustom yourself to believing that death is nothing to us, for good and evil imply the capacity for sensation, and death is the privation of all sentience... Death, therefore, the most awful of evils, is nothing to us, seeing that, when we are, death is not come, and, when death is come, we are not. It is nothing, then, either to the living or to the dead, for with the living it is not and the dead exist no longer.

Beautiful thoughts about calmly accepting death can be found in the work of Seneca:

> Bassus kept saying: "It is due to our own fault that we feel this torture, because we shrink from dying only when we believe that our end is near at hand." ... We do not fear death; we fear the thought of death. For death itself is always the same distance from us; wherefore, if it is to be feared at all, it is to be feared always.

The Stoics, especially late ones like Epictetus, argued that 'to perform philosophy means to learn to die' and that we have to accept life for what it is. Epictetus' follower Marcus Aurelius, who became a Roman emperor, was acutely aware of the fragility of life. The many wars that he was forced to fight as emperor clearly contributed to it. In his *Meditations* he denies the possibility of life after death:

> Though thou shouldst be going to live three thousand years, and as many times ten thousand years, still remember that no man loses any other life than this which he now lives, nor lives any other than this which he now loses. The longest and shortest are thus brought to the same. For the present is the same to all, though that which perishes is not the same; and so that which is lost appears to be a mere moment.

Ancient philosophers also treated the question of resurrection and eternal life, which became important after the rise of Christianity. Pliny the Elder gave a convincing answer to all dreams of future and existing monotheistic religions. I quote here from John Toland's *Letter to Serena*:

> But the Reasons of those who deny'd the Immortality of the Soul, whether Poets or Philosophers, are almost all comprehended in a narrow Compass by Pliny the elder, in the seventh Book of his Natural History. After the Interment of the Body, says he, there are various Conjectures about

departed Souls. But the State of all Men is the same after the last Day of their Life, as before the first; nor is there any more Sense in Body or Soul after Death, than before the Day of our Birth. But the Vanity of living Men extends to future Ages, and feigns to itself a new life in the very time of Death bestowing Immortality on the Soul; Come teaching the Transmigration of the same; others allowing Sense to those in Hell, and worshipping their Ghosts, and making a God of him, who is not at present so much as a Man.

...These are Allurements to quiet Children, and the fictions of Mortals that won't live without end. The Vanity of preserving the bodies of Men, it like that of the resurrection promised by Democritus; who did not revive himself. But what a prodigious madness is it, to think that Life can be renewed by Death.

These were great ideas, which, alas, were not destined to find a foothold in history. The continuous expansion of the Roman Empire, swallowing more and more territory, worsened the quality of its intellectual resources and undermined the morale of Roman society. Pretty soon there were fewer decent people than there were plebs and barbarians, and there was no need for eternal values, but there was a big desire for simple and primitive decisions. As social equality and eternal life.

As it always happens, the demand created the supply. In the fourth and fifth centuries AD, Roman culture, with all its pomp, theatricality, and burning desire for life, was overthrown by a new monotheistic civilisation, wild and incomprehensible to Romans. Not only did this new civilisation not value every moment of human life, but life itself lost all its meaning, becoming preparation for the long-awaited and desired death. But before worshipping death, the religion had to convince its adepts that death is not the end of everything, but the beginning. Thus was born a horrific chimera which still lives and flourishes today.

■ A Time to Uproot What was Planted ■

The cult of death can exist in a religious doctrine that has an important ritual and spiritual significance. Judaism is not like that (though not without exceptions), and its main provisions relate to life not in heaven but on earth.

Judaism sees death as a natural end to life and treats it realistically, not considering it a tragedy, or spending too much emotion on it. The book of Ecclesiastes states that there is '...a time to be born, and a time to die; a time to plant and a time to uproot what was planted...' (Ecclesiastes 3:2) At the same time, Ecclesiastes says that in a world devoid of meaning and full of injustice, death is the ultimate injustice.

In the Tanakh there is not one line which attempts to show death as good, but there are many attempts to praise life, starting with Moses: 'This day, I call upon the heaven and the earth as witnesses [that I have warned] you: I have set before you life and death, the blessing and the curse. You shall choose life, so that you and your offspring will live.' (Deuteronomy 30:19)

The Book of Psalms celebrates life and thanks God for a late death:

The sorrows of death have encompassed me: and the perils of hell have found me. I met with trouble and sorrow: And I called upon the name of the Lord. O Lord, deliver my soul. The Lord is merciful and just, and our God sheweth mercy.

The Lord is the keeper of little ones: I was little and he delivered me. Turn, O my soul, into thy rest: for the Lord hath been bountiful to thee. For he hath delivered my soul from death: my eyes from tears, my feet from falling. I will please the Lord in the land of the living.

In its attitude towards death, Judaism is strikingly similar to ancient paganism. This is not surprising. All the major ideas from ancient primitive tribes and paganism in relation to death and the dead body have not just remained intact, but also become harsher. It is worth recalling that Judaism was the first monotheistic religion and was born in a sea of many polytheistic beliefs. So the Jewish perception of death has retained more pagan ideas than other Abrahamic religions. In this respect Judaism is the direct heir of paganism, with its complete separation of the world from the underworld and notions of ritual uncleanness of the dead body. As in Antiquity, early Jewish cemeteries were located outside of the city.

Corpses were associated with the highest degree of ritual impurity. Absolutely everything associated with death and the dead body was considered unclean and therefore untouchable – blood, internal organs, murder weapons. Judaism has a hierarchy of sources of impurity emanating from the dead and the ways they disseminate.

Torah law strictly prescribes the deceased to be buried as soon as possible. Even for a criminal executed by a sentence of the court and whose body is to be displayed for edifying purposes, it is said, 'But bury him the same day.' (Deuteronomy 21:23)

In another part of the Torah, laws governing attitudes towards the deceased are as follows:

If someone dies in the tent, everyone in the tent will be unclean for seven days... If there is a dead body out in a field, whether the person died in battle or for some other reason, whoever touches that dead body, or its bones, or even its grave will be unclean for seven days.

The closer one is to God, the stricter the prohibition regarding approaching a dead body. Severe restrictions were imposed on the class of priests, the Cohanim.

A Kohen could not in any case approach the tombs of eminent saints, or even the graves of his parents. He was strictly forbidden from kissing the dead, taking them by the hand, asking the dead to take him with them. If a Kohen slept in the house in which someone died at that moment (without any consideration for the man of God), then he should immediately be woken up so he could leave.

If a Kohen is not sleeping and he finds out that someone has died, that the house is defiled by the uncleanness of a corpse, he is obliged immediately to retire, forbidden to stay in this house even for the short time it would take to get dressed. We vividly imagine a half-naked Kohen running out of the house, but it's still better than being caught by someone else's death when on the toilet.

The only civilised explanation for all these restrictions is found in the work of the French Jewish philosopher Emmanuel Levinas:

> Death is the source of impurity as it can easily take away all meaning from life, even when we think we conquered death with the use of philosophy! Indeed, every time we face death the meaning of our lives is at the risk of disappearing and being reduced to absurdity. The pursuit of pleasures of every minute – remember carpe diem, seize the day – becomes the only sad wisdom. Great deeds and great sacrifices lose all their splendour. Death is the principle of impurity.

I agree with Levinas that the inevitability of death reduces to absurdity the meaning of religious life in Judaism. However, from a religious point of view, this is logical: to a normal person the appearance of a decaying corpse reminds him that death is the end of it all. The person might not withstand this test and spend the rest of life taking part in every imaginable pleasure. Who, then, will pore over the holy books?

The lack of the cult of death in Judaism can be explained by a lack of developed ideas concerning the afterlife. Ancient Judaism didn't have a single coherent concept of the afterlife and its concepts of heaven and hell were equally vague and subdued. It effortlessly combined rational ideas from ancient philosophy, with calls to suffering and martyrdom the only routes to a happy afterlife, with confidence in the resurrection of all the righteous, and with even the Eastern ideas of transmigration of the soul.

Even in the Tanakh, this most important issue for any decent religion is mentioned only in passing. The Book of Job implies that Job believed death to be the greatest misfortune and that it had just one advantage: it puts an end to all other misfortunes. The afterlife is presented as the realm of worms and decay, with no chance of getting out. I might hope for the grave to be my new home. I might hope to make my bed in the dark grave. I might say to the grave, 'You are my father' and to the worms, 'my mother' or 'my sister' (Job 17:13-16); 'so he lies down and does not rise; till the heavens are no more, people will not awake or be roused from their sleep.' (Job 14:12)

Some vague ideas that death is not the end, but rather the beginning appeared in Judaism in the fifth to fourth centuries BC. No genuine monotheism can survive without it. Specific thoughts about the spiritual meaning of death, resurrection, and the coming judgement arose in Judaism by the middle of the fourth century AD, the time of completion of the Jerusalem Talmud, at about the same time as Christianity stepped on the scene of history.

Most likely this was not by accident. As the 'weakest' of the Abrahamic religions (weak in the sense of absence of statehood), Judaism was greatly influenced by its powerful neighbours and for almost two thousand years the Jews were forced to live in a hostile religious environment.

Judaism never gave any details of this sweet world to come and it was stated that the spiritual world cannot be fully understood by Man because the human brain is limited.

Many followers of Judaism say that they want, for themselves and their descendants, not aimless heavenly life but something much more significant – a full and eternal life on earth. This life begins with the coming of the Messiah – *Mashiach* – who will bring with him the moral way of life, and help to stop all wars and to rebuild the Temple, the dwelling place of the spirit of Yahweh. Along the way he will resurrect all those who have been waiting for him, and fill their new lives with common prayer and joyful sacred meaning. Only the righteous will be resurrected for eternal life. Sinners will remain dead.

The righteous don't need to wait for a Messiah to receive their well-deserved rewards: after the death of the body, the soul of the righteous is immediately sent by God to heaven, 'Gan Eden', which consists of two parts.

In the Lower Gan Eden the souls inhabit the bodies in which they were at death and they enjoy various types of spiritual pleasures.

In Upper Gan Eden the souls are in their true form and receive pure spiritual pleasure, which is much larger than the pleasures at the bottom. (Of course, what monotheistic religion would recognise the equality between the carnal and the spiritual/religious pleasures?) The levels of pleasure received depend on the religious achievements of the righteous: the more time he devotes to the study of the sacred books, the more the posthumous high.

Needless to say, a dying sinner ends up immediately in hell, which is called 'Sheol' or 'Gehenna' in Hebrew (a valley near Jerusalem where garbage was burned, but in this specific case the 'garbage' is the soul of the sinner). In Gehenna the soul of a sinner waits for deserved suffering and pain, the level of which depends on the value of his admitted sins (similar to Christianity). The Jews fall into Gehenna just for the time required to 'clean' them from their sins (just like labour camps in totalitarian countries), while the 'infidels', meaning unbelieving Jews and non-Jews, remain there forever.

It resembles Christianity. The Jews should have listened to Job and recognised Christ as the Messiah. In the first case they would not have wasted two-and-a-half thousand years praying, and in the second they would already have rebuilt the Temple of God, calling it the Temple of Christ the Saviour.

No need to criticise Judaism fiercely for this blunder. Yes, it never gave the afterlife special significance or value (especially when compared to Christianity). Yes, the believer does not know his fate after death. But this approach has an extremely important foundation: the concept of the afterlife is not necessary and therefore is not important; religion promises the believer full recompense for his deeds in this life.

The laws of Judaism do not concern the afterlife, but the earthly life: God will reward the righteous with family prosperity and material well-being, He will punish sinners with ruin and death. For this reason, Judaism has a favourable attitude to wealth, seeing it as a sign of God's kindness.

This is a tremendous achievement compared to Christianity and Islam – ancient Jews managed to devote their whole life to God without the allure of the afterlife. They followed moral commandments not for future gain, but solely for the sake of finding the meaning of life and order in it. It is important to acknowledge that death has always had spiritual and religious significance in Judaism. We mean the concept of sanctification of God's name, *Kiddush ha-Shem*, which over time, with the increased persecution of Jews, became the symbol of compulsory martyrdom. Death in the name of faith was the sacred duty and the only possible response by any Jew when forced to breach the fundamental prohibition of Judaism: idolatry, adultery, and shedding the blood of others. The Spanish Marrano Jews were sure that those who practised their faith secretly and died at the hands of the Inquisition were destined for a special place in heaven. One was also supposed to

The old Jewish cemetery off the beaten track.

The Hassids adopted a burial ritual according to the Christian rite for their dead
– the contrast with the image above is striking.

circumcise newborn babies at the risk of martyrdom. So after the recent problems with circumcision in Germany and its prohibition in Sweden, true European Jews are faced with a difficult choice.

Other signs of the cult of death and the cult of the saints are apparent in Hasidism, the democratic religious mysticism from the first half of the eighteenth century, which quickly spread through the Jewish world. Its success is not surprising: in contrast to traditional Judaism, with its emphasis on strict observance of religious rituals and the study of the Torah, Hasidism places emphasis on a personal understanding of God.

It was claimed that Man serves God not only by strictly observing all the religious rites, but also by sensing His presence everywhere and in everything: through enthusiastic and joyful prayer you find a true emotional connection with God, almost merging with Him to the point you can even 'see His face'. Through such communication you can achieve the ability of clairvoyance, miracle making, and prophecy.

Hasidism is particularly close to Christianity because it is focused on the uneducated masses of the poor. It insisted that faith is more important than learning. Hasidism places emphasis on righteousness – people whose sincere and ardent faith allows them to get closer to God than other believers. The righteous (or *tzaddik*) become almost saintly mediators between God and Man. The enthusiastic worship of the tzaddik miracle workers who promised deliverance from all evils and diseases brought the new teaching to the crowds of ordinary Jews. The people flocked to local saints, sometimes giving them the last things they had in the hope of receiving a miracle.

As in Christianity, the cult of saints was followed with a cult of their tombs. The graves of the tzaddikim became a place of pilgrimage; it was believed that their tombs possessed special healing powers and prayer there was especially effective. The cemetery and the graves of the righteous became places of fervent prayers, remembering the holy works and wisdom of the righteous. At some point even babies were brought to the graves of the tzaddikim to be circumcised.

Under the influence of Hasidism the balance between the rejection and the veneration of the dead in Judaism became no more, while the mystical attraction to death increased. Death itself started becoming holy. With the growing importance of death in Hasidism, the material side of life became secondary. For a proper Hasid the sad fate of the body is not important. Out of multiple passages on this subject, I choose to quote here from *The World was Created for Me* by Rabbi Aryeh Kaplan, which tells us about worms, as does the Book of Job, and about the punishment in the grave, just like in Islam.

> As you know, shortly after the burial the body begins to decompose. To see this is scary and painful. The Talmud teaches us that "Worms cause the same pain to the dead as the needle does to the living, as it is written": "And they alone cry for themselves." Kabbalists call this process *hibut hakever* – "punishment in the grave". What happens to the body in the grave may be even worse than Gehinom. But of course it all depends on the person. The stronger his connection throughout his life to his body and the material world, the more anguish after death. The hardest is the loss of the body to one who was focused on the material side of existence in his life. For those who live an intense spiritual life the fate of the body can be of no worry. They feel at

home in the spiritual realm and soon they forget about the body. We know that the tzaddikim are not worried about *hibut hakever*, because the life of their body had no significance for them. (Job 14:22)

Judaism is not alone in despising the body. All monotheistic religions condemn people of my kind – soulless, desperately loving their earthly lives, for whom the fate of the body is crucial, who are not ready to forget about it. Notice that these religions have long lost their egalitarian views that they suggest we voluntarily adopt the new 'spiritual' ruling caste presumably sent to us by Heaven. We'd better not accept it, because it can be stronger than all earthly tyrants.

▪ A King in an Unmarked Grave ▪

Islam can be accused of many sins, but a death cult it is not, and it also lacks a cult of saints.

The best evidence of this was the funeral of the sixth king of Saudi Arabia, Abdullah bin Abdul Aziz. They buried him in an unmarked grave in one of the public cemeteries in Riyadh without the honours typical for heads of state in any Western country, with just a simple tombstone featuring no inscriptions. Though I was familiar with the basic principles of the Muslim faith, this kind of funeral for one of the most powerful men in the Islamic world, or possibly the most powerful, was overwhelmingly impressive.

This equality in the face of death is the secret of the incredible popularity of Islam in the world. Since the Islamic doctrine is monotheism par excellence, it clearly and explicitly says that worshiping graves is a sin and idolatry, because an excessive veneration of the graves of the righteous makes them into idols worshipped besides Allah. To worship graves is idolatry, a sign of pride, the desire to stand out among other worthy Muslims. A Muslim should bow only before Allah, who will decide who is worthy of honour and who is not.

This fundamental concept is backed up by Islamic writings, such as in *The Book of the Unity of God* by Shaikh Imam Muhammad Abdul-Wahhaab:

> Imam Malik in the book "al-Muwatta" shared the hadith that the Messenger of Allah, peace be upon him and Allah's blessings, said: "O Allah! Do not make my grave an idol that is worshipped. Strong is the wrath of Allah against the people who turn graves of their prophets into mosques."

Salafis and Wahhabis were even calling to put a definitive end to idolatry and exhume the remains of their beloved Prophet Muhammed from his grave in the Masjid al-Nabawi mosque in Medina with the purpose of reburial in an unmarked grave.

That makes quite clear why the supporters of 'true' Islam are destroying the most valuable tombstones of Sufi saints: they believe that such monuments are inherently pagan and reflect the influence of the Christian world on Islamic traditions.

The grave of a Muslim should be distinguishable (marked by a low stone, lined with clay or marked by a small tree), but in any case should not rise above the ground much.

Marking the grave is only so it doesn't get lost, so relatives can take care of it and show respect to the deceased.

Everything else is a manifestation of unacceptable pride and sin. It is undesirable to write the name of the deceased on it, or to decorate, plaster, or highlight it in any way. Also out of the question is to place monuments and portraits of the deceased by the grave, or to adorn the tomb with pages with Quranic verses. The late king of Saudi Arabia may be warmly remembered. But no one will worship his grave; he is no longer with us and there is no need to feel sorry for him. He lived well and tasted all pleasures possible.

In Islam, as in Judaism, there is the notion of ritual impurity. This impurity comes from sexual intercourse, severe illness, and touching the dead, unless the latter dies as a martyr. The requirements for avoiding ritual impurity are the same for all Muslims, regardless of their spiritual rank. Ritual impurity is intolerable to a believer, as in this state he cannot pray, perform Hajj, or recite the Quran.

An impure person should redeem himself with a large ablution (*gusul*), except when the desecration was sinful (sexual abuse, drinking, etc.). The position on ritual impurity has, over many years, developed in a detailed way in Islam: If a person touches any part of his body to a cold corpse that has not had the three ablutions, then he has to perform ablution. Even if his nail touches the nail of the deceased, he will be required to perform ablution.

If a person touches a still-hot corpse, he is not obliged to perform ablution, even if the area of the corpse which he touched was cold.

The ablution performed after touching the dead is exactly the same as the ablution performed after intimacy or the release of sperm. If an underage child or a mentally disabled person touches a corpse, he will have to perform ablution after reaching adulthood or returning to a stable state of mind.

Islam wouldn't be a great monotheistic religion if it didn't separate the earthly from the celestial. Every Muslim should be aware of death: constant thoughts of death tear

Wadi-us-Salaam, Iraq. This is the largest cemetery in the world and spreads over six square kilometres and accommodating no fewer than five million bodies.
Look closely: it appears very similar to a former Jewish cemetery.

man from undue attachment to worldly concerns, and keep him from life's pleasures and sinful temptations.

On the other hand, these thoughts maintain the human fear of death and thereby strengthen the religion, which promises an afterlife in heaven with the carnal joys it prevents or limits during life on earth. Awareness of death can be supported by visiting graves: 'I have previously forbidden you to visit graves, but from now visit them, for they hold you from the pleasures of life and remind us of the hereafter.' (Sahih Muslim 2/672)

However, from the point of view of Islam, a person should not wish for death, even in intolerable conditions of existence. Man may not know what to expect. Only Allah knows when one is to live and when to die:

> And among these adverse consequences is that a wish for death is the manifestation of ignorance and stupidity, as Man does not know what will happen to him after death, it may be that he will fall from the frying pan into the fire and find himself in a worse situation associated with possible torment and horrors of the grave. (Sheikh Abdur-Rahman Ibn N. as-Sa'di)

Here it is necessary to explain to the reader what he means by 'possible torment and horrors of the grave'. In Islam, there is such a concept as 'azab al-qabr' or 'punishment of the grave'. After death, Man passes from the earthly world to an intermediate afterlife – the world of the grave – in which he awaits the day of judgement. The test by the grave is the beginning of supernatural life. There the judgement of the earthly life of the deceased starts.

The fate of true believers in Allah, who followed the Quran and Sunnah all their life, and the fate of Muslim sinners and infidels, are fundamentally different. If the person led a righteous life, his grave expands and becomes a semblance of the Garden of Eden, while if he was a sinner or infidel it narrows and becomes a kind of hell. Muslim sinners will experience the torments of hell and will be punished according to the sins of their life.

There is a connection between the world of the grave and the material world. Good deeds during people's life, the prayers of relatives, and a righteous life of their offspring can radically improve the situation of the sinners:

> Al-Bukhari related on the authority of Abu Hurairah, "Whoever accompanies the funeral of a Muslim, seeking the reward only from Allah, the Almighty, and he stays with it until he offers the funeral prayer and the burial is completed, will return back with two Qirat, each Qirat is equal to the mount of Uhud." (*Bulugh al-Maram* 569)

Allah decides what torments await the wicked and how long they will last. In any case, it is worst of all for infidels: for them the world of the grave is much worse than death and in the grave they'll experience loneliness, horror, and suffering, compared to which the evil of the earthly life is nothing and can even seem like paradise. In short, Muslims are intimidated by the torture and horror of the grave just like the Christians are by the sufferings and horrors of hell. And even more: the 'punishment of the grave' can start just right after death of a Muslim, while a Christian can wait till the Last Judgement. The punishment of the grave happens to every dead person, with the exception of martyrs fallen in Jihad for Allah. Martyrdom for the faith of Islam has a special place, so much so that the martyrdom in Judaism and Christianity seem insignificant.

The reason is clear and simple: unlike Judaism and Christianity, Islam was initially spread by its Arab founders with the sword and the main ideological principles of the new religion were first and foremost to ensure the combat readiness and bravery of the Muslim army. This meant making soldiers unafraid of death and ready to sacrifice themselves at any moment. In practice, this entailed two things:

Firstly, this death was considered honourable in Muslim society, which was important for the surviving relatives of the warrior.

Secondly, the Shahid warrior could be confident about his afterlife: he would avoid the 'horrors of the grave', fully atone for the sins of his relatives, and be immediately rewarded by going to heaven. In the Quran it is stated clearly and unequivocally:

> And never think of those who have been killed in the cause of Allah as dead. Rather, they are alive with their Lord, receiving provision, rejoicing in what Allah has bestowed upon them of His bounty, and they receive good tidings about those [to be martyred] after them who have not yet joined them. (Quran 3: 169-72).

One of the founding fathers of ideology of the Iranian revolution, Ali Shariati, writes in *Jihad and Shahadat*:

> A Shahid is one who denies his whole existence in the name of a sacred ideal in which we all believe. It is natural that all the sanctity of this ideal and purpose is transferred to his existence. However, his existence is suddenly turned into non-existence, but he absorbed the full value of the idea for which he gave his life. It is therefore not surprising that in the eyes of the people he has been sanctified.

It would be nice if this militant ideology was a thing of the distant past, but political events of recent decades show that the pursuit of martyrdom in Islam is as strong as ever. Especially since Muslim families, in particular the poor and uneducated ones, are very proud of their offspring who overcome the fear of death and become martyrs. So we should not expect that there will be fewer suicidal Shahids in the near future.

◾ The Religion of Death ◾

If we make every effort to avoid death of the body,
still more should it be our endeavour to avoid death of the soul.
Anthony the Great

Belief in immortality robs the world of its value.
Nietzsche, *The Antichrist*

Unlike Judaism and Islam, for Christianity the cult of death is real and has great spiritual significance. The glorification of death is an important feature of the Christian religion, which has managed to do the almost impossible: suppress the natural fear of death and make people passionately long for it.

To appreciate this phenomenal innovation of Christianity, which lies outside of rational thinking, we must begin with the Christian understanding of life and compare it with a polytheistic one. In polytheism, death was considered the natural end of an organic being of flesh and blood, destined to be born at one time and to decompose fully in another. In Christianity, earthly life, organic life, is not important as it is seen as preparation for another, much more important, afterlife, the eternal life. The body is prison of the soul. The soul wants to leave this prison; it wants to be free and therefore desires its death. A believer merits the salvation of his soul and resurrection of his body after the Last Judgement by his own death. For years I have wondered what state the body of a righteous person will be in when resurrected. What age and in what condition? If it is resurrected in a young and flourishing state – I cannot wait to be resurrected, too. If it is resurrected in the same state it was just before death – no, thank you, it is better not to resurrect me at all.

The Roman philosopher Celsus, who tried to show the absurdity of Christian doctrines, wrote in *The True Word*:

> It is equally silly of these Christians to suppose that when their God applies the fire [like a common cook!] all the rest of mankind will be thoroughly roasted, and that they alone will escape unscorched – not just those alive at the time, mind you, but [they say] those long since dead will rise up from the earth possessing the same bodies as they did before. I ask you: Is this not the hope of worms? For what sort of human soul is it that has any use for a rotted corpse of a body?... I mean, what sort of body is it that could return to its original nature or become the same as it was before it rotted away?

Indeed, the resurrection of the dead after the Last Judgement is the greatest miracle ever. Way cooler than the resurrection of Christ or the creation of the world.

In the *Octavius*, written by Christian apologist Marcus Minucius Felix, it is noted that Christians' hopes are in vain. Their God is simply weak:

> Neither do you at least take experience from things present, how the fruitless expectations of vain promise deceive you. Consider, wretched creatures, [from your lot] while you are yet living, what is threatening you after death. Behold, a portion of you – and, as you declare, the larger and better portion – are in want, are cold, are labouring in hard work and hunger; and God suffers it, He feigns; He either is not willing or not able to assist His people; and thus He is either weak or inequitable... Where is that God who is able to help you when you come to life again, since he cannot help you while you are in this life?

All these impeccable arguments were challenged by the ignorance of people who didn't want to listen. Nothing could stop the adepts of the new religion, who were ready to renounce everything in their life for a chimerical hope for eternal life. The type of reasoned statement I've just quoted became impossible by the end of the fourth century: the religion of love would strangle these authors before they even put down the pen.

A person will be allowed into Heaven only if he rejects the values of the earthly world. In my first epigraph – 'If we make every effort to avoid death of the body, still more should it be our endeavour to avoid death of the soul' – Anthony the Great suggests that all sins come from our unwillingness to abandon the world of the living. My second 'atheist' epigraph is a phrase from Nietzsche's *The Antichrist*: 'Belief in immortality robs the world of its value.'

In essence it's the same idea as St Anthony's, only with the opposite premise. Nietzsche places emphasis on the value of life, while St Anthony placed it on the value of death.

Nietzsche thought that belief in the special significance of death and immortality in the afterlife deprives the world of meaning and value. And vice versa: as soon as we fill the world around us with meaning and value, the belief in the afterlife becomes a chimera.

St Anthony declares that the abandonment of sensual desires is pleasing to God because only He allows a person to kill himself while still alive and become a living corpse (*un mort vivant*). The religious salvation from sin and death transforms into the salvation from life.

How did this idea of superiority of the afterlife to real life infect the polytheistic world? How and why did death become more important than life?

The Christian idea of victory over death appeared at the same time as the faith of the first Christians in the Second Coming of Christ the Saviour and the coming of the Kingdom of Heaven. Even if Christ did not conquer death definitively during his First Advent, then he will destroy it forever in his Second Coming. Death is not the end; it is not necessary to be afraid; real life begins only after death. Death is just a transition from one world to another, the transition from the momentary to eternity, from the unworthy earthly world into the world of the divine. Is it possible to imagine anything better?

Look at how religious philosopher Søren Kierkegaard is full of romantic optimism in his attitude towards death (in *Sickness Unto Death*):

> ...humanly speaking, death is the last thing of all; and, humanly speaking, there is hope only so long as there is life. But Christianly understood death is by no means the last thing of all, hence it is only a little event within that which is all, an eternal life; and Christianly understood there is in death infinitely much more hope than merely humanly speaking there is when there not only is life but this life exhibits the fullest health and vigour. His thoughts weren't new. Many

theologians have put forward the idea that a person cannot overcome the fear of death and live in peace with oneself without God.

I would gladly accept any God if he freed me from the fear of death. But there is a hitch: such an achievement is not free, for the believer must renounce the pleasures of earthly life and recognise all material problems as negligible. I am not ready for this. And I am not alone: billions of people do not serve any God and they do not declare war on life. And people lived in peace with themselves for millennia without the One God and the immortal soul.

I recognise that belief in a better afterlife weakened the fear of death and, in the situation of a bleak earthly existence, made death attractive. Nothing else can explain the insanity that came over the believers.

Christianity offered those willing to listen a transition from real life to the chimeric life. These listeners were mainly from among the poor and uneducated classes, but there were many of them and their faith that true believers in Christ would be saved was the main reason for the great success of Christianity in the Roman Empire.

If you make an effort, and for at least a couple of weeks put aside newspapers, cheap novels, detective stories, and social networks, and you find time to read at least half of the 27 books of the New Testament (don't worry, they are all quite thin; this is not the thick volume of the Pentateuch of the Old Testament), then it will all become quite clear. Through triumphantly proclaiming victory over death and allowing each individual to gain immortality, Christianity strives to attain victory over life. The victory over life and the praising of the value of death represent the two fundamental ideas of the Christian religion.

Christianity is a religion of death, a textbook on mortification, since it grew from contempt for life, worship of the dead, and the idea of post-mortem retribution. The image of Christ is strongly associated not with life, but with a painful death. His death is the central event of the Christian religious doctrine and the instrument of his death, the cross

The catacombs at the time of the arrival of the "cult of saints", 3ʳᵈ century AD.

of the crucifix, is the main symbol of the religion. Christianity considers pleasure a sin. Pleasure helps a person alleviate fear; it's an attempt to push oneself away from death, to turn away from it. And therefore it becomes a dangerous rival of religion. To turn away from the idea of death is tantamount to turning away from God and religion. Because people can die at any moment, they should always be ready to repent for their sins and go to heaven. So for a religious person thoughts of death are essentially thoughts of God, sin, and redemptive prayer.

In short, death should be respected and loved. Saint John Climacus says the following in the *Ladder of divine Ascent*:

> Just as bread is the most necessary of all foods, so the thought of death is the most essential of all works. The remembrance of death brings labours and meditations, or rather the sweetness of dishonour to those living in community.

Fifteenth-century Catholic monk Thomas a Kempis agrees in *The Imitation of Christ*:

> When a man of good will is afflicted, tempted, and tormented by evil thoughts, he realises clearly that his greatest need is God, without Whom he can do no good. Saddened by his miseries and sufferings, he laments and prays. He wearies of living longer and wishes for death that he might be dissolved and be with Christ.

Victory over life demanded a lot of effort in Christianity. Despite the striking personal example of Christ the Founder, it was difficult to knock ordinary people from a natural balance, to tear them from reality, to encourage them to reject the natural values of life. The believer had to suffer for his past sins, and to be afraid not of physical death and decay, but of the upcoming divine Judgement. Otherwise how could you get one to sacrifice to God the best part of his short life? And what do you save him from? To convince wavering believers, Christianity developed a number of muddy and difficult mystical ideas designed to show that death is more desirable and important than life. First, Christianity developed an idea of death as a salvation from sin. Christianity promises the believer to defeat not only death, but also sin. Or rather, to conquer sin and thereby conquer death. God will never forgive unrepented sin and will certainly punish it with torments of hell.

Christianity considers our mortality to be a punishment for the original sin. But in this context I simply cannot understand the ageing and death of animals, and feel especially sorry for pets, cats and dogs, and all the beauties of the zoo: lions, tigers, elephants, and giraffes. Did they, too, commit the original sin? A believer accumulates sins all his life, until his death, which religion considers to be a key moment of existence, when everyone will have to answer for their actions before God.

In *The Destiny of Man,* Nicholas Berdyaev, an existentialist philosopher of the last century, gives a picturesque definition of the importance of death:

> According to the Christian faith death is the result of sin, the last enemy that must be defeated, the ultimate evil. And at the same time death in our sinful world is good and valuable. It only causes us unspeakable horror not because it is evil, but because it has depth and grandeur that stuns our regular world.

In these circumstances death becomes the biggest fear for devout believers, as no one knows beforehand how his actions will be judged and whether the hope of Salvation and eternal life will come true. God has taken away our immortality and He can easily give it back. Or not. He decides.

That is why salvation from sin has become the main goal of a believer's life. For the believers who did not want to listen to the exhortations of the Church, religion added the threat of hellish torment to spiritual nourishment. Here's how it looked in one of the 'soft' interpretations, the second letter to the faithful of Saint Francis of Assisi:

> The body becomes sick, death approaches, and this man dies a bitter death. And no matter where or when or how a man dies in the guilt of sin without doing penance and satisfaction, if he is able to perform some act of satisfaction and does not, the devil snatches up his soul from his body with so much anguish and tribulation that no one can know it unless he has experienced it.

But fleeing from sin doesn't guarantee a blissful eternal life. You must give up all pleasure too, like Saint Ambrose recommends: 'If you die to sin you will be alive to God; but you will live when your dead body will have no lust.' Jesus Christ died on the cross; he died in the same world we will die in. Thus, he invited us to repeat his path. That is why, without exception, all Christian philosopher-theologians saw death as a joyful and

Caravaggio, Saint Jerome, 1605-1606.
Thoughts on death became "bedtime reading" for every saint.

happy event. The need for God is experienced as wishing for death. Remember the story of Sergey's grandmother? If I believed in God, I would also desire to die as soon as possible so as not to miss this amazing opportunity.

The idea that a righteous Christian will meet God after his death is still alive. Here's how Russell Grigg, a Christian missionary, answers the question of his book title, *Why Did God Impose the Death Penalty for Sin?*:

> If mankind was immortal, we would all be cut off from God for eternity. However, because of Christ's death on the cross and His resurrection, if we repent and have faith in the atoning work of Christ for us, our physical death then ushers us into the glorious presence of God in Heaven to be united with him for eternity. How wonderful of God that death, which was the ultimate penalty for sin, should be the very means whereby believers are restored to God and to beautiful holy perfection forever!

It all sounds so wonderful that I was immediately overcome with a desire to kill myself. It seems surprising enough that this author Russell Grigg hasn't done so himself.

But you cannot do it. In Christianity, as indeed in all other monotheisms, suicide is prohibited. Man has no right to dispose of his body during life and therefore after death the destruction of corpses is prohibited: the body must be 'returned' to the Creator in one piece, although talking about corpses as being 'intact' is strange. It is 'intact' probably during the first couple of hours. But it is worth asking a criminologist for how long a corpse resembles a man.

It is worth remembering that artificial maintenance of life, or the opposite – euthanasia – is a sin regularly practised by modern medicine. This itself should constitute a limitation of the power of God and thereby weaken the chances of the deceased to attain eternal life. But here the loving God gave us a break. You can 'legally' achieve premature death through voluntary suffering in His name. In addition, we are allowed to ask Him for an early death, especially if you're bored and dreaming of uniting with Him in heaven as quickly as possible. In case of positive consideration of our requests, He will decide how to grant it: a car accident, a stroke, or a cancer. And now, with a guileless heart, I can give you some examples of the Christian attitude towards death. There are a great number of these examples and some of them are so extraordinary that they can astound even the coldest and most callous person.

■ Memento Mori ■

I want to admit now that this chapter came about not as a result of the systematic analysis of religious sources in Christian theology, but by accident. One summer my then-girlfriend and I went for a small romantic getaway in the Eternal City of Rome, and naturally our travel itinerary included the famous Roman catacombs. We had long wanted to go there, especially my girlfriend: filled with the sublime and pure image of the first Christian believers, rebelling against the injustice and depravity of the Ancient World. In childhood she was told about the catacombs by her parents and read a lot about them in religious literature. One story even suggested that the tombs of Christian martyrs had the scent of lilies and roses.

She had a special place in her heart for the romantic secret meetings in the dimly lit corridors of the crypts. Her childhood imagination created paintings of spirituality on the walls of the tombs, illuminated by the flickering light of candles, with the timid symbols of the omnipotent and the all-seeing One God.

These catacombs were a shock, especially for her. They were not the romantic ancient burial sites, but a gloomy sanctuary of death. Rarely does it happen that in just a few minutes a child's beautiful dream becomes nothing. The idea of corruption, decay, dying, and death permeated Christian culture from the beginning of its existence.

The catacombs were dominated by the bitter cold and a frightening silence – after the warm autumn day on the bustling Roman streets we felt particularly uncomfortable.

The walls of the long, seemingly endless corridors and numerous small crypts (where believers prayed) were entirely composed of tombs: from the floor to the ceiling were endless rows of the clay cells, once filled with corpses. Death surrounds the observer literally from all sides: the concentration of graves in catacombs is many times more than the cemetery.

Many miles of underground graves are littered with human remains. The catacomb which we visited is not the biggest in the city, but it contained 13 kilometres of graves. The Christian tradition began without any doubt as a tradition of death.

Skeletons found in the Roman catacombs.

Most graves were subsequently looted and are now empty, and those untouched in the 20 past centuries contain only dust and bones. But in the first century AD all this magnificence was still fresh and exuded a strong stench. There were special air shafts to filter the smell of the dead bodies, but according to eyewitnesses this did not help much. So it's hard to imagine how the first places of worship of the first Christians smelled.

The first emotional reaction to the catacombs was terrible: wild rituals, celebration not of God the Saviour, but of the Stinking Death. The abnormality of this disgusting Alice's looking glass was in particularly strong contrast to what existed just a few metres above them on the surface – the hedonistic Italian culture.

Why did Christians choose the catacombs as a place for prayer among the dead? To answer this question, it is necessary to understand where the catacombs came from.

The catacombs existed long before the appearance of Christianity on the historical arena. Some of them are abandoned quarries, but most were excavated for ritual purposes. The catacombs served as places of burial for Jews and many other peoples of the Middle East. They were found in Carthage, Phoenicia, Asia Minor, Syria, Malta, Sicily, and Sardinia. To some extent this custom was natural for Romans, who had long buried their high-class citizens in underground family tombs – where they staged *columbariums* for urns containing the ashes, and placed the sarcophagi. The role of such tombs steadily increased from the first century AD in conjunction with the gradual disappearance of the custom of burning the bodies of the dead.

Nevertheless, for the Jews and the Gentiles the catacombs were not intended for religious rites and ceremonies, and they remained a rare phenomenon. Ancient society has always tried to protect itself from death and to mute the natural fear of it.

Christianity behaved quite differently, emphasising the transience of life and the perishing of the body. The decomposition of a corpse was regarded as proof of the principle of imperfection of flesh and a justification of the call for the abandonment of temporary earthly pleasures in favour of faith, the only way to God.

Death happily replaced life for Christians: the ancient lust for life transformed into a thirst for death. In the first centuries of Christianity's existence, religious life was focused on dying: less involvement in worldly life forced the reduction and suppression of desires. Therefore, in the framework of Christianity, the catacombs began to take up a lot of space (it is said that six million people are buried in them – this number drives me crazy) and find a religious significance. For the first Christians the burial became a matter of fundamental importance: how, where, and next to whom a man is buried became more important than how he lived. Those Christians believed that after resurrection they would live in the same religious community as in life. In this regard it is not surprising that the Roman catacombs have grown steadily and quickly became the source and main symbol of the Christian death cult.

A large part of the catacombs was dug by believers in new locations or as an extension of previously existing ones. This is evidenced by the images of gravedigger Christians, day and night picking at layers of tuff. Supported by faith, they lived in the bowels of the

NEQVE ILLIC MORTVVS

Skeleton accompanied by the inscription Neque illic mortuus ("Nor am I dead there"), the sculpture erected on the tomb of Giovanni Battista Gisleni (1670), Church of Santa Maria del Popolo, Rome.

earth as a monk does in his cell. Christian burials of the time were characterised by a fundamental equality of death: in the catacombs people from different families and social groups were buried together (just like in Islam).

Some wealthy Romans who had converted to Christianity gave up their family crypts for the mass funeral of fellow believers. The closed family tomb became a public cemetery or, more accurately, a community of the dead. Everyone, regardless of their place in the world, was awarded posthumous equality and ended up in the same place.

The living Christians of the time wanted to be closer to the remains of those lucky ones already dead, whose souls are in bliss near God, and they wished to be especially close to the holy martyrs – a religious doctrine claimed that the remains of saints had healing powers. The tombs of the holy martyrs transformed from a symbol of decay and dust into a symbol of victory over death; holiness eventually came to mean immortality.

After that, unsurprisingly, a cult of saints began to take shape, based on attributes of death. Saints were sometimes dug up, dismembered, and moved to new, more worthy locations. On the way people touched them and even kissed them.

Over time the border between life and death, established by Antiquity, was blurred. Death mingled with life; it became the most important part of life. The cemetery was moved to the centre of the city and became a centre of social life. The grave was the centre of life. It is easy to see the enormous contrast with the Jewish 'neighbours': their priests avoided contact with death, while Christianity was searching for it. Don't think

Jean Le Noir, The Three Living and the Three Dead, 14th century.

too badly of ancient society: the vast number of successful and educated people mocked Christianity and subjected its ideas to ruthless critical analysis. For them, death and the afterlife held no appeal compared to the earth surrounding them: the warm sun, the blue sky, the singing birds, the fish splashing in the pond. They didn't want to be under the earth.

The Byzantine historian Eunapius was terrified by the Christian traditions:

> For they collected the bones and skulls of criminals who had been put to death for various crimes, men whom the law courts of the city had condemned to punishment, made them out to be gods, haunted their sepulchres and thought that they became better by defiling themselves at their graves. Martyrs the dead men were called and ministers of a sort and ambassadors from the gods to carry men's prayers.

The persecution of Christians played a part in the development of the catacombs, even though its scale is largely exaggerated by official Christian historiography. Although the Roman Empire had freedom of religion (it was perhaps the last social formation of this kind for the next millennium and a half), the Christians could not openly meet at any place they desired during short periods of 'persecution'. They benefited from the special Roman law which recognised places of burial as inviolable for the administration. For this reason, until the appearance of the first churches in the third century AD, catacombs continued to be the main place for all religious ceremonies.

While writing this, I had a vision that at first Rome temporarily drove Christianity into the grave, but then the roles reversed.

After the historical victory of Christian civilisation, cemeteries emerged from the underground and turned into huge cathedrals, leaving the catacombs for guests and tourists. But the cult of death remains in all its splendour to this day.

In the fourteenth to fifteenth centuries, it became clear that Christ was not coming for a second time. Instead, the plague came many times, which, according to various estimates, took with each epidemic around one third to one half of the population of the affected territories; the smell of bodies wouldn't leave the towns for years. Together with a disappearing faith in the Second Coming, the fear of the plague intensified and greatly exceeded the fear of the Last Judgement. Moreover, historical events contributed to the weakening of the authority of the Papacy and heresy spread widely. There was also a partial collapse of traditional Christian values. Death was made flesh, finding inspiration in all the known texts of the Bible:

> I looked, and there before me was a pale horse! Its rider was named Death, and Hades was following close behind him. They were given power over a fourth of the earth to kill by sword, famine and plague, and by the wild beasts of the earth. (Revelation 6:8)

The famous French historian Georges Duby writes in *Age of Cathedrals*:

> When the idea of death in its roughest forms took hold at the centre of religious life, and began to control it, when the fear of disappearing from the face of the earth and the desire to prolong life led to the idea that the main way of imitation of Christ was the memory not

of His life, but of his death. At that moment the grave moved to the forefront, becoming what it already was for many centuries in secret, hidden behind the veil of serenity over the official Church.

In these circumstances a joyful meeting with God is not at the front of people's mind, as it was in early Christianity, but the horrors of death. It means that one had to think constantly about death. Death penetrated all spheres of human life. Memento mori. Remember you must die.

Johan Huizinga, in *The Waning of the Middle Ages*, wrote that:

> The medieval soul demands a more concrete embodiment of the perishable: that of the putrefying corpse. Ascetic meditation had, in all ages, dwelt on dust and worms. The treatises on the contempt of the world had long since evoked all the horrors of decomposition… To render the horrible details of decomposition, a realistic force of expression was required, which painting and sculpture only attained around 1400. At the same time, the motif spread from ecclesiastical to popular literature. Until far into the sixteenth century, tombs are adorned with hideous images of a naked corpse with clenched hands and rigid feet, gaping mouth and bowels crawling with worms.

Fragment of the Danse Macabre, Dominican monastery of Basel.

Crypt of the Capuchins, Rome, 16th-18th centuries.
"As we were like you, so will you be like us".

In *Inventing the Enemy* Umberto Eco quotes the Lenten Sermons of priest Sebastiano Pauli:

> As soon as this body, all things considered well put together and well organised, is closed up in its tomb it changes colour, becoming yellow and pale, but with a certain nauseating pallor and wanness that makes one afraid. Then it will blacken from head to toe; and a grim and gloomy heat like that of banked coals, will cover it entirely. Then the face, chest, and stomach will begin to swell strangely: upon the stomach's swelling a fetid, greasy mould will grow the foul product of approaching corruption. Not long thereafter, that yellow and swollen stomach will begin to split and burst here and there: thence will issue forth a slow lava of putrefaction and revolting things in which pieces and chunks of black and rotten flesh float and swim. Here you see a worm-ridden half an eye, there a strip of putrid and rotten lip: and further on a hunch lacerated, bluish intestines. In this greasy muck a number of small flies will generate, as well as worms and other disgusting little creatures that swarm and wind around one another in that corrupt blood, and latching on to that rotten flesh, they eat and devour it. Some of these worms issue forth from the chest. Others with I don't know what filth and mucus dangle from the nostrils: others, intermixed with that putridness, enter and exit from the mouth, and the most satiated come and go, gurgling and bubbling down the throat.

Indeed, it is not an appealing picture of Christian body decay. The only hope is that the soul, transparent and pure, observes all this horror from Heaven and rejoices that it has always believed in the best and had enough time to escape.

However, as paradoxical as it may sound, the fear of withering flesh and death did not mean the fear of the beyond and the recovery of ancient traditions: the inevitable organic decay of the human body emphasises the fundamental value of earthly existence.

It was at that time when, alongside the 'sublime' spiritual religion, an old neighbour reappeared – the long-forgotten mythological consciousness, with its inherent sarcastic Dance of Death. Dances of Death (*Danses Macabres*) were held mostly in cemeteries and helped people to come to terms with the harsh truths of life and death. Whoever you were in life, an Emperor, the Pope, rich, poor, big, small, you were all still heading for the same fate – death. It could come for you at any time. From this point of view, equality permeates the essence of the Dance of Death. In death you will lose all the joys of earthly life: power, fame, and worldly pleasures. From this point of view, the Dance of Death is inspired with egalitarianism and throws us back to the era of the Desert Fathers.

The crypt of the Capuchins houses the remains of nearly 4,000 monks. Due to the fact that the cemetery is small and that rest in sacred ground is a rare privilege, when one of the monks died, they would exhume the old skeletons from the grave and put a new deceased in their place.

At the entrance there is an inscription, where the cult of death was expressed at its best: 'What you are we were; what we are you will be.' ('*Quello che voi siete noi eravamo; quello che noi siamo voi sarete*'.)

The crypt of the Capuchins resembles an earlier inscription at the entrance to the chapel called the 'Chapel of Bones' ('*Capella dos Ossos*') in the Portuguese city of Evora: '*Nós ossos que aqui estamos pelos vossos esperamos*' ('We, the bones, are waiting for you').

Unknown Austrian painter, Portrait of a Man, 18ᵗʰ century.

The Christian death cult continued its triumphant march in the sixteenth to seventeenth centuries. A new genre of painting appeared, continuing the tradition of worship of death – *vanitas*. The term dates back to the great biblical verse. (If the whole Bible was like this, I would without any doubt start believing in God):

> Everything is so meaningless. The Teacher says that it is all a waste of time! Do people really gain anything from all the hard work they do in this life?
>
> All things continue the way they have been since the beginning. The same things will be done that have always been done. There is nothing new in this life.
>
> Someone might say, "Look, this is new," but that thing has always been here. It was here before we were.
>
> People don't remember what happened long ago. In the future, they will not remember what is happening now. And later, other people will not remember what the people before them did. (Ecclesiastes 1:2-3; 9-11)

A *vanitas* painting was an allegorical still life on the theme of the inevitability of death. In the centre of the composition there is always a skull, like in the creations of the famous modern German designer Philipp Plein. There is sometimes some rotten fruit, a symbol of the decay of all living things – even the tastiest and most useful – and an hourglass, a symbol of transience of life and ageing.

While finishing my study of the attributes of death in Christianity, I told myself that it would be much easier to worship death without God, simply addressing your admiration to it, without any intermediaries. It is too complicated to deal with God: He doesn't let you die as promised, He prohibits suicide, and you cannot understand Him with your mind. Isn't it better to worship death instead of God?

I am not the first person to think like this. For example, a death cult in its purest form emerged three centuries ago. In this cult death was not supposed to horrify. One should worship it as the supreme deity. I am referring to the fairly common religious cult of the Holy Death (Santa Muerte). In Mexico and the United States (among Mexican immigrants), the number of adherents has reached millions and continues to grow. To me, the reason behind its popularity is quite clear: everyone has met death and its power is undeniable.

Those who worship death claim that the Christian Church is prone to a caste system and punishment, and is bad at helping the poor and unhappy believers. Death, however, makes no exception for anyone and 'creates miracles, helps to feed your family, saves you from terrible diseases'.

With all its extravagance, this cult, born among Catholics angry with the Church, should not be placed in opposition to official Christianity. And such a wonderful initiative shouldn't be forbidden. At its core this cult is purely Christian and brings to its logical conclusion the most wonderful slogan of our old friend, Anthony the Great: 'If we make every effort to avoid death of the body, still more should it be our endeavour to avoid death of the soul.'

■ Hello Death, Our First Step Towards Heaven ■

The contempt for life is an absurd feeling, because ultimately
it's all we have – all of our existence...
Montaigne, *Essays*

All the monotheistic religions, despite the fundamental differences in approach, represent religions of death rather than of life: they transform the natural fear of death into the hope for eternal life in the afterlife. Religious consciousness is based on the staunch belief that death is not the end of everything, and can and must be overcome. Only the mortal physical body collapses with time and dies; the God-given soul and mind only get stronger and remain immortal. For this reason, there is no need to fear death: true believers will be resurrected later in a wonderful afterlife and will be rewarded with the full enjoyment of eternal life. Indeed, death is our first step towards Heaven.

If you do not believe that, religious faith becomes meaningless. What is it to be based on if not on the hope of personal immortality, if not of the body, then at least of the soul? How else to justify the self-imposed limits throughout life and all the sacrifice?

All religions resemble each other in their attitude towards life and death and they advance only three ideas:

– All earthly human existence has no value. It is only a preparatory stage, a temporary stop, a short transition period before the eternal afterlife, which will be happier than the life left behind on earth.

– Death must be exalted because it has meaning and purpose.

– Religious faith is good because it gives an understanding not only of life, but also of death. Death sometimes then becomes more attractive than life, which loses its meaning and value.

Indeed, look how attractive death is from the point of view of monotheistic religions:

– Death is the highest form of happiness, a proper end to a religious life filled with worship of God and service to Him. Only after death does the believer have a chance to come closer to his Creator and 'see His face'.

– Death has an important spiritual sense: it frees the captive soul from the body, which immediately rushes to Heaven. It passes from one lower spiritual state into another, a higher one.

– Death allows the believer to get rid of nagging problems and start a new, happy life.

One can believe in all this. One can believe in anything he wants, but this particular faith can cost him a lot.

Firstly, these religions replace the fear of death with another, no less wrenching fear – the fear of supernatural punishment, which threatens the faithful who do not follow the principles of moral conduct imposed by the Revelation, on the eternally established concepts of good and evil.

Secondly, along with fear of death, the believer is 'freed' from an earthly existence. Religion forces him to live on earth only for the sake of his God, who becomes the meaning and purpose of his entire life. In this case it's not surprising that a ritual suicide in the name of God becomes desirable.

Thirdly, fighting fear of death with religion is the credo of those who are either zombie fanatics or incapable of creating values, those who are weak in spirit and subconsciously looking for an easy path to immortality as compensation for earthly failures and suffering. Incapable of creating values, they seek them in the Revelation, in death rather than in life.

From this point of view, the specific ideas of every monotheistic religion do not matter. All monotheistic religions replace the fear of death with faith in the immortality in the afterlife. The only differences are minor details.

Judaism says that when the Messiah comes, only the righteous will be resurrected and will live forever in a perfect world. Sinners will remain dead.

Both Islam and Christianity believe that all the dead, even non-believers during their lifetime, will be resurrected, and the good among them will go to heaven and live with God while the bad ones will die again and remain in hell.

The version of Christianity that was adopted at the First Council of Nicaea in 325 AD states that the resurrection will happen during the Second Coming of Christ, whereas Muslims believe that it will happen after Judgement Day.

Forcing believers to accept the afterlife was not easy. There is nothing more natural than the fear of death, inherent in all of us, fuelled by a powerful instinct of self-preservation.

However, the idea of afterlife and the cult of death were mercilessly exploited by all Revelation religions and they have been popular for several thousand years. On the basis of this idea, like on some super-compost in a greenhouse, grew many generations of believers. This is understandable: everyone, including the author of this book, would like to alleviate the numbing fear of future non-being. How can you not love religion if it is fighting death and offers the gift of eternal life?

Some authors, noting the widespread cults of death and the subsequent afterlife, give a less romantic explanation of their origin. This interpretation, perhaps rather cynical, is far from religious spirituality and lofty ideals. In their view, as populations of ancient civilisations grew gradually, the problem of social control over individuals increased, since monitoring people required large resources. Monotheism arose as a necessary response to this problem. It created total invisible control, pushing people into socially acceptable behaviour, and did so free of charge.

Every believer, scared to death by inevitable post-mortem retribution if he violated socio-religious norms, was forced to monitor not only his actions, but even his thoughts and feelings. Fear of getting into hell was much stronger than any earthly punishment, not excluding the worst kind – the death penalty.

After reading this, I thought about the great force of manipulation. Alas, that distant era did not yet have bugging devices and CCTV cameras.

Asian religions are not far from Abrahamic religions when it comes to their attitude towards death. Death in these religions is positive, to be desired rather than feared.

Hinduism believes in an immortal soul which reincarnates into another body. Depending on the lifetime 'achievements' of the deceased, his soul can end up anywhere: from a god to an insect.

In Buddhism, death is only a stage in the chain of rebirth. Life and death flow into each other without end (at least it doesn't mention insects). Death is the best end of life, the desired path to the Ideal. So a proper Buddhist should not fear death: life itself is like hell. It is painful, sad, and full of desires and suffering. So we should not be sad when people die, but when they're born. When you die, you must be happy: the suffering of Man in this life has ended.

Buddhism is not looking for immortality: the dead have no one to connect with. There is no God. Buddha said on this topic: 'I went through many births, seeking the Builder of the house, but without finding him being born again and again is bitter.' So, Buddhism is a kind of monotheism, where the One God was replaced with the One Death.

Now I would like to present you my own position. I must have one, right? Here it is:

Man is free. Only his earthly life has value. The afterlife and the immortal soul do not exist.

Worshipping death is a crime against all of us. Death is not Good, it is not a happiness; it is the tragic end to everything.

The One God, the Big Brother, as monotheistic religions understand it, doesn't exist. That is why it is not possible to approach God and 'see His face'. Probably there is an omnipresent God the Creator, but it's a different story.

The phenomenon of wanting to die to meet with God just paralyses my mind. However, I must admit that I have never been a humanist, incapable of wishing death on someone else.

I am willing to support legitimate use of the death penalty against murderous terrorists and their minions, even the most insignificant.

I have no doubt that you can and even should wish death to a pervert or paedophile who raped a child.

I can understand the desire to sacrifice one's life for one's children or, in extreme cases, for a common cause.

I understand that one could hastily and briefly wish death on a boy from senior class who kicked you at recess with impunity.

But how can you wish death to yourself? How do you even brainwash humans to push them to such a pinnacle of madness?

So I have nothing else to do but to search for immortality in this life. And I found it. I like the ancient method of attaining immortality, which I found in an anthropology book: apparently, you have to carefully rub the body with the bark of a magic tree and there you have it, eternal life guaranteed.

But don't ask for the name and the place of this tree. I will never tell you.

CHAPTER IV

The Unbearable Joy of Suffering

Why do religious people accept unnecessary and unbearable suffering 'for God'? Have you ever noticed that as soon as the two small words above are placed next to the word 'suffering', any negative connotations are immediately replaced with positive ones? How has suffering, which had provoked only fear and disgust, suddenly become something worthy and admirable?

Why do believers think that suffering is pleasing to God and why do they not merely accept it, but positively seek it out? Isn't the vast amount of unavoidable suffering – all those natural disasters, wars, untimely deaths and dreadful diseases – enough for these people? As they wind their way to heaven, why are they happily making their own life hell?

How does the religious view of suffering manage to deny the human nature and its natural aspiration to pleasure? In general, how did the phenomenon of voluntary suffering appear in religious doctrine?

Nietzsche writes that in ancient times, it was usual to inflict pain on another. In this context, he formulates the following question: How did it happen that in the Christian era, Man began to feel unworthy, and where did his unnatural feelings of guilt (guilty consciousness) come from? How did Man begin to strive towards self-harm and atonement of this guilt by voluntary suffering?

■ The Happiness of the Eternal Return ■

My educated readers have undoubtedly already spotted the similarity of the title of this chapter to that of Milan Kundera's famous novel, *The Unbearable Lightness of Being*.

Kundera writes about the irresolvable contradictions of our life and the inevitability of suffering. On the one hand, life is easy in the sense that it's the only one we have. All our experiences happen once only without any repetition and there is no other life to follow this one.

> ...life which disappears once and for all, which does not return, is like a shadow, without weight, dead in advance, and whether it was horrible, beautiful, or sublime, its horror, sublimity, and beauty mean nothing.

On the other hand, Man has a gut feeling that life is cyclical by nature and this becomes a heavy burden for him as he recalls the inevitable mistakes of the past, while recognising the impossibility of putting them right and his responsibility for the future. That's why life is frequently unbearable.

Which one of us has not at one time found ourselves in a situation which is extraordinarily similar to something that happened decades ago? We meet a girl who bears an uncanny resemblance to our first love and regret all over again that we had not proposed to her back then. Couldn't our life have taken a different course then? We might be walking with different children today to the kindergarten.

Nevertheless we have no other life than this, nor will we ever have another, so only this life can bring us happiness. If we withdraw from the world and its heavy burdens, our life also loses its meaning. If every second of our lives recurs an infinite number of times, we are nailed to eternity as Jesus Christ was nailed to the cross. It is a terrifying prospect. In the world of eternal return, the weight of unbearable responsibility lies heavy on every move we make. That is why Nietzsche called the idea of eternal return the heaviest of burdens.

If eternal return is the heaviest of burdens, then our lives can stand out against it in all their splendid lightness.

> But is heaviness truly deplorable and lightness splendid? [...] But in the love poetry of every age, the woman longs to be weighed down by the man's body. The heaviest of burdens is therefore simultaneously an image of life's most intense fulfilment.

With all due respect to Kundera and his résumé of Nietzsche's ideas, I would prefer to let Nietzsche speak for himself. He speaks about the 'heaviest weight' in *The Gay Science*.

> What if some day or night a demon were to steal into your loneliness and say to you: "This life as you now live it and have lived it, you will have to live once again and innumerable times again; and there will be nothing new in it, but every pain and every joy and every thought and sigh and everything unspeakably small or great in your life must return to you, all in the same succession and sequence – even this spider and this moonlight between the trees, and even this moment and I myself. The eternal hourglass of existence is turned over again and again, and you with it, speck of dust!? Would you not throw yourself down and gnash your teeth and curse the demon who spoke thus? Or have you once experienced a tremendous moment when you would have answered him: "You are a god, and never have I heard anything more divine. If this thought gained power over you, as you are it would transform and possibly crush you; the question in each and every thing, "Do you want this again and innumerable times again? would lie on your actions as the heaviest weight. Or how well disposed would you have to become to yourself and to life to long for nothing more fervently than this ultimate eternal confirmation and seal?

Why did Nietzsche call the idea of eternal return, known since the Prehistoric era, the 'heaviest burden'?

As far as the people of Antiquity were concerned, time was infinite and cyclical; sooner or later the beginning of time will meet its end and the cycle will begin again. Time has neither a beginning nor an end. Human life is also cyclical and likewise takes the form of a wheel of time. The number of events in the life of any human being is limited and each generation is doomed to repeat them over and over again in the time between birth and inevitable extinction. The sole goal of human life is its own existence, which is filled not only with positive emotions and pleasure, but with problems, struggles, and suffering.

Although at first glance the concept of cyclical time appears both strange and complex, I encounter this all the time in my everyday life. I can give many examples: the night changing into day, the varying seasons, the phases of the moon, and the menstrual cycle. Repetition occurs not just in nature but in society too – economic cycles, for example (most of us have some experience of crises – the bankruptcy of Lehman Brothers still makes my flesh creep). A cyclical view of time doesn't allow the possibility of a final change; the time of eternity begins already in one's lifetime and in essence becomes 'time without time'.

For the ancient, mythologically inclined mind, cyclical time appeared particularly natural. The archaic man, our common 'primitive' ancestor, did not do anything that had not already been done by somebody else. Viewed from this standpoint, life appeared as an endless repetition of the deeds of our forebears – a fine basis for one's own actions and a source of personal strength and self-assurance. Not merely a re-enactment of a murky and vague past, his actions became a return to the initial truth, tried and tested by the experience of previous generations. The diversity of myths, gods and religious practices set the conditions for the diversity of modes of individual behaviour.

Nothing has actually changed; we can live like this today. Practically all pagan cultures and polytheistic religions which flourished in the territories occupied by Babylon (Mesopotamia), Ancient Egypt, Ancient Greece, the whole of the East, and North and South America, maintained this view of time, which in itself was based on the observation of natural cycles.

The main distinguishing feature of all polytheistic religions was their exclusive anthropocentrism. Initially, one's biological father was the object of veneration; this was then transferred to the head of the clan, then the tribe, the city, the state, and finally to the deities carved in the image of Man. Polytheistic religions recognised the existence of a massive array of gods and goddesses, each of whom was responsible for a different aspect of the universe's existence.

Sigmund Freud believed that the whole of humanity suffers from collective neurosis and seeks a mighty protector, God, for this reason.

One should not forget that polytheistic religions were nothing like religions as we know them today. Basically, the only distinguishing feature that separated the gods and goddesses from humans was their immortality and power; in all other aspects, they were very much like humans. They possessed the same virtues and failings; they could be just or unjust, benevolent or jealous. The pagan gods and goddesses were not known either for their essential munificence or wickedness. As in the case of humans, the gods' behaviour was relative. Depending on the current situation, today's benevolence became tomorrow's malice and vice versa. They quarrelled, lied, and slept with mortals. They could be noble and helpful or treacherous and murderous; everything depended on their free choice or even their mood.

It wasn't just the gods who had the freedom of choice – Man had it too. If a pagan god was satisfied with the sacrifice offered to him, he had to fulfil his obligations in return – to grant his petitioners a long life, healthy children, good harvests, and military success. Moreover, all this had to be delivered not in some unspecified point, but today or in the nearest future. Pagans placed a lot of value in the present and their own lives. If a god failed to fulfil his obligations, he was exchanged for another. The gods were viewed as Man's partners – senior ones, to be sure – but still someone with whom Man could – indeed *should* – enter into negotiations.

I would like to make another point, which is crucial for understanding both the pagan attitude to life and the monotheistic one which replaced it.

The pagan concept of the 'wheel of time and the eternal return' allowed for the comfortable existence of evil and suffering in the world; both of these notions were accepted as an inseparable part of the cycle of life. Nobody was much interested in their origins (just as I am not particularly interested in the origins of rain, fog, or tides).

There are many reasons for the existence of evil and suffering in the world: natural disasters, everyday mental anguish, falsehood, violence, injustice and humiliation, innate diseases, fatal illnesses and the agony attached to them.

Nature, which is not idealised, has interest in our individual happiness; it makes use of necessity, pain, passion, fear, and hatred to force Man to find his own sustenance, protect himself, and deal with other people. Possessing a physical body inevitably leads to suffering as the body grows old and sickly. This means that evil and suffering are a universal human experience. Today, scientists claim that if human life had been devoid of pain and that if suffering hadn't been possible, there would have been no room for evolution.

All people are eager to avoid evil and suffering, yet all know that this is impossible because suffering is an inevitable part of life. It's inevitable if only for the simple reason that each lived moment places us squarely in the past and advances our end.

The pagans were lucky: they didn't trouble themselves with fundamental questions such as their gods' responsibility for the existence of evil, nor did they feel the need to justify their actions. Although pagan gods often directed natural phenomena and interfered in the lives of men, they were neither all-powerful nor had any pretension to beneficence. Moreover, they had no desire to assume any responsibility for the evil and suffering in the world. Remembering how overcrowded the pantheon was, such pretentions would have caused fratricidal wars. For this reason the gods were obliged to share power with each other, rather like in today's democracy. All that was lacking were the celestial elections.

Each of these competing gods could symbolise order and chaos, evil and goodness, pleasure and suffering. Taken separately, none of them was omnipotent and so Man had nothing to gain by clinging to one particular god. Thus, you could have self-respect and live your ordinary life.

Elevating one God above all the others changed the situation radically. Materialistic religions were overturned, marking a decisive departure from anthropocentrism, which is away from Man per se towards 'idealocentrism' (pardon me for introducing this scary notion).

Spiritual fun and games were over: the material and spiritual realms were stacked up in fierce opposition to each other, the Ideal became the object of veneration and the supreme ruler, and linear time came to replace the cyclical one.

The idea of a life after death is entirely in contradiction to the cyclical notion of time. That's the reason why the ancient Jews promoted a linear view of time. The cyclical nature of time was rejected and the world hurtled to its end with great speed.

The linear view of time and its accompanying historical perspective first appear in the biblical account of the creation of the world. Historical events stop 'going around in circles'; that is, they stop repeating themselves according to an existing archetypal scheme and become an open line, fully controlled by the plan and providence of the One God. A strict separation arises between the past, present, and future. Time becomes orientated towards the future and gains a starting point – God's creation of the world, and a finishing point or the point of arrival – the Judgement. That is all; there is nothing else, nor will there be.

Humanity's destiny is absolutely clear, too: it is moving from the initial fall from grace to the final redemption. Any mistake could be costly; Adam and Eve disobeyed God and sinned only once and that was enough to be expelled from paradise and be deprived of eternal life. And now we are to suffer and to die because of them.

One's life choices and freedom are severely limited by the sacred history as shown in Revelation. This notion of time, which has been removed from the realm of Man and has thus become an attribute of God, changes everything. Man no longer belongs to himself, but becomes the property of God, an insignificant part of the divine will, no longer the centre of everything, but a fragile vessel guided by the powerful divine hand. Needless to say, one's worldview also changes; one perceives all the events in one's life – both the joy and the suffering – as an expression of divine will.

The linear concept of time also presupposes that history (and Man within it) has a divinely ordained purpose, that is, the transformation of Man into a kind of idealised state, which would make him seek his higher purpose and know God. The end of time means the end of everything: the world, time, and the universe. Even death itself, that ultimate enemy of Man, will be destroyed forever. The Almighty God will destroy all evil and suffering, and all sufferers will be richly rewarded. But most importantly, He will destroy death, Man's greatest enemy.

It sounds lovely, doesn't it? Before Judaism, nobody managed to invent such a marvellous tale. Famous Greek myths are nothing compared to this.

Christianity was happy to inherit the concept of linear time. St Augustine supposed that if time were cyclical rather than linear, Jesus Christ would be crucified and raised from the dead again and again, making his initial crucifixion and the wondrous Resurrection ineffective for the redemption of human sins. And yet we know that the incarnation happened only once and that Christ gave up his divine life for our sins once and for all. This unique, unprecedented event defines and directs the only possible course of the history of the world in general, and our own in particular.

And at the end of it all, the sacred goal, the height of redemption will be reached: 'Then comes the end, when he delivers the kingdom to God the Father after destroying every rule and every authority and power.' (Corinthians 15:24; John 6:39-40) Despite Augustine's bold statements about the implacably linear nature of the religious worldview, the naive concept of a cyclical time still managed to penetrate the unbreachable fortress of Christian philosophy. It wasn't an entirely alien concept to certain Christian apologists, and even some classical exponents of the Kabbalah.

Sacred events (such as the birth and crucifixion of Christ) take place only once, yet they are still marked by religious rituals which don't simply commemorate them but return the believer to that mythical time, allowing him to participate in the events himself. The rites and rituals repeated those events that held a sacred significance: the Sabbath mirrored God's deserved rest after the heavy labour of creating the world and the Communion was a recreation of the Last Supper Christ held with His disciples and the act of co-suffering with Him.

In the linear concept of time, the pagan notions of life beyond the grave were changed. The end was seen not as the sorrowful conclusion of a life's journey, but the bright future, the desired spiritual continuation of the unworthy life on earth and the door to paradise, inaugurating the long-awaited chance to meet God and to 'see His face'. What's more, if you lived righteously and believed fervently, the door would be left ajar and you would see the glow of the bright heavenly light of the future streaming out even in your lifetime.

In this way, the predetermined past (you can't change anything) became augmented by a predetermined future and the puppet-like believer found himself literally 'crucified' within God-controlled history. Rather like his hero Jesus Christ. I have not yet mentioned one important moment, namely a fundamentally different attitude towards suffering in monotheism and in paganism.

■ The Golden Age of Pleasure: When Suffering was Evil ■

Ancient civilisations with polytheistic beliefs at their core had one common characteristic: there was no place in their worldview for human sin or for suffering for the sake of redemption. These irresponsible civilisations had not yet become acquainted with the One God and His divine commandments. These civilisations had no concept of divinely inspired morality or of the strict division between good and evil.

Strange though it may sound to a believer in the One God, pagans managed perfectly well without a universal concept of morality, and even managed to create great cultures in these intolerable conditions. Good and evil were relative terms for them and changed along with society and its deities. Pagans had an easier life. They could blame one god for all their misfortunes and thank another for all their good fortunes. All civilisations maintained some form of common moral code against which human behaviour could be measured and a system of rewards and punishments enforced. Otherwise no human society could survive. Without life after death as a measure of life on earth, human existence was more joyful. There was no concept of eternity applying to the individual. The cyclical nature of time gave Man or his descendants another chance to return back to the source and to correct his mistakes, that is, to start all over again. And, if at first he didn't succeed, there was no final sentence to come into effect. The ancient pagans felt no need for voluntary suffering, which had nothing to do with gaining 'spiritual perfection' or the gods' approval, just as the notions of forgiveness and salvation didn't exist at all. Any normal man could see that suffering for the sake of gods was contrary to nature. Suffering and pain are evil by their definition as they represent a threat to one's life, and voluntary suffering is doubly so, being a battle against oneself. And so all civilisations that preceded monotheism did everything they could to keep themselves well away from suffering.

You'd have an easier job imagining a 10-storey-high bedbug than discovering a cult of suffering in the ancient world. If Antiquity had any cult at all, it was the cult of pleasure.

The ancient ethical system was a recipe for a happy life and was simple and humane: avoid suffering and strive for pleasure, which is good in itself. Man's main pleasure is his own human life; a lack of moderation in pleasure leads to excess, and with it inevitable suffering. This is rather similar to the advice a loving mother would give her son.

In any case, it's impossible to avoid suffering altogether; suffering is a natural factor of life, a senseless but unavoidable stage on the journey towards true happiness, so the best one can do is to remain emotionally neutral to everything that is transitory – pleasure as well as suffering. This said, the most sensible position is still not to imbue suffering with special meaning but to do everything in order to minimise it.

If all else fails, you can always blame the malicious gods. Antiphon, the Sophist philosopher of the fourth century BC, wrote: 'These actions which are against nature [i.e. asceticism] are the reason why people suffer more than they need to, experience less pleasure than they could, and feel more wretched when the reverse is possible.'

The vast majority of Greek philosophers considered Man's pursuit of happiness and pleasure to be the main criterion of morality and the driving force behind all human behaviour. A life that offers no personal advantage or sensory pleasure is a life without meaning. For example, the great Socrates was categorically opposed to traditions and moral prescriptions. Through them laws were held as just, only because they had a long history. Such tradition can contradict common sense and hinder one's enjoyment of life. It would be better to devote one's time to pondering one's place in this world.

Aristotle considered pleasure to be moral and the product of nature's empirical selection. All advantageous action is accompanied by pleasure and disadvantageous action by suffering. Pleasure and suffering are diametrically opposed. This is why pleasure is a necessary component of all goodness, and suffering is unworthy of an intelligent man. But further, it is agreed that pain is bad and to be avoided; for some pain is without qualification bad, and other pain is bad because it is in some respect an impediment to us. Now the contrary of that which is to be avoided, qua something to be avoided and bad, is good. Pleasure, then, is necessarily good.

Aristippus, one of Socrates' own disciples, claimed that the meaning of life is to be found in hedonism, the ability to extract physical pleasure under any circumstances. For, he said, the happier you are, the less suffering there is in the world. Sometimes, one can even endure suffering for the sake of one's posterity or to gain pleasure in the future. Only a sage is able to master circumstances to suit his own situation and this is why it is impossible to overcome suffering without wisdom and the right attitude.

Epicurus, the star of philosophy in the fourth century BC, was convinced that although pleasure is an inseparable part of a successful life, Man's safeguard against unnecessary suffering is to be found only in moderating his enjoyments (a happy medium). In this way, he will reach *ataraxia*, a state of detachment from any anxiety of mind, by deliberately distancing oneself from worldly cares. Excess does violence to human nature, which is why we must use reason to determine our own individual limits that distinguish pleasure from disorder and chaos.

> When we say, then, that pleasure is the end and aim, we do not mean the pleasures of the prodigal or the pleasures of sensuality, as we are understood to do by some through ignorance, prejudice, or wilful misrepresentation. By pleasure we mean the absence of pain in the body and of trouble in the soul.

One often pays dearly for pleasurable excesses; one risks one's health, the respect of others, and even one's liberty. Epicurus also maintained that all human misfortunes and disasters are caused by our ignorance of what constitutes true pleasure. People yearn for ever greater pleasure which they are unable to attain. This in turn causes them suffering as they are then unable to be satisfied by the pleasures they already possess. They spoil their pleasure by their fears of being deprived of it and thus increase their wretchedness. All this sounds very contemporary. You'd hardly believe that this was written in the fourth century BC.

In general, the Greeks and Romans preferred to use clear, comprehensible language, unlike most modern-day politicians.

The question of suffering is central to the thought of the Stoics, a subject much talked about at my school. Unlike Epicurus, the Stoics were much more attuned to suffering and had a more favourable view of the necessity to bow to fate. The Stoics insisted that Man must be reconciled to the suffering which he is powerless to avert and learn to bear pain and even death with courage and equanimity. It is only by limiting our desire for pleasure that we can achieve peace. Notice that they are not talking about renouncing pleasure, but limiting our yearning for it. Using the world's favourite pastime as an example, you are invited not to give up sex altogether, but to confine yourself to your wife or husband plus just the one lover – instead of the 10 you were used to before.

The ideal man is seen to be a dispassionate sage who respects only the power of his infallible reason and is troubled by neither excessive joy nor exaggerated grief. Strong emotions are seen as a failing; moreover if we pander to these emotions, the affliction becomes a chronic disorder of the soul which will ultimately destroy all healthy aspirations and pleasure.

You shouldn't think, however, that the Stoics hated life; they were rather a type of romantic philosopher who wished to equip Man with tools to deal with the 'unbearable complexity of being'.

The eminent Roman philosopher Lucius Annaeus Seneca, Nero's tutor and the contemporary of Christ, was also in favour of wise moderation in all things:

> If, however, you seek pleasures of all kinds in all directions, you must know that you are as far short of wisdom as you are short of joy. Joy is the goal which you desire to reach, but you are wandering from the path if you expect to reach your goal while you are in the midst of riches and official titles – in other words, if you seek joy in the midst of cares, these objects for which you strive so eagerly, as if they would give you happiness and pleasure, are merely causes of grief. [...] None but the brave, the just, the self-restrained, can rejoice.

Its philosophers were clear and concise in defining exactly what every man is in need of. This applies not just to the men of their times, but of our time too. Their thoughts remain fresh and contemporary – a heaven on earth without prior suffering is achievable even in our lifetime. Our society is also inclined to regard suffering as an unavoidable evil and does everything to minimise it. Based only on their teachings, we could have quite easily entered the modern world a few centuries earlier than we did. Some of us would have already inhabited Mars, many generations before the birth of Elon Musk, who is hoping to send humans there in 2018.

Sadly, it was not to be. The advent of the One God in His Christian guise demolished this civilisation and began to extol the virtue of suffering, that universal enemy of mankind. Moreover, it proposed something quite incomprehensible to the ancient consciousness – the notion that suffering should occupy a much higher ranking than pleasure on the scale of values. Suffering became the proof of goodness and spiritual perfection, and extreme suffering the best method of obtaining redemption, forgiveness, and salvation.

Nietzsche understood the intellect, the morality or the reason as a progress of the will towards power and the expression of the life instinct. For him, Christianity represented a failure of the life instinct within society and degradation in general. The hope of salvation, the value of asceticism, and the attempt to extract meaning (meaningless in itself) from human suffering were notions designed to extol weakness.

The most interesting 'philosopher of suspicion' was Freud. He explained the existence of religious beliefs by the displacement of Man's subconscious desires and was convinced that religion was a universal neurosis. In fact, religious rites resemble compulsive neurosis: both are distinguished by their uniformity, repetition and ritualism, and both are executed unconsciously.

I am in agreement with the approaches of Nietzsche and Freud but would like to add that, in my opinion, monotheism is an act of gross and blatant manipulation, perhaps an even greater manipulation than all the others that have preceded it.

I am convinced that monotheism appeared and separated from polytheism due to one reason only – to protect the weak. People are different, but they can all be divided into two broad categories – the strong and the weak. Strong people, in common with everyone else, also experience the burdens of life and natural suffering, but they are able to resist them, to fight them, and be reconciled to the finite nature of life. A strong person's burden is particularly heavy because he rejects all supernatural ideals such as God and the hope of continuing his life after death; there is no other world except for this one and Man has only himself to rely on. This struggle only makes him stronger, inspiring an even greater thirst for life on earth, thereby finding his hard-won happiness. A strong person feels no revulsion for an earthly existence and doesn't seek to shield himself from evil and suffering, but regards all of these as the best aid to building up his character and achieving greatness for his soul. I have good news: a strong person is neither a superman, nor a contemporary superhero like Spiderman or Catwoman; a strong person is you or me.

A weak person cannot deal with his own problems and that it is the reason why such people invented monotheism. Initially, the attraction of monotheism was confined to the weaker nations in general and weaker individuals in particular. Monotheism is born out of a culture of weakness anyway. The weak spent a long time searching and finally found a protector for themselves (this is not an accusation and from a purely human point of view completely reasonable; there are very few strong people in the world, the majority are weak). The powerful divine protector promised to comfort, reconcile, and make everything good – not in this life but hereafter.

It's no coincidence that the first occurrence of monotheism, that is Judaism, arose from Egyptian captivity. It's no coincidence either that after failing to gain a firm foothold in Palestine, Christianity flourished amongst Roman slaves and plebeians. For them, the concept of the One God was attractive. The main reason is that the One God was without a doubt far more powerful than any deity from the pantheon of the gods who in any case were perpetually fighting with each other like a street gang. It was never clear who to turn to for help. Make one mistake and appeal to the 'wrong' god and it's all ruined; it was all too easy to lose not just your wealth but life itself.

At first glance the emergence of the One God was timely and had advantages that should have appealed to the strong as well as the weak. There is no fear of making a mistake: everything is well described in the Holy Book and it's obvious who you are meant to appeal to for help.

But that's just at first glance. If you look more closely, the situation is far from rosy. The 'Mighty Defender' is not going to help for free. Assistance that you don't have to pay for is contrary to nature. No one ever helps anyone for nothing; everything has to be paid for and in this case the cost is particularly high.

You could pay off the old racketeer deities with rams, or in extreme cases with your own children. Often, there was no need to pay anything at all: you could politely explain to any god on the make that there are more of them where he came from and that you have to give to the others too. You end up like the gingerbread man who runs away from the little old man, the little old woman, the ploughman in the field, the cow, and the pig.

This won't work with the One God; you can't play with Him according to your rules, just like the fox who wouldn't be fobbed off and quickly gobbled up the gingerbread man, first one quarter, then half, then three quarters, until the whole gingerbread man had been consumed.

The One God is not your partner; He is your 'Master' and any bargaining with Him is impossible as a matter of principle. For this reason, He will demand much more from you in return for His protection than any number of insignificant beggar-gods. So what sort of pay can the weak and poor man, who has nothing of his own, offer the mighty and jealous God?

Only sacrifice. From the earliest pagan times, humanity has always known that divine favour is won through offering sacrifices. The pagans were used to sacrificing their enemy, their animals, and their children.

The One God, however, wants a far greater sacrifice – the whole of a believer's life on earth. And don't try to console yourself with the fantasy that you will be able to determine the level of sacrifice you offer. Even if you accept this kind of God and want to play by His rules.

▪ God Likes to See you Suffer ▪

Monotheism is a radically new type of religion based on the concept of the One God, the supreme ruler of humanity, animals and nature. The situation had obviously changed: instead of being obliged by the gods as before, the people now had obligations towards God. This looks a bit strange; normally people have children and feel responsibility for them, but here the One God has created people, towards whom He feels no obligation, but rather expects them to pander to and suffer for Him.

As I have already mentioned, in linear time the future is fundamentally different from the past because only an onward progress is envisaged, with a complete absence of any repetition. The death of the body seals the fate of the immortal soul and marks the passing of the final sentence – up to heaven or down to hell – for which there is no appeal.

This enormous responsibility spoils the believer's life on earth because of the need to earn the main attraction – eternal life in paradise – which is no easy matter. The believer is obliged to keep up with the divine commandments most rigorously, remembering that God is omnipresent. Also, one has to appease God by constantly repenting for one's sins – past, present and future – and must do everything possible to earn His forgiveness. What's more, one is expected to repent spontaneously, without waiting for God's invitation. Fortunately, there are enough sins to go round for each and every sinner and for everyone together. (I am less sure the same is true about blessings and happiness.)

It is precisely at this moment that suffering makes its appearance on the historical stage of the One God. This isn't some inevitable suffering from natural causes – this type of suffering has always existed – but primarily voluntary suffering imposed on oneself for the sake of God. One should not be afraid of death any more: the final aim of life does not consist in existence itself, but in life after death. Only the road filled with lifelong suffering can lead to God and paradise. Sinful, ephemeral pleasures do not bring eternal happiness and divine joy can only be found in worshipping God in the life to come. This is why I mustn't extol pleasure in the manner of the primitive Roman and Greek pagans, but rather suffering. In this way, the inevitable evil is turned into absolute good.

But what should one do if he does not have enough strength to spiritually grow by renouncing his base physical nature? In this sad case, God will most certainly help his poor servant by sending him natural catastrophes, diseases and the premature death of his beloved ones.

This is how, in a brief period of time, suffering was transformed from absolute Evil into absolute Good and a vivid source of religious happiness.

The acceptance of voluntary suffering is the most honourable, but also the hardest part of faith. Yet there is a silver lining: the severe suffering lasting the whole of the believer's life makes death seem like a welcome and joyful liberation from a heavy burden. It represents, if you will, an exalted religious romantic ideal which successfully shields the believer from the prosaic reality of life. These are the same ideals that nowadays explode every day, together with the belts of the suicide bombers who wear them.

■ Man is Born to Trouble ■

Judaism is above all a religion of God's Kingdom and His divine Law with all the rest, including human suffering, seen as only a vague and barely noticeable background. Judaism has an ambivalent attitude towards evil and suffering. This is hardly surprising: Judaism is ambivalent about everything; that's the nature of Judaism.

On the one hand, suffering can be interpreted as a punishment for human sin, the chief one being the sin of breaking God's Law. The destiny both of the righteous and the sinner depends on the balance of good or bad actions in this world. It is the same idea in all monotheistic religions: material joys in this world come at the expense of eternal bliss, while suffering is compensated for by that bliss.

The first ever mention of suffering as a punishment for sin occurs in Genesis. Adam and Eve disobeyed God and were punished by being exiled from paradise, after which they were inflicted by disease and lost their immortality. Even a law-abiding Jew who has kept all the ritualistic prescriptions is not exempt from falling into sin and receiving

Hans Memling, The Last Judgment, triptych,
right panel, 1467-1471.
This is what lust has done to us!

punishment. You don't even need to ask 'what for?' There is always plenty of sin to go around and humans always deserve to be punished for it. No military disaster seemed absurd, no suffering was in vain, for, beyond the 'event' it was always possible to perceive the will of Yahweh.

The few righteous men who, despite their blameless lives, still found themselves on the receiving end of substantial punishment were explained away by the Israelite sages and prophets. Alas, the Almighty God is not always just, but is occasionally malevolent, jealous, and vengeful. God is often silent and sends suffering to his people with an astonishing indifference:

> You sell Your people cheaply, And have not profited by their sale. You make us a reproach to our neighbours, A scoffing and a derision to those around us. You make us a byword among the nations, a laughingstock among the peoples. [...] All this has come upon us, but we have not forgotten You, And we have not dealt falsely with Your covenant. [...] Arouse Yourself, why do You sleep, O Lord? Awake, do not reject us forever. Why do You hide Your face and forget our affliction and our oppression? For our soul has sunk down into the dust; Our body cleaves to the earth. (Psalms 44:12-25)

Nevertheless, such is our God and we are duty-bound to give Him all honour and love and to expect reward both in this life and the next.

I am not sure whether this explanation was enough of a consolation to all the wretched and unjustly punished men, but I am quite certain it wouldn't be enough of a consolation for me.

On the other hand, Judaism regards the inevitability of suffering as a way to learn more about life, to grow spiritually, to come nearer to God and be vouchsafed to 'see His face': 'Yet Man is born to trouble, as the sparks fly upward.' (Job 5:7)

For centuries, Jewish sages have always maintained that some obstacles are conducive to a full religious life. They regarded righteous suffering as a trial sent by a loving God to teach people a moral lesson, and to strengthen their faith and resolve. Suffering elevates humanity, ennobles the spirit, and sanctifies and purifies the soul from the pollution of pride and coarseness, as suggested in the Midrash: 'He who does not know suffering, knows not what it means to be human.'

A Jew is cleansed from his impurity through suffering torments which, in turn, cause him to appeal to God once again: 'When thou art in tribulation and all these things have come upon thee...thou shalt turn to the Lord thy God.' (Devarim 4:30)

Judaism threatens Man with suffering; it needs suffering because without it there is no hope of returning Man back to God. Thus the original monotheistic religion states clearly that the transient pleasure of this life is the enemy of the eternal bliss and happiness to come.

I would add here that when a normal person is faced with terrible disasters, especially if he fears for his life, he is likely to turn to anyone at all – to any God and even the Devil in the vain hope of salvation.

The question of Man's reward after his death and especially its timing is complicated, while being suspiciously reminiscent of the well-known oriental parable of Hodja Nasreddin:

> Once upon a time, the Hodja boasted that he taught his donkey to speak. When the Emir heard of this, he ordered to pay the Hodja 1,000 coins on the condition that he show the Emir his talking donkey sometime later. At home, the Hodja's wife was distressed and cried out in tears, "Why did you deceive the Emir and take his money? When he realises that he has been tricked he will order you to be thrown into prison!"
>
> "Calm yourself, wife," answered Nasreddin, "and hide the money in a safe place. I have forty years to teach the donkey; in this time, either the donkey will die or the Emir."

Our case is simpler still; the believer is most likely to die first, and there will be no one to claim the reward at all.

Maimonides was convinced that the divine plan behind suffering and tribulations was to provide a secure framework for selecting and nurturing a spiritually healthy nucleus of believers. The presence of God's mystical power was a reminder of the temporary nature of tribulations and a guarantee that these would not result in the decimation of the Jewish race and its faith. All suffering is merely a transition stage to future spiritual perfection.

From what I've written above, you might conclude that God has little time for a small Jewish soul that is spiritually sick, and that it is perfectly acceptable to sacrifice a large proportion of the Jewish race for the sake of the faith and future spiritual perfection. Obviously, Maimonides' intention was to say and do what would seem most helpful – to encourage the wretched people in their distress – but the result was, in my opinion, quite different. Rather different from what was intended, I should think. Without wishing to do so, Maimonides delivered what is generally known as a self-fulfilling prophecy. And this prophecy concerned more than one distress. Alas, there were many of them in the history of Jewish people.

Indeed, it is not the way we talk about suffering, but the real suffering that matters. The most pertinent question here is not the Jews' relationship with evil but the way evil and suffering relate to the Jews. No hint of casuistry is intended in this sentence; the Jews are perhaps the only people in the history of mankind that have been subject to persecution from the time that their ethnic group first emerged. In this sense, the Jewish people can truly be called chosen. The Jews were expelled from Egypt, Palestine, England, Spain, Portugal, France, and Switzerland, and all of these expulsions were at the cost of hundreds of thousands of Jewish lives. However, all of these instances of persecution and death are nothing compared to what happened to the Jews in the middle of the enlightened twentieth century – the horror of the Holocaust. I would like to note that the concept of suffering as a means of spiritual growth and of drawing ever closer to God was passed on by Judaism to Christianity, its much more successful heir, much like a relay baton is passed on in a race. Christianity carried this baton far more readily than did Judaism and managed to cover a far greater distance doing so.

■ On Suffering, the Best Friend of Christian Virtue ■

*He who does not carry his cross
and does not follow Me,
cannot be My disciple.*
Luke 14:27

If you were to ask any Christian to describe the essence of his faith in a single sentence, he would almost certainly say 'Christianity is a religion of love'. This is the answer that's been hammered into his head since early childhood so he is likely to blurt it out without even thinking.

And that's a shame. If he were to stop and think even for a moment, he would undoubtedly see that there is another, much more apt answer to this question: Christianity is first and foremost a religion of suffering and death. It's precisely the cult of suffering and death – not the cult of love – that lies at the heart of Christian teaching. For Christianity, the value of Man's life is correlated only with how much he suffered: the Christian doctrine is permeated with different forms of suffering right across the board, from top to bottom.

This conclusion is inevitable after even the most cursory study of the works of the Fathers of the Church and medieval theologians, or after listening to the preaching of contemporary Christian authorities and examining the many religious depictions in churches and museums.

Suffering is Christianity's central premise and key value, a fact most evident from the religion's two main themes: the martyr's death of Christ and the horrors of the Apocalypse. It is clear in the common rituals and church services, in the experience of total seclusion, in the privations and extreme suffering voluntarily endured by religious fanatics.

The first and most important Christian image is of course the image of the Passion of Christ. In the course of the 2,000-year history of Christian ideological hegemony, this image has not only taken a firm root in the officially sanctioned everyday culture and collective consciousness, but it has also penetrated deeply into the daily life of ordinary Christian citizens. This image is familiar to everyone, including primary schoolchildren. It depicts the exhausted Christ, obedient to the divine iron will of God the Father, carrying His cross up to Golgotha. Sometime later, He is tied to this cross; He is scourged, tortured, and crucified. He dies – not forever, but in order to rise again quickly and ascend to meet the Holy Spirit and His divine father. That's it, we can go celebrate Easter.

The theme of Christ's Passion has become a daily reality, even a necessity to Christians throughout the world. In saying this, I don't of course mean those believers who attend church only to show off their new dress, their diamond necklace, or their Breguet watch complete with a crocodile-skin strap. I mean the real, sincere believers, especially our common ancestors who lived in the glorious days of old.

This promise remained largely unfulfilled, but Christianity managed to change the compulsion to avoid suffering so that a person voluntarily seeks out suffering. Suffering has become the life's main value, a cult, an idée fixe, an obsession, a necessity, a vital criterion for assessing reality, and the source of the greatest joy and pleasure.

Hieronymus Bosch, Christ Carrying the Cross, 1516.
Just imagine how difficult it was to preach to such a crowd!

All forms of suffering are welcome here: the pain of a wounded body streaming with blood, or in the throes of death. All kinds of physical abnormality are happily depicted. Open any book on the art of the Middle Ages and you will immediately find a mass of freaks and monsters there.

How did we get there? Is it possible that the whole of Europe has gone mad?

How did suffering and its memory become an exquisite joy?

What can explain the emergence of the radical cult of suffering in Christianity?

I will try to give answers to all these questions.

■ Christian Suffering as the Imitation of Christ ■

The Christian cult of suffering is nothing other than the reflection and recapitulation of the way of Christ, who endured suffering and torments and finally gave His life for the salvation of us all. Through His own death, He redeemed the sins of humanity, including the original sin, the biggest sin of all. Isn't a believer's offer of voluntary suffering a worthy response to this gift?

The Passion of Christ, imitated by the millions of tormented but exhilarated souls and painfully ravaged bodies, was an enticing prospect of a more exalted reality, salvation, and the sweetness of eternal life. Suffering was meant to be of priceless benefit for life on earth too – it was supposed to be a source of an enormous outpouring of love for one's neighbour.

Nothing can be as worthwhile as imitating the experience of our beloved Father, Teacher, and Big Brother. Martin Luther expounded this theme with aplomb; he saw suffering as the main point of faith and was in great fear lest the Christians remain ignorant of the suffering that will not fail to come:

> … on the Passion of the Lord You have also heard why it was that God the Father ordained it, namely that through it he wanted to help, not the person for Christ, for Christ had no need at all for this suffering; but we and the whole human race needed this suffering. […] We shall at this time speak only of the example which this Passion gives to us, what kind of cross we bear and suffer, and also how we should bear and suffer it […] Christ by his suffering not only saved us from the devil, death, and sin, but also that his suffering is an example, which we are to follow in our suffering. […] We should suffer after Christ, that we may be conformed to him. This must be the kind of suffering that is worthy of the name, such as some great danger of property, honour, body and life. Such suffering as we really feel, which weighs us down; otherwise, it would not be suffering.

That said, the believer could never attain the right level of suffering and would thus always remain guilty in the face of the loving God: '…bear in mind that every affliction, pain and sorrow of ours is nothing compared with the painful torment and wounds inflicted on the body and soul of our Lord during His passion suffered for our salvation.'

This explanation is so unreasonable that it merits no serious criticism. This is somewhat worse than placing the cart before the horse and expecting it to carry you to your bright future. Imagine a man first forging a sword for himself, then cutting off his hand and then blaming the sword for his suffering and worshipping it. So who was it that has 'forged'

Christ for himself and invented His suffering? It's not as if they both fell down from the sky? It's perfectly obvious that the urgent wish to justify the already existing suffering in the world preceded the religious cult that was founded on the basis of this desire.

This desire is easy to understand. Since Christ has suffered and risen from the dead afterwards, it would seem highly probable that every true believer who has also suffered would be raised from the dead in the same way. All he needs to do is to repeat Christ's Way of the Cross and await resurrection. One should be grateful that the faithful are granted a certain leniency in that they aren't required to undergo an actual crucifixion. You end up with a flawless logical proposition according to which the suffering of One God has been exchanged for the suffering of hundreds of thousands of His followers.

However, even this chain of logic, which at first glance appears so simple and sensible, even though based on unquestioning faith, has one major flaw. Christ was perfectly aware that He is God and spoke on the matter many times. This means that His death on the cross was not such a big sacrifice or particularly significant since He always knew that He was destined to rise from the dead and ascend into heaven. In reality He risked nothing at all, unlike all other Christians. I was happy when, rereading Nietzsche, I found the same ideas. In his books *On the Genealogy of Morality* and *The Antichrist*, Nietzsche accuses Christianity of littering the human consciousness with chimeras. In *On the Genealogy of Morality* he notes that whereas the ancient gods existed precisely in order to bear the responsibility for all the evil in the world, Christianity identified the main culprit as Man himself and sentenced him to an eternally guilty conscience in the form of 'self-crucifixion' and 'self-abuse':

> …everywhere the hypnotic glance of the sinner always moving in the one direction [in the direction of "guilt" as the sole cause of suffering]; everywhere, bad conscience, that "abominable beast", as Luther called it; everywhere, the past regurgitated, the deed distorted, the green eye on every action; everywhere, the will to misunderstand suffering made into the content of life, suffering reinterpreted as feelings of guilt, fear, punishment; everywhere, the scourge, the hair shirt, the starving body, contrition; everywhere, the sinner breaking himself on the cruel wheel of a restless and morbidly lustful conscience; everywhere, dumb torment, the most extreme fear, the agony of the tortured heart, the paroxysms of unknown happiness, the cry for "redemption". In fact, the old depression, heaviness and fatigue were thoroughly overcome by this system of procedures, life became very interesting again: awake, eternally awake, sleepless, glowing, burned out, exhausted and yet not tired, – this is how man, the "sinner", looked when initiated into these mysteries.

Despite the fact that Man himself is the source of his suffering, he is not able to be rid of it by himself. Nothing can be done without the Church as the intermediary: 'And he must suffer so much that he is always in need of the priest. Away with physicians! What is needed is a Saviour.'

Nietzsche is severe but just: it is a revolutionary achievement to convince Man that he is the source of his own suffering. It would be great to be able to do the same in family conflicts.

Another reason for the emergence of the cult of suffering in Christianity was the persecution of the Early Christians during almost three centuries. I have mentioned earlier in this book that the extent of this persecution was highly exaggerated in subsequent times

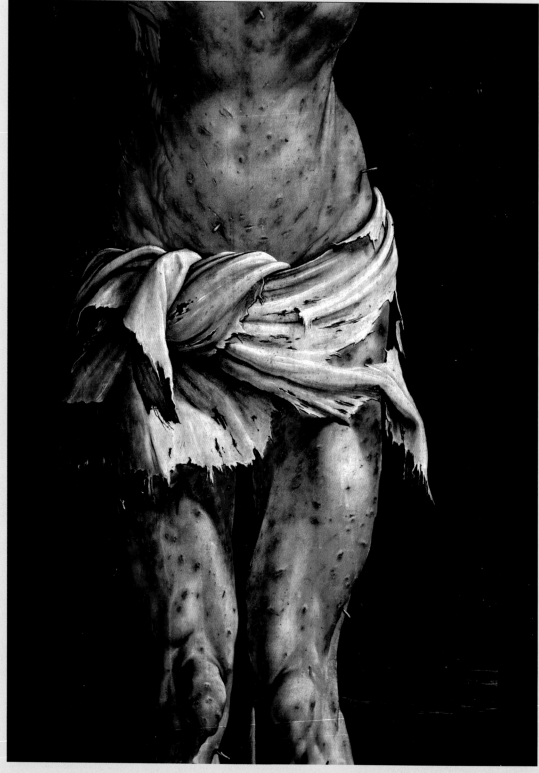

Matthias Grünewald, The Crucifixion, 1515.
No one could depict suffering and destruction of the flesh better than the Christian painters.

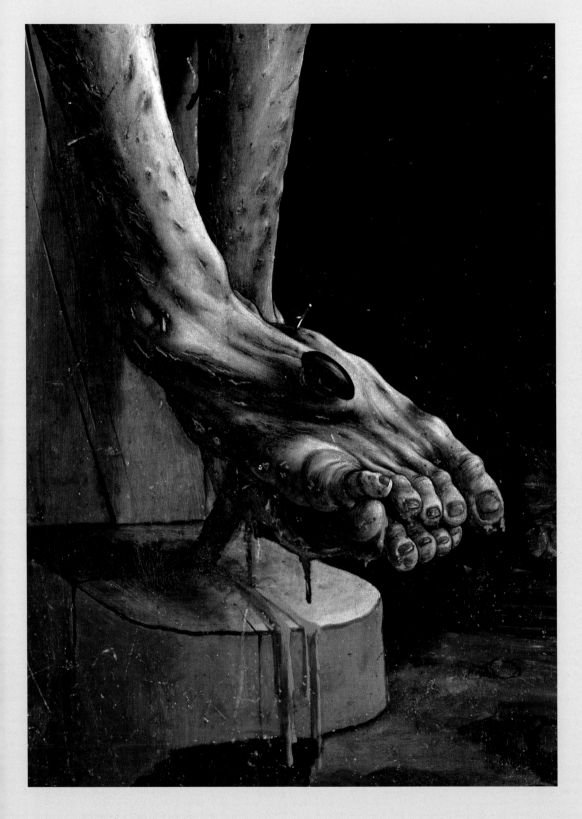

in the way it always happens in the wake of victorious spiritual or social revolutions. The martyrs' suffering quickly became a major attribute of the new religion and from its earliest days was considered to be the quickest way to God and salvation.

Suffering and tears go hand in hand. The New Testament places a great deal of emphasis on tears; Christ Himself never laughed and His teaching rapidly turned into a religion of misery and tears – those true friends of real piety. Life on earth was declared to be nothing more than a vale of sorrow and suffering whose true purpose was to prepare Man for his longed-for death and the future life beyond the grave.

So, to use the language of psychology, the people were presented with a systemic internalisation of negative attitudes. The world outside was viewed not as inherently good and as a source of natural happiness, but as a concentration of evil and suffering. In order to save their souls (first and foremost from others' lustful bodies), the believers were urged to renounce the world. This worldview is undoubtedly helpful for any monotheistic religion. Both Man and God should be separated from the world as much as possible: Man, to prevent him from being tempted by sinful desires which turn his attention away from God, and God to prevent Him from being exposed to direct sunlight. As soon as He is seen in clear light, He risks turning back into a piece of painted wood as in the old pagan days.

■ Christian Suffering as Means ■
of Attaining Spirituality and Approaching God

Christianity views suffering as an essential tool for achieving a spiritual state; without suffering, you can forget about spirituality and being close to God.

Saint Paul said that the fact that people experience suffering means that they are treated by God as His children. After all, is there a father who doesn't punish his son?

According to Ambrose of Milan, our tribulations are a sign of God's favour. He punishes us here on earth, just as a caring father should, in order to exalt us in Heaven. Therefore we must rejoice at this and weep bitterly when trials and suffering are not visited upon us. Let us lament our lack of trouble, tribulations, lament our good life, for we lack the sign that the Lord is with us. He grants us some small consolation in this life in exchange for the little good that we manage to perform by chance, but in the life to come we will receive eternal punishment for our sins. The famous Meister Eckhart claimed that 'the beast that bears you fastest to perfection is suffering'.

Erasmus of Rotterdam expressed the same ideas in *The Manual of the Christian Knight*:

> If the storm of temptation shall rise against thee somewhat thick and grievously, begin not forthwithal to be discontent with thyself, as though for that cause God either cared not for thee, or favoured thee not, or that thou shouldest be but an easy Christian man, or else the less perfect: but rather give thanks to God because he instructeth thee as one which shall be his heir in time to come, because he beateth or scourgeth thee as his most singular beloved son and proveth thee as his assured friend.

Christianity is being serious when it maintains that only the blind would not see the good of suffering. In fact, within every person there is a voice arising from his baser physical nature which opposes the high calling of the spirit. The human being is divided into two irreconcilable halves and this is the cause of the illness with which he is afflicted. Salvation through suffering ensures the healing of this illness.

What can I say? It is a paradox. Over the centuries, people of ancient civilisations lived a happy lie, looked for spiritual progress in sciences and pleasures, aspired to well-being, tried to avoid distress, poverty and diseases by all means, and did not know at all that, according to Christianity, they were gravely ill.

Does it mean that our ancestors were unspiritual imbeciles? Or is it those who maintain this position who are ill?

Only when Man is afflicted by disasters does he lose faith in his power and become convinced of his own insignificance. Only thanks to disasters does Man acquire the higher Christian virtues: the understanding of his sinful nature, and the virtues of patience and humility, which constitute the fundamentals of Christian morality and are commonly seen as being the best adornment for the soul. And this is close to the idea of loving one's enemies and blessing those who curse us. If one knows history a little bit, one understands that this 'blessing' has always been conducted not with a cross but with a sword.

Matthias Grünewald, The Temptation of Saint Anthony, 1515.
Suffering is a grace, a happiness, and a celestial joy.

I would like to point out that loving someone who hurts you is a well-known phenomenon. And funnily enough, the greater the harm, the deeper the love. Hostages fall in love with terrorists, inmates admire their jailers, and believers are ready to endure any form of suffering from their God.

Does this mean that overcoming suffering leads to an immediate cessation of spirituality? If that is so, why do we bother to build hospitals? And, on the contrary, if we do our best to get sick with the most horrible diseases, does that make us saints?

As Saint Paul said: 'The Lord disciplines him whom he loves.' (Hebrews 12:4-6)

▣ Suffering as Particular Grace ▣ and an Unearthly Joy

Eckhart asserts that Christians must have the greatest love of suffering as this is the only thing that God did during His sojourn on earth. The crux of the Christian message preached to this day from the pulpit and from dedicated religious channels goes as follows. Only suffering can bring nothing but joy and happiness; all of life's other advantages are insignificant and fickle. In fact, suffering like Christ is the biggest pleasure for a true believer.

Contemporary Catholic thought also agrees that suffering is conducive to Man's progress as it is only by suffering that we discover the shining beauty of goodness, while the Anglican theologian and poet C.S. Lewis agrees in *The Problem of Pain,* writing that 'God whispers to us in our pleasures, speaks in our conscience, but shouts in our pains: it is his megaphone to rouse a deaf world.'

I would prefer the Lord's shouts to bring me happiness or for Him to disappear altogether if he is minded to cause me suffering. Suffering is what I don't want.

▣ Man's Sinfulness is the Reason for Suffering ▣

Don't be surprised by the fact that, while in the previous section suffering was described as a special blessing, a source of happiness and unearthly joy, in this it is seen as a punishment for sin. Religion is not subject to the rules of formal logic because it is based on a belief in miracles rather than reason.

Suffering and sin are fused together; one suffers for one's sins, which are as prevalent in the world as the Devil. By the same logic, suffering is also prevalent – all the time and everywhere.

Let's just read what Saint Gregory the Wonderworker wrote:

> Whence come famines and tornadoes and hailstorms, our present warning blow? Whence pestilences, diseases, earthquakes, tidal waves, and fearful things in the heavens? And how is the creation, once ordered for the enjoyment of men, their common and equal delight, changed for the punishment of the ungodly… What is our calamity, and what its cause? Is it a test of virtue, or a touchstone of wickedness?

Christianity can't exist without sin; the more sin there is, the greater the suffering. The more there is suffering, the more there is Christianity. The Christian religion gives rise to great amounts of guilt and these feelings of guilt then engender the maximum levels of suffering. Man doesn't own either his soul or his body. Nevertheless, despite this, he is still responsible for the sins of both his body and his soul, which must be paid for by his suffering. We mustn't forget that God is the embodiment of goodness and He desires not the death of a sinner but his repentance and life. For this reason, a sin already committed is not automatically punished by suffering. Saint Augustine wrote that 'Christians must suffer more than other men; the righteous must suffer more still and the saints must endure great suffering. The closer a man is to God, the greater the amount of suffering he is sent.'

It cannot be otherwise: sin and suffering are the foundations of the religion rather than love. Let's imagine for a moment that humans are sinless and have always been so, or that they used to be sinful but are now magically free from it. What was the reason for Christ's suffering then? Whose sins did He redeem? What cause did His death serve? Why all the prayers and suffering? What exactly are we expiating? What are all these prayers for?

The believer must never be at peace; on the contrary he must at all times be agitated and nervous, have a guilty conscience, and ponder his inadequacy. You can't 'sell' the notional benefits of redemptive suffering to anyone else. Humans are always guilty before God and for this reason alone they must suffer, and struggle with the passions, lusts, and torments of their own flesh. By undergoing these extreme sufferings, the believer demonstrates his obedience to God, expiates his sins on earth, and buys from God the right to access paradise and the joy of eternal life.

The sensation of having a 'bad conscience', the feeling of guilt about one's discrepancy with the ideal, the shame of debt, and the desire to have it cancelled ('expiated'), reached its zenith with the formation of the most rigid restraint of all, the idea of the One God, as Neitzsche explains in *The Genealogy of Morality*. In the same way, it was here that the uncanny and perhaps inextricable link between the ideas of 'debt and suffering' was first crocheted together:

> …that will to torment oneself, that suppressed cruelty of animal man who has … discovered bad conscience so that he can hurt himself … this man of bad conscience has seized on religious pre-supposition in order to provide his self-torture with its most horrific hardness and sharpness. Debt towards God: this thought becomes an instrument of torture…

Of course, by this I don't mean that the majority of today's Christians thinks day and night about their guilt and that they desire to suffer as much as possible; contemporary Christianity is like a toothless old lion now, but once upon a time it used to leap up high and bite ferociously and continued to do so for at least the last 1,500 years.

The experience of guilt has permeated the people's consciousness to such an extent (and not just the people of faith) that thoughts of self-punishment have become commonplace. If Christianity had been able to maintain its hold on the world to the same extent for another few hundred years, all courts of law could have been safely abolished, with the believers all marching off to prison voluntarily. There is no shortage of suffering in prison.

Some contemporary Catholic theologians have become so brazen as to suggest that humans have a 'biologically based inherent feeling of guilt'.

Christ has shown the means by which sin is expiated. He suffered not for His own sin but for the sins of all humanity and now it is our turn to show Him how we suffer for our own sins.

■ Only a Life of Suffering ■ Can Lead Man to the Church

Never has a truer statement been made. It is much easier to manipulate unhappy people than happy ones. An unhappy person is easily led to any place of your choosing: he will swell the ranks of suicides, join a Satanist cult, a political party, or even follow you to the registry office.

A happy person is difficult to manipulate. He is self-sufficient. In his happy cocoon he needs little from anyone, and particularly the Church. And here we find ourselves turning to conspiracy theories and manipulation. Manipulation is the main mechanism behind all mass movements, both the social as well as the spiritual ones. And not just mass movements either; it concerns small-scale 'kitchen' revolutions too.

You see the signs of it everywhere: children manipulate their parents into buying them new toys by crying and misbehaving; the state manipulates its citizens with media propaganda. Why shouldn't the Church manipulate its believers as the Good Shepherd manipulates his sheep?

The Church has come up with a brilliant marketing plan for its services. It makes perfect sense to encourage people to embrace additional suffering (ill health and natural disasters are not going anywhere either) and 'load them up' with sins in order to keep them in a state of constant stress and fear. At the same time, they are bombarded with limitations and prohibitions in all spheres of life, starting with food and finishing with sex. Only then does Man want to go to church to seek consolation; when you have rotten luck, there are not many other places you can go. In this way, the Church is able to instil this entirely illogical notion that misfortune in this life means a state of bliss in the next. It astonishes me that the early followers of Christianity did not see this. And even more that, 2,000 years later, contemporary Christians persist in this lack of understanding. Why do so many of them still base their lives on suffering?

■ Suffering is Not in Vain ■

Christianity justifies the suffering endured during this earthly life with the chance of attaining true happiness in the life to come. Compared to this happiness, our life here on earth is a torturous wait, its value precisely in suffering for your sins.

It's obvious that the more suffering and the worse the conditions that humans find themselves in, the more they are ready to believe in a reward after death. After all, those who live well have their reward already – the Church Fathers and the Evangelists do not think about them. Blessed are those who weep, for they shall be comforted. (Matthew 5:4)

But what can be done with those who have little faith, or even no faith, or a desire to acquire the same in life after death? To prevent the spread of such foolishness – and to correct it wherever it has already appeared – the Church is diligent in instilling in its congregations from the earliest childhood the fear of the torments of hell, which it depicts vividly and in minute detail. The fear of the eternal and infinitely cruel punishment in hell is a useful antidote to the fear of any earthly suffering. If Christianity really believed in what it preached, namely that God is love and that happiness is to be found in faith and spiritual perfection, it would not feel the need to frighten the faithful in this way.

What conclusion should a true believer draw from all of this? The simplest and most logical one is that life on earth is transient and full of pain, whereas death is good and filled with the promise of hope. In this understanding, the cult of suffering is none other than the other side of the cult of death. Paul the Apostle considered all suffering as a small death, and his desire to share in Christ's suffering inevitably turns to sharing in His death too. He is explicit in identifying death in situations where it would have been more appropriate to talk merely of suffering: 'If, then, we have died with Christ, we believe that we shall also live with him.' (Romans, 6:8)

Gregory the Theologian expresses his ideas of the 'slow death of self' most beautifully and no less effectively than the Buddha.

Others again take joy in wives and children
And in mighty wealth's soon-to-be-lost acclaim.
Others enjoy the markets and gardens,
Or baths, and cutting a great figure in the city,
being paraded with high-sounding words, like one's followers
make a din and one can be pompous on the high stage.
Yes, many are man's pleasures in this many-sided life;
but happiness has been mixed with evils.
I, however, have died to this life; I bear but a meagre
breath upon this earth, and I flee from towns and men.
I hold converse with beasts and rocks, where, alone, away from others,
I dwell in the miserable, ramshackle little place.
One coat, no shoes, no hearth, I live on hope
alone, and am in disgrace to all worldly people.
My bed is straw, my blankets, reinforced sackcloth;
the dirty floor's dust is watered with tears.
Many are those who groan beneath iron bands;
While I've heard that some take ashes for their food;
yet others mix the drink with grievous tears;
others, packed about with wintry snow, stand
forty days and nights, like trees,
in their hearts already departed from this earth,
possessing in their minds God only.

That's why many great Christian authorities, including Pascal, have always advocated the constant remembrance of death, advising believers never to lose sight of it. Pascal himself managed this. He was often sick and happily died aged 39.

It's quite possible that a man who has managed to achieve such a state of detachment is really happy, but there can't be many of such unfortunates in the world.

▪ Sacred Masochism and Death-Bed Torments ▪

Holy Scripture insists on there being no reason to fear death and promises martyrs blessings after their death. It is also understood that the harsher the suffering on earth, the greater and sweeter the reward will be in heaven. This state of affairs forces one into the conclusion that it would make more sense to take matters into one's own hands and start looking for suffering now, rather than sit around and passively wait for the distant happiness beyond the grave. The most ardent believers came to see suffering as their main and only purpose. The believers were not simply enduring their existing misfortunes humbly, but actively seeking new ones. No one was complaining about pain any more, it became an object of desire.

A legitimate question therefore arises: wouldn't suicide advance longed-for death? But as we have covered, Man's life is not only in God's hands but *owned* by God and for this reason suicide is strictly prohibited. As far as God is concerned, suicide means terminating one's earthly suffering wilfully and without His permission – tantamount to criminal disobedience. So don't go looking for an easy way out.

On the other hand, self-torment is not forbidden, so it's hardly surprising that this sort of worldview of self-victimisation and suffering frequently leads to real masochism.

Just think of the early Christian desert dwellers and hermits; weren't they guilty of self-torture? Weren't they seeking Christian perfection through their acts of martyrdom and masochism? Wasn't it their martyrdom that made them into saints in the first place?

It looks as if the general idea was that extreme suffering would draw Man to God much in the same way as candlelight attracts gnats and mosquitoes. Or, perhaps, the way sticky flypaper traps kitchen flies. Saint Cyprian of Carthage expresses this idea in his treaty *On the Dress of Virgins*:

> Or, if she must glory in the flesh, then assuredly let her glory when she is tortured in confession of the name; when a woman is found to be stronger than the tortures; when she suffers fire, or the cross, or the sword, or the wild beasts, that she may be crowned. These are the precious jewels of the flesh, these are the better ornaments of the body.

Following Christianity's decisive victory over pagans and heretics and at the conclusion of the Crusader period, the fanatical believers were beginning to experience a shortage of thrills. The Middle Ages saw the development (predominantly amongst Catholics) of decidedly masochistic trends, encompassing longed-for punishment, humiliation, subjugation, and pain.

A new type of Christian masochism emerged which was simultaneously masochism and sadism, almost our well-known sadomasochism. For a normal person, both trends are a manifestation of an illness and mental aberration, but in the world of religion they were seen as a blessing, an act of healing and atonement. Historical literature is thick with pertinent examples of this topic, some of which we will reproduce below. Let's start with the monastic life.

Saint Dominic, the founder of the Order of Preachers (the Dominicans), insisted that the 'brethren' lash each other with whips. As for himself, he practised self-flagellation three times every night: once for his own sins, another for the sins of his contemporaries, and the third for the souls in purgatory. It was believed that flagellation could save one from the torments of hell in the next life. At the end of the twelfth and the beginning of the thirteenth centuries, this behaviour was taken outside to the streets and highways of the cities, which became filled with crowds of self-flagellating citizens. The rise of this practice is said to have coincided with the outbreak of the plague that engulfed Europe, with people attempting to ingratiate themselves with God by means of their whipped and lacerated flesh. The whipped parts of the body were often the unfortunates' sexual organs, as the source of sin and life itself, and this put the flagellants in a state of bliss. In any case, they practised asceticism; they had no sexual contact with women (history is silent on the subject of men), ate anything lying around, and slept on bare straw. It's not beyond reason to suppose that this self-torture was aimed at suppressing unfulfilled sexual desire. They justified their lifestyle by the fact that they expected the end of the world to come soon, and so wanted to imitate Christ in all things and please Him by their suffering. The Franciscan Saint Anthony of Padua is thought to be the founder of this movement. Please note that he is called a saint. Today he would be considered a paranoiac.

These masochistic penitential practices or the 'Foolishness of the Cross' reached their peak in the Modern Age at the same time as the Enlightenment and the rise of secular culture. It's quite possible that they were a conservative religious response to this. There are even some modern scholars who highlight this particular form of Christian masochism.

A Carmelite nun, Catherine of Cardona, wore iron chains on her bare body and flogged herself with chains and hooks on a regular basis. While being thus engaged, she experienced unearthly joy and divine visions. One could encounter similar practices among the Franciscans, the Dominicans and even the Jesuits. Nowadays, the practice of self-flagellation has been preserved only among certain Christian groups in the Philippines and the Shiite Muslims. Could you imagine anything similar in Antiquity?

So those who condemn Marquis de Sade and Sacher Masoch are being entirely unjust; those two were perhaps the most proper Christians of all, especially Sacher Masoch, who was determined to cultivate in himself a proper attitude to suffering and thus prepare for future life beyond the grave.

Let me make another point. Suffering is the most burdensome part of any human life. In this sense, it is 'worse' than death because in death one finds liberation from suffering. This is why the martyrs of old were able to embrace death so easily while today's terminally ill people have to fight for euthanasia, the right to end their life voluntarily. Any normal person is very fearful both of death and even more so of the suffering that precedes it. Pain and suffering are frequent precursors to death and are firmly associated with it. A Christian regards a painful death as the 'final chord' in his life of suffering, one to guarantee a life of heavenly bliss. Believers used to pray to die in the middle of the day and in great torment (as opposed to dying at night in one's sleep) because a death like that imitated the life of Christ and increased the believer's chances of ending up in heaven. A person's form of death was a way of assessing his righteousness. If a man's personal piety left something to be desired, the Christian God gave him a last chance to correct his ways and earn salvation.

For many believers, death became a joyful and longed-for event, heralding an imminent encounter with God.

Read this description of a nun's agony in the eighteenth century:

> She trembled with joy the more that her illness increased. She received the good news that her yearned-for hour was approaching…

And all of this was happening in Europe, in the sixteenth through the eighteenth centuries, at a time when the industrial revolution had already begun and the great thinkers of the Enlightenment worked and flourished. On the other hand, there is nothing

21ˢᵗ century, The Passion of Christ, Philippines
The Christian Church has never really lost its passion for suffering.

surprising in religious fanaticism; hundreds of suicide-minded Islamists are today no less joyful and hopeful.

The martyr-like death is described aptly by one Orthodox priest who himself was destined to die for his faith. And this was not in the eighteenth century, but just a couple of years ago:

> Of course the best Christian death of all is the death of a martyr, for the sake of Christ the Saviour… Whenever anyone got killed in the early Church, there were no letters of condolences. Instead everyone in the Church immediately sent congratulatory letters.

Just imagine, they were hurrying to congratulate them on acquiring another protector in heaven!

Christian religion requires the suffering to continue throughout the whole of the believer's earthly life, culminating in a torturous death. Only then can prayer, the Church, and God become one's only true joy and purpose.

I am absolutely sure that these considerations were at the root of the seemingly strange practice of having potential heretics and witches burnt slowly at the stake, rather than hanged. For the Christians of the time this form of death constituted an act of supreme Christian love for the condemned. The fearful torments increased their chances of being pardoned by the Lord and ending up, if not in heaven, then at least in a better part of hell.

◼ In the Land of the Blind, the One-Eyed Man ◼ is King, or, How the Cult of Suffering Emerged from the Cult of Weakness

Life is a well of delight; but where the rabble also drink, there all fountains are poisoned.
Nietzsche, *Thus Spoke Zarathustra*

What is my own theory of the origin of the cult of suffering in Christianity?

Christianity is a religion for those who, for a number of reasons, have not been able to overcome their own personal difficulties. And in fact, the poor and the oppressed have been suffering and deprived of many things because of their poor spiritual development, and it has always been difficult for them to reconcile with the idea that life will inevitably come to an end.

The slaves, the oppressed, the paupers, and the wretched have been subjected to suffering with such predictable regularity that hurt feelings and attitudes could not help but arise.

Christianity declared itself first and foremost a religion of universal equality, a religion of the poor and the oppressed. They were offered a chance of fair judgement and eternal happiness in exchange for behaving in a correct way and keeping their thoughts pure. The approach of Christianity to the problem of equality is quite obvious. Christianity is the religion of the weak and for the weak, and its solution is to create a divine cult of weakness. My main thesis is that the cult of weakness had naturally given rise to the cult of suffering. I say 'naturally' because the weak and the oppressed have always suffered; they suffered for every piece of bread, for having to depend on the landowner, or the squire, or the king, or the pharaoh. Their suffering was an unavoidable evil with which they became reconciled as they accepted their lot in the world. If you want to avoid suffering, then be prepared to fight, work harder than anyone else, prove your superiority on the battlefield, or impress your bosses, the pharaohs, with your skill and intelligence.

On the one hand, Christianity is a product of a social disease, and on the other, it is a rather sensible hypothesis. Unless the poor are furnished with their own theory that God created paupers, their privations and suffering would appear entirely for nothing. So Christianity came and explained to the weak and suffering people that far from being evil, their suffering was in fact a source of goodness and that God Himself had suffered in the same way. It may well be that the image of the suffering God arose at the same time. This image had already existed in other forms within pre-Christian cultures. There were a number of suffering deities who embraced a painful death only to rise again to a new life of joy. It is logical to suppose that a God like that would be better placed to understand and reward the believer's suffering. The image of a suffering God is, in any case, much closer to the suffering people than the image of a God who is sated, successful, and happy. Besides all this, a God who suffers is closer to the people if only for the fact that such a God is not a subject to envy. A God like this would always be popular in a society which lives according to the principle of 'I'd rather my cow die than the neighbour have two cows'.

Moreover, He suffered not for the sake of the mighty and exalted kings, pharaohs, or high priests, but for their own sakes – the weak and the oppressed. Naturally, this divine Revelation could not increase their endurance, but would undoubtedly bring certain moral relief.

It would be naive to suppose that the appearance of God with His explanations immediately alleviated all the suffering of those who came to believe in Him. As far as the suffering was concerned, nothing much changed; the suffering continued much as before. However the vector of this suffering assumed an entirely opposite direction. From merely denigrating themselves, the faithful moved towards an aggressive opposition to all powerful and rich people, as well as to secular values in general and individual freedoms: 'For every one who exalts himself will be humbled, and he who humbles himself will be exalted.' (Luke 14:11)

It is true that the mighty of this world have a problem with morals and spirituality in the Christian understanding of these concepts. Powerful people like to create their own values on which they then base their moral code. Powerful people like to live a full life on earth without much regard for the state of their soul, the existence of which they are, in any case, not entirely sure. By and large, they are not much bothered about having a soul at all and are liable to regard any inner torments as a sign of weakness or doubt about their chosen course of action.

The weak, however, need not only a soul but also a cohort of leaders and prophets for their very existence. They know all too well that they are incapable of constructing values independently and deriving a moral code from them. For this reason, they always borrow their moral code from the strong, while frequently accusing them of every sin under the sun and calling for their extermination.

What I mean is this: it wouldn't be so bad if the Christian cult of the weak concerned itself with forcibly pushing the weak into the ranks of the strong, as happens nowadays with the cult of political correctness. The problem was of a different nature.

The problem is that Christianity was the first global revolt of the weak against the strong. This means that the rise of the weak was accompanied by belittling the strong and being antagonistic towards them. The very fact of their belonging to 'the true faith', that is to weakness, supplies the weak with a sense of being equal in everything, as well as possessing a special status and the right to sit in judgement over the mighty, who are devoid of morals and 'spirituality'.

A simple moral condemnation of the strong soon led to their extermination. This state of affairs has been attested throughout human history. Nothing good came out of Christian ideas; the pseudo-egalitarian society that arose as a result was weak and dumbed down, having lost all of its values and culture. At least it got to keep the suffering.

■ A Buddhist's Happiness is in Renouncing Life ■

There is clearly a powerful cult of suffering within Buddhism. The literal translation of the word 'cult' means 'excessive care or veneration', 'strong attachment', 'cultivation'. I feel that this definition works both ways; a 'cult' is not only something we are excessively fond of or venerate but also something we excessively hate and want to flee from. In other words, I feel it defines all forms of excess – whether it be infinite respect or equally unbridled hatred – in exaggerating the faults of others or in diminishing our own. Isn't bowing down before an opponent's great power and invincibility a form of cult?

The most important point here is not Buddhism's attitude to suffering – whether it regards it positively or negatively – but the fact that it sees it everywhere and in everything. Because of this attitude, suffering has enormous significance to Buddhism and has taken over the globe.

I have tremendous respect for Buddhism. Over the last century, Western society has grown tired of Christianity and fearful of Islam. At the same time, society has become so enchanted with Buddhism that it accepts everything in it without any critical analysis, disregarding the poverty and instability of the Buddhist countries.

Buddhism considers suffering and pain to be an essential characteristic of being alive, and for this reason suffering affects not just humans but all living things who suffer in the eternal cycle of reincarnation, the Samsara. Buddhism does not separate human beings from other living creatures; Man has never been banished from paradise nor received any special mission.

All situations repeat themselves, everything is torturously homogenous; there is suffering in everything in accordance with the law of individual karma, the sum of all our actions in life. On its own, karma has absolutely nothing to do with sin; Buddhism knows neither sin nor absolute evil.

Buddhism also has no concept of pleasure, the opposite of suffering. Suffering and happiness are not antitheses of each other, but rather the two sides of the same coin.

No positive moment in a person's life, no instance of pleasure and joy can exist in separation from suffering; suffering encompasses all of them. Buddhism even calls the unpleasant sensations 'the suffering of suffering' and the pleasant ones it calls 'the suffering of change'. In other words, pleasure is also suffering, except when we either don't realise this, or realise this far too late. This is easy to explain: there is no single human condition on earth that can satisfy in all respects and give that person lasting happiness and peace. Of course, a person can experience pleasure for a short moment – especially physical pleasure – but this moment is fleeting; you can't freeze-frame it and it quickly disappears, causing new unsatisfied desires and greater suffering. All life's pleasures are short-lived and relative while suffering is absolute.

According to the Buddhist doctrine, the cause of suffering is our attachment to material benefits and illusory desires, or rather yearning – in other words, our zest for life pleasures. The yearning for pleasure is insatiable. Besides, this yearning is not simply a desire for happiness but also a rejection of unhappiness. If people didn't have desires, they wouldn't suffer either.

This yearning for life, this appetite for the passions, and this rejection of the unpleasant are all a result of faulty vision and a lack of understanding of the nature of things. Man closes his eyes to the ocean of suffering around him and is unwilling to accept that the cause of all this suffering lies within him and only he can remove it. Listen to these wonderful words of Buddha, it's almost poetry:

> This, Bhikkhus, is the noble truth of ill: birth is ill, decay is ill, disease is ill, death is ill, association with the unloved is ill, separation from the loved is ill, not to get what one wants is ill, in short the five aggregates of grasping are ill.
>
> This, Bhikkhus, is the noble truth of the source of ill: the craving which causes rebirth is accompanied by passionate pleasure, and takes delight in this and that object, namely sensuous craving, craving for existence and craving for annihilation.

Buddhism would never have become so attractive and successful if it had simply laid out the extent of the immeasurable suffering without offering its own unique 'carrot', a way of eliminating this suffering. Buddhism offers to free man, to snatch him out of the storm of suffering. In order to do this, he must renounce his desires, distance himself from temporal reality and generally reject life. This is the only way to free oneself from the fetters of karma and to escape the cycle of reincarnation. This carrot is called the Noble Eightfold Path, a means of reaching the state of bliss where there is no longer any suffering, or Nirvana.

By extending this logic, absolute Nirvana is reached only at the point when the human body is utterly destroyed, since evil, which leads to suffering, is at the heart of all being. Buddhism pauses either at the foot of the mountain or at the edge of the precipice and defines Nirvana as a state of non-desire, non-consciousness, and non-life, but also a state of non-death.

◼ Buddhism and Stoicism ◼

On the one hand, Buddhism places the subject of suffering at the centre of its teaching, much like the majority of the Ancient Greek philosophers, especially from the Epicurean and Stoic schools. Also, Buddhism developed much closer to the Age of Antiquity. I have reasonable suspicion that the Epicureans and Stoics borrowed some of their ideas from Buddhism. Siddhartha Gautama, who later became known as Shakyamuni Buddha, was born and was active in the sixth to fifth centuries BC while Antiphon and Aristotle began to teach only in the fifth to fourth centuries BC. Epicurus was even later on the scene, acquiring his wisdom only in the third century BC. Of course there was no air travel back then, but still, two-hundred-odd years is a sufficient time lapse to allow any idea to migrate from India to the Mediterranean. In any case, the influence of Buddhism on Hellenic thought is much more plausible than the other way round. That is why it may seem as if Buddhism, with its recognition of the cyclical nature of time, its rejection of the One God, together with its noble tolerance of other religions and worldviews, makes it similar to ancient philosophy, in particular to Stoicism. It is believed that some ancient philosophers recognised the inevitability of suffering and were seeking ways to escape it by calling for moderation in consumption – just like the Buddhist ones.

However, this similarity is only on the surface and in any case doesn't apply to Greek philosophy as a whole, but only to its Stoic 'division'. The divisions between Buddhism and Hellenic philosophy are deeper and much more significant than any seeming congruence. In this, I am in complete disagreement with such philosophers as Berdyaev and Spengler and even Nietzsche.

Nietzsche, a keen admirer of ancient philosophy, approved of the fact that Buddhism saw suffering as a characteristic of being, which was nevertheless 'beyond good and evil': Buddhism is the only genuinely positive religion to be encountered in history, and this applies even to its epistemology (which is a strict phenomenalism). It does not speak of a 'struggle with sin', but, yielding to reality, of a 'struggle with suffering'. Sharply differentiating itself from Christianity, it puts the self-deception that lies in moral concepts behind it; it is, in my phrase, beyond good and evil. For some reason, Nietzsche was unable to see that the people of Antiquity did their best to rid themselves of suffering, whereas in Buddhism it had taken a firm hold within Man. Most probably, Nietzsche hated the Christian doctrine so much because of what it destroyed that he was willing to stand for any religious or philosophical doctrine with a slight resemblance to that of his beloved Greeks. He did not really care about Buddhism's obsession with suffering. He had suffered his whole life and obviously thought that Man couldn't avoid suffering no matter what he does.

The love of Buddhism, felt by the German historian and philosopher Oswald Spengler, was inspired primarily by his rejection of the importance of historical time. He believed that every culture has to be born, develop, and die. I like this theory very much but I am also rather frightened by it. Where are we now? Are we in our happy early childhood or in the senility of old age? Spengler considered Buddhism and Stoicism to be related movements of a dying secular age; both philosophies lack metaphysical constructs and both are based on almighty reason. Exactly where in Buddhism he espied secularism and especially the almighty reason remains unclear.

I disagree that Buddhism is equivalent to Ancient philosophy. An examination of the principal differences between Ancient philosophy and Buddhism shows us the following.

Buddhism states its positive attitude to reason and its opposition to the acceptance of ready dogma. However, the Buddhist mindset is not directed towards life on earth, as is the case with the Ancients, but towards choosing 'the right faith' and rationalising certain religious practices. One is invited to use one's dispassionate intuition rather than reason in order to discover the truth of things.

Ancient philosophy exalted a life of the senses and developed a multi-faceted cult of pleasure. The Ancient ethical system considered suffering to be evil and pleasure good. Buddhism rejects sensual life and in this regard it is a complete antithesis to the thoughts of the Ancients. Buddhist ethics do not allow for any fundamental distinction between suffering and pleasure; both are seen as evil. Goodness is equated to detaching oneself from both suffering and pleasure.

Finally, Ancient philosophy couldn't conceive of any life other than a purely secular one, whereas Buddhism clearly emphasises a religious lifestyle, which is placed above secularism. A secular lifestyle is clearly a concession to those who are weak of body, will, and spirit. Otherwise, where would all these Buddhist monks come from?

So, in my opinion, Buddhist philosophy has nothing in common with an Ancient one. But in its focus on suffering, it has aspects in common with Christianity.

■ Buddhism and Christianity ■

Many Christian apologists fiercely deny any resemblance between Buddhism and Christianity and even accuse Buddhism of cowardice; instead of saving the world as Christ had wanted, the Buddhist runs away from it.

Berdyaev, failing to recognise Christianity's spiritual kinship with Buddhism, writes that Buddhism is afraid of suffering and renounces the human personality in order to be delivered from suffering.

It is true that, at least formally, suffering is understood differently in Buddhism and Christianity. For Christianity, suffering is good; one mustn't try to avoid it, but instead seek it out, as bodily and spiritual suffering are necessary for cleansing the soul from sin. Through his suffering, Man can approach God and even 'see His face'. The way of such suffering imposes limitations on oneself and even a complete rejection of all ephemeral, defective, and sinful temporal pleasures that are destructive to the body and soul.

Buddhism regards all suffering as a type of evil that has nothing to do with sinfulness or morality and which must be eliminated from one's life. It is impossible to approach God, since God-the-Creator simply does not exist.

Buddhism also denies the existence of the unalterable and eternal soul and thinks that believing in the latter is a cause of suffering and confusion: a person who believes such things does not understand his essence. This is logical, as the person fears for the fate of his soul after death, which causes him suffering, as he is always displeased with himself.

Buddhism has no fears of the soul being marred by the stain of pleasure. It makes mild appeals to those who wish to make spiritual progress that they should deny pleasure, but always allows the possibility of returning to pleasure in case their spiritual life is not as happy as planned.

Nevertheless, when you focus your Nirvana-weakened gaze, it becomes obvious that Buddhism is much closer to Christianity than would appear at first glance. Both religions focus heavily on suffering, and this fundamental point of reference gives rise to many other similarities:

Just as in the case of Christianity, Buddhism is sceptically inclined towards the world around us – the world full of illusion, evil, and suffering. For this reason, its wish is for the individual personality to be subsumed by religion:

> Attraction comes from meetings with,
> and from attraction dukkha's born;
> see danger of attraction then,
> fare singly as the rhino's horn.

Like Christianity, Buddhism preaches a life of asceticism and self-denial to the point of renouncing all sensual pleasure. Buddhism is certain that passions rob Man of his freedom and bring about suffering. The Buddhist Nirvana, which is similar to the Christian state of sanctity, is an environment in which all things that are temporal, secular, animalistic – indeed the whole of our illusive physical world – are stripped of all power and value, and the person inhabiting it enters a certain personal state free of desires.

Buddhism – in common with Christianity – has no time for Man. Christianity considers Man to be sinful and worthless while Buddhism maintains that the personal 'I', the ego, doesn't in fact exist. It is interesting to note that with all his hatred towards Christianity and love for Buddhism, Nietzsche still claimed that Jesus was a Buddhist who had appeared in the land of the Jews.

Mara, the Buddhist devil, similar to his Christian counterpart, tempted Gautama Buddha with visions of beautiful women, the better to destroy his spiritual life.

Finally, in common with Christianity, Buddhism has given birth to the enormous, contagious, poisonous and parasitic fungus that is monasticism. In certain historical periods, the overall number of monks was comparable to the whole population of 'believing' countries.

What conclusion can we make from all this? It's quite obvious that Buddhism – just like Christianity – is not a religion of life, but of death.

▪ Suffering is the Infidels' Destiny ▪

There is no general cult of suffering in Islam. It is not considered as being in any way key to the ethical system, and is seen in a broadly negative light – as a form of evil, an absence of joy, torment, and punishment – as harm, in other words. Many different people suffer in Islam – pagans, heretics, sinners, the traitors of Allah, and those who allow injustice to take place – but never the 'real' faithful Muslims. The latter will be protected from suffering by Allah, who will also bestow eternal bliss on them in paradise. In this way, pleasure is closer to Islam than suffering, although instead of suffering, Islam imposes a mass of limitations on the life of the believer, such as prayers five times a day and a long period of fasting.

The Christian idea that suffering elevates Man, enabling him to grow spiritually, to advance towards God, and to ease his access to paradise is rather a marginal notion for Islam.

This notion existed within Islam in its early stages of development, but usually only in those Islamic movements which were most influenced by a Christian worldview; for example, Sufism. However, it didn't take hold within classical Islam; one's soul can be cleansed only by ardent faith in Allah and the faithful following of the precepts of Sunna. Physical and spiritual torments have no part in this.

Islam's lack of a culture of suffering can be explained by the history of its origins. Unlike Christ, Prophet Muhammad did not suffer and was not persecuted or harmed in any way. From the beginning, Muhammad's method of spreading his teaching was subtle and carefully thought through. First, he preached only in secret and converted only the closest people around him. Later, when the movement had gained strength, he addressed himself to the people as a whole. This meant that there were no martyrs of the faith during his lifetime. In fact, it was the unbelievers in Allah, rather than the Muslims, who had to take cover against the mighty onslaught of the new religion.

The Prophet wanted to make following the new faith easy and pleasant. For this reason, Islam appealed for moderation in everything, even in its call to serve Allah. There is no need to exhaust yourself; all you need to do is to keep to the rules he wrote down and rejoice in the reward which most certainly awaits the righteous in heaven.

Moreover, there is no single standard of orthodoxy within Islam; neither can there be, because faith should be tailored to the individual circumstances of every man. Allah's unwillingness to see men suffer is reflected both in the Quran and in the Hadiths.

> There has come to you a messenger from among yourselves, concerned over your suffering, anxious over you. Towards the believers, he is compassionate and merciful. (Quran surah 9, ayat 128)

The message of this is that any attempt to undertake anything which is above one's strength (for example praying day and night to the point of exhaustion or fasting on a daily basis) invariably has an adverse effect, as it causes Man to lose his strength and be unable to perform even moderate acts of piety. In this sense, Islam is fundamentally different from Christianity with its cult of suffering and extreme asceticism. The Christian believer is expected to engage in a constant struggle with himself and thus prove his faith to God.

Islam, which was conceived as a religion for warriors, did not take up the notion of either the original sin or redemptive suffering. This allowed Muslims to preserve the integrity of their human nature so that there was nothing in it that had to be overcome. Suffering is not seen as a result of sin, but rather as an aid to conquer sin.

> I visited Allah's Apostle while he was suffering from a high fever. I touched him with my hand and said, "O Allah's Apostle! You have a high fever". Allah's Apostle said, "Yes, I have as much fever as two men of you have". I said, "Is it because you will get a double reward?" Allah's Apostle said, "Yes, no Muslim is afflicted with harm because of sickness or some other inconvenience, but that Allah will remove his sins for him as a tree sheds its leaves."

As far as atoning for the sins of others is concerned, Islam would regard this as a complete incongruity – everyone is responsible for himself before Allah. From a historical perspective, this religious worldview appeared most reasonable and made Islam an attractive option in the eyes of many nations.

Nevertheless, suffering is inevitable in any case and a faithful Muslim should do all he can to endure it with fortitude and to draw useful lessons from his misfortune for the future.

Abu Hurayra, one of the most famous of Prophet Muhammad's companions, revealed that the Prophet declared that 'the example of a believer is that of a fresh tender plant; from whatever direction the wind comes, it bends it, but when the wind quietens down, the plant becomes straight again. In the same way, the believer is tried by means of many misfortunes but remains patient'.

Practically speaking, it means the believer should not express his dismay whenever he is confronted with an unpredictable turn of events. A Muslim must accept suffering with faith and hope, neither resisting it nor asking for the reasons why. He should receive his portion of suffering as the will of Allah and praise Him when it comes to an end (or when he dies). Allah knows about everything and would never subject a person to a trial that is beyond his strength or send more misfortune on him than he can bear. For this reason, one should never accuse or speak against Allah if one is visited by some undeserved misfortune or unexpected illness. It is quite possible that this is a deliberate test sent by Allah which must be borne with all dignity.

All suffering and every injustice will be generously recompensed by Allah both in this temporal world and in life in heaven (this idea is rather similar to Christianity's).

The only people truly deserving of the most fearful and terrible suffering are those who don't believe in Allah. Allah has no compassion towards them whatsoever (today, we really can see the absence of this compassion in Somalia, Nigeria, and particularly in the Islamic State).

> And slacken not in following up the enemy: If ye are suffering hardships, they are suffering similar hardships; but ye have hope from Allah, while they have none. And Allah is full of knowledge and wisdom.
>
> …In addition there will be maces of iron [to punish] them. Every time they wish to get away therefrom, from anguish, they will be forced back therein, and [it will be said], "Taste ye the Penalty of Burning!" (Quran surah 4, ayat 104; surah 22, ayat 21-22).

Ashura.

However, despite its generally negative attitude towards suffering, Islam allows (indeed welcomes) suffering for the faith and reserves a particular mention for shahids (martyrs), although from a historical perspective their numbers have been relatively few (from a historical perspective only; nowadays, we have more martyrs than we need). Apart from the faithful who have died fighting the infidel and in internal disputes, the ranks of the martyrs have also been swelled by the prophets and the ulama (scholars). To die for Allah's glory, for the sake of strengthening the faith, or indeed in order to defend one's homeland and family, is an honour that can become a Muslim's whole life's purpose. Moreover, it is irrelevant whether the shahid suffered or met with an instant death; the only thing of importance is the positive outcome in the end. Unlike in Christianity, the value of one's death is not increased by the suffering that preceded it.

Through his death, the shahid declares his unfaltering faith in Allah and in return receives from Him a handsome reward, forgiveness of all his earthly sins, and a guaranteed place in paradise near Allah's throne. He even requires no washing prior to burial. So martyrdom in Islam is a highly attractive deal with God.

> Those who have left their homes, or been driven out therefrom, or suffered harm in My Cause, or fought or been slain, – verily, I will blot out from them their iniquities, and admit them into Gardens with rivers flowing beneath; – A reward from the presence of Allah, and from His presence is the best of rewards. (Quran surah 3, ayat 195)

They say that the martyrs are envied even by prophets, because they are safe from the punishment of the grave and secure from the great terror, they can choose their place in paradise, get married to 70 dark-eyed virgins and make successful intercession for 70 of their relatives. They will rejoice so much that on Judgement Day they will ask to revive them and allow them to die as shahids once again.

This really sounds most attractive. So it's little wonder that there is no shortage of shahids wishing to avail themselves of such lavish promises of reward and there are thousands of excited Muslims on standby ready to blow themselves up together with the 'enemies of Allah'.

I wouldn't mind becoming a martyr myself if I wasn't such an incorrigible atheist. A martyr's death without suffering makes dying for Allah supremely easy. Abu Hurayra reported that the Messenger of Allah, may Allah bless him and grant him peace, said, 'Martyrs only experience the blow which kills them as one of you might experience the prick of a sting.' (At-Tirmidhi)

Islam recognises two categories of martyrs: those who are already recognised as martyrs in this world (dying in the way of Allah, in a jihad) and who will receive an immediate reward; and those who might be recognised as such in the world to come (dying from natural causes or disease).

We say 'might' because the benefits arising from martyrdom in the world are not extended to this second category and their posthumous fate will depend on the state of their faith – one resurrects in the same state he deceased.

Unlike in the Christian tradition, Islam has never had much time for self-flagellation. There is, however, one rather significant exception. By this I mean the Shiite ritual of Ashura, a bloody imitation of the suffering and death of the descendants of Caliph Ali, Prophet Muhammad's son-in-law. This ritual, which is still widely practised in many Muslim countries, receives plenty of news coverage in the world media, so there is little point in devoting much time to it in this book.

I have covered all there is here about the curious phenomenon of religious masochism and the desire to inflict suffering on yourself.

Even if this self-flagellation seems to be the peak of absurdity and does not make any sense for any reasonable person, it is more than easy to implement it in your life. Leading a ferocious battle against your natural needs and pleasures will be enough. And then you can occupy yourself with the suffering of the saints – as we already know, there is never enough of it.

CHAPTER V

The Great Battle
Against Pleasure

> *Sooner murder an infant in its cradle than nurse unacted desires.*
> William Blake, 'Proverbs of Hell' from *The Marriage of Heaven and Hell*

This key chapter is devoted to asceticism, which for centuries has struggled against our right to pleasure. Asceticism is one of the oldest and most important practices in human civilisation. It always finds new loyal fans, smoothly moving from one culture to another. The famous French expression about the eternal monarch, slightly paraphrased, is a good fit: 'Asceticism is dead, long live asceticism!', 'Austerity,' 'penance,' and 'ascetic' – what do these terms mean, how did they arise and, most importantly, why do they exist?

The ascetic lifestyle is described in detail in many historical sources and just as many works of art. In all cultures and religions asceticism has similar features – a conscious rejection of natural needs, pleasures, luxury, ostentatious humility, as well as strict temperance in situations where most people would not want to restrict themselves.

However, after what I experienced in Israel, my lack of understanding of asceticism turned into a complete rejection of it, and I was filled with a burning desire to understand its essence.

■ A Purely Jewish Story ■

I first encountered asceticism during a visit to Israel. I had for long waited to see the Holy Land and Jerusalem, to swim, as Christ did, in the sea of Galilee, and to visit Eilat.

It was one of my first trips abroad and my girlfriend grumbled discontentedly that normal people would have gone to a better place: to Paris, where her favourite writer Hemingway lived, to Barcelona to see Gaudi, or to Rome, which speaks for itself.

The battle over countries and cities continued for several months, and in the end the Jews still beat Gaudi. I suddenly remembered that I had a school friend now living in Israel.

The woman's name was Avital.

She had thick bluish-black hair, huge black eyes, and an ocean of energy.

As a young girl in school, she continuously fidgeted, laughed into her hands, told her neighbour ridiculous things, and wrinkled her nose in a funny way. She liked to dress in short shorts, tight-fitting short T-shirts over nothing, and white trainers with blue socks. Avital was very active: she did ballet, rhythmic gymnastics, acrobatic rock-n-roll. Any party invariably ended at her house where she and her guests would drive her poor parents insane.

Needless to say that by fifteen, Avital was the most popular girl in school and at least half the boys were hopelessly in love with her. The girls were even worse: their external enthusiasm and ostentatious affection could not hide their jealousy, quite understandable in this situation.

Finding Avital in Israel took just four phone calls. She was very surprised and pleased to hear from me. The only thing that surprised me was that she did not make the slightest attempt to invite me to her house or show us the glory of life in the Promised Land. In the end, we agreed to meet at my hotel. Avital came to visit us with her husband and their two daughters as promised. She called the room from the front desk and told me that they were waiting for us downstairs in the lobby, which was full of kids and tourists due to the school holidays. I could not find them immediately, although I repeatedly approached black-haired slender middle-aged women and asked them all the same question. Avital came up to me first. The amazing girl from 22 years ago had turned into a pudgy woman with thick glasses, one shoulder clearly above the other, and instead of the thick blueish-black hair, she was wearing a red wig with eternally curled hair. She was dressed in a baggy, calf-length, dirty-pink suit under which she wore thick grey synthetic stockings and old-fashioned shoes with low heels. This was the outfit of a woman who had stopped caring what she looked like, or what others would think of her appearance, many years ago.

The head of the family, David, was around forty-five. He was of small stature, thin and bent, in a traditional black suit, hat, and white shirt. Their daughters (fifteen and sixteen), while possessing young and beautiful faces with large expressive eyes, were already pudgy and crooked.

The situation had the energy of a meeting of porcelain figurines on the shelf and my girlfriend, known for her ability to find a way out of any predicament, suggested we start our meeting with some friendly lunch in the restaurant. David said that Tel Aviv was not the city where a religious person could eat, but he hoped that the restaurant at the hotel was fully kashrut. It is necessary to explain that all restaurants are kosher in Israeli hotels – this happened historically and hasn't changed.

The entrance to the restaurant had a large plaque with the inscription in Hebrew and English – 'GLATT KOSHER'. This means not just kosher, but absolute kosher; Moses himself would not refuse such a meal. But because the restaurant was inside a hotel, or perhaps because the plaque failed to convince my friends, David questioned the waiter and the manager for fifteen minutes, demanding a piece of paper with the signature of a specific rabbi. In the end they only ordered salads, drank a little red wine, and spent thirty minutes with rather strained faces.

They were nice people to talk to, in no small part because they withstood the huge number of questions I had for them. David was born in the former Soviet Union into a family of mechanical engineers. In his early youth he was very fond of long-distance running, football, and hiking. But his main hobby, as befits an intelligent Jewish boy, was reading classical literature and encyclopedias. Then he was dragged into the army, specifically an artillery regiment. After the army David enrolled at a technical college where, after three years, a kind person explained to him that he was not just a man, but a Jew. This meant Judaism, not just a religion among all other religions, but the only and undeniable truth. And all the servants of this truth are obliged to live in Israel. So he went to a kibbutz, which is the traditional start on the way to Israel for most new immigrants. In the kibbutz David met Avital. From the kibbutz they moved straight to Bnei Brak, the main centre for Orthodox Judaism in Israel, and in seventeen years of marriage had seven children – six girls and one boy. The rest is typical: Avital stayed at home with the children, while David studied the Torah. How Avital got to Israel and what happened to her, Jane did not dare to ask. After discussing David's history and their children, I tried to turn the conversation on to world politics and culture. This intention led to nothing good: they were not interested in anything except religion, the life of their communities, and raising their children in a religious spirit. They knew almost nothing about what was happening in the world. They did not know the famous actors, music artists, or writers. They didn't watch the movies we thought were brilliant.

In order to protect themselves and their children from content harmful to religious people, they had abandoned TV, internet, and music long ago. They refused all the non-kosher evil achievements of civilisation. The thing we found the strangest was that they absolutely were not ashamed of their ignorance.

Starting a conversation about sports was absolutely pointless too: it was enough to see them and their two daughters. How the two young girls coped with a life without fun, we could only guess, but at least the parents did not forbid them from talking to each other.

The conversation inevitably faded and, wanting to defuse the situation a little and to raise a topic that would be fun all round, I asked how often they went as a family to the beach. Almost every resident of Israel is quite close to the sea, my interlocutors especially – the center of Bnei Brak is just five miles away from the sea.

Avital did not expect a question about the sea, but, after a pause, replied hesitantly that sometimes she went to the beach with the children. She only wished that all the family members weren't so very busy and could go there as often as they would like. Her husband, by contrast, took a firm position, saying that he did not go to the beach out of principle. He said it was because he had a catastrophic lack of time. Anticipating my bewilderment at the idea of a person with no job having no time to himself, he hastily added that he needed to be praying in the synagogue before sunrise, after sunrise, and in the evening, and a lot more time is spent on the study of the sacred books. He got home no earlier than nine or ten in the evening, and had to go back to the synagogue at five in the morning. Seeing our bewilderment at such a large amount of religious work, he softened a little and, with a guilty smile, said that every day he felt that he was very close, and that very soon everything would finally become clear, but then again he realised a bit was missing, and he had to get up a little earlier, pray more and even harder. Obviously, at this point I saw the divine truth, in the form of a cat which in vain tries to catch its own tail.

When they finally left in a car, I felt as good as the righteous in paradise. My interlocutors most likely did too. From my room window I saw the perfectly clear sea. Three-hundred metres to the left of our window, a few dozen young men and girls were riding kites on large frothy waves. Tanned, with perfect postures and toned muscles, they were laughing and speaking in a language incomprehensible to me.

After dinner, I made a call to another of my friends who was especially friendly with Avital. From her I learned the story of what happened to her. When she was 17, her parents sent her to an educational religious camp for six weeks. Religious teachers promised a 'slight acquaintance' with the Jewish tradition and a lot of other useful and pleasant entertainment. Entertainment could be found in the city, that's not what she went there for. The main idea of her parents was simple and quite clear: protect the decent Jewish girl from the arrogant claims of her sexually active peers, at least for a time. They regretted this idea immediately upon her return from the camp.

From then on Avital stopped using light switches and an elevator on Saturdays; luckily her healthy heart allowed her to climb the stairs to the twenty-third floor without difficulty. They also had to buy a second set of pots, dishes and cutlery – they wouldn't starve their only child! Forever gone were gymnastics, rock-n-roll, along with short shorts, T-shirts over nothing, the healthy thinness of a teenager, and laughter. In two years she emigrated to Bnei Brak.

Her parents, an absolutely secular couple, were appalled, but there was nothing they could do. Five years later they also moved to Israel, taking along the kosher kitchenware and a fear of talking about religion: for grandparents, the fear of separation from grandchildren is worse than excommunication. A purely Jewish story.

I hadn't fully appreciated the importance of asceticism in matters of faith and its influence on the lives of not just believers, but all of us. In short, I did not see it as the enemy. But in the process of exploring the basic principles of Christian doctrine, I saw in religious penance not only my enemy, but yours.

Atheists want people to live natural lives, fulfil all their lawful desires, and receive all required pleasure, while religions want them to live in faith and hope, while pleasure will be had in the afterlife, which means never. The theme of asceticism is without any doubt extremely important since it affects hundreds of millions of believers voluntarily sacrificing quality of life for the sake of an illusory hope.

Normal people are by nature more prone to excess and intemperance than to asceticism. In, for example, ordering a plate of meat and fries in a restaurant, and in the end using bread to collect the remainder of the sauce on the plate, or finishing an open bottle of wine even though you didn't want to.

Nevertheless, we are always given examples of extraordinary ascetics, the very existence of whom must demonstrate the incomparable advantages of the ascetic way of life. Besides a large number of famous religious figures (Anthony the Great, Hilarion, Basil the Great) the great names of Socrates, Diogenes, Newton, Kant are mentioned, but somehow such ascetics as Adolf Hitler and Pol Pot are forgotten. I am very interested in the fact that not only religion, but also some political movements have managed to impose very strict austerities on people. The number of people following all the ascetic rules of life, like the characters in my Jewish story, is enormous. Slowly the phenomenon of asceticism transformed in my mind from domestic habits and ceremonies like food, clothing and entertainment, into something on the level of existential global problems. It was quite clear that in exchange for the hardships, something very serious and very valuable was offered, something a believer would find absolutely impossible to refuse. But before you go searching for this 'value' in history, it should be understood in general terms what constitutes human needs and enjoyment. Otherwise, it is quite unclear what exactly ascetics give up.

■ Pleasure and Needs: What was Maslow Afraid of? ■

It is wrong to think that human pleasure, as a rule, is redundant. Pleasure is a natural reaction to fulfilled demands. The demand expressed is the lack of something necessary to our existence and is manifested in the feeling of tension, an unbalanced state of mind. Pleasure signals the successful implementation of biological debt.

Pleasure is the reward for maintenance of life. Pleasure is guaranteed: a hungry beggar eating a crust of bread after a long search and wait will receive no less pleasure than the rich man from some exquisite food at the most expensive restaurant. Another example: women get much more pleasure from sex (compared to men) and that they pursue it more is not an accident. Nature compels them to reproduce and pays a generous compensation for the pain of childbirth and the hardships of childcare.

The supreme authority in this matter is Abraham Maslow, the twentieth-century American psychologist, who created the famous Hierarchy of Needs. This pyramid was cited and described so many times that its image has long overshadowed the famous pyramid of Cheops. To describe it in a nutshell: at the foot of the pyramid are basic physiological needs and closer to the top are spiritual needs (e.g. creativity and self-actualisation).

Maslow said in *Motivation and Personality* that 'basic needs must be satisfied, otherwise we get sick'. I tend to believe him: that all the people living a full life are mentally healthy, while those who call on us to restrain ourselves painfully for the sake of 'attaining spiritual perfection' are sick. Man is sacred and his pleasures are, too.

I'd like to outline my own point of view on Maslow's pyramid and the importance of the needs in it. Without diminishing the necessity and advantages of spiritual fulfillment, it is recognised that the most important needs are basic, and fundamental to human survival and metabolism. Man, as the top animal, has genetic programmes, biological instincts, and an invariable set of basic needs, including food, drink, sleep, sex, air, and physical activity.

Basic needs are the most important, unlike spiritual needs, and nothing can take their place. It is impossible even to replace one with the other: food can never replace water and vice versa. If these needs aren't satisfied everything immediately collapses, starting with the spiritual. With spiritual needs, oddly enough, things become much easier. All of them can be easily refused without any threat to one's own existence. Human history is replete with examples of how the most highly educated and highly elevated quickly became animals when deserted on an island, or as long-term prisoners for primitive tribes, or in the army, especially during wars.

In addition, spiritual needs are easily replaced with one another. For example, the need for reading the Bible daily can simply be replaced with a need to read the Quran. Hundreds of thousands of Western Europeans make this transition every year and do not experience any issues. We can live without meeting the need to read a good book, attend a symphonic concert, or go to church, but the need for food and the removal of toxins is indispensable. Each of us had to learn this the hard way. I, for example, am not capable of writing a single line on an empty stomach.

Sexual desire is a little easier. This natural need can, in principle, be shifted: the need to sleep with a particular woman/man can be replaced with the need for another, but giving it up completely does not work. Such a restraint risks harming your physical and, especially, mental health.

The biological nature of Man is the foundation of his existence and no spiritual aspirations can be fulfilled without meeting the needs at the base of the pyramid. Maslow discussed this in *Motivation and Personality*: If our noblest impulses are seen not as check-reins on the horses, but as horses themselves, and if our animal needs are seen to be of the same nature as our highest needs, how can a sharp dichotomy between them be sustained? How can we continue to believe that they could come from different sources?

I believe that Maslow's obvious caution and reverence towards the highest requirements are associated with fear of religious opinions. He apparently became afraid of his own thoughts. It is difficult to accept the fact that 'the roots of higher needs' are as thick as the 'roots of the lower needs' and that they 'nourish the soil of our biological nature' just as well. So, I strongly disagree not just with the superiority of the higher, spiritual needs over the lower base ones, but with their alleged equality. The physical and spiritual are inseparable and in this coupling the physical takes distinct priority.

It is obvious to any sensible person that you must first satisfy your basic needs and then, if you have the desire, move towards spirituality and self-actualisation.

As claimed by Maslow himself, aspirations and human values do not come from the outside, but rather from within. In addition, it is obvious that the 'primitive' and practical Maslow did not believe in divine grace, which in the Christian paradigm alone can fill a man with something valuable. Necessary pleasures are not subject to moral evaluation.

This idea is simple at first glance, but it is extremely important for understanding the fundamental differences between secular and religious views of the world.

To fight against pleasure is to fight a losing battle: pleasure is the essence and meaning of earthly life, battling it is useless; it's as possible to renounce pleasure as it is to renounce breathing. Restricting needs and pleasure with impunity is only possible within some reasonable limits, the search for which defined Greek civilisation for centuries. Go beyond these limits even a little and the deprivation of basic needs violates a natural balance and leads first to suffering, and then to the development of neuroses.

■ Why Epicure is Great ■

The word 'austerity' is of Greek origin and means the presence of a sense of measure in consumption and passion, in diligent hard work, and in exercise for the body and soul. In short, nothing exceptional, mysterious, or mystical.

A sense of measure was one of the four major ancient virtues, along with wisdom (prudence), courage, and justice. The Greeks insisted on the need to control human passions, including the limitation of self-love.

Ancient virtues, including the principle of moderation, relate to principles of harmony, welfare, and the Golden Mean; these are based on reason, rationality, and reasonableness. The Greeks imagined Man balanced in his rightful place between animals and gods as part of a harmonious cosmic order. Philosophy was invented by the Greeks not for the pleasure of empty and vain thinking, but to answer the main question of human existence: what to do with your life and how to overcome the fear associated with imminent death. The Greeks gave to this question a clear answer: we need to do everything possible to live in this world, here and now. So the philosophy of Antiquity is primarily the art of living well and Greek austerity is the road to happiness and daily joy.

In principle, moderation is not bad because too much can be as bad as too little; it can be harmful to humans. Desires can never be fully satisfied and pleasure is potentially redundant and needs to be monitored and controlled. Excessive can't be good by definition.

In Aristotle's ethical system of moderation and limitation, natural needs are also central. It introduces the principle of 'nothing in excess', which is known as the 'Golden Mean'. It is recommended to limit particularly strong passions and pleasures, as they tend to grow uncontrollably. Reasonable desire in principle cannot be aimed at the impossible and unattainable, as in this case it would not be conscious, but stupid (in this regard, we have a suspicion that the idea of resurrection from the dead and the afterlife in heaven could not have been implemented by Aristotle).

The principle of moderation applies not only to the intellectual elite and government leaders, but to all people because any rational person will always choose a middle ground that is the mean between extremes. For statesmen, moderation was particularly recommended, as exemplary control of the ruler over himself allowed people to count on his self-control and wisdom in difficult situations.

Excess and disparity were synonymous with ugliness and lack of beauty by the Greeks.

The most important aspect of the Greek concept of temperance was its lack of connection to self-restraint for the sake of principle or to show off a mystical spirituality. People of the ancient world prayed to the gods, not for forgiveness for their sinful pleasures, but for the revelation of even greater carnal pleasures (if you are at this moment thinking of Christianity, then you are right). In the public consciousness after Antiquity, already in the grips of divine law, the word 'fun' began to hint at something if not completely negative, then clearly redundant and not very important for the individual and society. Without pleasure you can easily live a respectable life of a worker bee, gathering honey for the hive.

Greek moderation was purely human, one might even say egotistical. A healthy lifestyle will allow for longer enjoyment of its benefits. Better to endure some suffering associated with the restriction of pleasure than to suffer more in the future and enjoy these same pleasures. Such austerity *à la grecque* is not a struggle with oneself, it has no external 'spiritual' purposes and constitutes 'preparation' for pleasure.

For example, why regularly gorge if you want to have a long life? Why have too much sex if you want to retain the ability to have sexual intercourse until old age? You have got to manage your resources. A temperate man does not seek idle pleasure at the wrong time, but conversely when the time is right he does not deny them either.

Almost every Greek philosopher has said something in favour of pleasure and against excesses; they were constantly searching for the 'Golden Mean'. The Cyrenaics were the first Greek philosophers who proclaimed a simple and understandable idea: pleasure is good and it is necessary to strive; suffering is evil and it must be avoided. The founder of this school, Aristippus, said: 'If extravagance were a fault, it would not have a place in the festivals of the gods.' However, he moderated this idea: 'It is not abstinence from pleasures that is best, but mastery over them without being worsted.'

Stoic philosopher Epictetus believed that 'The most pleasant may become the most unpleasant, if one transgresses measure'. Roman philosopher and poet Juvenal, well-known for his winged words, shares Epictetus' opinion: 'Desire only so much as hunger and thirst, cold and heat demand … keep a sane mind in a healthy body.'

The chief expert on pleasure, and at the same time the most convinced ascetic, was Epicurus. His doctrine is the apotheosis of spiritual development and morality. It is sad that the Christian civilisation turned Epicurus into an enemy of the soul, an egomaniac, and a profligate.

Epicurus founded his philosophy on pleasure, believing that happiness consists in the full satisfaction of all desires. Man has a natural desire for pleasure, and a no less natural aversion to suffering: 'Pleasure is our first and kindred good.'

Epicurus gives a clear classification of desires, dividing them into two groups. The first group includes the natural physiological desires, which, in turn, are divided into the vital (hunger, thirst, sleep) and the natural, but not essential, such as sexuality. The second group includes 'vain' needs: wealth, fame, recognition. Realisation of natural desires leads to pleasures of the flesh, which are inherently strong and brief. When a person is looking for such pleasures, he suffers and remains eternally unsatisfied as the thirst for such enjoyment is, in principle, insatiable. The second group includes sustainable and long-term enjoyment associated with intelligence, harmony, and peace, the most important of which is the pleasure of the mind – philosophy. But reason and philosophy are not needed without context. They are a means to self-knowledge and maximum enjoyment of life. Epicurus would certainly like Maslow's pyramid, but unlike the latter, he would never apologise for 'our instinctive, animalistic nature'.

A positive attitude to pleasures did not prevent Epicurus from being a real ascetic (a Greek ascetic is not much like a Christian ascetic) and considering reasonable abstinence to be the main key to human well-being. As he states in his *Letter to Menoeceus*: 'You cannot lead a life of prudence, honour, and justice, which is not also a life of pleasure. For the virtues have grown into one with a pleasant life and a pleasant life is inseparable from them.'

He also said that not much is needed for a full life. This is why we eat a little cheese and not the entire pot, or a handful of barley and not the whole trough. It is a pity that at the time nobody was interested in following the advice on healthy food. Epicurus could have been a Jamie Oliver of Ancient Greece!

It is not necessary to moralise and accuse those who are entirely absorbed in excessive consumption of resources and sensory experiences. Nothing should be banned. Our individual needs are different, universal norms do not exist. Everyone should take care of themselves and determine the limits of their pleasures: 'The wealth required by nature is limited and is easy to procure; but the wealth required by vain ideals extends to infinity.'

Epicurus' form of temperance is fundamentally different from that of Aristotle, who sees it as one universal category, resting on the understanding of its place in society, which depends on the individual. Epicurus is an extremely anthropocentric philosopher: the man of Epicurus refrains only for his own sake and for the sake of future enjoyment. And then, far on the philosophical horizon, all society's problems can be found. The only people Epicurus unreservedly condemned were the lazy and idle. He would not have liked a life devoted to idle prayer.

The main idea of the Ancient philosophy lay in the glorification of the human being, development of his human spirituality and domination of the body.

Unfortunately, the great Ancient civilisation collapsed under the pressure of violent monotheism in a historically short period of time. It was easy to deal with the influence of Judaism, which existed on a very small territory and had a negligible number of believers, but the impetuous and massive spread of Christianity finished it off. A completely different environment appeared where religious asceticism replaced all other forms of spiritual practices. The path chosen by this asceticism led in a completely different direction.

A rational attitude to Man and to the world, typical in the Antiquity which laid the foundations of secular asceticism, could not have survived the conditions of Christian civilisation. Could not and did not survive. But let's be just: the ideas of ancient asceticism have never completely vanished from Western civilisation. But its manifestation became a pleasant exception. One of the major thinkers of the Enlightenment, the liberal Christian John Locke, shared the philosophical views of Epicurus and encouraged Man to be as he is. If God created Man with so many needs, then they must be met for full compliance with the Creator's design. Eighteenth-century philosopher Claude Helvetius followed Epicurus, saying that '…pleasure be the only object of Man's pursuit'. (*De l'Esprit*, or Essays on the Mind) Man 'need only imitate nature, in order to inspire a love of Virtue. Pleasure informs us of what she would have done, and pain what she forbids, and Man will readily obey her mandates.' (*De l'Esprit*, or Essays on the Mind) He concluded that we need a third thing to guide ourselves – the love of oneself, which is the primary impulse of all humans and engenders the pursuit of happiness.

This is stated so beautifully that there's a wish to shut all books on theology and ethics. We could not live according to Helvetius. Western civilisation continued on a different route taken more than 2,000 years ago. But before I pass to the story of this ascetic adventure, I would like to talk briefly about the secular asceticism which is still largely inspired by the ideas of Antique asceticism.

■ I Am My own God ■

Secular asceticism is primarily a lust for better life, here and now. It aims to help Man enjoy every moment of life and to become successful in it. In order to achieve this, Man should know himself; he should develop his personality and find his place in this world.

Secular asceticism assumes a balanced, informed practice, the rejection of excess, which can destroy your health and distract you from achieving your goals, and rejecting this also offers help in achieving an intellectual clarity of thought, as well as inner peace, which results in satisfaction and a high social status.

Secular asceticism does not have as its goal the subordination of the body to the spiritual; it never separates body and spirit and considers the person as an indivisible whole. Secular asceticism is about exercising self-control and willpower, freeing oneself from the influence of short-term emotions and moods and casting off the fleeting, useless, and empty. And sometimes it is about punishing oneself for one's failure to become better at enduring suffering. Our vitality helps us overcome the fear of losing what can be irretrievably lost (health, money, comfortable living conditions, a sense of gratification, and especially what will be lost by all – our very lives).

Secular asceticism is the natural thirst for perfection. In this context ambition and even vanity in reasonable quantities are positive characteristics.

It should be noted that contemporary secular asceticism is not the voluntary renunciation of desires and pleasures without a counterpart. To let one's quality of life deteriorate without any counterpart would be stupid. Any reasonable rejection of a pleasure involves trying to get something more important and valuable.

In practice this means full concentration of efforts on establishing the values of civilisation at the social level, that is, achieving outstanding results in politics, science, culture, and sport, as well as the personal: one's own intellectual improvement, a healthy lifestyle, and the well-being of one's family and children.

Such asceticism always surrounds us, and forms of secular asceticism are very varied.

Politicians refuse a normal human life: free movement, communication with people they choose to communicate with, and a full family, all to the benefit of their burning desire to become the leaders of their peoples.

Athletes are the real ascetics who, striving to reach Olympic heights and achieve records, limit 'bad' food and wine, go through hours of training from the age of five, and lose their normal childhood pleasures – entertainment, fun, romance of youth.

Musicians, actors, artists, and writers strive to clear their brains and stimulate the creative process with privacy. This is well illustrated even by my example: to write this book I had to combat laziness, give up most entertainment, reading for fun, and travelling around the world for many years.

For those who have no talent for politics, no prominent traits for achievements in sport, and no obvious creative abilities, austerity is also useful.

It is useful to eat small amounts of tasteless food if you do not have a very active life. Then you will remain an XL, and not an XXXL by the age of forty. This savage habit will allow you to fit in one aeroplane seat and protect your arteries from cholesterol.

It is also better not to stay seated with a book in front of the fireplace for too long, or to surf too much on the internet, or to watch TV or drink beers with your colleagues. It is better to go for a walk every day and in any weather for at least five kilometres. And all this so you have the opportunity to be healthy and meet not only your great-grandchildren and great-great-children.

I even have some ideas about feminine asceticism. Women's lot is much harder than men's in pretty much everything and asceticism is no exception. The female body is destined to fade faster than a male one. If a woman wants to preserve it without hiding behind make-up, stylish clothes and expensive jewellery, she should expose herself to an extremely strict diet and intensive physical exercise.

Secular asceticism can be considered instrumental asceticism since it is not the ultimate goal in itself, but simply a tool to accomplish goals.

And another important point: secular ascetics are busy with themselves. In propounding values they want to become immortal through the legacy they will leave behind. This is a very old idea: Man becomes God, if he is able to create a world in his own image. I would like to continue with the transformations that asceticism has known in monotheistic religions. Let's start with the religion where asceticism occupies the biggest place, namely Christianity. In comparison to other religions, asceticism in Christianity is much more important: universal and even compulsory, with man acknowledged as defective and sinful.

■ Gravedigger of the Ancient Asceticism ■

Christian asceticism has the most direct relationship with us, i.e. those living in countries in which Christian culture played a huge role in the development of our civilisation.

The condemnation of pleasure in monotheistic religions goes back to the Old Testament, the Book of Genesis. According to it, Adam and Eve were expelled from paradise by an angry God for the 'terrible original sin' – the tasting of the fruit from the Tree of Knowledge without permission. They were the first to discover they had bodies and that these bodies could deliver them a lot of pleasure. The jealousy and wrath of God was fully justified: before the Fall He naively believed that the only true pleasure was the pleasure of seeing Him and talking to Him.

The belief in this small and seemingly harmless fairy tale was a death sentence for pleasure. This fairy tale formed the basis of the religious doctrine and was the main reason for the rejection of human nature and the world. The idea behind this rejection was to overcome all bodily ambitions, especially lust, the worst enemy of God. All types of pleasures came under attack, even those that were associated with meeting the most basic needs of the body: gluttony, exercise, even rest (those expelled from paradise do not deserve relaxation). Well, at least drinking and urinating weren't banned.

Christianity, though it originated in the bosom of Judaism, was formed within the Roman Empire in the beginning of the first century amidst the centre of ancient culture. So by and large it only had the right to claim the status of an heir to ancient civilisation. However, Christian asceticism cannot be considered the successor to Greek asceticism. The principle of the 'Golden Mean' – moderation in pleasure and passion with the potential for even greater pleasure – was transformed by Christianity into a principle of decisive and uncompromising struggle against human nature and its natural sensual desires. Moreover, Christian asceticism is essentially the upside-down version of the Greek one. Despite fierce criticism of the heritage of the 'godless' pagans for centuries (just take a look at Arnobius), the credibility of ancient culture remained very high. Just discarding it completely was unthinkable, even impossible: here and there you could see abandoned amphitheatres, statues, beautiful buildings (although often without roofs), the medicine was in Latin, and astronomy in Greek. For the simple and uneducated Christians there was a need to find clear and understandable explanations originating in Ancient culture, namely Ancient philosophy.

So Christianity returned to the favourite concept of Ancient Greek philosophers – human virtues. Christianity formally retained the four basic Greek virtues: prudence, justice, courage, and chief among them, temperance (asceticism), calling them 'cardinal' virtues, and on this foundation it began to claim the status of successor of great Antiquity.

Christianity immediately said it recognised Greek virtues but considered them too 'natural' and therefore quite 'primitive'. Christianity's interest lies in the search for supernatural virtues, which can only be achieved with the help of Christian asceticism and the Holy Spirit. In this regard, Christianity has created an extra three virtues above (above, not next to) the traditional Greek four – faith, hope, and love.

Faith, hope, and love are not lamentable virtues, provided that their object is Man alone. Alas, these three virtues in Christianity are associated not with Man, but with God: faith was understood as superhuman patience in waiting for the fulfillment of divine promises, hope was founded in the irrational idea of resurrection from the dead and eternal life in heaven, but love had no relationship to human senses, instead it was towards God.

Using this simple technique, Christianity was able to bring about the death of Greek austerity all the while pretending to be its heir. The anthropocentrism of the ancient world was thrown aside with the rest of ancient culture and ethics, based on a rational faith in Man, and turned into religious ethics based on an irrational faith in God.

The new mutated austerity and the corresponding new lifestyle has led our civilisation to disastrous consequences. Besides the everyday concerns of human life, it was invaded by such anti-human concepts as 'original sin', 'the kingdom of heaven', 'divine grace', and 'living communion with God'. Normal life lost all dignity and was replaced with ascetic 'feats' such as the tireless reading of the Scriptures and choosing poverty with the goal of deliverance from the powers of the material world. Chastity replaced the joy of carnal love. The knowledge of God replaced poems, plays, and exploits of heroes. Obedience to God stood in place of a healthy ego and self-development. The search for suffering in imitation of the Saviour and humility before him had replaced the search for good health and joys of life. Faith in God devoured all that was truly human.

It doesn't take much to prove that such a rebirth of austerity would horrify any educated ancient man. The ancient man would surely think that in Christianity the ideal was not penance, but folly, because at its core is the desire for the impossible and unrealisable.

■ Birth of Christian Asceticism ■

The starting point of the whole concept of Christian virtue is the words of Jesus Christ: 'Be perfect, therefore, as your heavenly Father is perfect.' (Matthew 5:48)

The only source of such perfection is love for God, the manifestation of which must be humiliation and a full rejection of oneself, and he who doesn't want that is unworthy of Him: 'People who think they are better than others will be made humble. But people who humble themselves will be made great.' (Matthew 23:10-11)

Christ not only requires obedience to the Commandments and the Law – other prophets before him did too – but also constantly encourages his followers to show signs of personal attachment to him, by imitation of his life: 'Those who will not accept the cross that is given to them when they follow me are not worthy of me.' (Matthew 10:38)

The main topics of this simulation are distance from the world, mortification of the senses, and the rupture of family ties. A complete rejection of the most precious things in this earthly life: 'My kingdom does not belong to this world.' (John 18:36)

Even if monotheistic religions are known to be jealous, the following statement is pretty astonishing: 'If you come to me but will not leave your family, you cannot be my follower. You must love me more than your father, mother, wife, children, brothers, and sisters – even more than your own life!' (Luke 14:26)

To demonstrate what it means to abandon 'his own life', Christ, before the start of his pastoral activities, followed in the example of Moses and spent forty days in the desert (according to Luke) fasting and experiencing various temptations.

Although he could have skipped fasting: being God he felt no desires of the flesh and fasted only to set a good example to others and their future followers.

Based on the emotional words of Christ, theologians rather quickly created a religious doctrine that has led to an unprecedented flourishing of asceticism. The most important task for every Christian was declared to be the rejection of the surrounding material world, which obscures the true existence of God. From now on human existence made sense only in Christ. One had to transform the nature of one's unworthy human flesh to 'spiritual' flesh, to imitate the image of Christ the Saviour. Violence towards oneself, the voluntary transference of pain and suffering, will necessarily lead to the reward of future spiritual perfection. And one should never forget that personal efforts never suffice: one can become a true ascetic only thanks to divine grace infused by the holy spirit. Only this can clean, refresh, heal, and transform Man so he can be saved. Without grace, asceticism and all hardship and suffering would be completely useless and futile.

Already the earliest Christians believed that the whole point of earthly life was to prepare for the Second Coming of Christ, which would mean the end of the world and human history, as well as the resurrection of all the righteous for spiritual existence alongside God. For this reason, Christianity considers worldly life as an obstacle to salvation. More than the other monotheistic religions, it devalues the earthly world, which it fears and hates at the same time. This fear and hatred shine through clearly in the writings of all the Fathers of the Church who saw deliverance only in the renunciation of the world, in voluntary trials, hardships, and painful mortification of the flesh, resulting in a constant struggle against carnal temptations and especially against the allure of women, the source of devilish sexuality. In worldly life it is impossible to eliminate concerns over the post-mortem destiny of the soul: the devil's temptation, caused by the animalistic nature of Man, haunts Christians everywhere. John Chrysostom, spoke very clearly in *Homilies on Matthew* about the joys of life.

> Yet for all this some are so cold and senseless, as to be always seeking only the things that are here, and uttering those absurd sayings, 'Let me enjoy all things present for a time, and then I will consider about things out of sight…' Oh excess of folly! Why, wherein do they who talk so differ from goats and swine?

The author's deep confidence in the existence of a sweet afterlife is apparent and this confidence dictates the hatred of life and its blessings. Although it's the second half of the fourth century and the victory of Christianity is only a few decades away – a blink compared to the millennium of developed paganism – all Greek and Roman culture with its reverent attitude to human life has been sentenced to death. Its remains evaporate quickly under the scorching sun of Christian fury, ready to destroy everything.

For a true Christian there is nothing more important than to purify his soul by destroying everything human in himself. As Jean of the Cross, a Christian saint of the sixteenth century wrote in *Ascent of Mount Carmel*: 'It is necessary to stop the enemy [that is temptation] at the gate [of external feelings and desires], so he could not enter inside and destroy the city.'

The principal agreement with the radical idea of austerity was not just something declared in the Church and in the confessional, but something to be proven: only practical penance can 'release the soul from the shackles and tyranny of the body'. Therefore, from the first days of the new religion on the stage of history, the relaxed Ancient world started to be infested with new habits and ascetic practices.

It is practically impossible to study all the aspects and particularities of asceticism in one book. That is the reason why I decided not to prove that asceticism has existed in all forms of Christian religion. I will skip fifteen centuries to look at the sinful passions of two greatest ascetic philosophers of the modern history – Blaise Pascal and Søren Kierkegaard. Nobody has better summed up the essence of Christian asceticism than these two.

Pascal described the disgusting nature of pleasures this way: the human body is temporary, finite, and mortal. A person is not capable of finding the truth. He loves only himself, drowning in unimportance, unaware of his insignificance in the infinite (which is probably good), and he is miserable since his existence is meaningless. One should therefore look for deeper things than pleasure, which will bring him true religious happiness.

According to Pascal, Man should refuse all pleasure. It is sinful because it distracts our attention from the only important thing in life – the preparation for death and the salvation of the soul. He vehemently denounced any attempt 'to turn away from death' – people should not forget that they will face merciless judgement.

All this, I'll admit, is a bit dull, but at least it's sublime. Personally, I have not really noticed that people who love themselves and who know how to get satisfaction from every moment of their lives are miserable. In fact, one can consider them as role models of earthly happiness. When Pascal abandoned science and dedicated himself to religion, he became a gloomy hermit, lost his joy for life and constantly suffered. Religion doesn't seem to have brought him any relief. God didn't help him at all. Probably, He didn't like Pascal.

The views of Pascal were also shared by the nineteenth-century Danish philosopher, theologian, and writer Søren Kierkegaard.

The philosopher-preacher aimed to understand the hierarchy of Man's priorities and to determine what was vital: pleasure or eternal life. Kierkegaard called for a return to true Christianity – the Christianity of suffering, sorrow, grief, and despair (he had an interesting opinion about his own religion – pure pleasure to read for an atheist!).

According to Kierkegaard, the desire for pleasure is impossible to satisfy, and distracts you from understanding yourself and finding the meaning of life. Sooner or later, Man plunges into despair, even if he refuses the fruitless passions and pleasures and aspires to find stability in the strict laws built on absolute ethics and reason. For example, a person can seek love in the marriage hoping that being a good spouse and imposing voluntary restrictions on himself will bring value and meaning to his life. But this path also leads to despair. The man can refuse not only enjoyment, but also ethics, and begin to follow only what 'God tells him', even if it brings suffering. Why? Because religion allows him to discover the 'divine' through 'fear' and 'trembling'.

I have three comments. Firstly, I did not notice that Kierkegaard had any notion of human happiness in his philosophy. Secondly, I can't not mention the amazing frankness of Kierkegaard about the prospects of a respectable family life. Thirdly, I feel the emptiness and sadness from the loss of the enjoyment, but do not see the benefits that religion can bring through 'fear' and 'trembling'.

It is also very unfortunate that neither Pascal nor Kierkegaard did not say anything specific about the enjoyment that will be waiting for the righteous in the eternal life. Will they be rewarded by the beauty of virgins and passionate pleasures of the flesh?

I have finished with the principles and now I am ready to turn to the most interesting and entertaining part, namely the practical implementation of Christian asceticism.

■ Retreat from the World and Mortification of Flesh ■

The only way for an ascetic to cease any contact with sin is separation from the world. Initially ascetic practice was used by marginal 'heretical' sects such as the Gnostics and Manichaeans, who were afraid of 'becoming dirty from the sinful material world'. Then, in early Christianity, disorganised Munis or, as they are commonly called, Desert Fathers, started to appear.

The phenomena that pagan civilisation considered sure signs of mental illness began to be perceived as the ultimate religious service. Almost all the saints of the early Christian Church were ascetics.

For these people the primitive life on earth seemed utterly useless. They said their mortal bodies were the locks of the spirit and they subjected their bodies to severe austerities not because they didn't like their bodies, but because they wanted to give these bodies to heaven and to glory.

Saint Paul promised eternal life to those who mortified their flesh: 'Therefore, brethren, we are debtors, not to the flesh to live according to the flesh; for if ye live according to the flesh ye shall die, but if ye through the Spirit do mortify the deeds of the body ye shall live.' (Romans 8:7-13) He gives a good piece of advice to his flock: 'Mortify therefore your members which are upon the earth.' (Colossians 3:5)

Mortification of the flesh consisted in sexual abstinence, seclusion from the world for secret fervent prayers to God, subjecting oneself to unbearable heat and cold, night vigil (battling sleep), strict fasting, solitude, and silence. If someone talks to God, they are not supposed to talk to human creatures. But the most important part was the suppression of sensual desires and a struggle against temptation and demonic forces. Demons were everywhere, so much more than mosquitoes.

Hatred towards purely human passions and joy was so great that it extended even to the service of God. The senses, even towards Him, were pleasures that could destroy the believer:

> The beginning of true life in Man is fear of God. And he abhors being in someone's soul along with the soaring of the mind [passions] … He who grieves [Christ] and gives freedom to their feelings, he is like the sick man who suffers bodily, while the mouth is open for harmful eatables. (Isaac the Syrian)

There were extraordinary talents among those who retreated from the world: ascetics St Anthony and Paul of Thebes lived in the desert alone from 70 to 90 years respectively, and Dorotheus of Gaza practised austerities of the desert for 60 years: he barely slept and only ate once a day some bread with wild herbs. Dorotheus lovingly spoke of his body: 'It's killing me, I will kill it.'

From the second half of the first millennium, the ascetic ideal captivated the vast Christian world. In place of the collapsed Roman Empire the Ascetic Empire arose and flourished. The Fathers of the Church did everything possible to deliver the faithful from addiction to earthly pleasures and joys, like the washing of the dirty flesh, delicious food, decorations, spectacles, laughter and, of course, the chief pleasure of the flesh – sex. It was assumed that devoid of all pleasures Man forgets earthly life and turns to God, happy to rush to the Church. Soon, the common people saw the extreme uncleanliness and irrational behaviour that is similar to dementia as the supernatural manifestations of divine presence.

The horrible filth and even putrefaction of a human's body became a symbol of sanctity and an object of veneration for thousands of people.

The Stylites were hermits who lived on the flat tops of towers and columns for years; they were very proud of themselves. The founder of the new, extreme form of ascetic pillar-dwelling, Simeon Stylites, stayed without dismounting for 37 years on top of the column and had set the example for numerous others. His contemporary, Jacob of Serug, considered the gangrenous foot of Simeon as an object of divine spiritual beauty and especially admired the superhuman vitality of the Saint who was observing the destruction of his own sinful flesh with joy. Simeon's disciple, Antonius, wrote in *The Life of Saint Simeon Stylites*:

> His body became infected because of the weight and roughness of the rope, which was cutting him to the bone. It buried itself into his flesh, as soon became apparent. For one day the brothers went out and caught him giving his food to the poor. They came back in and told the abbot. "Where ever did you get this person from?" they asked him. "We can't abstain from food as he does. He fasts from one Sunday to the next, and gives his food to the poor, and there is a most horrible stink coming from his body which is more than anyone can bear. Maggots fall off him as he walks along. His bed is full of maggots."

From a religious point of view, this behaviour is not surprising: for monotheism the actual survival of the believer is not very important (everything is in the hands of God). Most important is not physical, but 'spiritual' survival, and dedication of one's life to the service of God. In this way, the issue of spiritual life takes absolute priority over the physical: without the 'survival' of the soul, that is, Salvation, the existence of bodies has no meaning.

I was tempted to join in the admiration for the exploits of the pillar-dwellers, provided I was told how and where these people washed themselves and took care of their natural needs. As a result of their intense spiritual life, were they able to rid themselves of the universal need to shit – this shameful manifestation of human nature?

The Desert Fathers and the Stylites movements did not last long. The fledgling Church could not afford the spontaneity of Christian asceticism, which led to disorganisation and a lack of spiritual control. The gigantic institution of monasticism replaced these phenomena.

Mortification of the flesh flourished in monasteries. The founder of the Jesuit Order, Ignatius Loyola, imposed all sorts of horrors on his poor flesh: wearing a garment of sackcloth over a rough hair-shirt, binding around his loins a girdle composed of prickly nettles, sharp thorns, or points of iron, fasting on bread and water every day, allowing himself no other indulgence than a dish of bitter herbs mingled with earth or ashes, cruelly beating his bare breast with a heavy stone, and resting his weary limbs on no better couch than the hard ground with a stone serving him for a pillow.

In the process, he picked up a number of painful diseases, but terrible weakness and constant fever and pain did not make his spirit yield. Admiring followers gave Loyola the title of Saint and if I had it my way, I would give him the title of Mad.

■ Body Care and Sport ■

The ancient world considered self-care and general hygiene a duty, one of the main pleasures. Rome had a number of baths. Despicable pagans not only bathed several times a day, but followed the disgusting custom of anointing the body with perfumes.

The Christian God replacing paganism did not agree with such barbarism and considered baths and pools as hotbeds of pagan debauchery. The 'dirty' trend began among Christians long before the Fall of Rome and the recognition of Christianity as the state religion. Clement of Alexandria (second century) wrote: 'Going to the bath for pleasure is not in the nature of things: shameless pleasure should be completely banished from our mores.' He was echoed by the pupil of Tertullian, Cyprian of Carthage, Bishop and theologian from the third century:

> What however shall be said of those who frequent the public baths, who to prying eyes expose a person dedicated to modesty and chastity. …You reply "that every one should look to the purpose with which he goes thither: that for yourself you merely think of washing and refreshment." Such a reason is no defence, no excuse for light and wanton conduct. A washing like that instead of cleansing does but defile you, instead of purifying does but sully. (On the Dress of Virgins)

Every true Christian is well aware that the sinful flesh deserves no care, contempt even. The sinful body deserved severe punishment and the easiest way was to deprive it of its purity: it is not easy to love a body that is painfully itchy. The rite of baptism immersed the human body in holy water, which was supposed not to be washed off. Besides, why wash in the absence of a normal sex life? There's nobody to smell you, after all. The baths disappeared quickly: water and austerity were never friends. As a result, the culture of public baths in the West was in decline for several centuries until it became a trend once again with the crusaders coming back from the former East Roman Empire.

Constant companions of asceticism were chronic bodily stench and itches. In the worst-case scenario, you could always hide the stench with perfume. This has its own indisputable logic: scabies leads to suffering and, therefore, spiritual purification. Modern man would have a hard time imagining the stink of the 'Holy'. Dirt, lice, and fleas became signs of zeal in worship. The ubiquity of fleas and lice in medieval Europe is well known. A widespread phrase in French recently became the title of the book by a very popular linguist: '*mettre la puce à l'oreille de quelqu'un*', which literally translates as 'to put a flea in somebody's ear' (the people from that time were well-acquainted with the feeling of a flea in the ear), and this had a host of meanings: to warn, to summon, to give food for thought, and even to contemplate love for someone.

Some write that the loser Pope Clement VII died from scabies. Dirt led to terrible epidemics like the plague that wiped out a third of the population of medieval Europe, more than any war. The Church, however, declared the plague as punishment for faltering faith in God.

Sport was not spared either. The fate of physical exercise in Christianity was at first better than the fate of baths, which immediately became considered 'frills'. Clement of Alexandria writes in *Christ the Educator* that gymnastic schools, in contrast to baths, were part of a reasonable lifestyle. The gymnasium is sufficient for the needs of young boys, even if there is a bath at hand… It offers considerable benefit to the health of the young, and besides, instils in them a desire and ambition to develop not only a healthy constitution, but also a wholesome character. If physical exercise is engaged in without distracting them from more worthwhile deeds, it is entertaining and not without profit.

It is only strange that he does not care about how the gym sweat is to be washed away. As far as we know, there were no baths and showers in homes. As for 'more worthwhile deeds' – no doubt the saint is referring to prayer.

Sport was glorified and widespread in Antiquity, especially in Greece, but did not last until the Middle Ages. Sport had to step aside. Nothing could distract the believer from praying!

That is why humanity so highly appreciated Baron de Coubertin's idea to restore the Olympic games, which in fact was the restoration of the lost relationship with the ancient way of life.

■ Condemnation of Decorations and Costumes ■

The negative attitude of Christianity towards dresses, jewellery, spectacles, and fun could be explained by the fact that they are temptations of sinful pleasures and distractions from God.

The hierarchs were particularly irritated with bright clothes, especially revealing ones. For centuries Christian preachers literally wore rags. Tertullian believed that women should put aside their festive garments and try to please not men, but God. As for husbands, they will have to make do with what they have, or rather the memories of what happened many years ago. For everyone who disagrees with him, he only has two words: 'You must.'

> …you have to try to be adored by no other besides your husbands; they can like you just as soon as you will cease to care about how to please others. Fear not; a husband can't feel contempt for his wife [sure can!]. He liked her enough when the the body and the soul forced him to select her as his wife.
>
> You will please *them* in proportion as you take no care to please *others*. Be without carefulness, blessed: no wife is *ugly* to her own husband. She *pleased* him enough when she was selected (by him as his wife).
>
> Let none of you think that, if she abstains from the care of her person she will incur the hatred and aversion of husbands. Every husband is the exactor of chastity; but *beauty*, a believing (husband) does not require, because we are not captivated by the same graces which the Gentiles think (to be) graces [either we're all not Christians, or we never were]. [But many wives are "ugly to their husbands and do not please them!" This happens to many men after a couple of years of marriage. "She pleased at some point, but not anymore."]

However, I fully agree with the following statement from Tertullian in his *On the Apparel of Women*, since it sounds very modern:

> I see some (women) turn (the colour of) their hair with saffron. They are ashamed even of their own nation, (ashamed) that their procreation did not assign them to Germany and to Gaul: thus, as it is, they transfer their *hair* there!

In the same book Tertullian also denounces men who want to please and to look younger, who in doing so forget God's will not to:

> If it is true (as it is) that in men, for the sake of women (just as in women for the sake of men), there is implanted, by a defect of nature, the will to please…to cut the beard too sharply; to pluck it out here and there; to shave round about (the mouth); to arrange the hair, and disguise its hoariness by dyes; to remove all the incipient down all over the body; to fix (each particular hair) in its place with (some) womanly pigment… while yet, when (once) the knowledge of God has put an end to all wish to please by means of voluptuous attraction, all these things are rejected as frivolous, as hostile to modesty.

Not far behind Tertullian is Clement of Alexandria, who believed that women should be clothed from head to toe. I suspect this might come from the Islamic custom. He did not understand or acknowledge (or, more likely, feigned the latter) that people really want to like each other:

> Let the woman observe this further practice: except when she is home, she should be completely veiled, for her appearance will be dignified only when she cannot be seen. …No part of the body of the woman should remain unveiled. …But the limit of their wishes should be the wish to be adored only by their husband.

Clement does not specify what women can do to be liked by their husbands besides displaying physical beauty, though he most likely meant devotion to God and the smell of sweat. Apparently, Clement was familiar with the smells of that time and their community. That is why, not commenting on women's hygiene, he gives women good advice: 'Woman should be fragrant with the odour of Christ. Let her be ever anointed with the heavenly oil of chastity, taking her delight in holy myrrh, that is, the Spirit.'

I naively don't want to think that Clement's woman would exude the smell of the unwashed body beyond religion. Clement has, however, many ideas I completely agree with as an ardent defender of natural beauty and wild nature. In *Christ the Educator* he asks:

> Do we need to ask Him about finery and dyed wools and multicolored robes, about exotic ornaments of jewels and artistic handiwork of gold, about wigs and artificial locks of hair and of curls, and about eye-shadowings and hair-plucking and rouges and powders and hair-dyes and all the other disreputable trades that practise these deceptions?

> …Again, it is absolutely forbidden them to add artificial hair, for it is unholy for them to add someone else's hair to their own, putting dead locks in with their own.

> …But to wear indoors "a garland gathered from the meadow in full-bloom" is not done by men of good sense. It is not right to appropriate to oneself the first green shoots of spring, and to encircle the head at banquets with rosebuds or violets or lilies or any other similar flower.

Saint Catherine of Sienna, fresco, c. 1462.   *Botticelli, Venus, detail from the Birth of Venus, 1485.*

■ Hatred for Feasts, Fun, and Laughter ■

The collapse of paganism marked the end of fun and the advent of sorrow and crying.

Instead of searching for joy, Christianity offered the spiritual search for 'the meaning of life', which meant looking for sins in oneself and others. Cyprian of Carthage, expressed a wonderful understanding of Antique culture and his admiration for it in *On the Public Shows*:

> Idolatry, as I have already said, is the mother of all the public amusements; and this, in order that faithful Christians may come under its influence, entices them by the delight of the eyes and the ears. …Those Grecian contests, whether in poems, or in instrumental music, or in words, or in personal prowess, have as their guardians various demons.

All kinds of sinful entertainment were condemned, especially theatre. Again, the most precise and vivid description is offered by Tertullian. In his opinion, Christians should abstain from theatre because they mention pagan gods and deny the principles of purity and moderation. According to Tertullian, believers should not watch or listen to things they have no right to practise because 'harmful things infect us with their harm'. He possesses honesty enough to recognise the 'power of pleasure' and the fact that many of his contemporaries shunned Christianity because of the fear of losing all entertainment (in my opinion, it would be wiser to avoid all religion):

> Ye who have testified and confessed that you have done so already, review the subject, that there may be no sinning whether through real or wilful ignorance. For such is the power of earthly pleasures, that, to retain the opportunity of still partaking of them, it contrives to prolong swilling ignorance …The views of the heathens who in this matter are wont to press us with arguments, such as these: That the exquisite enjoyments of ear and eye we have in things external are not in the least opposed to religion in the mind and conscience; and that surely no offence is offered to God, in any human enjoyment, by any of our pleasures, which it is not sinful to partake of in its own time and place, with all due honour and reverence secured to Him. …How skilful a pleader seems human wisdom to herself, especially if she has the fear of losing any of her delights!

John Chrysostom talks about entertainment much more harshly and bluntly. He lives in a world of a victorious Christianity, and his confidence is founded in the power of his religion and the power of the Church. The pagan traditions need no reverence anymore. His other statement convinced me that he was rightly known as a wordsmith. He speaks so openly and so well in *Homilies on the Gospel of Matthew* that I almost wanted to return to the fold of Christianity:

> Wherefore they that sit by should not laugh at these things, but weep and groan bitterly. *What then? Are we to shut up the stage?* it will be said, *and are all things to be turned upside down at your word?* Nay, but as it is, all things are turned upside down. For whence are they, tell me, that plot against our marriages? Is it not from this theatre? Whence are they that dig through into chambers? Is it not from that stage? Comes it not of this, when husbands are insupportable to their wives? Of this, when the wives are contemptible to their husbands? Of this, that the more part are adulterers. So that the subverter of all things is he that goes to the theatre; it is he that brings in a grievous tyranny. …And lasciviousness, whence is that, and its innumerable mischiefs? You see, it is thou who art subverting our life, by drawing men to these things, while I am recruiting it by putting them down. *Let us then pull down the stage,* say they. Would that it were possible to pull it down; or rather, if you be willing, as far as regards us, it is pulled down, and dug up.

William Bouguereau, The Youth of Bacchus, 1884.

Jan Styka, Saint Peter preaching the Gospel in the catacombs, 1902.
Two ways of spending your free time. There's really no accounting for taste,
but you can't deny that fresh air is better for your health.

After reading this, I was mentally transported to that time and immediately realised that the theatre and circus came to an end. And that's a pity, these capital spaces would be useful for exercises in scholasticism: debates about the number of devils at the sharp spire of the temple always attracted large crowds of people. Did Chrysostom believe in what he wrote? It's likely that he did. He was completely absorbed, fascinated, under the spell of religion. He was almost a fanatic.

From the Church's point of view, to forbid the feasts was a logical step. The point is simple – the faithful must be protected from any non-religious life. So you needed to forbid people from gathering in any place except the Church. Otherwise it would be difficult to control their thoughts and behaviour.

Laughter (not only during feasts but in daily life, too) became a sin because it was considered a direct product of the Devil. Although Christ cries three times in the New Testament, he never laughs.

The Christians believed that laughter is accompanied by 'vile actions', since it's coming from the base of the abdomen, the part of the body close to the 'dirty' sexual organs. But anyway, what is there to laugh about without tasty food, fancy dresses, fun sports, entertainment, and plenty of sex?

In his Rule, Saint Basil of Caesarea said the following about laughter:

> The Lord, the gospel teaches us, doomed himself to all bodily suffering... however, the gospel stories testify that he never engaged in laughter. On the contrary, he declared miserable those who engaged in laughter.

John Chrysostom echoes him and suggests those who are inclined to laugh without reason to think about their sombre future:

> If you also weep thus, you have become a follower of your Lord. And these things I say, not to suppress all laughter, but to take away dissipation of mind. For wherefore, I pray you, are you luxurious and dissolute, while you are still liable to such heavy charges, and are to stand at a fearful judgment-seat, and to give a strict account of all that has been done here?

Isaac the Syrian uses an interesting and highly cultured turn of phrase, although he's not clear what the low actions are that he's talking about: 'Any low action done with considered thought is not to be avoided. If you are compelled to laugh, do not show your teeth.' The monastic order of the Middle Ages, struggling with laughter, introduced corporal punishment to tackle the problem in *Rule of the Four Father*: 'If someone will be caught laughing or joking, resolve that in the name of the Lord himself he is to be punished with the whip of humility for two weeks.'

■ Condemnation of Gluttony and Praise of Fasting ■

The Christian religion, with its way of aggrandising hardships, could not ignore food. Some early and very influential Christians considered gluttony as an issue no less fundamental than adultery, and condemned it more than lust. This makes a lot of sense

– food as pleasure is much more available than sex. Interestingly, my father, a great lover of women, was fond of saying that food is the greater pleasure because of the frequency of its consumption and the unlimited variety of sensations it affords. The most elementary, most pressing human need was opposed to God. In the fundamental Epistle to the Romans, the Apostle Paul writes: 'Destroy not the work of God for the sake of meat. All things indeed are pure, but it is evil for that man to eat what causeth offense.' (Rom. 14:20)

The condemnation of those who 'eat what causeth offense' is quite modern. It could become a credo for all dieticians if it was only about the health and possible reduction of the sexual attraction of the consumer due to a large belly. The problem was not the health or a belly. It is just that all gourmets are simply blasphemers and atheists. Paul is echoed by Clement of Alexandria in *The Teacher*:

> '…we eat only to live. Eating is not our main occupation, nor is pleasure our chief ambition… Surely, excessive variety in food must be avoided… this perversion of taste due to some misguided culinary adventure or foolish experiment in pastry cooking. Men have the nerve to style such self-indulgence nourishment, even though it degenerates into pleasures that only inflict harm.'

Probably Clement was referring to the same sinful desire that overcomes after a delicious evening at a restaurant with a loved one.

In cases of the complete inability to avoid pleasure with food – you never know what the situation is: enemies might make you eat, and it's impossible to disobey your terrifying boss – it's recommended that 'over an abundant table remember the death and suffering of the Saviour'. Very similar to the way Judaism calls to think of the Torah during sex.

To curb the food orgies of ancient paganism, religious practice introduced fasting – limits on types and amounts of food consumed. In itself, fasting is more positive than negative. The benefits of limited fasting were obvious to mankind long before the advent of monotheism, but it wasn't the kind of fast that was prescribed to patients of Ancient physicians, and not modern fasting either, which means losing ten pounds only to gain twenty in two to three months.

Religious fasting is not intended to improve health; this is a secondary function. Fasting is a form of penance and religious austerity, the purpose of which is to increase the efficiency of prayer and look for greater closeness with Christ the Saviour. It is assumed that the pangs of hunger will force a person to think of the soul, and that they will not allow him to forget the main purpose and meaning of life on earth.

In addition to food restrictions, fasting necessarily includes limitations on activities and communication with the outside world – silence, solitude, and intense prayer. It's a pity that human nature could not devote itself entirely to God and live without food and sex all 365 days of the year.

Children under 14 were exempt from fasting since instilling the sacred importance of the fasts was almost impossible because of their desire to enjoy the blessings of life every day. People over 60 were exempt – why risk the life of a respectable believer?

The ban on food has another meaning, maybe the most important: a hungry man loses sexual desire, which in itself is a lot worse than the desire to fill the stomach. In men, food and sex are intertwined. Saint John of Cronstadt said the following on this issue:

> Our body requires very little to maintain its health and strength, and if you eat food and drink more than what is needed, then nature will increase and excrete as excess through the eruption of seed; from that there will be irritation of the genital organs or the need of nature to satisfy urges, a requirement which you should blame on yourself. Don't drink lots of sweet tea and do not eat a lot of sweets, it also entails the eruption of the seed.

It's possible that St John believed that this eruption was the proverbial original sin. I used to think that the eruption of the seed led to new life, but in fact it led us to the expulsion from paradise and towards death. To be sure, any fast included sexual abstinence.

The weak-willed people who did not want to follow the prohibition of sex during fasts were told that because of the impurity of marital relations on fast days children could be stillborn and wives could die in childbirth. The Christian Church has always been a first-class manipulator and the Holy Fathers were the top PR agents.

John the Forerunner, icon, 16th century.

◾ The Ban on Sinful Thoughts ◾

The believer must give up not only everything that can cause pleasure, but refrain from thinking about it at all, nipping all the desires in the bud. From the point of view of the divine doctrine, such a ban is absolutely logical, for thoughts and fantasies, especially sexual, bring sinful pleasure.

The best illustration of this are the words of Christ: 'You have heard that it was said, "You must not commit adultery. But I tell you that if a man looks at a woman and wants to sin sexually with her, he has already committed that sin with her in his mind.' (Matt. 5:27-28)

This famous statement has received countless number of reactions which are all pretty obvious. Not only adultery is worthy of condemnation, but carnal desire in and of itself, and even the lustful glance. And the thoughts of Man, according to the teachings of Jesus Christ, must be pure *and* free from bodily passions and animal lusts.

Unfortunately, our human weakness makes this prohibition absolutely impossible: even the greatest saints are clearly human. Man, though higher, is still an animal, and has 'animalistic lusts', even in prison (we personally are very proud of our animalistic lusts, and do not advise you to neglect them). But for true believers even life outside of prison is hard and absolutely all of them become sinners, in need of the aid of the Holy Church.

◾ Condemnation of Wealth and Praise of Poverty ◾

Studying Christian asceticism, it is impossible not to mention poverty, which, along with suffering and deprivation, is one of the main ideals of Christianity.

The idea that poverty is desirable and even necessary to achieve certain moral, spiritual, and intellectual goals appeared much earlier than Christianity itself. For example, it was generally accepted in Buddhism, but applied only to monks.

Only in Christianity, especially in the early years, was poverty elevated to an ideal. Otherwise where would the well-known passage from the gospel of Matthew come, where Christ clearly explains that poor people are closer and dearer to him than the rich: 'And again I say unto you, it is easier for a camel to go through the eye of a needle, than for a rich man to enter into the Kingdom of God.' (Matt 19:24)

This idea was further developed in the writings of the disciples of Christ and became less an opinion and more an attack: 'For thou sayest, I am rich, and increased with goods, and have need of nothing, and knowest not how thou art wretched and miserable, and poor, and blind, and naked.' (Revelation 3:17)

The position of Christ is understandable. If a rich man renounces earthly life, he has a lot to lose: money, fame, vanity, pleasure. It is very difficult to forget the earthly and to surrender completely to God.

Wealth is a serious obstacle on the road towards faith in Christ and the spiritual life of Man.

It is possible that Christ bet on the poor because he did not succeed with the rich and became disappointed in them as potential supporters of the new doctrine. The rich did not want to give up their earthly pleasures even in exchange for promises of more powerful celestial pleasures. There are few counterexamples, although the Church has always praised poverty and indulged the distribution of wealth to others.

But the poor, whose lives contained few pleasures, were happy to abandon something they never had. In his position even the faint hope of changing his situation sounds divine: he 'loses' his poverty, his misery and suffering, and gains eternal life. Much later Karl Marx expressed the same idea in the *Communist Manifesto*: 'the Proletarians have nothing to lose but their chains'.

To make poverty a virtue in the minds of believers in Christian mythology you can even find expressions like 'God is the poorest among us': I saw such a tag myself in Brazil, in the historical centre of San Salvador. Betting on the poor was a brilliant PR move: there are always more poor people than there are rich, and they have always shown a high degree of gullibility. The praise of poverty was very reasonable and provided high-speed distribution to religion, akin to a forest fire.

The assumption that poverty carries with it a higher level of morality is in contrast to common sense and the accumulated experience of mankind. On the contrary – poverty clearly distorts the moral character of Man and devalues his life. But nobody has the right to condemn them for it or cast stones: poverty entails years of sacrifice that destroy the human psyche, a lack of education, culture, and free time that could be spent on self-development and the creation of your own values.

Poverty is envy and hatred; it's the propensity for violence and the highest rates of offences against other people: murder, rape, armed robbery. Disrespect for the lives of others is quite natural and understandable: one's own life is not worth anything either. This has been the same in all civilisations, including Rome and Palestine at the time of Jesus. This poverty formed the breeding ground for the spread of Christianity at first, and much later Christianity's blood relative – Marxism and other bloody egalitarian utopian social theories of the twentieth century including fascism.

The praise of poverty has so permeated the entire culture of Christian civilisation that sometimes you could even contemplate a question: if poverty is so good and virtuous, then why do we fight it? Why all these discussions at the UN, the outreach programmes? After all, if we succeed in this struggle then no one will go to heaven! The world will be populated by only the rich and very rich surrounded by large camels, but heaven will remain completely empty.

◼ Asceticism Today ◼

The passion and the excesses of asceticism are not in the distant past, in the glorious times of early and medieval Christianity, those times full of frantic faith in God that looked for the joy of encountering Him and hated His enemies. Asceticism, a little changed, continues its missionary work with the same tenacity and perseverance. Asceticism was, and remains to this day, the basis of religious morality, an attempt to take away one's nature.

Modern religions fervently defend the need for asceticism. Just type 'asceticism' or 'austerity' into Google and you will see thousands of fresh articles on this subject.

Of course, nowadays selling people the idea of global asceticism is becoming harder and harder. For example, modern Christianity has been forced to pipe down on the topics of feelings, privacy, and entertainment. The faithful are offered a 'soft', 'positive' kind of asceticism (does this mean that before it was negative?), intended to 'regulate their instincts and needs', not to torture their body. They say that austerity is not a life in a cave and a state of permanent fasting, but the ability to regulate one's instincts. Isn't this remarkably similar to the Greek desire for moderation? There is a complete sense of a return to the times of Greek civilisation. It is not clear why it was necessary to destroy ancient civilisation so thoroughly and why we have wasted two thousand years and no less than one hundred generations of people.

But even the new softened view of asceticism continues to break lives and steal the fleeting pleasures from a large number of believers. Asceticism is always with us. Penance should last a lifetime, because Man is inherently worthless, his nature damaged by original sin so that he is weak and morally compromised.

The main task of every believer is to struggle against sin which prevents strengthening one's union with God. The struggle against original sin is at the foundation, although in the era of radioisotope analysis, the internet and nano-technology, believing in this fairy tale becomes quite impossible. But people do believe.

Not long ago, I read an interesting blunt statement by Pope John XXIII, which almost mortified my flesh:

> On a spiritual level the gospel and the whole ascetic tradition of the Church demand one follows the practices of mortification and penance, which guarantee the superiority of the spirit over the flesh, and provide effective methods of atonement for sins deserving of punishment, from which no one is free, not even Jesus Christ and his immaculate Mother.

I did not know that Jesus and Mary had sinned!

The desire to preserve asceticism in our society leads to absurdity and arrogance. The Congregation for the Institutes of Consecrated Life and Societies of Apostolic Life even says that 'Asceticism, which assumes a limitation on following base impulses and spontaneous primal instincts, is an anthropological need even before it's purely Christian.' In other words, Man naturally and happily engages in a struggle against his animalistic nature in search of 'Christian virtues'. I think that anthropological needs, if they actually exist, are based on genetic programmes. And genetic programmes are in turn based on impulses and instincts, their purpose is survival and reproduction, and they do not care for asceticism or any other religious or secular principles. I absolutely dismiss the connection between the rejection of worldly pleasures and spirituality. To insist on such a connection would mean that all secular spiritual life, which created science, technology, genius literature, and sublime art, is not spiritual and holds no value to a believer and his Church. But the primitive, poorly educated priests, a good portion of whom are infected with manic paedophilia, are spiritual. I wonder how mentally healthy people can listen to this and remain in the bosom of the Church.

But I do not reject all the claims of modern religious asceticism. There are things I like a lot, maybe because they fit in a secular framework and may not be asceticism, but just a part of good manners.

I am talking about the calls not to criticise, not to discuss people behind their backs, not to backbite, not to yell, not to kill, and not to interrupt or convince those who are not willing to listen or accept what is said. It is only strange to hear this from a religion that always criticises atheists and other religions, which constantly argues loudly and strongly from every corner, as well as from the rooftops and towers of any tall building.

■ Do the Act with the Fear of God ■

For centuries the Church argued that every true believer has an 'ascetic instinct', and fulfilling it is only possible within a monastery and nunnery, the best place for Christian life.

By severing all contact with the outside profane world, the monastery became the ideal of privacy and the best place to pacify the unruly flesh, to fast, and to pray incessantly. This struggle led to the removal of many talented people from society and the formation of a new broader social class – ascetic priests and monks who, in the name of faith, refused not only all pleasures, but also refrained from living among normal people.

According to the authoritative opinion of John Climacus, the sixth-century Byzantine theologian and philosopher, avoiding the world is the foundation of a believer's life. How else is it possible to escape from the shameful passions nourished by insidious hormones, the existence of which offends God?

> Equanimity is good, and its mother is the retreat from the world. Those who abandon everything just for the sake of the Lord must not have any connection with the world… Those who abandon everything should not touch anything for the passions desire nothing better than to return…

'Passions desire nothing better than to return' – I fully agree with this phrase. If a man sees a young busty girl, or smells the scent of roast meat, he will not want to continue to live in a stuffy and smelly cell. The charter of the quite moderate Catholic order of Saint Benedict says on this subject:

> The monastery should, as far as possible, be organised in such a way as to produce everything needed, to have water, a mill, a garden, and various crafts so that the monks are not forced to go beyond its walls, which is detrimental to their souls. This suggests that normal human life is incompatible with Christian life and detrimental to the spirituality of the "saintly people".

The monastery should not remain complacent. A monk should be ashamed that he is a man and that for all his desire he could not fully reject the signs of life, showing vile human nature in the form of natural needs. Isaac the Syrian says this on the subject in his Ascetic Discourses: 'With propriety proceed to the fulfilment of necessary needs, with fear before the Angel keeping you and do the act with the fear of God, and force yourself to do so until death, even if it unpleasant to your heart.'

Naturally, an anti-sexual religion that demands absolute purity from its ministers of religion could not put men and women in one place, and therefore built separate monasteries.

'Spiritual' women had more requirements than men: under the influence of religious madness they took a vow of lifelong virginity, even if they lived beyond monasteries among the laity. In exchange for voluntary renunciation of sexual life, for being a wife to a man and a mother to children, they were promised the status of a model of Christian sanctity. The violence against oneself and suppression of the instinct of motherhood became a virtue.

Monastic orders were many and each represented its own vision of the ascetic doctrine. For example, the order of St Benedict and the Franciscans condemned luxury, while the Dominicans protected religion from heretics.

Fully reliable data on the number of monks during the height of Christianity does not exist, but many historians argue that at certain times mendicant monasticism in Europe made up one fifth to one third of the total population.

Christian mythology has retained an incredible number of stories about the contribution of ascetic monks to the development of human civilisation and argued that after the collapse of the Roman Empire the monks taught the barbarians to write, to count, and to build. What they built together in the seven centuries of the Dark Ages remains a mystery to this day. It is more likely that our civilisation was created by human vanity and money.

In addition to the monks serving God through asceticism, isolated from society, there are friars who live among us and spread God in our society with their good example. Friars observe a vow of poverty, abstinence, and obedience, live by charity, and usually travel a lot, imitating the wandering monks of the Middle Ages. I'd like to note that there are not many religious employees nowadays. So we have nothing to fear: we will be able to feed them easily enough.

■ How Buddha Ate Cow Dung ■

Abrahamic religions were not the pioneers of temperance and austerity. It was present in other cultures, not only in Antiquity, but also those in the East. The attitude towards asceticism is particularly interesting in Buddhism, which itself is now a real trend in the West.

The core of the relationship between Buddhism and asceticism can be easily expressed in a few words: Buddhism rejects austerity because it is pointless suffering that does not lead to spiritual growth or enlightenment. Of course, the Buddhist practice includes a lot of restrictions, but it actually calls not for suffering but for the eradication of it:

> There are these two extremes that are not to be indulged in by one who has gone forth. Which two? That which is devoted to sensual pleasure with reference to sensual objects: base, vulgar, common, ignoble, unprofitable; and that which is devoted to self-affliction: painful, ignoble, unprofitable. Avoiding both these extremes, the middle way realised by the Tathagata – producing vision, producing knowledge – leads to calm, to direct knowledge, to self-awakening, to unbinding. (Dhammacakkappavattana Sutta)

The Buddha himself spent several years trying to find spiritual truth in extreme austerity but found nothing in it and was completely disappointed.

But he relates this himself in a stunningly truthful short story. This story was well written, thorough, and precise, but also filled with such emotions and colours that I would put it among the best short works in the history of world literature.

> Sāriputta, I recall having lived a holy life possessing four factors. I have practised asceticism – the extreme of asceticism; I have practised coarseness – the extreme of coarseness; I have practised scrupulousness – the extreme of scrupulousness; I have practised seclusion – the extreme of seclusion.
>
> … I was an eater of greens or millet or wild rice or hide-parings or moss or rice-bran or rice-scum or sesamum flour or grass or cowdung. I lived on forest roots and fruits, I fed on fallen fruits. I clothed myself in hemp, in hemp-mixed cloth, in shrouds, in refuse rags, in tree bark, in antelope hide, in strips of antelope hide, in kusa-grass fabric, in bark fabric, in wood-shavings fabric, in head-hair wool, in animal wool, in owls' wings. I was one who pulled out hair and beard, pursuing the practice of pulling out hair and beard. I was one who stood continuously, rejecting seats. I was one who squatted continuously, devoted to maintaining the squatting position. I was one who used a mattress of spikes; I made a mattress of spikes my bed. I dwelt pursuing the practice of bathing in water three times daily including the evening. Thus in such a variety of ways I dwelt pursuing the practice of tormenting and mortifying the body. Such was my asceticism. Such was my coarseness, Sāriputta, that just as the bole of a tinduka tree, accumulating over the years, cakes and flakes off, so too, dust and dirt, accumulating over the years, caked off my body and flaked off. It never occurred to me: "Oh, let me rub this dust and dirt off with my hand, or let another rub this dust and dirt off with his hand" – it never occurred to me thus. Such was my coarseness… I would go on all fours to the cow-pens when the cattle had gone out and the cowherd had left them, and I would feed on the dung of the young suckling calves. As long as my own excrement and urine lasted, I fed on my own excrement and urine. Such was my great distortion in feeding.
>
> Now I recall having eaten a single rice grain a day. Sāriputta, you may think that the rice grain was bigger at that time, yet you should not regard it so: the rice grain was then at most the same size as now. Through feeding on a single rice grain a day, my body reached a state of extreme emaciation. Because of eating so little…the hair, rotted at its roots, fell from my body as I rubbed. Yet, Sāriputta, by such conduct, by such practice, by such performance of austerities, I did not attain any superhuman states, any distinction in knowledge and vision worthy of the noble ones. Why was that? Because I did not attain that noble wisdom which when attained is noble and emancipating and leads the one who practises in accordance with it to the complete destruction of suffering.

This passage needs a little explanation. Usually people identify themselves with their body and to weaken this attachment Buddhism gives its own assessment of the human body. The body is subject to ageing and death, it is the source of uncleanliness. It is not just the stool that is unclean; the whole human body is unclean: bones, cartilage, muscles, hair, skin, organs of digestion, respiration, circulation, nerves, brain, blood, lymph, semen, saliva, bile, etc. Neither the body nor its components are our original nature and for this reason the attachment to the body is one of the misconceptions of our mind.

This is an interesting move, which looks more sophisticated and efficient at manipulating believers than promising them the afterlife. People can hope and wait for the promised afterlife but remain very attached to their body and its sinful pleasures. In disconnecting the body, Buddhism pushes a person in the direction of ascetic religious and spiritual practices.

The failed austerity of Buddha, in terms of food, clothes, dirt, and stench, is strikingly similar to the circumstances of the life of the great Christian ascetics. It is a pity that they didn't trust us, their descendants, with their invaluable life experience.

It comes as no surprise that the Christian Church is not fond of Buddhism. In reality, it is the right attitude – nobody is fond of their competition. Denouncing your competition is the best way to improve your own position. I found a couple of interesting explanations for the negative attitude of Christianity towards Buddhism on the popular Catholic site, All Monks.

According to it, Buddhism is a criminal doctrine since it doesn't recognise the existence of the One God and denies divine Revelation. In this sense, Buddhism is very close to Paganism.

The essence of this belief is atheism and agnosticism since it completely ignores God, denying dependence on Him, as well as denying the obligation of obedience, gratitude, and love towards Him.

Buddhism obviously exaggerates human capabilities and thereby fights against all kinds of spiritual control. It relies on the false idea of a person's self-sufficiency in the harmonious world and suggests not following God, but reason and experience. Supposedly Man himself is able to give up all his desires voluntarily, while staying completely happy. From the point of view of Christianity, these people lose all motivation to practise virtue, and society drowns in anarchy, disorder, and moral degradation.

Besides that, Buddhism does not recognise the fundamental importance of sin. It calls to avoid sin in everyday life only because it causes negative effects, entirely ignoring the fundamental meaning of sin as the complete opposite of the spiritual and the divine. In secular life Buddhism easily permits the deadly sins of polygamy and divorce.

Especially deplorable is the claim that a person must first obtain empirical knowledge of the world and then decide for himself whether he wants to follow the path of Buddha or not. It is here that false asceticism originates. Such uncontrolled austerity fast becomes fanatical and even insane.

The real, true Christian asceticism is based on the understanding of the essence of Man and his purpose, and recognises his commitment and responsibility to God. He is directed by the light of divine revelation, which reinforces, through divine grace, the will of Man to control his baser passions and resist the Devil's temptations in the world. And, most importantly, true asceticism necessarily requires the repentance of sins and thus gives Man not the gloomy solitude of Buddhism, but a happiness and love for humanity. Such noble asceticism developed the spirit of sacrifice and fabulously enriched the human race. Responding to the point of view as stated above seems gratuitous. The main idea behind this point of view is the doctrine according to which a person who doesn't recognise his sinfulness and doesn't want to spend his life repenting for these sins is not really a human being. I promised myself long ago that I wouldn't comment on such obvious nonsense under any circumstances.

There is only one question which still tortures me. I really want someone to explain to me how exactly Christianity miraculously enriched the human race?

He who accepts the pleasures of this world is deprived
of the pleasures of the world to come, and vice versa.

Avot de-Rabbi Nathan

For some reason it is assumed that there is no austerity in Judaism. This statement is far from reality. Isn't this statement an example of austerity? If we were religious Jews, we would be much offended for our native religion. Judaism was the first true monotheistic religion, remaining so to this day. Within the Jewish religion pleasure is also the enemy of God. Pleasures distract from godly thoughts and from the most important thing in human life – the study of the Torah. It is obvious that a person accustomed to luxury and pleasures won't be able to live without them and will be constantly distracted from godly pursuits. It is not surprising that the repressive character of Judaism towards the body is as bad as the Christian one. Addressing this issue in Judaism completely, coherently, and logically – as was the case with Christianity – is simply impossible. The Jews lost their statehood and were scattered all over the world, exposed to different cultural and religious influences, especially from the mighty Christianity (the situation is unique – the child teaching the parent!). For this and other reasons, Judaism in the era of the Pentateuch (around the seventh century BC) and Judaism in the era of the completion of the Babylonian Talmud (the end of the fifth century) are quite different from each other, not to mention the Judaism of the late Middle Ages. Within Judaism there were different, often opposing, views on austerity.

Starting from the second century BC, sects appeared in Judaism with extremely ascetic orientations (the Essenes, the Nazarites), preaching the renunciation of wine, complete sexual abstinence, and high purity regarding food. The biblical tradition has preserved for us a lot of wonderful ascetic stories. Ezekiel lay on one side for 390 days, eating only bread. Isaiah walked naked for three years. (Isaiah 20:2-3, Ezekiel. 4:5) The prophet Elijah wandered barefoot in a coarse cloak of camel's hair, Jeremiah completely abandoned women, and Jonah waited for God's voice under the scorching sun.

All these stories have only one thing in common: in reality they never happened, but nevertheless each of them gives us a great excuse to drink in honour of their heroes.

Especially notable were the silent Essenes who believed in celibacy more than marriage and stopped sexual relations with their wives after pregnancy; who did not wear any jewellery, and wore their clothes until they were in tatters. We have no information about the smell of their clothes, but I found another curious custom in many sources: at all festive meals and religious holidays the Essenes wore white robes. The doctrine of the Essenes is reminiscent of Christianity: the fine soul of Man is imprisoned in the evil body and after death it goes to heaven (righteous souls rest in the paradise of the blessed fields and the evil and sinful dwell in cold and darkness).

Some say that during the fifteenth and sixteenth centuries the Jews had such rigid ascetic practices as the rituals of mutual castigation, but this remained marginal and did not become an example for most believers. One person was situated on the floor, head to the north, feet to the south – or sometimes vice versa – and the other, while remaining in a standing position, struck the first with 39 blows to the back with a belt made of cow leather. The one receiving the flogging repeated the thirty-eighth verse of Psalm 78 three times. At the end of this operation, 'the surgeon' is converted in turn into the patient. Jews were lucky that this practice stayed marginal and didn't become a model of behaviour for the rest of believers.

Asceticism was extremely important for the survival of Judaism as a religion. One should not forget that Judaism developed during the fight against the 'corrupting' influence of Hellenism, particularly devastating for Jewish youth. It is the history of a polemic battle against Greek philosophy and its inherent secular lifestyle. Now it seems all this is not of great importance, but then it was vital to the worldview of the Jews, the existence of the religion and its state.

To illustrate the controversy between the Jewish and the ancient world, I have for you an excerpt from the Book of Wisdom. It begins with a lengthy exposition of the ancient views on life from a man mourning his own mortality and desperately wanting to live here and now, and ends with the Jewish comment on it:

> The time of our life is short and tedious, and in the end of a man there is no remedy, and no man hath been known to have returned from hell: For we are born of nothing, and after this we shall be as if we had not been: for the breath in our nostrils is smoke: and speech a spark to move our heart. Which being put out, our body shall be ashes, and our spirit shall be poured abroad as soft air, and our life shall pass away as the trace of a cloud, and shall be dispersed as a mist, which is driven away by the beams of the sun, and overpowered with the heat thereof:
>
> And our name in time shall be forgotten, and no man shall have any remembrance of our works. For our time is as the passing of a shadow, and there is no going back of our end: for it is fast sealed, and no man returneth. Come therefore, and let us enjoy the good things that are present, and let us speedily use the creatures as in youth. Let us fill ourselves with costly wine, and ointments: and let not the flower of the time pass by us. Let us crown ourselves with roses, before they be withered: let no meadow escape our riot. Let none of us go without his part in luxury: let us everywhere leave tokens of joy: for this is our portion, and this our lot. (Book of Wisdom of Solomon 2: 1-6)

A very strong poetic text! I especially liked the expression 'use the creatures as in youth'. The position of Orthodox Judaism is quite predictable. It is always the same for all monotheistic religions: primitive and categorical. Why join in the discussion and strain with mental activity if it is said once and for all? For they have said, reasoning with themselves… they knew not the secrets of God, nor hoped for the wages of justice, nor esteemed the honour of holy souls. For God created Man incorruptible, and to the image of his own likeness he made him. (Book of Wisdom of Solomon 2: 1-10, 22-23)

If you do not recognise the immortal existence of the soul, the Holiness of the righteous, and the rewards awaiting one in the afterlife, all religious doctrine instantly loses all meaning. And then the whole pyramid of Jewish life loses meaning and sustainability.

The Torah must be contemplated, with the heart trembling before the Almighty, with minimal daily mercantile business, to combat the redundancy and giggling, meekly accepting all the sufferings that are sent by the Almighty, rejoicing over one's lot. If it is impossible to avoid having fun (e.g. during sex), its origin should be declared as divine and God should be continually thanked for it. In general, the same plaintive song: This is the way [of understanding] the Torah: bread with salt you eat, and [even] water to drink in moderation, and sleep on the bare ground, and let your life be hard, but work on the study of the Torah. And if you do that, 'happy are you and good is bestowed upon you': you are happy in this world and good is bestowed in the world to come. (Midrash Shmuel)

And citing Mishna:

Our Rabbis have taught: 'A man is forbidden to enjoy anything of this world without a benediction, and whoever does so commits sacrilege. Whoever enjoys anything of this world without a benediction is as though he had partaken of the holy things of Heaven; as it is said, "The earth is the Lord's, and the fulness thereof."' (Talmud, Berachot 35A)

Rabbi Shlomo Ganzfried writes in his famour *Kitzur Schulchan Aroukh*:

This means that even in the paths you follow for the sake of your physical needs, you must know G-d and carry out these functions for His name's sake, blessed be He. For example: eating, drinking, walking, sitting, laying, getting up, sexual relations, conversation – all the needs of your body – should all be (for) your service of your Creator, or as something which leads to His service.

One shouldn't get satisfaction even from sleeping:

It is not necessary to say when one has the opportunity to study Torah and observe mitzvot, although one is tempted to go to sleep for one's own pleasure, that it is not fitting to do this. Rather, even when one is tired and must sleep to rest from one's weariness, if it was for physical enjoyment, this is not praiseworthy. Rather one should intend to give sleep to one's eyes and to one's body rest for the sake of one's health, so that one will not become confused during Torah study due to lack of sleep.

Judaism did not forget spectacles, fun, and dance. There is a Talmudic ruling (Gittin, 7a: the Gemara) that after the destruction of the Temple it is forbidden to listen to any music except that which is necessary for the proper performance of the commandments (such as the music that accompanies the prayers during weddings and other festivals). For Maimonides, a 'woman's voice is a shame' and he never really hides his 'love' for music. It reminds me of the negative attitude towards music and dance in the countries professing a Wahhabi form of Islam, for example, in Afghanistan, Sudan, Somalia or ISIS.

Also well-known is the position of Judaism towards food. Believers should observe kashrut. Regarding kosher, everything is pretty clear and there is no need to spend time searching for deep mystical explanations in the holy books.

Firstly, following the imposed restrictions, people do not focus on the food, and instead on God, 'lifting up simple consumption to the high plane of ethics and spirituality'.

Therefore, simply eating food in order to live, typical among the primitive Roman and Greek Gentiles, becomes a sacred religious act for the believer.

Secondly, non-kosher food (for instance seafood) is forbidden because it 'provokes' unwanted sexuality, distracting Man from learning the Torah. God probably does not need such a boost, but some young men would be happy to have it.

Maimonides talks about this in *The Guide for the Perplexed*:

> The thirteenth class includes the precepts concerning forbidden food and the like; we have given them in Hilkot maakalot asurot; the laws about vows and temperance belong also to this class. The object of all these laws is to restrain the growth of desire, the indulgence in seeking that which is pleasant, and the disposition to consider the appetite for eating and drinking as the end [of Man's existence].

This opinion of the highest Jewish authority made me very happy. I am not Jewish but saw the prohibition on eating pork as something positive. Pork, although tasty, is a meat that's difficult for the body. My position on seafood is quite different. I always felt sorry for those friends and acquaintances I saw looking in the direction of fresh oysters, risotto with seafood, and lobster on the grill, who repeated that they'd never tried it and didn't want to.

Of course, nobody believed them, but nor did they want to inadvertently hurt the religious feelings of these good people for whom the short-term pleasure of a measly shrimp would permanently close the road to eternal spiritual truth.

Now when it has become clear what the real reason for this ban was, I can lightheartedly persuade my companions to break this rule for the greater sexual happiness of their wives and mistresses.

One thing is good: the attitude to (kosher) wine in Judaism is generally positive because, as Shlomo Ganzfried brilliantly points out in Kitsour Schoulhane Aroukh, 'Wine strengthens the natural body heat, improves the digestive process, helps evacuate waste products, and helps the body health.'

But his doesn't apply to young and strong men because for them it is 'adding fire to fire' to cause sexual desire and distract them from religion.

In Orthodox Judaism there is another point of view. For the sake of spiritual perfection, Man does not have to give up the joys of everyday life. Ascetic self-restraint is as undesirable as satisfying all our desires. The desire to deprive a man of all pleasures is a mistaken one, for it leads to the violation of his physical and spiritual health. Austerity and asceticism are opposed to the desire of God to give people the opportunity to enjoy their earthly life. In Judaism there is not as much repression of the body as there is in Christianity. And Judaism does not have monks. A person is prohibited from imposing additional restrictions, except those already in the Torah (there are more than enough of them!). It is said in the Jerusalem Talmud, Tractate Kiddushin (4:12, 66d): 'You will one day give reckoning for everything your eyes saw which, although permissible, you did not enjoy.' Naturally, all these concessions are given only for the sake of a more successful repetition of the divine law.

Ultra-orthodox Jews during the Mayim Shelanu ceremony.
It's a shame that religion is not compatible with a sane lifestyle.

Maimonides, too, supported this view:

> Therefore, our Sages directed man to abstain only from those things which the Torah denies him and not to forbid himself permitted things by vows and oaths [of abstention]. Thus, our Sages stated: Are not those things which the Torah has prohibited sufficient for you that you must forbid additional things to yourself? (Mishneh Torah, Sefer Madda, De'ot, 3)

This softness from the harsh Maimonides can be explained in two ways. Maybe the Torah already forbade almost everything and in the future the universal spread of asceticism would endanger the existence of Jews on earth. Perhaps the great thinker was outraged that a person who received the freedom of choice between 'permissible' and 'prohibited' would become filled with the sin of pride. Man has no right to choose his lifestyle and his way of serving God.

The attitude of Judaism towards women's beauty, dresses, and jewellery is far more liberal than in Christianity, although there is no real glorification of the human body and its beauty. The most important role of beauty lies in the proper fulfillment of the commandments (Mitzvot) concerning the relationship between Man and God. Sages recommended that unmarried girls take care of their appearance since beauty has a great importance in the early stages of dating, when marrying, and when maintaining the marriage.

After the Jews returned from Babylonian captivity in 582 BC the law obliged dealers to deliver cosmetics to all the little villages to help the local women preserve their attractiveness in the eyes of their husbands. If a woman took a vow not to wear bright and beautiful clothes – her experience should be promoted, it is very helpful for the family budget! – her husband could cancel his vow lest she inspire him with disgust from her wretched appearance. Sages said that one who sees himself created in the image of God will not neglect his appearance. Proverbs are even more severe: 'If the garment of the Torah scholar has a spot, he deserves to die, as it is written: "All who hate Me love death".' (Proverbs, 8:36) It is clear how Judaism (and Islam, too) seeks to regulate all the most basic and natural aspects of human life. I was particularly irritated with the interdiction 'to walk haughtily erect, with neck fully outstretched'. The meaning of the passage above is clear: people should not be proud of themselves, but of their God.

Such an attitude to the body disappointed me – numerous generations of anti-Semites drew images of crooked Jews in black religious robes. I was much more drawn to the young sporty Israelis with heads raised proudly, who can be seen everywhere with surf boards, or playing volleyball, or with a gun on their shoulder.

■ Ascetics in Burkinis ■

In terms of asceticism (among other things), Islam is much closer to Judaism than it is to Christianity. There is no conception of the original sin in Islam and thus there is no need to merit the pardon of Allah. In contrast to a Christian, a Muslim is not torn between body and soul, instinct and mind. According to Islam, the energy of instincts is pure and therefore it is not subject to moral judgements. It allows Man not to neglect his instincts; not to oppress them.

The question of good and evil of instincts becomes important only when it concerns the social order which, according to Islam, has to be regulated by the religious laws. Man has to control his instincts so that they serve not only his egoistic objectives but also some authentic and sacred aims.

I like this methodology, except for one point: I consider as sacred normal profane values and objectives and do not see any need for religious laws.

Nevertheless, asceticism of the Christian type, which singles out a small group of 'especially correct' believers above the overwhelming mass of others, never took off in Islam. Islam does not share the Christian concept of the sinfulness of the flesh and does not require sexual abstinence and celibacy from its priests, although moderation in worldly life is considered a virtue. Islam has no institution of monasticism, which it regards as a purely human innovation, not related to divine law. Christian monasticism is seen as a strange deviation of Man from his own nature.

A Muslim in the modern world can become a monk if he wishes so and may even earn respect from other believers. But it is a different kind of monk. In Islam a monk can marry, lead an active sex life, and own property. The difference from other believers is that he believes the main business of his life is prayer and spreading religious teachings. This kind of a monk is called a 'zuhd'. The zuhds appeared in the tenth to thirteenth centuries. They believed in 'oblivion in the heart of everything except Allah', and their goal is not killing one's own flesh and rejecting the world, but practising elevated piety, shifting one's focus from the human to the divine, and becoming indifferent to material well-being. Here are two vivid and imaginative Islamic quotes. Wahb Ibn al-Ward wrote: 'Zuhd is for the earthly things that are not yours. Zuhd is no sadness about worldly things which were missed, and no happiness for worldly things which are acquired.' And Abu Idris al-Khawlani wrote:

> The renunciation of the world is not through prohibition of what is permitted and not with wasting of one's property. Indeed, renunciation of the world is when you rely more on what is in the hands of Allah than what is in your own hands, and when trouble befalls you rather wish to obtain the reward (in other world) than to bring back what is lost.

Asceticism in the fullest sense of the word existed in Islam only in the early stages of its development, in Sufism, which was influenced by ascetic Christian doctrines. Sufism is a form of mystical Islam, seeking to incite men towards continuous moral and spiritual improvement, to purify them and their hearts from defilement, encourage the influence of the spiritual world, and thereby weaken that of the physical world.

A successful disciple can become perfect and even mentally 'see' the name of God inscribed in his heart. All this is achieved by reflection on the metaphysical foundations of existence (Sufis such as Hasan Basri even believed that 'an hour of thinking is better than a night of prayer'), by strict adherence to the injunctions and the Sunnah of the Prophet Muhammad, and by fasting.

Christian asceticism and early Sufism do in fact have a striking resemblance: the cult of poverty and material deprivation, the feeling of nature corrupted by sin, the expectation of the end of the world, susceptibility to suffering and sexual abstinence, celibacy and complete renunciation of the world, long hours in vigils and additional prayers and fasts.

Sufi was the faithful follower of the Prophet, Amir Ibn Abdullah at-Tamimi, who was indifferent to worldly goods and preferred celibacy, prayed standing up at night, and suffered from pain caused by swollen knees. The only thing he was sorry about was that Allah did not give him the ability not to sleep so that he could worship Him day and night.

Classic Sunni Islam has always accused the Sufis of excessive tolerance and love of peace, worship not only of God, but also of Holy Men, pagan superstitions, magical rites and, most importantly, the lack of observance of the divine law – sharia. In recent years, Sufi shrines and mosques have been destroyed and hundreds of Sufis have been killed in Pakistan, Somalia, and Mali.

However, Islam is strict and certain life restrictions apply to every believer without exception. It commends moderation in all things and requires prayer five times a day; there's an annual month-long fast during daylight hours (Ramadan); special clothing for women which covers the body and hair. On the Tel Aviv beach, close to Jaffa, we saw Arab women bathing in the sea covered from head to toe. Female Jews bathe similarly.

I don't think they were particularly comfortable, but everyone is free to do as they want. In 2016, this clothing (which has a special name – burkini) provoked a real scandal in France where they tried to forbid it.

Islam also prohibits certain foods and alcohol: 'Say, "I do not find within that which was revealed to me [anything] forbidden to one who would eat it unless it be a dead animal or blood spilled out of the flesh of swine".' (Quran 6:145)

Muslim propagandists explain that the ban on blood and pork is about health: both quickly breed bacteria and parasites. Alcohol is banned for 'moral' reasons as it leads to loss of self-control, forgetting God, and potential crimes. Also, general moderation in food is commendable for a Muslim. A hadith attributed to Yahya Bin Muaz ar-Razi says: 'The light of wisdom is hunger, while satiety furthers from Allah.'

> The Prophet said: '…And nothing does Allah reward more than hunger and thirst.'

Islam never had an aversion to the body: 'Health is the wealth of the body.' (Abu Darda) The Quran says that the body must be kept clean and contains a lot of regulations about hygiene, although Muslims in poor countries often don't follow them.

There is some ambiguity about laughter. On the one hand, laughter is not forbidden, but in some hadiths, it is stated that it is undesirable, as it kills spirituality and piety. In any case, laughing is not allowed during prayer. But you can cry.

One of the founders of Sufism, Abu Hamid al-Ghazali, writes beautifully about laughter in *Wonder of the Heart*: 'One laughing because of one's youth will cry because of their old age, one laughing because of their wealth will cry because of their poverty, one laughing because of his life will cry over his death.'

I have nothing to add, Islam can be beautiful and poetic, but I still prefer the joyful and carefree laughter of the Ancient Greeks.

■ Monotheism and Asceticism ■

Asceticism is not a universal phenomenon. Even if all ascetic practices are characterised by their desire to control the human body, achieve a higher spiritual state and overcome the fear of death, the asceticism of Antique society and of secular societies are very different from their religious analogue. It is possible to distinguish between those forms of it that are positive and those that are negative.

Positive asceticism is based on love of worldly life. It does not deny the misery and suffering of everyday life (as can be seen in Greek tragedies) but insists that earthly life is beautiful and worthy of admiration.

In positive asceticism, one can eat healthy and delicious food, play football and go out sometimes.

Negative asceticism completely transforms the notion of asceticism. Controlling one's body, achieving a higher spirituality and overcoming the fear of death are no longer means of making life better by being happy, but goals which have nothing to do with common human values. Negative asceticism is not fond of earthly life and does not aspire to make it better. On the contrary, it aspires to make it unbearable since the goal of this asceticism lies beyond our existence, with the chimera and death.

In negative asceticism one does not eat healthy and delicious food, does not play football, does not go out. One prays a lot. Day and night. All types of religious asceticism (i.e. asceticism in Judaism, Islam, Christianity, and even Buddhism) are asceticism of negative kinds. Even though the asceticism differs in every form of monotheism, the main idea is always the same – disdain of the imperfect earthly life and constant praise of the ideal, chimeric life after death.

All monotheistic religions claim that there is an insurmountable opposition between the immortal soul and the mortal body, and yet the fate of the soul depends entirely on the earthly behaviour of the body. The soul is closer to God than the body, and this proximity imposes a responsibility for all actions of the body. It is the soul's destiny to love God, to approach him after death, reunite with him and 'see his face'.

So, if you think that you are one and indivisible then you are greatly mistaken. In a perfect world all of us would be issued two passports – one for the soul, a noble heavenly blue, and the second for the body, probably black. After death Man leaves the second one in his grave and takes the first one in order to present it to God and his ministers.

It goes without saying that a person who believes in the celestial world cannot fully respect the earthly one. For all the bodily joy and pleasure that the sensual, earthly world can give us is incomplete, ephemeral, and sinful. Religions encourage people to do everything possible to free themselves from the yoke of bodily needs and release the immortal soul from the sinful body, the 'prison of the soul', and thus achieve the main goal of life – a return to 'spiritual freedom'.

Man alone is incomplete, ephemeral, sinful, and holds no right to love himself nor to autonomy. He does not have the privilege to create his own laws and values, and to live in accordance with them.

For religions all values are enclosed in the divine doctrine. Man should not spend his life seeking pleasures but try to conform to God's laws. Human life itself is worth nothing without God.

But I have good news: Man has one sacred right – the right to obey his God in everything. Who would ask for more?

The reader could ask: What is the criteria for this separation? How can a person understand whether the asceticism before him is positive or negative?

The distinctive trait of positive asceticism is having a limitless respect for a human being, for his desires and needs, his pleasure and suffering. Such a doctrine loves Man and aspires to teach him a reasonable way of life which makes his existence brighter and happier. Positive asceticism does not seek to transfer us from a natural human state towards something different.

Negative asceticism does not trust humanity, and therefore seeks to take the believer away from a normal human existence and subject him to fundamental and irreversible changes through perverted and painful practices. But in the case of religious asceticism we are dealing not just with physical self-mutilation (depriving the body of what it requires), but also spiritual (separation of the imaginary spirit from the body and giving it the other functions that don't exist naturally).

The religious ascetic is unworthy of divine majesty, and to leave this world he must transform into a different higher state; he must be purified, reborn, and become a completely different person; to die like a man of the old earthly world and be reborn in the new heavenly world as a man of God.

Preparation for death during life is the essence of religious austerity, which sees life only as a 'temporary postponement of death'. All an ascetic wants is to become a 'living corpse'. The goal was to 'cleanse' a person, 'regenerate' him, and spiritually transform him into a new 'higher' being, capable of overcoming physical death and achieving immortality while still living. But the 'higher being' has never been created.

To understand the difference between negative and positive asceticism, I propose to return to the pyramid of Maslow. Monotheistic religions claim that everything in Man comes from God, including basic needs, which are secondary and dependent on the 'spiritual' ones. Monotheistic religions do not recognise the fact that human desires are the primary and fundamental motivation of all human action and that without them Man is no longer Man. So they essentially turn the pyramid upside down. The base becomes something that has always been incremental, supportive, but certainly not essential for physical survival, namely the 'spiritual'. They engage in a real war against real basic needs.

I personally prefer to live down on the lower levels of the pyramid of needs and enjoy meat, fish, fruit, wine, sun, sea, and love. Religious ascetics do not live like we do, and not even where we do. They choose as their main place of residence the top of the pyramid. They are moved exclusively by a religious need to adore and worship their God.

Every sensible person understands that this crazy idea does not work and never will. The despicable and sinful body is the reason why an ascetic falls from the spiritual peak into the boiling carnal desires at the foot of the pyramid of needs. As a result, there is nothing truly human anymore in the pyramid of Maslow. It is no surprise that the believer who is deprived of many basic needs and most pleasures becomes a psychopath, who is at dire risk that the upside-down pyramid standing on its tip will sooner or later drop right on his head.

The builders of the tower of Babel did not reach God and neither did religious ascetics. Instead of an 'ascendant' state and the appearance of divine bliss in life, ascetics were rewarded with an endless and painful Sisyphean task – the heavy inefficient labour of tormenting oneself with temptations of the body and a constant sense of dissatisfaction for the sake of the soul. There was a tremendous waste of human effort, passion, and life; the priceless human potential that could and should have been directed at creating something useful for human society was squandered.

Where did this negative attitude towards the most basic of human pleasures come from? Why is God against a delicious lunch at a Michelin-star restaurant, a light detective novel, or passionate sex in the woods?

Why has pleasure become an enemy of God? Is it not possible to combine pleasure and faith in God? Isn't the condemnation of natural pleasures just an unfortunate accident?

No, it is not. The negative attitude of religions to human pleasure is not an accident or a whim. All monotheistic religions, at least to some extent, deny the right of its believers to receive purely human pleasures, and some even see pleasure as its worst enemy.

This attitude to pleasure is quite understandable and justified. It's actually quite straightforward: choose God or the enjoyment of life, there's no middle ground.

Almost all monotheistic gods are very jealous and vindictive. This fact has long been observed and described in detail, but if you have any doubts, reread the main books of the Old Testament.

The jealousy of God fully applies to human pleasure. God recognises no pleasures besides the pleasure of serving Him. Getting pleasure from anything else is an insult to God and undermines His power.

Selfless love for God can only exist through abandoning self-love.

Therefore, it was logical to sacrifice oneself, to proceed to a voluntary renunciation of one's desires and pleasures. Passion for pleasure is incompatible with a passion for prayer and in practice means the denial of the superiority of the divine soul and the divine hierarchy of values over the sinful body.

Pleasure takes Man's precious energy and time, which should be fully devoted to God and His religion. Pleasures are sinful by their nature because they make believers think about something other than God. In fact, pleasures steal Man from God. The main task of asceticism consists precisely in making a believer free for constant prayers and spiritual life.

Asceticism can vanquish the sin. Sin became a convenient tool to manipulate the religious masses. With the hope of 'salvation from sin', a number of new members engaged in the practice of asceticism. Instead of searching for virtue in the development of positive aspects of human personality, once necessary for a full life, Christianity proposed to seek virtue in repenting imaginary sins and 'crimes' against God, as well as in negative sides of the human personality, in the dark corners of the soul, which are always plenty.

In Christianity the universality and inevitability of sin leads to the universality and inevitability of austerity – lifelong efforts to clear and punish yourself in order to destroy sin and to earn God's forgiveness. All people are 'infected' with the original sin, all are imperfect and guilty before God, including the saints. That is the reason why believers must dedicate their lives to their purification and punishment in order to break the spell of the sin and merit the pardon of God.

It is not clear why God created people who are so bad. Being omnipotent, he could have created someone better and less sinful. As compensation for their tremendous sacrifice the ascetics receive deliverance from the fear of death and a more than generous reward. All true believers will be rewarded with the eternal pleasure, with the eternal felicity! But not in this miserable life, only after they die.

Not paying any attention to the lack of evidence about the untold pleasures of heavenly life, religious ascetics continue to believe in this chimera and happily break their human lives in its service. They live in the earthly world not as sensual bodies full of joy, but as shells deprived of life. Visit any temple or in any premises for religious worship and you will observe a great number of such shells – ghosts of former lives and bodies.

I am convinced that eternity cannot be found in the illusory hope of heavenly immortality, but only in our earthly life. Pleasure allows us to touch eternity without waiting for death. Earthly pleasure, though limited in time, continues to live in memories and can reach unprecedented intensity, defying the power of God. In everyday life people perceive themselves as a point in time and space and are always 'sandwiched' between birth and death. Philosophers believe that only two things can break us out of this sad prison – love, both the Platonic-spiritual kind and the sensual-sexual kind; and art – music, poetry, and literature.

Who has not experienced great sex, exciting us so completely that everything else in life loses value? This short moment of eternity resurrects sometimes in our memory and never leaves us until death.

Who has not 'flown' to the edge of the universe during a symphonic concert? The time of sublime pleasure feels like it has a completely different nature and quality compared to ordinary time in everyday life. This is especially so after the concert when you get back home to the smell of urine in the stairwell and old slippers in the hallway.

Apollo Belvedere, statue.

Bartolome Murillo, Christ the Man of Sorrows, 17ᵗʰ century.
Two types of asceticism compared: the first ancient
and the second Christian.

Strong emotions, no matter with what they're associated, help to 'break' time and when the past, present, and future merge at one point in time, all problems and diseases disappear and the only important memories in old age are an old bench, plump salty lips, and an ink spot on a school skirt, the one and only time in eighty years when the soul and body were one and illusory eternity came into being. Intense pleasure washes away the mundane and the sense of linear time. Man acquires superhuman strength, forgetting about God, about his own mortality, and even the feeling (alas, only for a short time) of being God.

Intense pleasure brings eternity, the infinity of freedom, the absolute, a sense of completeness and universality – these are the inherent metaphysical attributes of God, but they are actually 'buried' in our nature, 'buried' so deep that getting to them is not available to everyone. These pleasures are pure in their essence, useless to all but their recipient and only serve themselves. They have no absolute or relative morality, self-interest, or any holy duty or higher purpose. This is why religions hate human pleasure. And they are right to hate it.

Don't they challenge God by opening their own road to eternity without his permission?

Does not the short but very powerful feeling of total freedom make Man god?

I would like to end this chapter by quoting Nietzsche, who believed that the ascetic ideal in religion serves to give some sacred meaning to suffering. Hard to say it any better.

> For an ascetic life is a self-contradiction: here an unparalleled ressentiment rules, that of an unfulfilled instinct and power-will that wants to be master, not over something in life, but over life itself and its deepest, strongest, most profound conditions; here, an attempt is made to use power to block the sources of the power; here, the green eye of spite turns on physiological growth itself, in particular the manifestation of this in beauty and joy; while satisfaction is looked for and found in failure, decay, pain, misfortune, ugliness, voluntary deprivation, destruction of selfhood, self-flagellation and self-sacrifice.

CHAPTER VI

Sex is God's
Greatest Enemy

But I tell you that anyone who looks at a woman lustfully has already committed adultery with her in his heart.
Matthew 5:28

All pleasures are enemies of God by default. It is therefore obvious that the biggest and most popular pleasure – the sexual one – must be God's Enemy Number One. And yet, for a long time I've resisted looking at this.

Maybe it's because sex filled the pages of newspapers, magazines, popular novels, and publications, so that any author avoids discussing sexuality. I remember hiding a copy of *Fifty Shades of Grey* someone gave to me in a cupboard filled with old newspapers. But this topic cannot be avoided here. As fate would have it, it caught up with me in Cambodia where only 2 per cent of the population are representatives of monotheistic religions, and Christians are one fifth of that. About 60,000 among the 16 million in population. That was fate!

▪ An Unexpected Meeting ▪
with a True Christian Missionary

This meeting occurred during a visit to Angkor. Covering an area of 200 square kilometres, with approximatively 50 temples, it's the largest religious site in the history of humanity. It scares me to imagine how much money was spent on it. Every Cambodian could have had a house made from gold!

My friends and I came to Angkor during the low season. The selection of tour guides was limited and we chose a very unusual person. Alexander was ethnically Korean, born in the former Soviet Union. After its collapse he lived in China, South Korea, and Thailand. Due to events I will go into later, he left everything five years before and arrived in Cambodia.

Our tour was more than six hours, during which Alexander described to us not just the history of the construction of Angkor but also many details about his life and the habits of the ancient inhabitants. We started with a gigantic temple complex, Angkor Wat (my girlfriend has kept the memory of this outing as large calluses on her heel). Then we admired Shiva bas-reliefs at the temple of Banteay Srei and grew numb from the supernatural beauty of the ancient sanctuary of Ta Prohm.

Everyone was very tired and wanted to get back to the hotel. However, near the exit from Angkor, we were drawn to another dilapidated temple carefully wrapped in beautiful dark-green moss.

At this moment our story begins. Our guide expressed no desire to accompany us – the 'official' part of the programme was over – and stated that there was no need to examine another 'pile of rocks'. We had to look at the temple on our own and upon returning to the car we felt somewhat awkward, as if we had offended Alexander. Still not sure about what our mistake was, I said that I deeply regretted anything I might have said to offend him. Alexander said that we did not hurt anyone, but the unclean pagan idols disgust his God. He explained that he was a deeply religious Pentecostal Christian living in Cambodia as a missionary. It was not his fault that the Khmers would worship dead stones and don't know the true God. After a few minutes of conversation, he felt our genuine interest in him and completely thawed. Soon, Cambodia, the Khmers and Angkor were forgotten as we spent many hours discussing individual spiritual transformations with the help of the Baptism by the Holy Spirit, his own journey to hell and heaven, and the healing of the terminally ill.

I wanted to know why and how he became a religious person. According to Alexander, he survived clinical death at the age of 40. His breathing had completely stopped, he realised he was dead, his soul left his body, and it rushed into a tunnel at the end of which he saw a ghostly light. During his time in the tunnel he clearly saw episodes from his life. His soul then flew out of the tunnel, flew to the stars, and stood among them, experiencing the presence of a powerful being. Despite the fact that at the time Alexander was not yet a pious man, his essence – his soul – began to offer prayers to God for salvation.

There was no answer, but the miracle happened. Soon his soul flew with the speed of light from the stars back to the ground, which from a tiny speck transformed rapidly into a huge ball with oceans and forests, until it closed in on his lifeless body with a nurse next to it trying desperately to resurect the body to life. The soul entered the body rapidly. And after a long operation there was a full recovery.

Soon after his clinical death, Alexander had a strange dream. He entered the massive Roman Golden Gates. There were beautiful girls, who surrounded him. At this moment, his son-in-law, a professional hunter, threw him a gun. The girls were gone. Then a huge eagle with golden feathers and a medallion on its breast flew over him.

When it sat down in the centre of the gate, he heard the voice of the hunter: 'Sasha, shoot!' Alexander pulled the trigger; a shot rang out. He hit the bull's eye on the medallion. The eagle turned and spoke to him in a human voice: 'Do you want to live in glory and be held in high esteem?' He said 'no' and woke up. In fear he ran into the kitchen where he fell on his knees and began to pray: 'Lord, forgive me, I'm afraid.' And then he again heard the same voice, the voice of the eagle, saying to him: 'Do you want to see the Face of God?' He again replied: 'No, no, I'm afraid!' because he remembered that the beginning of wisdom is the fear of the Lord. Only about a year later was he able to interpret the dream. The eagle was an angel, the medallion on the breast of the eagle the sin of adultery, the girls represented his sinful relations with women. And a miracle happened: faith in Jesus and prayer removed the yoke of his sin and saved him from the horror of adultery.

This dream helped Alexander understand that his clinical death was the result of an immoral lifestyle, especially the random drunk cheating on his third wife whom he loved but to whom he did not make love. Worse yet, after hearing his story about the journey to the stars she demanded he move to another apartment. The woman did not want prayer, but daily sex, and did not want to heed the words of James:

> But each person is tempted when they are dragged away by their own evil desire and enticed. Then, after desire has conceived, it gives birth to sin; and sin, when it is full-grown, gives birth to death. (James 1: 14-15)

Any further dialogue with Alexander was very difficult. I asked him a number of questions, which he could not answer immediately, almost never gave direct answers, and sometimes became angry.

'Alexander, do you have a wife in Cambodia?'

'No.'

'So is your local girlfriend living with you? We've heard many good things about Cambodian women – loyal, caring, and smooth-skinned.'

'I have no girlfriend.'

'For five years?'

'Yes.'

'But if you do not have sex, how do you satisfy your sexual desire?'

'I do not have any sexual desire! In Colossians, Apostle Paul makes it clear that it is necessary to kill the sins of the flesh: fornication, uncleanness, passion, evil desire, covetousness… In accordance with the will of God it is necessary to keep your vessel in sanctification and honour, not in lustful passion like the godless Gentiles!'

'But this cannot be! You are a healthy man, you have genitals, and your organism continuously produces sperm and pumps hormones into the blood, which demand that sperm be poured out in some way. Are you healthy?'

'I am well, and my sexual organs and sperm are all normal. But I have no sexual desire. God helps me not to have it. The Apostle Paul in his epistle to the Corinthians clearly states that the fornicator sins against his own body, while he who copulates with a prostitute becomes of one body with her.'

'And where does the semen go in this case?'

'I do not know where. I have no sexual desire in my body because there is no Christian love towards a woman. I have not yet found the right one. But I have the desire and joy of prayer. Again, to quote Paul. "The body, however, is not meant for sexual immorality but for the Lord, and the Lord for the body.' (1Corinthians 6:13)

'But you want more children?'

'I do! I'll find myself a good woman here, get married to her in church tradition and God will return sexual desire to me. For desire before marriage is from the Devil, and after – from God.'

To my mind, this final affirmation was most interesting. Sexuality happens to be separated from human nature. Apparently, with God's help, sexuality can easily be 'switched off' and just as easily 'turned on'. Like an electric switch.

How did monotheistic religions accomplish the impossible, namely separating a person from one of their main physical functions? I finally understood why Alexander's third wife had left him. It is difficult not to think that he lost his mind. However, I think it's fair to say that it was his religion that made him completely crazy. Though Alexander is a good guy, his fourth wife will have a very hard time.

After this conversation I realised that I could not ignore the topic of sexuality and would have to spend a few months of my life writing this chapter. I shall start with the time when the idea of One God was unknown and sexuality was not a sin that needed to be mortified.

Why did this separation happen? Or rather, why did it not occur in previous monotheistic civilisations, where sexuality was seen as an important and integral part of a person?

■ Sex before God ■

It is difficult to accept the fact that monotheistic religions separate sexuality, a natural manifestation of human nature, from the other human physical needs. This feeling must have been experienced by the great Montaigne who, in the midst of wars of religion, wrote his famous maxim on the subject:

> What has the act of generation, so natural, so necessary, and so just, done to men, to be a thing not to be spoken of without blushing, and to be excluded from all serious and moderate discourse? We boldly pronounce kill, rob, betray, and that we dare only to do betwixt the teeth. Is it to say, the less we expend in words, we may pay so much the more in thinking? For it is certain that the words least in use, most seldom written, and best kept in, are the best and most generally known: no age, no manners, are ignorant of them, no more than the word bread they imprint themselves in every one without being, expressed, without voice, and without figure; and the sex that most practises it is bound to say least of it.

Although the role of instincts in human behaviour is a topic of heated debate, no one dares to deny that sexuality is an integral part of life and a basic human need. I'd add that it is the best part of life: it is impossible to deny the power of sexual desire and the great pleasure that its satisfaction brings. It's absurd to compare humans and animals as essayists like to do. The average person has a lot more sex than animals, primarily for pleasure. The desire to reproduce is only a small part of the desire to have sex.

Love came to Man long before the gods did, not to mention the One God. All ancient societies were characterised by absolute sexual freedom. Sex organs were seen as mysterious mean of human species reproduction and a symbol of the fertility cult. They represented the sacred object. For example, a phallus was represented almost everywhere: on private houses, everyday life objects, and in public places. One can also find the representation of female sex organs in the most ancient artefacts of human culture. Indeed, the polytheistic religious cults did not forbid, but actually encouraged sexual intercourse.

The polytheistic gods craved pleasures and were subject to dreadful passions. They were depicted on the bas-reliefs of ancient houses and temples proudly displaying their hypertrophied phalluses and vaginas. The latter were considered sacred at the dawn of civilisation. And from the point of view of nature these organs are no different from legs or arms.

Some historians believe that 'in the beginning God was a woman'. In the Sumerian, Phoenician, and Armenian civilisations there was the cult of Astarte, or Ishtar, associated with female sexuality, reproduction, and cosmic wisdom. The Sumerian hymns compare the vagina of the goddess to the 'Boat of Heaven' and describe with enthusiasm the 'precious gifts' of her womb. The priestesses of the cult were said to have intercourse with men during specific days. They encouraged orgies, because they believed that this would allow men to 'attain the divine'.

In Ancient Babylon, a father could feel proud if he offered his only daughter to the temple where she'd become a 'god's spouse', or to put it simply, a 'temple harlot'. There was nothing disgraceful about it, and those women even preserved the right to their father's heritage. Herodotus in his *Histories* says the following on this subject:

> Now the most shameful of the customs of the Babylonians is as follows: Every woman of the country must sit down in the precincts of Aphrodite once in her life and have commerce with a man who is a stranger…whatever it is she will not refuse it, for that is not lawful for her, seeing that this coin is made sacred by the act: and she follows the man who has first thrown and does not reject any: and after that she departs to her house, having acquitted herself of her duty to the goddess, nor will you be able thenceforth to give any gift so great as to win her. So then as many as have attained to beauty and stature are speedily released, but those of them who are unshapely remain there much time, not being able to fulfil the law; for some of them remain even as much as three or four years…

This form of worshipping gods may seem quite exotic, but I think the majority of the male population would gladly join such a cult. It is nobler to go to the temple than to prostitutes or a lover while hiding it from your spouse. By the way, the word 'orgy' acquired a negative connotation due to the efforts of monotheistic religions. In the ancient societies, this activity was highly respected. A well-known specialist in ancient civilisations Mircea Eliade writes in *Treatise on the History of Religions*: 'It's the orgy that pushes the sacred energy of life… An orgy in a certain sense turns a person into a kind of seed, because abandoning norms, limitations, and individuality, giving yourself up to spontaneous cosmic powers, a person transforms into seed.'

The same attitude can be found in Ancient Greece, where society did not dictate to its citizens the correct sexual conduct for their private lives. Every adult could decide what to do with his body. The notion of 'morality' didn't apply to sexual life but only to injustice and crime. Sex was considered a biological norm and the most powerful source of pleasure. Romantic love without sex was not for the Greeks. This crazy idea appeared much later. The Greeks thought a sexually satisfied man to be more moral than an ascetic since the former is not envious or irritable.

Starting with Homer, the Hellenic culture is favourable to all aspects of sexuality: to gods' eroticism and their sexual relationship with men and women, to onanism of both genders, group sex, sadomasochistic rituals, female and male homosexuality, zoophilia in all its forms, and the mysterious rites of Dionysus.

The cult of the naked, especially male, body also appeared in Greece. Our flesh is an exterior form of spiritual harmony and the sensual beauty makes our spiritual beauty visible. To cover the genitals in artistic reproductions was something unnatural and would suggest that genitals were shameful. The body, the flesh, needs constant care: for instance, by shaving armpit and pubic hair as many do nowadays (let's not forget that after the defeat of paganism no one shaved anything for many centuries). You do not need to be ashamed of nudity, but rather of a dirty or decrepit body.

In some respect the Ancient Greeks and Romans were even too progressive. For instance, men did not really respect the idea of monogamous loyalty: they needed wives only for reproduction. Conjugal love was usually associated with friendship. However, maybe that's not so bad, since the Greeks greatly appreciated friendship. In their view, love of a man towards a woman was secondary because it was dictated by the nature of Man and for this reason was banal, animalistic, and even unspiritual. Sensual and sublime love cannot be limited by reproduction and it meant relationships outside the family are profound in a different way – with another man's wife, a concubine, or with a male lover. However, it doesn't mean that homosexuality was the dominant form of sexuality or presented a threat to the family. In Ancient Greece no one ever questioned the obligations of a father and a husband.

This idea has a right to exist because it doesn't contradict the formal logic. Moreover, from the point of view of our society, this idea is more than welcome! We should probably even introduce a new term – a 'Greek marriage'. Why not? In the Ancient Roman orgies, homosexuality and zoophilia were tolerated. In the Roman Republic and during the early Empire, the Romans favoured the household, the family and its traditions. As the imperial power increased and the wealth of the nation grew, the austerity of military culture and sexual asceticism gave way to Oriental and Greek influences. Uninhibited sexuality, often quite aggressive due to the violence of gladiator games, became fashionable. However, the term 'sin', let alone a 'sexual sin', was never a part of Roman life. The term 'lust' had only positive meaning. A lot has been written already – read Foucault – about the sexuality in Ancient Greece and Rome. But what about the East?

In China, the cult of the phallus and the elements of sexual orgies can be traced back to the Neolithic age. Both the dominant philosophical systems, Taoism and Confucianism,

Lucas Cranach, The Golden Age, 1530.
Back when Man knew nothing of sexual shame, he led a very pleasant existence.

do not consider sex to be something bad or sinful; they see it as everyone's personal affair. There is only one difference in their approach. Taoism is favourable to sexuality, while Confucianism imposes some restrictions on showing nudity, despises romance, and demands women to be loyal and never jealous. The Confucians believed that the passion in the sexual act was an exchange of energy between a man and a woman. Many manuals on the art of love advise not only to copulate regularly without ejaculating, but to constantly change partners, preferably during the same night. Indeed, copulating with one woman doesn't have any rejuvenating effect. A minimal effect can be attained with ten partners; a positive effect with 12, and 93 partners will grant you immortality. This method was called 'healing one person by another' and was considered the path towards health. Two thousand years later we continue to deny the evidence and to believe in the fairy tale of monogamous loyalty.

In Hinduism, all gods of the pantheon, including the ascetic Shiva, experienced powerful sexual desire before they created the world and men.

Buddhism, ever battling desires, believed that combat with unsatisfied desire means more evil and suffering than if it is satisfied. Some Buddhists said that orgasms were a great help in penetrating the subtle levels of consciousness. It is interesting to mention that homosexuality or adultery were rated only three on a scale of one to ten of the negative attitude towards sexuality. Telling friends about the adultery was rated five. They probably believed that there was nothing to do about adultery. Everyone cheats but telling about it in vain humiliates the Buddhist and therefore must be condemned. Nine and ten were reserved for seducing nuns and monks, and copulation with Buddhist saints.

Japanese culture has never mixed sex and sin, and has always put sexual satisfaction on a pedestal, believing that it can dramatically improve one's life on earth.

All this does not mean that the pre-monotheistic communities I described did not have certain restrictions on sexual behaviour – they have always existed and will exist everywhere. However, they knew that sexual desire could manifest itself so powerfully that it would distract a person from other goals and objectives. In this regard every culture produced its own methods to curb excess sexuality by redirecting it: working together, hunting, or war. But no one tried to deny people their sexual gratification.

In almost all primitive and developed societies, there is a universal ban on incest. The reason for this ban doesn't lie in some moral norms. The incest simply makes any civilisation impossible. It undermines the social stability of the lineage, tribe, and family.

What conclusion can we make? Simply, that morally healthy societies did not separate sexuality from other physiological needs and make it taboo. Sexuality is a basic biological human need and so can't be considered under moral categories; can't be described as being good or evil; is not to be judged by people or gods. For this reason, battling sexuality with moral preaching is as useless as fighting the urge to eat, drink, urinate, and defecate. Such prohibitions can only create perverts and mentally challenged people.

To be sure and confident in my conclusions, I studied the main sources on ancient religions and the most important law codes of the last millennia: the Code of Ur-Nammu, the Laws of Lipit-Ishtar, the Laws of Eschnunna, and the Code of Hammurabi. I also studied the Laws of Manu.

I found many things in those laws: protection of royal properties, real estate transactions, detailed trade rules, family law and heritage. Everything was as regulated as it is nowadays: monogamy in marriage and rules of divorce, punishment for adultery (death penalty for both criminals) or for raping another person's wife (death penalty for the criminal), incestuous relationship between a father and a daughter (nothing too severe, a father was excluded from the community and a daughter was not persecuted). Ancient Indians (Manu) seem to be the most violent: a wife who committed adultery shall be devoured by dogs; second marriages were strongly prohibited; and even small offences like seducing a guru's wife were to be punished by death or castration. On the other hand, polygamy was tolerated. I didn't find any restrictions in the domain of licit sex. Once again, the Laws of Manu happen to be the most severe: they punish a man who copulates with a female animal or has anal sex with another person with a short fast.

At the end of my studies of sexuality in the Ancient world, I started to doubt. Indeed, I presented to my readers the version that has been corroborated with historical account of facts, archeological excavations and other profane 'nonsense'.

Where is the faith in all this? Is it possible that the One God does exist and that the passage to the monotheism has been a natural and inevitable step for humanity? Is it possible that His laws, including those concerning sexuality, are the only path to the bright future in paradise? In this case, I accuse Him of oppressing the sexuality of his believers in spite and I simply must present a more positive theory for the believers and for Him. God created Man. There were no millions of years of evolution. The bones of dinosaurs, sabre-toothed tigers, and mammoths we are constantly unearthing were deliberately buried into the earth by the One God to test our faith in Him.

If this is true then things look bad for sexuality, because it is closely connected with the most terrible tragedy of the created mankind – the Fall.

What happened to Man? Human beings led a happy and harmonious life for centuries in pagan civilisations, and then, all of a sudden they were transformed into wretched monsters who constantly needed God's help.

■ Lust's Death Sentence, ■
Or, Where Did the Guilty Serpent Come From?

Before starting a medical treatment, doctors ask about the first signs of illness – indeed, it is necessary to understand what led to a serious illness. I have also tried to find this first sign, an omen of the future oppression of sexuality. How did religions become an instrument of oppression and control of sexuality? How did they manage to successfully manipulate men with interdictions?

How did they manage to convince people that the most natural thing, something from the very depths of the human, something banging like a hammer in the brain, is bad and sinful? How was the need for another's body replaced by prayer?

I believe the fundamental difference between pagan and monotheist civilisations is their attitude towards lust, or luxury.

The term *luxuria* comes from Latin which means the presence of vitality, rapid growth, desire (libido), passion, imagination, abundance, wealth, and luxury. It referred to sexual pleasures, the dearest ones for a human being. Aristotle refers to luxury as 'an impulse to achieve the pleasing things'; Plato sees in it one of the mortal parts of the soul situated in the lower part of the stomach, which creates the appetite and the sexual instinct. However, the notion of luxury is extremely ambivalent. As François Mauriac said beautifully in *God and Mammon*, 'The desire to suffer is also a luxury.' All ancient nations and religions considered luxury and lust to be a sign of a human's health and a virtue: a sign of love for oneself.

Judaism has never had a positive attitude towards luxury, but it was unambiguously condemned by Christianity after the collapse of paganism. It is associated with the Biblical seduction. It is the enemy of mankind, society and God. Luxury – a love for life and sex – is incompatible with the love of the jealous God of Judaism and Christianity. A true believer can have only one strong desire, namely a desire of God and his Church. Any strong desires which are not connected to faith are harmful. It is impossible to love both oneself and the Creator. Luxury ceased to refer to a life full of pleasures and became synonymous with licentiousness, indulgence of a desire that's too strong (especially if sexual), and fornication. The early Christian writer St Jerome replaced the noble *luxuria* with 'extravagance', an extreme folly. But another word stuck in canonical Christianity and in our joint history – 'lust'.

The Old Testament condemns lust in many ways:

It led to the Fall of Adam and Eve. It was the reason for their banishment from paradise. People fall sick and die because of it.

It made the Hebrews adore the Golden Calf and refuse God's nourishment. They did not want to be nourished exclusively by faith in God's promises and were dreaming about some ordinary Egyptian mutton.

The Prophet Daniel says the following: 'O thou seed of Chanaan, and not of Juda, beauty hath deceived thee, and lust hath perverted thy heart.' (13-56)

In the Old Testament, it characterises people who want to possess something and tend to appropriate it by using violence: 'You shall not covet your neighbour's house. You shall not covet your neighbour's wife, or his male or female servant, his ox or donkey, or anything that belongs to your neighbour.' (Ex 20-17)

So that's how the word lust became monstrous and the overwhelming majority of modern people forgot that the horrible word itself is not negative or threatening to human existence. In modern encyclopaedias, the word 'lust' means pretty much the same thing as *luxuria* – a sense of longing, need, desire, and passion for anything: food, power, sex, and even knowledge. It is not incompatible with the meaning the Ancient Romans ascribed to it: the penchant for all pleasures one can have. The love of life. If you feel that you have no more lust, then be assured: you have died, or will die very soon. Now I have looked at lust, and before I turn to the Fall, I would like to tell you the tragic story of one of its main characters – the Serpent.

It is no coincidence that Judaism chose the serpent for the extremely honourable role of tempter of the first people.

– Snakes are some of the oldest symbols of the material culture of humanity. Perhaps it's the most complex, versatile, and powerful symbol. Snakes were connected to almost anything: eternity and cyclical time. The snake curled in a ring and devouring its own tail symbolised *Ouroboros*. Life, death, and immortality. There are reasons for the legends about eternal lives of snakes (they shed their old skin, renew and start a new life). Male and female procreation. Snakes promote breeding because they look similar both to a penis and an umbilical cord. The snakes are often present in the representations of the sex goddesses. For example, one of the main goddesses of the Minoan civilisation is represented bare-chested and holding snakes in her hands. Fertility: the various goddesses of the earth in unconnected ancient cultures are holding snake-phalluses. The snake symbolises sensual temptation, an invitation to an orgy after a difficult harvest.

– Destruction and protection. Snakes are powerful, potentially dangerous, and can breed chaos and death if you inadvertently come into contact with them. But a skilful approach gives strength and health. And for this reason snakes are also the symbol of medicine. Evil. In the Babylonian *Epic of Gilgamesh* the hero travelled a great distance for a plant of eternal youth and found it, but it was immediately stolen by snakes. The snake is a central symbol for paganism and for this reason it had to become the main symbol of pagan evil, illicit sexuality, and the enemy of the One God.

Of course, another pagan symbol of fertility and obscene sexuality could have been chosen – a hare or rabbit, any horned animals, or the insatiable and lustful pig. But these animals never could become the epitome of demonic powers. They never had much intelligence. There was nothing mysterious about them. Unlike snakes, people never respected or feared these animals.

The snake thus has never had any strong competition. Because of that it was chosen as the destroyer of mankind. Everyone knows what happened: the serpent tempted Eve to violate the prohibition, Eve persuaded Adam to eat the fruit of the forbidden tree, and for this they were expelled from paradise to earth. After that, the snake quickly lost all its positive traits (it remained, however, a symbol of medicine) and turned into the hideous symbol of temptation, sexual sin, and imminent death. The Devil himself appears in the Old Testament as a serpent.

In Judaism, the Serpent doesn't just represent the source of the world's evil. Because of him, the people lost God's gift of eternal life, and he represents qualities that are considered negative in mass religion, namely wisdom and cunning: 'The snake was the most clever of all the wild animals that the Lord God had made.' (Genesis 3:1) Because of these qualities the Serpent was able to suggest a compelling argument in his seduction – he said if the first people violated the rule, they would live forever, with knowledge of good and evil.

Firstly, the cunning serpent tempted the virgin Eve because he 'lusted for her' and his unclean seed inside her became her first menstruation period (so this is where the religious prohibition of sexual intercourse during menstruation came from!). Then it was Eve's turn to become the Serpent for Adam and as a result they were both banished from paradise. The Serpent got his share – God cursed him before all the cattle and the beasts of the field and forced him to 'walk on your belly' and 'eat dust for all the days of thy life'.

It is possible that the Serpent knew what to expect, and never regretted what he had done. James George Frazer believed that even if he 'is cursed by God and condemned thenceforth to crawl on his belly and lick the dust', he is the winner in this story, because 'serpents contrived to outwit or intimidate Man and so secure for themselves the immortality which was meant for him; for many savages believe that by annually casting their skins serpents and other animals renew their youth and live forever.'

The Rabbi Moshe Weissman advances an absurd but interesting theory of how Eve seduced Adam.

The serpent proposed that the first men try the taste of Evil, so that they could repudiate it afterwards and attain a new degree of holiness. He started with convincing the woman, for women are easy to be seduced and convinced. When Eve ate the fruit, she understood that she had made a great mistake and that she would die. However, it was not death that frightened her, but the idea that God would create a new wife for Adam.

The Goddess of the Serpents, from the Palace of Knossos, 1500 BC.

244 Tortured by jealousy, Eve made Adam eat the forbidden fruit. I would like to mention that Eve turns out to be a very mean creature, because not only did she make Adam eat the forbidden fruit, but she also gave it to all the birds and animals and so deprived them of their immortality.

In Christianity, the Serpent is synonymous with the Devil. It is often portrayed at the foot of the cross as a symbol of original sin, in the scenes of the temptation of Christ, and under the feet of the Virgin Mary. Since the original sin was committed by Adam with the use of his penis, the analogy between the penis and the Devil is obvious.

Now, after telling you about the Serpent, I can concentrate on the sinister role that sexuality played in the Fall.

■ The Downfall of the Ancient Phallus ■

How is it that something so unthinkable in civilisations preceding monotheism was accomplished – making people use so much of their energy not to seek natural sexual pleasure, but to seek out their 'sexual sins'?

The Old Testament tells us 'God created mankind in his own image, in the image of God he created them; male and female he created them.' (Genesis 1:27) If we accept the biblical version of the creation of Man, the fate of sexuality is unenviable right from the start since it is directly connected to the biggest tragedy in the history of the created Man – the Fall, the expulsion from paradise and the loss of immortality.

The biblical story of the Fall is known to everyone. Adam and Eve could live in paradise, eating the fruit from any tree except the tree of knowledge of good and evil. God chose an apple as the symbol of temptation, a pagan symbol of spring, fertility, youth, love, and longevity. I don't know about you, but I find this choice highly suspicious.

It was later, when men lived far away from God on earth that God placed the knowledge of good and evil first on the list of things humans have to do. When people lived in God's backyard and saw Him every day, the concept of evil didn't need to be known. Most likely, that knowledge would spoil the image of God. Of the three religions, the only intelligible explanation of the prohibition imposed by God is given in the Quran: 'Your Lord did not forbid you this tree except that you become angels or become of the immortal.' (Quran 7:20)

The treatments of the Fall in Judaism, Christianity, and Islam are quite different and the more obvious the link between the Fall and sexuality, the more negative the attitude towards sex in the religion in general. Although in terms of formal logic it all looks quite strange: God gave Man genitals and cannot blame him for wanting to use them.

Judaism believes that the first people had sex before the Fall, since during their creation God commanded them to 'be fruitful and multiply'. Fulfiling this commandment without sexual intercourse is quite difficult. In the Fall, it's not the sex between Adam and Eve that's important, but the human desire to violate the prohibition of God and to be free in forming His knowledge of the world.

For Judaism the Fall is about the sin of pride and curiosity, an attempt to rob God of His most important attribute: power.

Judaism does not recognise the fundamental Christian concept of original sin, passed on to subsequent generations as an inheritance. In the Judaic interpretation, the repercussions of the Fall are limited to people from the Old Testament. They had to work hard for the extraction of food, suffered difficult pregnancies and childbirths, illness and, most importantly, mortality. On the other hand, the Fall of Adam and Eve from the primitive life in paradise resulted in a life of the spiritual and ethical, so it's not all bad.

In Christianity, the damned heavenly apple transformed from a symbol of the illegal acquisition of knowledge into a symbol of illicit sexual contact. The biblical concept of cognition is interpreted as a loss of innocence for Adam and Eve and sinful pleasure without God's permission.

The Fall in Christianity is therefore first and foremost a sexual sin. It is this sexual sin, called the original sin by Augustine, that has become a key point of the Christian doctrine and which leads to the need for the redemptive mission of Jesus Christ. If Eve had not eaten the apple and did not seduce Adam with it, the first human beings would not have found that they have bodies that could give them a lot of pleasure. And had not Adam engaged in lustful sex with Eve, Christ wouldn't have to hang out on that cross 'for our sins'.

I tried to understand the essence of this terrible sin and still couldn't manage it. I am particularly sorry for Adam. Not only was he the victim of Eve and the snake, but he was declared responsible for this!

How far-reaching can one silly action be! If Adam had pulled himself together and resisted temptation, we wouldn't have felt pain, would have enjoyed immortality, and had a happy life in heaven. This argument is relevant today. Many family tragedies come from a single illicit sexual act. This does not mean that we urge you to refrain from something you want so bad; this is a call for greater caution, and the timely suppression of treacherous messages from your phones.

In Islam, the Fall plays a much smaller role than in Judaism and Christianity, and there is no sexual component to it.

Firstly, Islam recognises that our ancestors would find it very difficult to avoid temptation. The temptation offered by the Devil, to become angels or immortal, was great and so attractive that fighting it was not humanly possible.

Secondly, Islam does not agree that the disobedience of our ancestors filled everyone afterwards with sin and perverted us all. Man is born in a natural state of purity, and everything that happens to him after his birth is the influence of external factors. Adam and Eve screwed up once and after they repented they were not just fully forgiven but received the right to rule the world.

Thirdly, the Quran says that even before the creation of the first people, Allah prepared a place for them on earth, so that living here is not the consequence of the Fall, but the original plan of God.

Despite the differences in interpretations, they have certain things in common. The relationship between Man and God changed as a result of the Fall. The first men lost their close contact with Him and started to feel shame and guilt for the sin committed by them. And in all three Abrahamic religions, the inevitable consequence of the Fall is a sense of shame about the nude body.

The book of Genesis says that before the Fall, Adam and Eve did not experience shame: 'Adam and his wife were both naked, and they felt no shame.' (Genesis 2:25) It was an age of innocence, people lived in harmony with their human nature without fear of God. It's unclear if they had sex then since they forgot to write about that in the Bible, and the opinions of Jewish and Christian commentators on the issue diverge. I personally think that it is possible to have any kind of sex and still maintain complete innocence, especially if you do not know that sex is a bad thing. To declare sexual pleasure a sin, it was necessary to make a person feel ashamed of their genitals, despite the fact that God gave them to Man. Separating the genitals from the rest of the body is the same as separating the sexual function from other physiological functions.

And that's where the serpent comes in. The serpent robbed them irrevocably of the age of innocence, bringing instead the shame of nakedness before God (for subsequent generations this shame became congenital): 'Then the eyes of both of them were opened, and they realised they were naked; so they sewed fig leaves together and

Matthias Grunewald, The Dead Lovers.
Carnal love never leads to anything good.

made coverings for themselves.' (Genesis 3:7) For God the fig leaves were not enough, so He came to the rescue: 'The Lord God made garments of skin for Adam and his wife and clothed them.' (Genesis 3:21)

St Augustine was convinced that the genitals were to blame for the transmission of original sin, and so they should be hidden, not only from others but also from oneself. Exposed genitals increase the risk of sinful thoughts and sinful desires. Observing someone else's genitals is without any doubt even worse. The modern-day practices present on Tinder, Grindr and Snapchat are the best proof. Moreover, Augustine seems to have believed that the sexual organs were not necessary for reproduction:

> Far be it, then, from us to suppose that our first parents in Paradise felt that lust which caused them afterwards to blush and hide their nakedness, or that by its means they should have fulfilled the benediction of God, "Increase and multiply and replenish the earth".

Islam is more tolerant towards sex compared to Judaism and Christianity, but also shares a negative attitude towards nudity. The Quran says that the Devil tore the clothes from the bodies of the first people to show them their private parts: "And when they tasted of the tree, their private parts became apparent to them, and they began to fasten together over themselves from the leaves of Paradise." (Quran 7:22) On the other hand, the Quran is sceptical about the protection given by the leaves and says that "a pious garment is better".

And so the One God found another enemy – nudity. It is guilty because it brings sexual pleasure to a person. It was a beginning of the new era: the ancient cult of the phallus, the same phallus one could see on the bas-relief carvings and marble statues, came to its end. Two new monotheistic cults replaced it: the cult of shame for having genitals and the cult of guilt for the sexual pleasure they bring. The limitations and suppression of sexuality that stem from the idea of the Fall were vital to monotheism. All the provisions of Abrahamic religions are intended to show Man his duty before God, his guilt before God, and his dependence on God. If not for the Fall, Man would have remained in paradise and the Abrahamic religions would have lost all their power and would probably not end up in the anthologies of ancient tales and myths. But in the eyes of billions of people, the Fall happened and religions did not lose their power; they gained it. It was sexuality that lost strength, quality, and taste, and I am going to show you this with examples from specific religions. Before this, I would like to share some seditious ideas. The notion of sin appeared as the consequence of faith in the One God. Thus, one can conclude that if the One God and His laws do not exist (a very reasonable assumption, right?), the very faith in Him is a fundamental sin which is so serious when it comes to its consequences for humanity that it can be called original.

After committing this original sin, our foolish ancestors lost all the pagan joy of life as well as self-respect. They became pious, filled with sentiment of their inferiority, and shame and guilt for no one knows what.

What do you think of it?

Masaccio, Adam and Eve banished from Paradise, 1425.

▪ The Prophets Have Never Had Sex ▪

'One out of a thousand die out of all ill people,
and that one of a thousand is from too much sex.'
Kitzur Shulchan Aruch, Sixteenth century

Amid Christianity's apparent hatred towards sex. Judaism is often framed as a religion that refers positively towards sex. But this is not true, or at least not quite true. It was with Judaism that the misadventures of sexuality started.

One of its greatest apologists, Philo of Alexandria, expressed this very well in *On the Migration of Abraham*. He urges to 'Depart therefore from the earthly parts' which pre-supposes giving up all sexual activities – and to return to the asexual spirituality: 'O my friend, fleeing from that base and polluted prison house of the body, and from the keepers as it were of the prison, its pleasures and appetites, putting forth all your strength and all your power so as to suffer none.'

There is another precedent: according to some Talmudic sources (and I perfectly under-stand that in the giant Talmud one can find anything), Adam abstained from sex after the Fall for several years.

More significant evidence of negative attitudes towards sex is found in the story of the Jewish exile from Egypt. Judaism welcomes abstinence as a sign of spirituality and close-ness to God. Abstinence – opposed to sexual activity, which is earthly and ordinary – is a special sacred state, the state of the service of God.

A proof of Judaism's negative attitude towards sex can be found in the behaviour of our common superhero, Moses. For some reason, he refused to have sex with his wife while preparing for the main conversation of his life, his conversation with God. Maybe Yahweh did not like the sexually active, maybe an unsatisfied man is prone to violent fantasies and visions, and it is easier to find something sacred in his restless sleep. It should be noted that Moses extended the requirement of abstinence to all his people: 'Then [Moses] said to the people, "Prepare yourselves for the third day. Abstain from sexual relations".' (Ex. 19:15)

Maimonides goes even further and attributes total and permanent abstinence from sex as the condition for Moses preserving the 'Splendour of the Most High':

> When prophecy departs from all the [other] prophets, they return to their "tents", i.e. the needs of the body like other people. Therefore, they do not separate themselves from their wives. Moses, our teacher, never returned to his original "tent". Therefore, he separated himself from women and everything of that nature forever. He bound his mind to the Eternal Rock. [Accordingly,] the glory never left him forever. The flesh of his countenance shone, [for] he became holy like the angels.

Evil Kabbalistic tongues say one shouldn't pity Moses. As compensation for the loss of an earthly sex life, Moses found sensual ecstasy with God himself, and even copulated with the energy of the divine presence – Shechinah.

Anyway, in the biblical text, abstinence is regarded as a symbol of spirituality, a prereq-uisite for prophetic revelations and a way to approach God: everything must be subordi-nated to the communication with the Almighty. The lust interferes with it. It is the *Yetzer*

Hara, or the abuse of the things that are important for survival like sexuality, which is required for marriage and the birth of children, or spending money to create wealth, etc.

Judaism is more clement with ordinary people, not prophets, and for them it restricts sex to marriage with the goal of procreation. It should be remembered that sexual intimacy in marriage (sex is appropriate only in a marriage sanctified by God) is given to man not for his pleasure, but in order to honour the divine commandment. God and sex are back on a war path! In addition, according to the Talmud, the successful execution of this commandment requires fulfilment of certain conditions: the 'Shema' prayer should be read before performing a sexual act, the room should be completely dark (*in candle fire lives a special demon that spoils the male seed*) and no part of the groom or the bride's body should be exposed from under the covers. The same Talmud tells of Rabbi Eliezer who performed his conjugal duty with such horror and fear that it seemed the Devil himself was making him do it. God and sex are back on a war path!

Maimonides writes that 'the beginning of all wisdom is the containment of bodily lust to what is necessary to sustain the body' while recognising the power of the evil lust, 'for most people there is nothing harder in the entire Torah than to abstain from sex and forbidden relations'.

The main manual of everyday life, *Kitzur Schulchan Aruch*, written by the Rabbi Schlomo Ganzfried 150 years ago, is very clear: 'One shouldn't have relations while standing nor when sitting, nor on the day one goes to the bath house, nor on the day one's blood is let. Nor on the day he starts out on a journey, nor (should one) have relations while travelling on foot, and neither before or after these events.' (Kitzur Shulchan Aruch 150:15)

Or: Anyone who is addicted to having sex, old age comes upon him. His power fades, his eyes darken, and a bad smell comes from his mouth. The hair on his head and his eyebrows, and his eyelashes falls out. The hair of his beard and his armpits, and the hair on his legs gets thicker. His teeth fall out. Many other troubles apart from these come upon him. The wisest of the doctors said, One out of a thousand die out of all ill people, and that one of a thousand is from too much sex.

Also, any kind of oral sex is discouraged: 'And even more so, one who kisses there, which is transgressing on all these, and also transgresses "don't make yourself abominable".'

Even minimal sexual intimacy requires humility and a special approach in its realisation: During intercourse he should occupy himself with Torah matters and other holy subjects, and even though he's forbidden to read aloud, thinking is allowed.

I have a hard time imagining sexual pleasure while thinking about the words of the Torah, and I cannot imagine any spiritual pleasure from the Torah during sex. Although I'll admit that this advice can be very helpful: when a man is thinking about something else during intercourse he can avoid premature ejaculation and make his partner have an orgasm. Talking aloud about other things during sex is good advice too, because your partner could be very frightened. So it can be said that the Talmud is the first sexology textbook.

Many things the sages of Judaism say completely overlap (in tone) with the statements of Christian scholars. Mishna Berakhot (Folio 24a) says: 'If one gazes at the little finger of a woman, it is as if he gazed at her secret place.' It is a great sin to 'look at even the small finger of a woman, with the intention of getting pleasure from her' or to 'listen to a woman's voice, or look at her hair'. It is recommended not to 'look at your wife's breasts, not at where her shame is' or at 'cattle, animals or birds when they mate'. These authors do not seem to care where women look and what they think about. But it would be very interesting, as women's lust might easily outdo men's!

Judaism has a very negative attitude towards homosexuality and bestiality. The latter was particularly prevalent among nomadic Gentiles, from whom the Jews originated. If bestiality was not ubiquitous, it would not be included in the Torah! 'You shall not lie down with a male, as with a woman: this is an abomination. And with no animal shall you cohabit, to become defiled by it. And a woman shall not stand in front of an animal to cohabit with it; this is depravity.' (Leviticus 18. 22-24)

This prohibition applied to men, women, and animals, and its violation was punishable by death. For people it is understandable, but why blame the poor docile animal? Why kill it?

Moreover, licit sex is also complicated.

Firstly, Judaism forbids sex during menstruation, which is associated with impurity and sin, and for seven days after. This is the best proof that sex has nothing to do with pleasure and is allowed only in the days when there is high probability of conception. (Leviticus 15:25-30)

One shouldn't marry infertile women for the same reason. The Jerusalem Talmud explains that sex without the possibility of conception, for pure hedonism, is intolerable for genuine Jews. Philo of Alexandria agrees: 'Those who sue for marriage with women whose sterility has already been proved with other husbands, do but copulate like pigs or goats, and their names should be inscribed in the lists of the impious as adversaries of God.'

And even clearer is the attitude of Judaism towards involuntary nocturnal emissions which should be avoided through all possible means. The Jewish law Halacha blames nocturnal emissions on impure thoughts of intimacy. For Judaism, nocturnal emissions are a sin of which the person is guilty. The only salvation from this sin are the words of the Torah, namely the Shema prayer, which states that the only worthy object of love and loyalty is God alone. Halacha forbids sleeping on the back and on the stomach and requires one sleeps only on one's side, as well as riding only a saddled horse. The man that has experienced nocturnal emissions is considered 'impure' until the night and must bathe.

Based on the testimonies of former Orthodox Jews in American and French media, little has changed for them. The sexual life of young Jews was bad back then, or rather non-existent, and so it has remained today. Orthodox Jews are forbidden from talking to members of the opposite sex before marriage; you cannot even look at girls, and have to cross to the other side of the street from where their school is located. The only outlet was, and still is, daily masturbation. A more potent outlet today – the wind of modernity has reached the Orthodox corners of the world and has ruthlessly brought to it the depraved internet and its porn sites.

The only ray of light came to Jewish sexuality from the Seventh Lubavitcher Rebbe. Menachem Mendel Schneerson found a way out of the difficult situation, recognising sexuality as the only experience in human life when he faces God, the only experience that allows him to become truly God-like.

■ Islam: The Best Sex is in Paradise ■

I have always found Islam's attitude towards sex mysterious.

On one hand, there's the charming promiscuity of the Golden Age of Islam, full of erotic tales from Scheherazade to Sheikh Nefzawi's book *The Perfumed Garden*, the latter a hymn to erotic pleasures with detailed descriptions of the sexual organs and captivating belly dancing, and stories about the sexual adventures of noble people, alongside warnings about harems and sexually transmitted diseases.

On the other hand, there are strict rules against natural relationships between men and women, against meeting, courtship, and seduction, and there are many sexual taboos from the depths of an extremely conservative patriarchal culture, including the prohibition of making love naked. The most severe laws against adultery included the punishment of stoning.

On one hand, you have women's bodies completely wrapped in a burka. On the other hand, you have women wearing a light hijab with a lot of facial makeup and tight jeans or trousers.

Unlike Christianity, Islam recognises sex as one of the main attributes of the human being. It pleases Allah since it is a realisation of His will and plan. Indeed, He created men and women anatomically different and subdued them to the powerful sexual desire which is no less natural than hunger and thirst. This desire is allowed without any need for procreation and cannot and should not be repressed in this world, nor in the next. Both men and women are entitled to sexual pleasure, since the foundation of a strong family is a fulfilling sexual life in marriage. A man that might get an orgasm much faster than a woman is obliged to restrain his feelings and devote a lot of time to flirting and foreplay. Thus, the cult of platonic love has never existed in Islam and lust is tolerated in it.

Al-Ghazali writes in his *Book on the Etiquette of Marriage* that without sexual desire Man would have been less perfect. It is desirable that he should have intimate relations with her once every four nights; that is more just, for the [maximum] number of wives is four which justifies this span. It is true that intimate relations should be more or less frequent in accordance to her need to remain chaste, for to satisfy her is his duty.

I completely agree with Al-Ghazali's assessment of the fragility of monogamous relationship in which a woman is not satisfied. I can only admire the strength of Muslim husbands who fulfil their marital duty with four wives every day during the decades. Such men should have benefited from the calmer and cleaner environment!

However, the situation is not that simple. There are two more important aspects to consider in Islam's attitude towards sex. Firstly, sexuality must be limited so that it doesn't go beyond the bounds of its legitimate place in the social order. There is an antagonism between the sexual desire of a believer and the social order. Free from the fear of God, carnal passions lead to unacceptable sexual deviations and dishonourable deeds.

Secondly, one should not forget that the lust ordered by Allah serves to fulfil God's plan not only here on earth, but also in heaven. An earthly lust is weak, temporary, and incomplete compared to the powerful and dazzling lust which awaits believers in paradise, the realm of lust. Lust is given to humans only to show them what it will be like in paradise and to incite them to observe rigorous religious practices and to adore God.

> 'For after death the righteous will enjoy the pleasures of love even more than in earthly life. Allah will not only let them have their 'old' wives, but will also give them new ones. On thrones woven [with ornament], reclining on them, facing each other … And [for them are] fair women with large, [beautiful] eyes, the likenesses of pearls well-protected.' (Quran 56:15-23)

Women will not menstruate or have other natural secretions, which will allow them always to be clean and ready for intercourse: Women of Heaven are unlike the women of this world. They have no menstruation or post-birth bleeds, they don't spit or blow their noses, do not urinate or defecate. This follows from the word of the prophet: 'And they will have therein purified spouses, and they will abide therein eternally.' (al-Baqarah 2:25)

The masculine strength will increase many fold. The Holy Prophet said: 'The believer will be given such and such strength in Paradise for sexual intercourse. It was questioned: O prophet of Allah! Can he do that? He said: 'He will be given the strength of one hundred persons.' (Mishkat al-Masabih, Book 4, Ch. 42, No. 24)

The promise of a wonderful life after death made life on earth appear worse, and highly increased the appeal of Islam as a new religion. This was a wonderful marketing strategy! I like the fact that Islam recognises and appreciates sexual pleasure. The only difference between me and Islam is that I believe that human beings got pleasure as a result of evolution and they do not owe it to anyone, while Islam believes that it was granted to them by Allah. Islamic sex is not only a means of procreation and pleasure, but also a form of worship of the Almighty. Islam thus forbids evading one's marital duties and instructs one to read special prayers before sex. Regarding things permissible in sex, there is a presumption of innocence: everything which is not prohibited by the Quran is allowed. As a result there was a fairly liberal environment for sex. Islam encourages variety in caresses and sexual positions and allows mutual masturbation. There is no ban on oral sex, although theologians' opinions on the subject differ.

Some, like Sheikh Ahmad Kutty, perceive it only as a prelude to the main course. For others, an oral sex act is permissible with the consent of both husband and wife provided that no liquid gets into the mouth.

Regarding 'no liquid gets into the mouth', I must say that this is difficult, and for this reason other scholars point out that oral sex is associated with the possibility of men's sperm getting into the woman's mouth or female secretions getting into the mouth of a man, and there is no single opinion on the issue of the purity of sperm. Some scholars consider it clean (like saliva and mother's milk), while others compare it to blood and urine, recognising it as unclean. The ejaculation of male seed in the woman's mouth is *makrooh* (undesirable). If ejaculation does occur in the mouth, the spouses need to perform *ghusl* (ablution). The mouth should be rinsed as swallowing the seed is not allowed in any situation. There is another point of view according to which a Muslim needs their mouth only for eating and praising Allah.

In contrast to Jewish and Christian traditions, family planning and contraception is allowed in Islam. Most Muslims think it's permissible to practice *coitus interruptus*. They refer to the Quran surah: 'You may ejaculate outward, but everyone who should be created before the Day of Judgement will be created regardless.'

In any case, modern Islam allows the use of the rhythm method of contraception (intimacy during days deemed safe in a woman's menstrual cycle when a woman is not ovulating) and condom use. However, Islamic scholars do not recommend the constant use of contraceptives by couples who could have healthy children since birthing children is one of the main purposes of marriage. Moreover, the use of contraception also slows down the growth of the Muslim population. The Prophet said: 'Marry the loving and fertile, for I will compete with the other Prophets with the number of my followers on the Day of Qiyama.'

One of the parameters that show the true attitude of a religion towards human sexuality is how they interpret involuntary nocturnal emissions. Unlike Christianity and Judaism which consider this to be a sin, Islam believes that there is nothing shameful about emissions, since they occur spontaneously and are not the result of human action. Involuntary ejaculation in dreams does not violate the sacred Ramadan: 'Ejaculation that occurs during sleep does not ruin fasting even if it happens during the day'. However, the emissions are *Janabat*, leading to a state of defilement, and after one a Muslim needs a ritual bath, just like after intercourse. Nevertheless, Islam imposes strict rules in sexual behaviour, and violating them is shameful for the person and disgraceful to the family and community. Completely banned in Islam are:

Adultery. Islam recognises only sex among those legally married: 'And do not approach unlawful sexual intercourse. Indeed, it is ever an immorality and is evil as a way.' (Quran 17:32)

Homosexuality is considered a grave sin but is still widespread in the Muslim world. There is a following hadith: 'As for the one who plays with the boy as if he had a relationship with him, he must not marry his mother.' (Sahih Bukhari, *The Book about Marriage*). The prophet said: 'He who would kiss a boy with passion is similar to one who committed adultery with his mother 70 times. He who committed adultery with his mother once is similar to one who committed adultery with 70 virgins. And he who committed adultery with a virgin is similar to one who committed adultery with 70 women.' (Al Ravandi)

Anal sex, even with your own wife. The Quran, however, does not state this prohibition and it is based only on hadiths: 'Allah will not look at a man who has anal sex with his wife.' (Reported by Ibn Abi Shaybah, 3/529, and At-Tirmidhi classified it as an authentic hadith, 1165)

Intercourse during menstruation and soon after birth. This interdiction also has many concessions compared to Judaism and Christianity. When a woman is on her period the man is allowed to enjoy any part of her body (and do everything except intercourse) with the exception of the vagina. The wife can also bring her husband to ejaculation with her hand.

Intimacy during a pilgrimage to Mecca, while fasting, in the presence of other people, and within the walls of the mosque. It is also forbidden to have intercourse with a child and if there is an unwrapped Quran nearby. These prohibitions are not much different from similar prohibitions in other monotheistic religions.

Exposed genitals, which are a sign of disrespect to God. Getting fully naked is undesirable even for men in front of men. Nakedness is called '*awrat*' and includes everything between the belly and the knees. I have noticed that Muslim men do not undress in the sauna with each other. On the authority of Mu'aawiya ibn Haida, who said: 'I said: "O Messenger of Allah, which of our nakedness is allowed, and of which must we beware?" The Prophet answered, "Guard your nakedness except from your wife or those whom your right hand possesses. (So it is permissible for both spouses to look at and touch the body of his or her companion even the private parts). He said: "O Messenger of Allah, what about if the relatives live together with each other? The Prophet answered: "If you can make sure that no one ever sees your nakedness, then do so. He said: "O Messenger of Allah, what about when one is alone? The Prophet said: "Allah is more deserving of your modesty than are the people".'

Islam is without doubt the least oppressive monotheistic religion when it comes to sexuality. However, the situation is not that simple. Freedom of sexuality doesn't belong to Man. Allah granted lust and He must be continuously praised for it. Secondly, despite the equal rights in bed, Muslim women are under total control of men, and not only their husbands but also all their male relatives, including their brothers and even sons. Life is not easy when you have to hide your whole body, except for hands and face, when it is 40 degrees outside. I know nothing about being proud to belong to the true faith, but it is clear that wearing a T-shirt is better for your body.

■ The Crucified Sex ■

'I plainly consecrated altogether to the Lord,
when I not only strive to keep the flesh untouched by intercourse,
but also unspotted by other kinds of unseemliness.'
Methodius of Olympus

Compared with all the other Abrahamic religions, Christianity has always been the most negative towards human sexuality. It has declared a crusade against it. Christianity was the only Abrahamic religion, among all religions, that transformed sexuality from the basic instinct into a symbol of Evil and death, a sinister trait of sinful human nature. It is the anti-sexual religion *par origine*, *par définition* and *par excellence*.

This naturally follows from the Christian doctrine. Christianity asserted and continues to assert that the source of all human problems is the original sin, the sin of disobedience for which God punished the first men by making sex shameful to them and sinful to him. The first men were guided by lust when they copulated without the permission of God.

Christianity asserts that sensual temptation, lust, and sexual pleasure did not exist before the Fall; they were the negative side-effects of the breach of the divine order by Adam and Eve. The 'infection' of the original sin does not allow a reasonable control over our sexual desires. Any sexual activity leads to aggravation of the terrible consequences stemming from the sexual crimes of our ancestors and destroys the soul.

A purely Christian, spiritual love of God is not compatible with carnal love, which is a criminal desire to get pleasure from the excitement of the flesh.

As this absurd idea was accepted, a huge number of other absurd ideas were born from it. These ideas are foreign to a normally functioning brain.

The original sin led to the banishment from the paradise, to suffering, illness and death. Thus, sexuality is not the beginning of life, it is not a pleasure which brings children to the world, as thought all human cultures, but its tragic end: 'Therefore, just as sin entered the world through one man, and death through sin, and in this way death came to all people, because all sinned.' (Romans 5:12)

The New Testament has an extremely negative attitude towards lust. The connection between lust and sin can be found in the Gospels and the Epistles of the Apostles: 'This is all there is in the world: wanting to please our sinful selves, wanting the sinful things we see, and being too proud of what we have. But none of these comes from the Father. They come from the world.' (John 2:16) Evil cannot tempt God, and God himself does not tempt anyone. You are tempted by the evil things you want. Your own desire leads you away and traps you. Your desire grows inside you until it results in sin. Then the sin grows bigger and bigger and finally ends in death. (James 1:12-15)

According to St Paul, 'The acts of the flesh are obvious: sexual immorality, impurity and debauchery; idolatry and witchcraft; hatred, discord, jealousy, fits of rage, selfish ambition, dissensions, factions.' (Galatians 5:19-20)

In any case, after the adoption of the sexual interpretation of the Fall, Christians were gripped by the fear of sexuality which became an enemy not only of God but of Man, since it led to him to be driven out of paradise to earth, led to all diseases (not only STDs), and the painful spasms of orgasm led straight to hell. So, in Christianity, sexuality was condemned and it became a symbol of all human misery and mortal sin. Literally mortal, leading not only to physical, but also to spiritual death, since lust is inevitably associated with mental anguish, guilt before God, and the Holy Spirit leaving the body. It is not surprising that during the first centuries of Christianity all true believers were absolutely convinced that the path to immortality lay in the complete renunciation of sex.

The battle against sex and sexual pleasure became the central issue of faith, and abstinence became the greatest virtue. It became clear to every Christian that sexuality, especially a passionate one without a reproduction purpose, is the Devil's work, an obstacle on the path of service to God. It should be banished without mercy.

Sexuality no longer belonged to the human but became a disgusting and shameful manifestation of his animal nature. The idea that sexual life is necessary, that without sex a person is neither happy nor healthy, were declared to be the instigation of the Devil. Carnal love, the kind associated with sexuality, is not true love.

The Christian theologians were obsessed with sinful sex, lust, limitless female voluptuousness and debauched heathens. The negative attitude towards sex has been present in all Christian confessions for more than fifteen centuries. Particularly striking is the fact that these quotes are not from primitive fanatics, but from wise, insightful, highly educated people – the Fathers of the Church – who often occupied the top positions in the Church. They had excellent knowledge of ancient philosophy and science and spoke many languages: Greek, Latin, Hebrew, and Aramaic. But these statements seem to me like the greatest nonsense in the history of human culture, and if someone said something similar today they'd be sent to a psychiatric hospital. When I was reading these theories, I felt as if I was myself in a psychiatric hospital.

Saint Augustine believed that sex organs obeyed not the person they belong to, but only lust. Lust lives its own life. In *On Marriage and Concupiscence* he saw the signs of rebellion against God in copulation:

> Well, then, how significant is the fact that the eyes, and lips, and tongue, and hands, and feet, and the bending of back, and neck, and sides, are all placed within our power but when it must come to man's great function of the procreation of children the members which were expressly created for this purpose will not obey the direction of the will, but lust has to be waited for to set these members in motion, as if it had legal right over them, and sometimes it refuses to act when the mind wills, while often it acts against its will!

The religious frenzy of Augustine against sexuality goes even further in *The City of God*. According to him, the first men who inhabited paradise before the Fall were created without any sexual desire. To commit the act of conception neither man nor woman needed sexual arousal, and excitement was the consequence of lust after the original sin. Adam and Eve could copulate without 'a shameful desire' and their sexuality expressed itself through mutual religious devotion and a bodily union without lust. Based on this Augustine concluded that sexual intercourse was 'fundamentally alien to the original definition of humanity':

> That we are to believe that in Paradise our first parents begat offspring without blushing. The correct members, like the others, would move through the act of will and the husband would infuse the bosom of the wife without passionate unrest, in full calm of the body and soul and retaining chastity as soon as such a need would appear, and seed would be planted in the bosom of the woman without her losing virginity. So both sexes committed the act of copulation and conception through an act of will, not shameful desire.

Augustine writes about this special intercourse in such a convincing manner that I thought that he was present when the first men copulated! Clement of Alexandria stated

Gian Lorenzo Bernini, The Ecstasy of Saint Teresa.
No man could make a woman feel such pleasure!

that '...anyone who does not abstain [sexually – author's note] is dead before God. Left by Logos and the Holy Spirit, he is a corpse.'

St John Climacus believed that:

> The snake of sensuality is many-faced. In those who are inexperienced in sin he sows the thought of making one trial and then stopping. But this crafty creature incites those who have experienced the sin to retry it through the remembrance of their sin.

During the Middle Ages Saint Thomas Aquinas was considered to be the main 'specialist' of lust. The religious frenzy of Early Christianity had calmed down, and it was time for cold and thoughtful analysis. In *The Parts of Lust* of his *Summa Theologiae* Aquinas states that even if sexual desire and venereal pleasure are natural, they must be considered as lust and therefore a consequence of the Fall, a mortal sin and a serious obstacle on the path of virtue.

Just imagine, my dear readers, how many times you have already committed this 'natural' yet mortal sin this year! And I am sure that you are far from giving up that pleasure! Indeed, lust is humanity's worst enemy!

According to Thomas Aquinas, lust has many species: 'love of this world' and its pleasures; hatred of God who interferes with pleasure and imposes the spiritual ones, aversion towards the future world and blindness of the mind which leads to erratic behaviour and a penchant for obscenities (is he talking about my favourite jokes?). The most terrifying according to him is that lust makes him or her believe that he or she is self-sufficient and can become God for oneself. The Church is right: such aspiration can be healed only with fire.

Another Medieval author warns that lust is only similar to fever: the body and soul searching for pleasures are subject to infernal tortures, and all of this in vain – the furious passion is getting only stronger.

And what about Protestantism? Martin Luther says that faith cannot tolerate lust and tries to get rid of it. When he comments on the Galatians, he says that 'you will never be without sin, for you have flesh. Despair not, but resist the flesh'. There is another problem: 'Carnal lust is not the only work of the flesh, and so he (*Saint Paul*) counts among the works of the flesh also idolatry, witchcraft, hatred, and the like.'

It is surprising that after thousands of years of massacring heretics, and of the omni-present propaganda of 'spiritual values', that there could be someone in the Europe of the sixteenth century left to hate because he adored another God!

Hatred of sexuality in Christianity reached ridiculous levels. Some scholars even argue that the sensual Song of Songs found a place in the biblical text through the Devil's machinations (more likely that it got there not because of the Devil, but because of booze. A wine-drunk monk could have mixed up the texts and the wrong one got in). Other scholars were strongly against this interpretation and suggested the text should not be interpreted literally, but figuratively. This is the opinion of Origen, Augustine, Gregory the Great and many others. They still cautioned against reading the text before achieving a certain level of religious spirituality.

In practice this meant that the breasts, hair, neck, belly, and belly button described in the Song of Songs are not parts of the female body, but spiritual symbols relating to Christ and his Church. For example, the words 'Let him kiss me with kisses of his mouth' should be interpreted as a devout soul interacting with the divine word.

After reading this I thought that it's good the Song of Songs does not mention a penis. What would the Fathers of the Church have come up with in that case? Which spiritual symbol would this penis represent and how would one explain what a kiss on it meant?

Nothing changed with modern Christianity. Lust is still one of the seven mortal sins for Catholics and one of the eight mortal passions in the Orthodox Church. The Church is not ready to give up being superior to biology. Hypocrisy has never left the Church.

Pope Jean-Paul II went beyond absurdity, stating that 'lust is fundamentally different from natural desire of sensual love between a man and a woman'. However, how would an eternal virgin know anything about it? No wonder that with this kind of thinking among the highest religious authorities, millions of Christians back then and today are happy to comply with these wonderful humane commandments. Just remember our Cambodian guide.

If you thought that the Christian doctrine of sexuality is based only on appeals to proper asexual behaviour and moral exhortations, then you are gravely mistaken. Monotheistic religions wouldn't survive a day without whips. Almost all Church authorities intimidated believers by promises of the terrible torments of hell. And it was not just acts that were punished; thoughts about the act were, too. The source of sexual sin isn't action, but sinful looks and fantasies, the lust of the eyes, which is unequivocally condemned by Christ himself, and it is worth repeating the gospel of Matthew: 'But I tell you that anyone who looks at a woman lustfully has already committed adultery with her in his heart.' (Matthew 5:28)

Even John Chrysostom relied not just on his fantastic eloquence, but also on more efficient methods exhorting to protect the young from lust with 'suggestion, exhortations, fear and threats'. He points out that adulterers who only touched the object of lust with their eyes will be punished: 'Since, although thou hast not touched her with the hand, yet hast thou caressed her with thine eyes; for which cause this also is accounted adultery, and before that great penalty draws after it no slight one of its own.'

The provisions of Christian religion, which deny the basic human instinct – sexuality – are stupefying in their insanity. The severe consequences for hundreds of millions of people could be qualified as a crime against humanity. This is the case of the chimera demonstrating its mighty power and its savage grin.

Theory is theory, but in practice Christianity had to create a new way of life for its believers. A way of life that would allow them to confront powerful sexual temptations. This new way of life was absolute chastity. Not a simple abstinence from sinful sex, but a virginity preserved for the entire life.

The Virgins Do Not Burn

*'Am I plainly consecrated altogether to the Lord, when I not only strive
to keep the flesh untouched by intercourse, but also unspotted by other kinds of unseemliness.'*
Saint Methodius of Olympus
The Banquet of the Ten Virgins, or Concerning Chastity

Before talking about virginity, we need to compare notes. We need to define what virginity means, which women fall under the definition, and how virgins were treated in various communities. From a physiological perspective, female virginity is nothing special. It is the small mucosa. The hymen is intended to protect the internal reproductive organs from infection. The attitude towards virginity changed throughout history, but in the civilisations that existed before monotheism, virginity wasn't really valued and people believed that the hymen wasn't special or sacred, otherwise it'd be impossible to explain why nature didn't just give them to human females, but to many other vertebrates, including elephants, horses, and of course apes as well. People treated virginity neutrally and didn't really ascribe much moral meaning to it, let alone divinity. The idea of retaining virginity by turning away from sex seemed absurd and was rarely implemented.

The idea of chastity and the state of virginity affiliated with it was always valued in cultural and religious tradition. One of the obvious reasons is that a couple of minutes suffice to make virginity completely disappear. It especially concerned the unwed women whose chastity added to their desirability. The loss of virginity was interpreted as the loss of original innocence and 'purity', the process somewhat poetically called 'defloration', i.e. the loss of the 'flower'.

Virginity itself was analysed in two aspects. On one hand, a virgin definitely has a higher socio-economic value compared to a non-virgin. The man received the right to the first use of a thing. He is sure that he is the most worthy and the true father of the children, or at least their first child the virgin gave birth to. The woman was deemed a material object, property, no different from other such things. This attitude towards virginity is confirmed by many rituals and traditions.

On the other hand, a virgin is more valuable than a non-virgin because she represents an untouched vessel filled with sexual energy. It wasn't a lack of sexuality that was valued in chastity by ancient civilisations, but its opposite – a higher sexuality. Virgins temporarily abstained from sex not because of some moral considerations or because they wanted to cast away their sensuality, but because they did not want to prematurely dissipate their natural sex energy and preferred to ultimately share with the chosen male the waterfall of their intense sexuality. The pent-up sexual energy can manifest itself as the dangerous and deadly power of unbridled erotica, typical among virgin goddesses: Athena, Artemis, Hestia (Vesta).

Virginity itself was also endowed with religious significance. The most famous cult was the cult of the vestal virgins in the Roman Empire, the main job of whom was the support of the holy fire in the temple of the Goddess Vesta. Romans thought that the virginity of the vestals gave them the gift of prophecy and was directly related to the well-being and security of the state. They took this very seriously and the loss of virginity by a vestal that gave an oath was punished by a horrible death: she was buried alive in the ground. To calm our readers, I remind them that there were never more than six vestals for millions of people in a huge empire. Virginity wasn't popular among other women.

The only reasonable explanation why this strange and violent cult existed for centuries may be that the preservation of virginity by adult women is a daunting task verging on impossible. This anomaly requires an iron will and diabolical patience. Because of this the virgin priestesses offered other people an example of self-sacrifice and unprecedented resistance. By the way, why not return to this wonderful cult and have vestal virgins in the US and Europe in order to boost patriotism? The value of virginity in monotheistic religions becomes religious. In Judaism, the value of virginity turns from a hidden future sexuality into a rejection of sex itself.

Christian civilisation went further, transforming chastity into a universal moral ideal. The principle of the 'new thing' did not catch on. The body and soul belong to God and the Church, and not to men: 'Now the body is not for fornication, but for the Lord; and the Lord for the body.' (1 Cor. 6:13) It's not the woman that gives the man her virginity, but God. After the conclusion of a marriage He graciously gives him the right to deflower this, and only this, woman.

It goes without saying that sexuality as a powerful creative force was rejected. In Christian civilisation virginity is never analysed in this way (I am actually surprised that even nowadays most men do not remark on the intense sexuality of virgins, as if two thousand years of Christian ideology have really blinded them). In this regard, we note that before Christianity entered the historical arena, virginity itself was never a sacred symbol of moral purity and the universal model for all women. Nor was it the subject of compulsory worship and even mass paranoia. The principal and sacred duty of any woman was to lose her virginity at the right time in order to become a wife and mother.

Christianity has turned history's attitude towards virginity upside down: not only women but also men are obliged to preserve their virginity. Virginity and celibacy are proclaimed the undying ideals of the good religious life for women and especially for men. They are transformed into the object of worship. Christ never entered marriage and praised 'those who choose to live like eunuchs for the sake of the kingdom of heaven'. (Matthew 19:12) His best disciple Paul said, 'It is good for a man not to have sexual relations with a woman' (Corinthians 7:1) and 'Are you free from such a commitment? Do not look for a wife'. (Corinthians 7:27)

John the Apostle was rejoicing on his deathbed because he never got married and stayed not with women, but with God: 'You who has preserved me also till the present hour pure to Yourself, and free from intercourse with woman; who, when I wished in my youth to marry, appeared to me, and say, I am in need of you, John.' The ideology of the founders of the new religion led Christians to abstain from sex. This kind of life was especially popular among the early Christians in the second to the fourth centuries, for example, Justin Martyr and Tatian lived in a state of the strictest preservation of virginity and refused conjugal relations in marriage. One of the first historians of the Church, Eusebius of Caesarea, and the writer-ascetic Jerome believed that the biblical adage 'Be fruitful and multiply' does not apply to Christians who have no need for natural reproduction because Christ will return for the Second Coming, the world will end, and everyone will be saved. According to Jerome, 'Virginity is natural to Man while marriage is a result of the Fall.'

In practice, refusing sex meant refusing family and children, but no one seemed to care about it: the purity of the ideal demands sacrifice!

Female virginity was not forgotten. This is what John Chrysostom says about it in *On Virginity*:

> Those that married have more peace of mind; and secondly because the flame (of passion) ever rises high, the subsequent copulation fast puts it out. A virgin, not having the means to put out the flame, though seeing that it flares up and rises, and not being able to put it out, is trying only in the fight against the fire not to burn herself. What can be surprising that – to wear a hearth within oneself and not burn, nourish the flame in the recesses of the soul and keep the mind intact? She is not allowed to throw out these coals of fire, she is forced to endure in her soul something that, according to the writer of Proverbs, is impossible to sustain according to bodily nature. What did he say? Can one go upon hot coals, and his feet not be burned? (Prov. VI, 28) But she goes and bears the torment.

It turns out that virginity and chastity are not true if they are not based on 'true faith', Augustine wrote in *On Marriage and Concupiscene*:

> For though consecrated virginity is rightly preferred to marriage, yet what Christian in his sober mind would not prefer Catholic Christian women who have been even more than once married, to not only vestals, but also to heretical virgins.

To my mind, any normal man would first take into account the appearance of his future wife.

Indeed, virginity stopped being some innocent mucosa. It became a universal moral ideal which symbolises the aspiration to overcome worldly desires, the victory of the spirit over the body and the purity before God. The best illustration of this baseline principle is the fate of the Virgin Mary who gave birth to God, resurrected and ascended to Heaven. Is there a better example of a Christian life?

The paranoid attitude of Christianity towards sexuality is well-known and well-described. But one of the most important aspects of this paranoia has not received enough attention nor an adequate evaluation. I am talking about medical effects of abstinence for both sexes.

Freud maintained that the suppression of instincts often has an enormous destructive effect on people since the unmet desires develop into complexes and neuroses which lead to deviant behaviour. Particularly dangerous is sexual frustration, which bears the threat of extremely negative physiological consequences – issues with the reproductive organs, insomnia, depression, which all lead to aggression. Personally, I have no doubt that the lion's share of murders could be reduced, or even prevented altogether, if the murderers had had normal sex at the right time.

The situation is no better for 'late' women. Even though contemporary society influenced by the old religious dogma still believes that one should not hurry with losing virginity, late defloration, not to mention lifelong virginity, has an extremely negative impact on women's health. Moral principles contradict the basic needs of the body, and the *BFF* of an innocent girl, the hymen, becomes the worst enemy of an adult woman. The negative impact of late defloration is much more considerable that any negative effects of early sexual activity. Medical studies suggest that the optimal age for defloration from a physiological point of view is 15-18 since around the age of 20-22 the connective tissue of the hymen begins to lose its plasticity. After 24-25 years of age virginity cannot be considered normal: the morphological changes in the vagina can lead to difficulties during penetration. However, this is not the most important. Physiological anomalies in a virgin's body result in severe and irreversible anomalies in the structure of her personality. Pessimism, anxiety, instability, conflict with herself. It creates the necessary conditions for borderline mental pathology. Such clinics have long been filled with these young women; they even reserved special buildings for them. Problems with the late loss of innocence aren't specific to women. According to another study, men who lose their innocence after 20 years of age have problems with arousal and reaching orgasm. Of course, nowadays the situation is not as tragic as it was a couple of decades ago. The majority of present-day virgins, even those who belong to the strictest religious communities, see virginity not as a 'sacred symbol of moral purity', but a 'technical element' – the presence of the hymen – necessary for a successful marriage. For those women, masturbation, oral, and anal sex are considered 'foreplay' and do not mean the loss of physiological virginity.

In case of an error or too much carelessness, 'technical virgins' can see a surgeon to help them. Or they also can tell their naïve suitors with enthusiasm that virginity is lost not in the moment when the hymen is broken, but when a woman consents to receive sexual pleasure in any form. And, of course, this was not the case: the poor girl has never wanted or consented to any of this! It would be so much better, and more honest, if they did not have to justify themselves. Why should a man do whatever he wants before marriage and a woman should not? A man should be happy that a woman who has some sexual experience has chosen him!

Despite being very liberal in any other domain, I must say that I do not like such 'technical' virgins for moral reasons. I do not like liars. Here I support the Virgin Mary, who didn't have any kind of sex. Whether everything I have just said applies to this specific case must be decided not by me, an atheist, but by you, my dear readers.

■ The Sweet Dream of the Immaculate Conception ■

> *Once you eliminate the impossible, whatever remains,*
> *no matter how improbable, must be the truth.*
> Sherlock Holmes

I became interested in the doctrine of the Immaculate Conception not because I suddenly felt a burning interest in Christian theology or the desire to criticise religious doctrines. I am only interested in scientific disciplines ruled not by faith and spirits, but by intellect and practical evidence.

The criticism of religious doctrines themselves isn't necessary in this book either since religion is not really present in my life. And if such criticism exists in this book, it's out of the necessity to defend secular values. I would like to note that no other tenets of Christianity (and there are over a dozen) are considered in this work. A single dogma is the exception – the dogma of the Immaculate Conception. It is possible that in this I was influenced by Nietzsche who once said that the Immaculate Conception is 'faith within faith'. It is a pity he did not add his favourite *par excellence*.

The dogma of the Immaculate Conception is the only case in human history when it is not the conception that matters most, but an adjective describing it. It is virginal (*Virginalis Conceptio* in Latin) since the Mother of Jesus Christ, the Virgin Mary, conceived him by being inseminated by the Holy Spirit through her ear. It is important that Jesus was conceived without any male sperm. We do not have any information concerning the divine one. Probably, God transferred Mary his genes in the same way He created the first men, namely in His own image.

Just to be clear, I would like to say that I highly respect the Virgin Mary, a very noble and distinguished woman, and that I wrote this text not to criticise her, but to protect all other women who have never managed to repeat her path.

This task is facilitated by the fact that in other Abrahamic religions the doctrine of the Immaculate Conception of God does not exist. And in contemporary Christianity it is not in the foreground. Good schools try not to discuss the issue in religious classes, so as not to lead to a lot of questions and ridicule on the part of students. The Immaculate Conception refers to a painful subject for all adolescents; it's obviously implausible, in contrast to the laws of nature, and sounds like a miracle from a child's fairy tale. However, when it comes to its plausibility, it is the same as with any other dogma.

The doctrine of the Immaculate Conception is a miracle and as such it is not different in any way from other pagan miracles, such as people turning into stone and sea elephants speaking. But there is a fundamental difference between pagan and Christian miracles. For one thing, pagan miracles have always served the interests of gods, not men – they are a violation of natural law, of which only gods are capable. Secondly, pagan miracles had no apparent purpose other than the desire of pagan gods to show off their power and are therefore devoid of morals.

Miracles in monotheistic religions always carried a moral judgement, which was later converted into a binding moral law. These are classic examples of the philosophy of suspicion, which accuses all religions of creating the conditions for the artificial birth of faith.

The tendency of religions to create artificial 'miracles' is even recognised by some theologians, especially modern ones. They explain this as follows. Belief and disbelief, atheism and religion, are twins that grew up in one family. They are based on the same facts, but these facts are used for a completely different interpretation. Of course, it may seem surprising that people continue to believe in something that is clearly absurd. Faith does not apply to the ordinary world, with its ordinary laws, but to the metaphysical world, based on the idea that the spiritual does not obey the laws of the material.

From a religious point of view, any event, including the most natural and normal process of birth, becomes a miracle if the religious interpretation of the situation dominates. In the case of the Immaculate Conception, this means that the ordinary, something that happens millions of times per day, becomes extraordinary and divine. From this point of view anything can be declared a miracle, including the satisfaction of natural needs.

I perfectly understand that the point of any faith is to reconcile the irreconcilable. The great Tertullian expressed this in his short and brilliant phrase *'credo quia absurdum'*. So, it is not surprising that the statements 'virgins can't get pregnant' and 'the Holy Mother of God has always been and always will be a virgin' do not contradict each other in the minds of faithful Christians. It is a very logical point of view and it makes me wonder how the intellect of those believers work. But I don't want to debate with them.

Christianity is a leader when it comes to the number of miracles that aren't compatible with rational thought. It starts with the most important miracle – a God-man descended from heaven. This is in turn divided into the wonders of the Immaculate Conception, the Resurrection from the dead, and the Ascension back into Heaven. The earthly divine cycle has ended, Christ returned whence he came – to God the Father and the Holy Spirit. All three of these miracles are in flagrant violation of the fundamental principle of monotheism, of the One God that exists as the God-idea. It cannot in principle have a physical presence, and for this reason it is even forbidden to depict it. And here the idea of God not only comes down to earth, but with the help of his junior partner, the Holy Spirit, inseminates a human virgin who is His creature as all people on earth. It doesn't sound very right from a moral and legal point of view.

To these major miracles you have to add the smaller and less significant ones: healing the terminally ill, lepers, and the blind; the resurrection from the dead; casting out demons; turning water into wine. If you believe in at least one of these miracles, it is possible and even necessary to believe in anything. It is not clear how priests combine faith in these 'Christian miracles' with their condemnation of popular superstitions – a heritage of pagan times – such as not lending money after the dawn, or not crossing the path of a black cat. Unlike the Immaculate Conception, debts and black cats actually exist and they are not miracles.

Christianity did not discover the wonderful idea of the Immaculate Conception – its existence in Christianity throws it deep into its pagan origins. This idea has existed since ancient times in many cultures, due to the sexual ignorance of primitive people who did not connect the concept of sexual intercourse, mainly a group activity, with the birth of a child. To avoid infertility, women participated in various magical rituals with water, plants, stones, and other totemic objects, which were then thought to be the father of a child. I must say that it's time to give up the most harmful myth – the myth that savage pagans are stupid and backwards while those who believe in One God are enlightened and conscientious. The ability to have a huge mountain or a mighty river as the father of a child captures the imagination no less than the fatherhood of the Holy Spirit. All primitive tribes without exception wanted their gods and heroes to avoid the hassle of natural conception and birth. Otherwise, how do they differ from ordinary mortals and how can they justify their right to leadership on earth and in heaven?

In later pagan mythology, a huge mountain and a mighty river were replaced by gods who were meant to be first in everything. This is why sexual contact between smart, beautiful virgins and gods was considered possible and even normal. The exceptional beauty and intelligence of a future mother gave hope for beautiful and smart children, those that people would be proud of and relate to. Myths of this kind of conception were very common in the pagan world, through all times and among all peoples, including those in Ancient India, Asia Minor, Ancient Greece and Rome, Ancient Egypt, and South America.

Every nation wanted to make their gods more sacred, so each pagan god had to be born from a virgin, or at least have an unusual or a non-standard conception. Many gods, heroes, and sages were conceived by gods from virgins. Here are the most interesting examples of sacred conceptions:

– Buddha was born to a famous royal family, but the paternity of the Raja was always in doubt. On the night of his conception, the queen dreamed of a white elephant with six tusks entering her. Experts on Indian culture are positive that this white elephant is of no less sacred value than the Holy Spirit.

Isis and Horus, 715-332 BC.

Icon depicting The Holy Mother of the Passion, 16ᵗʰ century.

– The Indian god Krishna was born entirely immaculately, not from a sexual relationship between his mother Devaki with her lawful husband Vasudeva, but from the life-giving beginning transferring from the head of Vasudeva directly into the womb of his wife.

– A virgin Indian girl named Kunti gave birth to her son Karna, fathered by the sun-god Surya. It is worth noting that after birth she remained a virgin.

– The main Ancient Egyptian goddess, Isis, the symbol for femininity and motherhood, managed to conceive her son (the god Horus) from her divine husband Osiris, the god of rebirth and king of the underworld, whom she resurrected herself. Incidentally, the sign of the Virgin Mary as well as Isis is a crescent moon and the image of Isis holding a child influenced the iconography of the Mother of God.

– The goddess of death, Coatlicue, the widow of the old Sun and the personification of Earth (much like our close friend the goddess Cybele), after giving birth to many children gave them the vow of chastity. Yet she did not fulfil it as she accidentally caught a ball of hummingbird feathers falling from the sky, hid it on her breast, and became pregnant with Aztec god Huitzilopochtli.

– The founders of Rome, Romulus and Remus, were born from the vestal virgin Rhea Silvia, a virgin by definition, and the god of war Mars.

Still, the main laurels of divine and Immaculate Conception belong to the characters from Greek mythology, especially the king of the gods Zeus:

– The virgin Maya gave birth to Hermes, the god of trade, from Zeus.

– Having swallowed his pregnant wife, Metis, Zeus gave birth from his head to the goddess of war, Athena.

– The god of wine, Dionysus, was conceived by Zeus and the princess Semele. After a provocation by Zeus's wife Hera, Semele, the mother of the child, temporarily died and Dionysus stayed in Zeus's thigh. The death was temporary because later her grown son pulled his mother from the kingdom of the dead and made her immortal. The last part is very reminiscent of another Son, who also made his mother – Virgin Mary – immortal.

– Zeus became a quail and thus took the virgin goddess Leto. The result was the goddess of hunting, Artemis. She was different from the other goddesses in two respects: her eternal virginity and extreme cruelty. This confirms my idea that the deprivation of sex quickly makes a person (or god) a maniac.

– And finally, the most famous example, illustrated by many artists from Rembrandt to Klimt. Zeus turned into golden rain and so penetrated the dungeon of the girl Danae, kept there by her father. It would be more correct to say that he penetrated the girl, not the dungeon, and as a result Perseus was born. Alas, a simple mythical hero, not another god in the pantheon. I am not aware of the way of life and moral character of Danae before this, but there is every reason to believe that she was a virgin too, since she was hidden in the dungeon long before her puberty.

I also started to look for examples of the Immaculate Conception and found a very good story in the Phrygian mythology. Although it's much less known and popular, it's much closer to the pure image of the Virgin Mary and the divinity of her child. It's based on the myth of Agdistis, not a mortal hero like Perseus, but a true god accidentally born from Zeus and the Phrygian Mother Goddess Cybele. Born from divine sin, Agdistis had both male and female sexual organs, meaning he was androgynous. His androgyny was seen by other gods of the Greek pantheon as a symbol of a wild and uncontrollable nature, and they were forced to castrate him. The blood from the removed penis of the unfortunate god sprinkled and fertilised the earth, and on that place an almond tree, symbol of existence, grew. Nana, the virgin daughter of the river god Sangarius, gathered ripe almonds from the tree and hid them in her bosom. The almonds disappeared and she miraculously became pregnant, and after a time allotted by nature she gave birth to a beautiful god named Attis.

The beginnings of the doctrine of the Immaculate Conception were difficult and blurred. Before describing the dogma of the Immaculate Conception, I would like to draw your attention to the fact that today's complete identification of this doctrine, the image of the Virgin Mary with Christianity has no direct relationship to Christ himself. All the texts of the New Testament are written interpretations from the end of the first and the beginning of the second century AD. It is possible that Christ considered himself a mere human prophet, like Muhammed, and did not pretend to be conceived from God nor to resurrect or ascend to Heaven. I am sure that it would have benefited Christianity since the latter would have remained strictly monotheistic as a religion, and for that reason would seem more attractive and reliable.

The idea of an Immaculate Conception is found by Christian theologians in the Old Testament's prophecy of Isaiah: 'Therefore the Lord himself shall give you a sign; behold, a virgin shall conceive, and bear a son, and shall call his name Immanuel.' (Isaiah 7:14)

In the Gospels of Matthew and Luke, the concept of the Immaculate Conception in Mary sounds even clearer: 'She was found to be pregnant through the Holy Spirit because what is conceived in her is from the Holy Spirit.' (Matthew 1:18; 1:20) The angel answered, 'The Holy Spirit will come upon you, the power of the Highest hover over you.' (Luke 1:35)

Somehow this important, fundamental idea in the new religion was not mentioned in the Gospels of Mark and John, or in the Epistles of Paul. It is particularly surprising that there is nothing from Paul, who discusses all the little nuances of Christian doctrine in scrupulous detail.

The position of the Virgin Mary herself is pretty strange. Despite a visit by the Archangel Gabriel, she either did not believe in 'divine' pregnancy or considered it undesirable for a married woman. Immaculate Conception is actually very hard to believe. Just imagine yourself in Joseph's place, or in the place of any husband who returns home after a long trip or time in prison and receives such an explanation from his beloved wife. I think in any case that Mary did not realise she gave birth to God.

In early Christianity, the doctrine of the Immaculate Conception was hardly popular, especially as women weren't very popular. The explanation is simple: it was the fault of the woman, because of her irrepressible sexuality, that Man committed the original sin and lost eternal life. Compounding this is the attitude of Christ towards his mother. He lacks not only worship, but even external respect. It seems he knows her price and expresses his attitude clearly. Someone told him, 'Your mother and brothers are standing outside, wanting to speak to you.' He replied to him, 'Who is my mother, and who are my brothers?' Pointing to his disciples, he said, 'Here are my mother and my brothers. For whoever does the will of my Father in heaven is my brother and sister and mother.' (Matthew 12:46-50)

One could of course consider these words to be the usual rhetoric of any exalted preacher ready to reject publicly everything that does not serve the main cause of his life. But a sliver of doubt regarding his true attitude to his mother remains. Despite the fact that the cult of the Virgin Mary was venerated by the vast majority of the many billions of dead Christians and the two billion living ones, that number does not include the very first, most important, and influential Christian – Jesus Christ. His opinion is always going to be more significant than the collective opinion of all other Christians put together, and for him she remained a simple human mother. This is why for a long time the Church Fathers could not decide on the nature and status of Mary.

The consolidation of the doctrine of the Immaculate Conception and the deification of Mary herself, which transformed Mary the Mother of Christ into the divine Virgin Mary, started only in the second century. This had well-founded logic, but when you come up with something absurd, you can no longer stop; one absurdity inevitably leads to another. Let's look closer.

The myth of Christ solidified with time and Christ himself transformed from a simple prophet wandering through Palestine to an omnipotent god whom it does not behove to have a simple woman as a relative. She's not just a mother, she's the mother of Christ! The cults of the Mother Goddesses, widespread in the East since time immemorial, battling Christianity constantly, also played a role. Everyone knows the best and most economical way to battle and expand is to absorb. Do not forget that Christianity is based entirely on Judaism, in which woman was born from the first man's rib, suffered from menstrual impurity, and because of that was relatively low in religious and social status. Was it possible for an ordinary Jewish woman to give birth to the Christian God? Of course not! One woman had to be elevated among all others, others who are by definition second-class beings, or even third, and behind cattle. Mark her with a great mind – no one would believe it. With beauty – there are other beautiful women. This mark would have to be extremely exceptional, for example, absolute asexuality and such an unusual way of conception.

Christ the God-man was sent to earth to atone for the sins of men, primarily the original sin, which is full of sexual connotations. Was it possible that the Saviour of mankind, the Redeemer of the original sin, could have been conceived in the original sin itself? With a sinful woman? So, the doctrine of the Immaculate Conception was the result of a necessary choice: either we change the whole doctrine of the God-man, or Jesus should be immaculately conceived by his mother, and not from a sinful man, but from a divine and immortal being – the Holy Spirit fits the role nicely. Baby Jesus conceived through the Holy Spirit was human, but since he was not conceived through sex, the original sin, which passes from one generation to another and makes us all suffer, was not transmitted to him.

The doctrine of the Immaculate Conception is vital to religion since it allows us to 'clean' and exalt God, as well as to introduce the ideal of asexuality, if not militant *anti*-sexuality, into daily life. Sexuality itself had to become a grave mortal sin and the only way to defeat the hideous pagan cult of the phallus. This is the reason why the Christian myth of the Immaculate Conception went much further than previous pagan myths and became very different from them. It can be said, to use the language of dialectics, that quantity became quality and the pagan cult of the phallus, symbolising fertility of nature and Man, was overthrown.

People still have phalluses, to the greatest sorrow of religions, but the cult is no more. It has become surprisingly easy to pray to God: having a phallus without the cult of the phallus, one can easily devote one's entire life to religion. Thus began the great era of austerity. But the holy place is never empty and in place of the cult of the phallus, a new cult was born: the cult of virginity and asexuality, which were made into the highest virtue. Both the Virgin Mary and Christ himself, the one who came to redeem the terrible sexual sin, were declared the ultimate symbols of purity. Indeed, sinners can't atone for the sins of others.

The fundamental denial of sex touched on the genitalia themselves, which were suddenly directly related to the original sin. What the infamous pagans proudly portrayed in the most prominent places became in itself impure, indecent, and obscene. Otherwise, why was it necessary for the Holy Spirit to enter the Virgin Mary's body, not through her vagina but through her ear? The fruit of the Immaculate Conception, baby Jesus, didn't develop in her ear, but in the womb, which is obviously closer to the vagina.

The most important thing in this doctrine is that Mary was a virgin before the Immaculate Conception and remained one after birth, till the very end of her life. While some early titans of Christian thought tried to resist the disproportionate (in their opinion) exaltation of Mary, and rejected the thesis of her ongoing virtue, they argued that the Immaculate Conception was a one-off and afterwards Joseph and Mary lived like all other married couples and even had other children.

Tertullian believed that after the birth of Jesus, Mary and her husband Joseph had a normal sex life. Origen claimed that Jesus had brothers and sisters, and John Chrysostom and Augustine even doubted the innocence of Mary after Jesus's birth – it was hard to believe for even such staunch Christians as themselves. In that distant era Christianity still stood on the ground with both feet and clearly understood the nature of women and their impetuous sexuality. A proof for this point of view can be found in the Gospel of Mark: 'Isn't this the carpenter? Isn't this Mary's son and the brother of James, Joseph, Judas, and Simon? Aren't his sisters here with us?' (Mark 6:3)

Later, the Catholic Church explained that in those remote times the terms brother and sister referred not just to real brothers and sisters, but also to nephews, nieces, cousins and step-relatives (brothers and sisters). The Church continues to vehemently deny that Jesus had brothers and sisters, since this would mean the Virgin Mary participated in lowly sexual intercourse after the birth of the God-man, and is therefore not the ideal of Christian purity. Who then could be the role model for nuns, the Brides of Christ? This can lead to the idea that Mary became pregnant not from God/the Holy Spirit, but from her boyfriend, and this happened long before her marriage to Joseph.

In general, the issue of women's chastity and the real number of male partners always aroused intense interest. Women are very reluctant to admit their real number of previous partners and the number might differ for the confessional and for her future husband. Some time ago, I read in a fundamental French research paper (more than one hundred pages) dedicated to the notion of faithfulness, that in Ile-de-France a woman of 50 years of age has no more than 4 to 5 sexual partners. After reading this I did not know whether to cry or to laugh. Such worthy modesty was caused not just by wanting to hide old sinful mischief, but also wanting to fit into the Christian asexual ideal (still present in the genetic memory), which one is taught from one's diaper days. For this reason, over the centuries, there was a tradition to attribute the birth of a child to any phenomena except natural sexual intercourse. This tradition is firmly established in the sexual education of children who were brought by a variety of large birds (like storks) or found in gardens, for some reason typically under a cabbage leaf. One of the most popular stories reads: A little boy was given a task at school to write an essay on the origins of his family. He decided to first ask his grandmother, to find out how she came into the world. Grandmother said she was found in a cabbage patch. 'How about Mom and Dad?' – 'Cabbage'.

The boy asks his parents and gets the same answer. They, as well as their son, were also found in cabbage. After the interviews the boy wrote in his essay, 'I was born in a very unique family. For the past three generations, defying all the obvious delights of sexuality, my family reproduces only vegetatively.'

To protect and support the concept of the Immaculate Conception, a lot of hefty works were created that a mind spoiled by a university education is not quite ready to comprehend. Just to list them would take thousands of pages. So I chose just one argument.

The first alleges that the virgin birth is happening around us at every moment, in every part of the world, all the time. Insects (ants, bees, and some others), plants, trees … they use virgin birth as a way of reproduction. It means the phenomenon of parthenogenesis or 'virgin reproduction', in which the female ovum develops in the mother's body without any fertilisation. This very rare phenomenon does exist (although not found in mammals), and many love to cite species of fish, birds, and lizards as examples. There are some rare lizard species, mainly monitor lizards and geckos, in which only females exist.

Unfortunately, the adepts of this theory did not come to the logical conclusion that it's not just people that are perverse, but almost all wildlife, while the Virgin Mary leads a small but brilliant tribe of the immaculate. If this ideology finds its adherents, soon we will see statues of geckos in churches and houses.

During the Middle Ages, a woman was understood through the contrast of the mother Eve and the Virgin Mary. Eve represented ordinary women, those relatives of the temptress, while Mary remained an unattainable ideal. Later on, Eve became the object of even more fierce criticism, which brought her the honourable designation of 'Daughter of the Devil'. This is a very honourable designation indeed, since diabolical female sexuality has always been appreciated in good male society. The theologians thought that the Virgin Mary is the 'innocent' Eve, the first (and last in our opinion) absolutely 'correct' woman, there to eliminate the consequences of the sinner's offence. As a result the ever-growing cult of the Virgin Mary affirmed itself in 1854 when the dogma of the Immaculate Conception of the Virgin Mary was established.

But be attentive! In this dogma of the Immaculate Conception of the Virgin Mary nothing is said about the virginal conception of Mary by the Holy Spirit. This dogma states that she was released from original sin by God. This limitation of the scope of the doctrine itself was a great victory for the Holy Church. In the fourth century, long before the dogma was established, some radical elements attempted to push a heretical idea that the Virgin Mary was also conceived by a virgin mother and the Holy Spirit. We'll stop there, since you can trace this to her parents, then to the parents of their parents and so on. Till we arrive to the first men. No, there won't be any first men anymore and one will have to rewrite the divine history!

The Catholic doctrine of 1854 says that the Virgin Mary was conceived by normal parents in the normal sexual way, but by God's grace Mary did not receive the original sin. She was redeemed before conception in anticipation of the future merits of her son. Disputing with the Orthodox Church, the Catholics justify the need for the doctrine as follows: the Immaculate Conception by the Blessed Virgin Mary is an inevitable consequence of two other tenets recognised by both Catholics and the Orthodox Church, namely the dogma of the Fall of the human race personified by Adam and the dogma of the Virgin Mary birthing the God-man. Indeed, if you do not remove the Virgin from the general human herd it would mean that she was born through original sin. The Saviour, feeding on her nature in the womb, would inevitably have his share of sinful nature. And since the original sin makes Man a slave of the Devil and if that sin remains in the Virgin Mary, the Saviour would be the son of a slave of the Devil. To make the mother worthy of the Son of God, two thousand years after his birth, she's enrolled in the list of the immaculately conceived, so we know she didn't get him dirty.

Of course, this wasn't the end. The new fairy tale gave birth to the next one with sad inevitability. Mary, born in integrity and officially freed from original sin, lost the ability to die peacefully, because death is the punishment for each of us for the original sin of our common ancestors. We had to accept the new dogma, the dogma of the immaculate, sorry, supernatural death of the Virgin Mary. This was successfully done by the Vatican on 1 November 1950. According to the new dogma, Mary, who died of natural causes and was then buried, miraculously ascended to heaven. At least when apostles opened her tomb they didn't find the remains of the Virgin Mary, but an empty space. Mary went to her son alive.

This is how the cult of the Immaculate Conception and cult of the Virgin Mary Mother of God originated and developed in Catholicism and almost eclipsed the cult of Christ. The Virgin Mary became a symbol of the greatness of Catholicism while her image became more popular than the image of Christ. According to my personal observations, the cult of the Virgin Mary is particularly strong in southern European countries like Spain, Portugal, and Italy. Could it be connected to the hot sunny climate and the early maturation of girls with their sexuality bristling in all directions, which is absolutely impossible to fully control? And the male disappointment: she might have been a virgin, but there are so many rumours going around. Girls are always much more practical and from an early age they are well aware that the Virgin Mary is unattainable; they can only imitate her and wait if not for God, then at least for their Joseph.

The cult of the Virgin Mary was literally omnipresent: numerous religious orders were founded in her honour, new rites devised, and chapels, churches and cathedrals built. Mary rose far above all the other saints and became the queen of heaven and protector of the highest protector of the people before God, from whom the most inveterate sinner has the right to seek help. Art shows it too: many legends were invented, such as the ideas that the strangest and most lost people could be saved through the Ave Maria prayer. One of them, an alchemist, magician, occultist, astrologer, soldier, writer, and demonology writer, likely just a very talented adventurer from the fifteenth to sixteenth centuries, Heinrich Cornelius Agrippa (Agrippa of Nettesheim), dedicated his most brilliant panegyric *The Glory of Women* to her:

> Princess of all, shines forth the blessed Virgin Mary, Mother of Christ, at whose beauty the Sun and Moon stands amazed, from whose glorious countenance, such a lustre of chastity and holiness floweth, as that it was able to dazzle the minds of all men, no man for all that, at any time through the temptation and enticements of so stupendous a beauty, falling in the least thought.

The fate of the Virgin Mary wasn't as great for the Protestants, who recognise the dogma of the Immaculate Conception of Jesus by the Virgin Mary, but do not recognise its logical continuation, the dogma of the Immaculate Conception of the most Blessed Virgin Mary. It is not clear what they see as the fundamental difference. In our opinion, both the first and second dogma have the same degree of plausibility, but everyone decides for themselves to what degree. However, one can offer a number of very plausible explanations to this paradox:

The simplest. The dogma of the Immaculate Conception of the Virgin Mary was developed three centuries after the bloody split of Protestantism from Catholicism. It is very doubtful that Protestants would accept anything coming from Catholics who had already massacred millions of their brothers in faith.

The most romantic. If you don't deify the Virgin Mary and consider her a normal human woman, every woman could potentially give birth to God. Isn't this thought quite inspiring?

The most reasonable. For Protestants, ardent supporters of hard work and personal achievement, the fact that the Virgin Mary gave birth to their God is clearly insufficient to create a cult around her personality and unthinking worship of her. In their understanding, Mary was a woman generously gifted by divine grace who deserves some admiration. Not perfect and, in principle, not free from evil and sin; which sin exactly, it is not clear. Probably the original one.

With this I conclude my description of the basics of the doctrine of the Immaculate Conception. I will not deny that the presentation of this relatively small issue proved to be very difficult for me, a person mutilated by the sin of rational thinking. Therefore, I am happy to pass to overtly personal conclusions.

It doesn't feel right to refer to the myth of the Immaculate Conception by the strict, serious, and binding term of a 'religious concept'. It seems to be a concept separate from the menacing commandments of the religion that loves us so much, and more like a fairy tale that an indulgent grandmother would tell her grandchildren before bed. This fairy tale returns to haunt you after you graduate from university and your first failed marriage, when you really want the extraordinary achievement of the Virgin Mary to be repeated by your own teenage daughter.

Nevertheless, the belief in virgin birth shared by hundreds of millions of people is not as harmless or innocent as it seems. It is definitely much more dangerous than other good stories such as exorcisms and turning water into wine. At least they don't get in the way of people's lives. This is completely different. What in religious theory looks like an inspiring concept becomes its complete opposite in daily life. And behind the grandmother's sweet face lurks the distinctly predatory snout of a wild beast.

The doctrine of the Immaculate Conception, especially in its Catholic version, is directed against life itself. It is anti-human, both in name and nature. The immaculate part of the phenomenon is the exact opposite of natural grace, and so of everything human: physical and mental health, self-respect, and balance of natural instincts. Both of its two protagonists, Christ and the Virgin Mary, were born not by the natural processes of life, but by supernatural means. That is why this dogma is the foundation of morality for those who love God, but don't like the earthly world. What is good about it?

The doctrine of the Immaculate Conception became so deeply rooted in our civilisation that it managed to poison the sex lives of a huge number of religious and non-religious people because it made them consider their own flesh, which is constantly striving towards sexual pleasure, as sinful. Nietzsche argued that the idea of the Immaculate Conception ruined not just the conception, but also the human, since it denies the fundamental importance of human sexuality as the basic cause of life. Nevertheless, I must admit that the doctrine of the Immaculate Conception is one of the most effective in terms of marketing. By taking the normal human word 'conception' and adding the word 'immaculate', all other conceptions have become evil once and for all; the fruit of those conceptions included.

When it comes to its impact, the doctrine of the Immaculate Conception is indeed a powerful religious concept. By glorifying a single woman, it managed to ruin the lives of hundreds of millions of other women deemed unable to conceive in a similar way, and who thus give up their natural sexuality. The belief that the Immaculate Conception has

Jean Fouquet, Virgin and Child surrounded by cherubim and seraphim, 1452.

actually happened set the bar so high that no other woman in human history could reach it. Because of that, all women except one became unworthy sinners incapable of living according to a religious ideal.

Finally, the doctrine of the Immaculate Conception is the most improbable religious concept, the adoption of which results in the complete and final rejection of the mind. It is usually said that faith begins where reason ends. In its implausibility the Immaculate Conception is clearly more absurd than the idea that last night a group of aliens landed in your backyard and that this morning you were in line at the supermarket with them waiting to pay for beer.

In conclusion, the doctrine of the Immaculate Conception became a valuable ideal for the Church. It played the crucial role in the final formation of the rigid anti-sexual moral and the concept of Christian marriage. It is a radically new type of marriage in which Joseph represents the ideal of patience (married life without sex must be quite unbearable), while the Virgin Mary represents ideal asexuality and motherhood. The Virgin Mary embodies divine asexuality since mortal women can't bear it. The reproductive function of women cannot be separated from another equally important function – the sexual.

■ Christian Marriage, or a divine Threesome ■

Alas, not all believers had the fortitude of spirit to reach these heights of chastity. So God made an indulgence for people inclined to the sexual sin, the essence of which was clearly expressed by the apostle Paul: 'Now to the unmarried and the widows I say: It is good for them to stay unmarried, as I do. But if they cannot control themselves, they should marry, for it is better to marry than to burn with passion.' (Corinthians 7:9)

The contemporary of Augustine, St Jerome, was convinced that Adam and Eve were virgins before the Fall and when they were banished from paradise they were immediately married: 'And as regards Adam and Eve we must maintain that before the Fall they were virgins in Paradise: but after they sinned, and were cast out of Paradise, they were immediately married.' Who exactly united them in the absence of the Church is a mystery. Probably, God himself.

However, this was not a passionate marriage. The negative attitude of Christianity towards sex is best seen in the only place it's allowed – in a Christian marriage. Its main objective consists not in satisfying the flesh but in struggling against a 'diabolical sexual desire'. This is why a true Christian continues to be the grave of sensual love, the 'cure against lust'.

The astute reader may argue that any marriage is a grave for sensual love since it is always violent. At least, it becomes violent at some point. People, no matter what oaths they make to each other when they wed, get tired of each other sooner or later, lose mutual desire, and with it passion. Being married for decades, we break ourselves and our sensuality for the sake of social stability, children, and mutual support in old age.

Nevertheless, there's a big difference between a secular and canonically Christian marriage.

In the former, spouses are supposed to do everything in their power to keep up the passion and love for the marriage bed. They even go to sexologists to get help.

The latter is the complete opposite: we have to 'tame the flesh' as soon as possible and become simple friends. So, a true Christian marriage is not the marriage you dream up when you're a teenager; it's very different. Despite what those deceived by Satan think today, marriage is not about mutual sexual arousal and satisfaction, but about abstinence and having children. The model Christian marriage is asexual. The fact that the best marriage is a marriage without sex stems directly from the words of Apostle Paul: 'It is good for a man not to have sexual relations with a woman.' (Corinthians 7:1) The main purpose of Christian marriage is not to kindle lust, but to love God and live in His service. That is why it's called the holy sacrament: the couple gets married in front of God and then is mysteriously united as one flesh not only in earthly life but after death, in the life beyond the grave. There were even stories of numerous miracles associated with this kind of love. Like the bones of a wife in a coffin shifted to the side to make room for the corpse of her dead husband, or vice versa, a husband's bones come to life and embrace his recently passed spouse (a gloomy proposition: even after death you can't get away from the loathed wife!).

Stories about spouses loving each other deeply in chaste and spiritual marital unions were overwhelming in the Christian faith from the moment of its inception. Rejecting one's sinful carnal nature, the husband and wife reached the heights of spirituality and found perfect true love. St Augustine expressed the opinion that sexual intercourse can be completely excluded from married life without any harm, supporting that with the story of the marital life of the Virgin Mary and St Joseph:

> This disease of concupiscence is what the apostle refers to, when, speaking to married believers, he says: "This is the will of God, even your sanctification, that ye should abstain from fornication: that every one of you should know how to possess his vessel in sanctification and honour; not in the disease of desire, even as the Gentiles which know not God."
>
> The married believer, therefore, must not only not use another man's vessel, which is what they do who lust after others' wives; but he must know that even his own vessel is not to be possessed in the disease of carnal concupiscence.

Achieving the ideal marriage was not easy. John Chrysostom was convinced that marital austerity was very difficult, much more difficult than the austerity of a monk, since it was necessary to suppress urges in the presence of a wife who was prepared for sex.

According to Martin Luther, one has to satisfy physical needs from time to time. But without 'satisfying the lust' (I have never really understood how he distinguished needs from lust). If the flesh becomes too lustful, it has to be restrained with the Holy Spirit. If it doesn't work out, there is only one way to solve the problem – get married to fulfil God's will! Through the holy sacrament of marriage God gives you permission for limited sex, and always remains with you in the marital bed, controlling how you fulfil the requirements of the faith, and reminding you that Christian love is first and foremost love towards God.

I, with my twenty-first century depravity and permissiveness, would call a man who loves God more than he does his wife… to put it mildly… crazy. So don't forget that you are never alone in the marital bed, there are three of us, like in group sex from university days. But the situation is worse: the belief that God is always watching you is not conducive to passionate sex… It is like living in Orwell's *1984*.

There are some other crimes against faith and the Church. It is obvious that sex without God's permission, meaning pre-marital sexual relations, or infidelity in marriage, is equivalent to treason before God and considered among the worst sins. Hardly surprising. It is, however, astonishing that the desire for your wife is a serious and heinous crime against God, too. The Church Fathers stated that it is actually worse than adultery. The true adulterer is not the one who sleeps with another man's wife, but the one who is searching for sinful pleasures with his own wife, and thus betrays God.

I had a hard time understanding this point of view. How is it possible to compare sexual practices in a legal marriage with adultery, which has always been condemned not only by religious but also worldly laws? Then, I realised that as bizarre as this may seem from the point of view of our worldly logic, it is absolutely comprehensible from the religious point of view. An adulterer in a marriage has either forgotten that God is present in his marital bed or has never understood the sacrament of the Christian marriage: God has given him permission to have sex with his wife, but this permission is valid only for passionless sex which doesn't make God jealous.

On the other hand, God has never given anyone permission to have sex outside of marriage; and has never considered this kind of sex to be a sacrament. This is why He is not present during such copulation and He has no reason to be jealous. Hence, the crime against Him is much smaller.

In addition to showing love for God, the Christian marriage has another purpose: birthing into the world godly children. This marriage connects physical virginity to the 'spiritual purity' of the bride, future wife, and mother. 'Unnecessary' sexual desires are indecent and should be suppressed in favour of the strictly limited use of sex only for reproduction. This should stop completely after the birth of the required number of children. Then the woman returns to the ideal of her youth, the completely asexual Virgin Mary, wholly committed to the service of her husband and the rearing of children born in the right Christian spirit.

Clement of Alexandria furiously denounced 'the indiscriminate throwing of seed, completely unnatural and counter-logical'. He said: 'For Man coition without the goal of procreation is not permissible. Coitus without the goal of birthing children goes against nature. Coitus did not bring any benefit to anyone. He is happy who was not hurt by it.' Because even in marriage it brings danger, unless it is with the goal of having children.

Augustine agrees with Clement of Alexandria and states that 'the marriage of believers converts to the use of righteousness that carnal concupiscence by which "the flesh lusts against the Spirit".' (Galatians 5:17) Only Christians can be saved from the horrors of lust and have children who 'may be born again and become sons of God':

Martin Van Maele, illustration from the series "The Great Danse Macabre of the Living", 1905.

Martin Van Maele, illustration from the series "The Great Danse Macabre of the Living", 1905.

> A man turns to use the evil of concupiscence and is not overcome by it, when he bridles and restrains its rage, as it works in inordinate and indecorous motions; and never relaxes his hold upon it except when intent on offspring, and then controls and applies it to the carnal generation of children to be spiritually regenerated, not to the subjection of the spirit to the flesh in a sordid servitude. (*On Marriage and Concupiscence*)

As proof, Augustine gives the killer argument: animal and bird couples copulate not to satisfy their flesh but solely to reproduce themselves. Probably, those animal couples told him about this during confession.

The Holy Fathers' opinions didn't remain on paper; they were brilliantly realised in everyday life. Christianity has always strictly forbidden sex with a woman during days when she could not conceive a child, especially during menstruation. Priests explained that intercourse with women during the prohibited days could lead to the birth of sick children – epileptics, lepers, and even those possessed by the Devil.

It was not permissible to have sex with pregnant women. Conception had already occurred and any sexual intercourse after this God-given miracle offends Him and causes great harm to the physical and spiritual health of not only the spouses but also of the unborn child. Artificial birth control methods were also forbidden (in the days before condoms this meant *coitus interruptus* – the sin of Onan), as well as sex with women who had started the menopause. One can only imagine how angry those women were! It goes without saying that Christianity also prescribes obligatory abstinence on Sundays and during religious holidays, Wednesdays, Fridays, and all fasting days. Fasting days are called fasting exactly for this reason: you cannot have any pleasure during this time! Strict observance of all these limitations would allow people to have sex no more than five or six days in a month, exactly during the period when it is possible to conceive a child.

The restrictions applied not only to quantity but to quality of sexual relationships. Only one sexual position, the most convenient for pregnancy, was allowed. Man, as stated in the Bible, was leading: the woman lying on her back, the man on her, both making no sound. The position with the woman on top is a great sin, an affront to God, not to mention doggy style ('bestial lust'), which resembles the despicable natural world and sinful homosexual contact.

Religion strictly prohibited all other sexual perversions: mutual masturbation (using the hands of the wife), masturbation (using your own hand) and other kinds of sinful sexual activity: foreplay, kissing, and so on. The Church prohibited oral and anal sex with a particular violence (choose the wrong hole by mistake when drunk, and everything goes down the drain; you have become an adulterer!). Indeed, from all these activities one can get sexual pleasure, but cannot become pregnant and have a baby. In fact, the mouth and the anus are not suitable for the noble goal of having children. No such cases have been attested in human history, even though almost everyone uses those organs for sex purposes!

The fact that homosexuals are incapable of childbearing largely explains the religion's hatred towards homosexuality. According to Scripture, homosexuality is a grave form of debauchery since it does not serve the continuation of life and hence is punishable by death. Scripture does not recognise that it's rooted in the biological properties of some people. Although, as it is common in life, religion vehemently rejected homosexuality, while a number of its priests happily engaged in the practice.

The real purpose of these restrictions is clear. Christianity has to do everything possible to suppress the natural sexual desire or, at the very least, severely compromise it. Then, monotony will eventually kill the sex drive and the nausea arising from the boredom of marital sex will finally put out not just sexual passion, but any form of sexual activity in marriage. Only then does a powerful desire to pray to God come forward.

To be fair, it wasn't just Christianity that tried to suppress sexual passion in marriage. Its heirs, the atheist totalitarian ideologies, had the same objective. According to Wilhelm Reich, one of the favourite disciples of Freud, those regimes wanted to 'purify the masses', reinforce 'family ties' and banish the 'sin of the flesh'. It was the same rhetoric: 'Everything that doesn't serve the reproduction purposes is immoral.'

To support my conclusions, I would like to refer to *The Twelve Commandments of Revolutionary Sex* by Aron Zalkin published in 1924 in the USSR:

> A purely physical sexual attraction is unacceptable from a revolutionary proletarian point of view… Healthy revolutionary offspring will be had through the most optimal use of your energy and through good relationships with other comrades by the worker that will start his sexual life late, who will remain a virgin until marriage, who will create a sexual connection with someone close in terms of class and love. Who will be prudent with sexual intercourse, preforming them only as the final form of deep comprehensive social and personal emotion.

And the most beautiful quote which makes me think about the attitude of Christianity towards the heretics: 'Sexual attraction towards someone from an antagonistic class, who's morally disgusting or dishonest, is a perversion similar to the sexual attraction of man to a crocodile or orangutan.'

George Orwell parodies the Christian doctrine in *1984*:

> The only recognized purpose of marriage was to beget children for the service of the Party. Sexual intercourse was to be looked on as a slightly disgusting minor operation, like having an enema… There will be no loyalty, except loyalty towards the Party. There will be no love, except the love of Big Brother… All competing pleasures will be destroyed.

The contemporary Christian Church continues to praise chastity in any form, be it virginity or holy celibacy, and recommends dedication of oneself to God with an 'undivided' heart. Also, it is not surprising that the centuries-old flourishing of the prostitution industry started with the implementation of the anti-sex morality. A modern person has a hard time understanding why the Christian idea of struggling against human nature has lasted for so long. It's doubtful whether the interpretation of the Fall as sexual sin would have survived for so long if not for some other sources that constantly give it new powers. It is especially difficult to understand today when hundreds of millions of people who consider themselves to be Christians live a completely unchristian life: nearly all of the population practice sex outside of marriage, if not oral, anal and homosexual sex.

■ Sex is God's Worst Enemy ■

How could such a natural thing as human sexuality become God's worst enemy? Why, in the powerful and highly cultured pagan civilisations that preceded monotheism, were there no restrictions on human sexuality (except for incest, which had a bad influence on social stability)? And why, after the advent of monotheism, did negative attitudes towards sexuality become universal? Why did monotheism demand restrictions and even the rejection of sexuality, not just for the elite clergy, but for all believers?

This was not an accident. Monotheism's struggle with sexuality was inevitable. The institution of religion, while irrational in many areas, is consistent and logical in its attitude towards sex. Monotheism fought fiercely for its anti-sexual ideas but chose not to give any explanation: restrictions imposed on sexuality are dictated by sacred books and for this reason there's no need to give any explanation to the public.

As for me, I am convinced that the restrictions that religions impose on sexuality do need explanation. Since I do not recognise any laws of sacred books, my explanation must be based not on its laws, but on those real and quite materialistic reasons that made religions introduce these restrictions.

Control of the sexual sphere allows you to manipulate believers. The religious person's ambition is to reunite with God and religion's ambition is to convert as many people as possible to their faith. The success of any doctrine hinges on the ability to manipulate their followers, not on the contents of the doctrine.

The goal of manipulating believers existed before monotheism, but now its importance increased a great deal. Now the number of followers wasn't in the hundreds and thousands, but in the many millions. And now the doctrine had become so estranged from human nature that it had to be justified in a convincing manner. So convincing in fact that everyone would believe that they themselves had caused this gap with nature. In order to control the actions and thoughts of Man, religions had to make him leave his normal state or, to put it differently, to dominate his basic instincts. I have mentioned earlier that a happy person is difficult to manipulate, especially in terms of religion. Earthly pleasures make a normal healthy person indifferent to the charms of a promised afterlife; he remains deaf to the preaching of religion. Why would a happy man spend many hours going to church when he has a fun girlfriend, a river, delicious fried meat, and an interesting book? To lure people into church, religions have to rely on the unhappy and the unsatisfied (a good example of this is the amazing success of Christian cults in poor developing countries in Africa, Latin America, and Asia), and they have to do everything possible to make them unhappy. They must deprive them of pleasures, instil self-doubt, and break ties with their relatives and other non-religious people. All physical and intellectual resources, and all desires of the person have to be transformed into prayer and religious worship. The only channel of communication must be the religious community.

In this context, choosing sexuality as the subject of violent criticism is very reasonable.

Firstly, the struggle against sexuality confirms religion's power. Only exceptional power can make human beings refuse one of the greatest pleasures in life. Sexual desire is the most powerful manifestation of human life; it is an affirmation of life in its purest form. You can even safely say that sex is life because sex is the only way to continue it (the opposite does not follow, life is not just sex. There are a lot of useful and nice things in life besides it).

Secondly, sexual pleasure isn't compatible with true faith in God. Once absorbed in carnal pleasures, a person wouldn't rigorously observe religious rites and respect the religious norms. Sexuality has always been a challenger and rival to God, both in terms of its significance in human life and in the strength of emotions it inspires. Love gives a person inner harmony, saves him from nervousness and fear, leads him to a state of relaxation and happiness. But once you deprive a person of sex, you can do with him whatever you want. The renouncement of bodily pleasures has always served as a source of religious inspiration and the foundation of all religious dogmas. In order to achieve this, divine commandments and covenants of previous generations explain that sexual desire is a mortal sin, which will be severely punished in the afterlife.

The formation of a neurotic fear of one's own sexuality leads to a discord with the surrounding world and makes one susceptible to manipulation – makes one a sort of formless clay. Freud explained very well that sexual hunger quickly leads man to hysteria and there is one small step between hysteria and religious zeal.

The person begins to hate himself while continuing to commit sexual sin and starts to regularly visit church with the purpose of getting rid of sexual addiction. It becomes a feedback loop: the more a person hates himself, the more God loves him.

This kind of manipulation has been used not only by religions, but also by egalitarian secular totalitarian regimes, which shared the religious hatred towards any independent pleasures and especially towards sex. All the sexual energy of a man belongs to the party, the state, the people… anyone else but the man himself. Particularly striking are the similarities between Christianity and communism. In Christianity the highest form of virtue was love for God, and in the communist states towards the Party, the leader, and the homeland. Christianity promised eternal life after death, communism promised a bright future for the next generations.

So not only God, but also dictators want to share your bed. George Orwell perfectly described this phenomenon in *1984*: It was not merely that the sex instinct created a world of its own which was outside the Party's control and which therefore had to be destroyed if possible. What was more important was that sexual privation induced hysteria, which was desirable because it could be transformed into war-fever and leader-worship.

Sexuality is a rebellion against God and an illicit pleasure. Let's try to conceive of God in the way He has been seen by the contemporary forms of monotheism and try to understand what He thinks.

God is very jealous. Nobody and nothing should even attempt to obscure Him and be compared to Him. God does not need rivalry, and therefore He naturally considers all pleasures except prayer to be His enemies. Moreover, sexual desire and sexual pleasure are so intense that during the process partners forget about God as they are completely absorbed in each other. In fact, it is impossible to simultaneously satisfy your sexual needs and give God attention He is allotted: human emotions are limited. You spend some on sex, you have less for God.

Sexuality of the believers offends the asexual One God. This situation can be observed throughout human life. For example, older people who lose interest in the opposite sex and become asexual are usually very irritated at the sight of the open expression of young people's sexuality. From a human point of view it's understandable: those deprived of the opportunity to receive the main pleasure of life will be jealous of those receiving it beyond measure.

It is the same with God. His predecessors, the pagan gods, had human traits including gender and sexuality, as well as a variety of sexual partners. For them human sexuality was natural and uninteresting. The One God is a genderless universal idea. However, there is a suspicion that, having lost his own sexuality, he became envious of the sexuality of others. If he does not have sex, then would He be glad that you have sex?

For the One God there is no better gift than abstinence, it is the way to imitate your spiritual leader. It makes sense. Engaging in sex near an asexual God feels somewhat indecent.

The asexuality of the One God manifested itself immediately when He first appeared among God's chosen people, the Jews. Initially He was male, but gradually His sexuality was relegated to second place and He became an abstract creative being. No wonder He said He created Man and Woman in His own image and likeness (Genesis 1:27). It is clear that God lacks a clear gender.

In cases where the One God does have a gender (for example He is similar to a man, like in the case of Christ, the God-man), He does not engage in sex. So the issue of Jesus Christ's gender identity has not been resolved definitively.

Sex reduces fear of death, and God becomes unnecessary. Sexuality is a powerful force, embodying the desire to continue your kind and giving the illusion of personal immortality. The more partners and children, the greater the thirst for life, the less the fear of death. The sexual act is an attempt to overcome the fear of mortality on your own without the help of God, to overcome it in a way other than believing in a mythical religious afterlife. It undermines the power of God, and His monopoly on eternity.

If the fear of death can be overcome or at least substantially suppressed without the help of higher powers, then what is the need for religion with its judgemental God whom you serve your whole life to get a spot in heaven? In this case God becomes useless. For this reason sexuality should be offered to God as a sacrifice, to prove loyalty to religion, and to show love for God and His Church.

Sexuality is opposed to spirituality. Since their foundation, the monotheistic religions have tried to captivate people with the ideas of spiritual transformation. Basic instincts of the human body were opposed to the sublime values of the 'soul'. (I haven't marked 'body' with quotation marks because I am convinced that it does exist. I cannot say the same about the 'soul'). In order to achieve their goal, religions had to oppress sexuality. Sexuality tempted Man in many different ways in order to make him abandon rigorous spirituality. But Man is greedy by nature and it is very difficult to turn down religion's proposal of a very advantageous exchange: give God all your sexuality in exchange for a guaranteed eternal life.

This was the start of the grand idea in which sexuality kills the soul. We can imagine how, when they hear this idea rustle its wings, the legislators, philosophers, and artists of powerful ancient cultures are turning over in their graves. This remarkable humanitarian idea has spread its wings for the two thousand years of Christian civilisation, inspiring many generations of romantic fools all over the world, and it will continue to fly over our heads until someone can find the strength of spirit and firmness of hand to finally shoot it. Maybe you, my dear readers, will succeed in it?

What do I think about sexual oppression in monotheism? Many things.

I don't share the opinion that sexuality is sinful. I find it quite difficult to imagine how obtaining sexual pleasure can be a sin against your own body, except in cases when there's so much pleasure that it can harm health. Nor do I accept the idea of the existence of the One God-Big Brother itself and the spirituality which is linked to it. Nor do I care to know whether this God is a man or a woman.

On the other hand, I firmly believe that the oppression of sexuality is a refusal of life, a crime against oneself. Any condemnation of sexuality in general and of sexual pleasure in particular means condemnation of life itself. If sex is the apotheosis of life, religion is the apotheosis of death. So even though God created all of us, He is also against life, or at least life as we understand it.

Religions have learned the simple truth: the more they oppress sexuality, the more powerful they become. It could be said that religions are nourished by energy, taken from Eros. The real problem is that sexual energy taken by religion vanishes into nothing: instead of creating value it is entirely spent on the mindless reading of the Revelation. Everything is already said in the Revelation, and it is impossible to create anything new. Prayer, unfortunately, creates no new value.

However, I have good news: no matter how much religion tries to weaken sexual desire, it is impossible to overcome nature. Sociological research shows that the majority of true believers fall for sexual temptation and continue to participate in sexual life, like the despicable atheists and agnostics. Yet they do so with less pleasure since they feel guilt and shame for their betrayal of God, the divine law, and the Church. It is precisely this guilt and shame which spawned the monster that was religious penance, and which successfully poisoned the lives of hundreds of millions of people. It was penance that made sin, shame, and guilt become parts of everyone's lives, for who among us has not lusted after someone?

So now it is time for all of us to think and finally make a choice: sex or God.

■ Return Our Lust To Us! ■

As for me, I have already made this choice. I choose sex. Those who have decided to choose sex, but don't know how to drive away the religious fog, know that I am ready to help you!

The method I would like to suggest is very simple and has always been used by children before adult society transforms them into small robots. Freethinkers of all times have used the same method. It consists in accepting as ideology the simple rule: do the opposite of what you are said to do. One would say '*aller à contre-courant*' in French.

For example, when a child is asked to go in one direction, he runs in another one with joy. A freethinker can be summoned to accept a dominant ideology, but he chooses to follow an opposite one. This can work out in our case. Religions, especially Christianity, tell us that in order to live a virtuous life and attain heavenly joy, we have to limit or renounce all natural sexuality that they call lust or sinful concupiscence. As for me, I suggest you accept and love lust with all your heart in order to abandon religion and get back your self-respect. In return, you will obtain sexual freedom and the right to passionate human sex and bright carnal love.

You will finally be able to do what you have done all your life without hiding or being ashamed or feeling guilty. You should reappropriate lust and abandon yourself to the

*Lust in Romanesque art: a woman
with breasts bitten by snakes.*

miraculous pleasures of life! Abandon yourself not to what they angrily call 'impure joys' and 'dirty lust', but to what it is in reality – 'noble passions' and 'limitless imagination'.

I am absolutely sure that if we had no lust, we would still live in the Stone Age. Indeed, lust is a sign of vitality and interest for the outside world. It is something that keeps us alive and pushes us forward. Isn't it lust for innovations that made Steve Jobs create the Apple empire? Isn't it Elon Musk's lust that pushes the rockets which will help us to conquer Mars?

Today all the necessary conditions for lust's rehabilitation are gathered. However, this rehabilitation started a long time ago, in the nineteenth century, with the first erotic postcards and Gustave Courbet's painting 'L'Origine du monde' (1866) which wasn't exhibited for more than 120 years. It seems they feared that visitors had never seen female sex organs.

In conclusion, I would like to say that I was serious when I wrote this. There is no irony or sarcasm in my manifesto of lust. I even invented a slogan: 'Return our lust to us, and we will return your God to you.' It seems like a fair exchange to me.

CHAPTER VII

Thou Shalt have no other Gods Before Me

Aunque la mona se vista de seda, mona se queda.
You can't make a silk purse out of a sow's ear.
Spanish Proverb

Every sphere of human existence is woven from a particular tangle of ideas. In religion, one of these ideas is the institution of holiness, made unduly sacred and held above rational analysis. Only God is superior to it. This concept demands an immediate deconsecration. I am positively sure that any idea – no matter its origin or its propagator – must be critically analysed.

One has to understand and to explain how it happened that there are extraordinary beings, demigods, among us, more or less equal human beings made of the same biological material and moved by the same passions and objectives. If they do really exist, one has to abandon everything earthly immediately and try to become a saint. If the phenomenon of sanctity doesn't exist, then we can gain some time in prayers and save some money in church candles.

The monotheistic religions, especially Christianity, make great use of the fact that people automatically associate holiness with some kind of perfection. Every one of us, even avowed non-believers, is filled with reverence, trepidation, and admiration when confronted with recognised saints or a promising aspirant for this grand title. This happens automatically, involuntarily, and unconsciously. Nobody teaches us to react like this. Like being scared of big dogs. Even without a sign saying, 'Beware of the dog!' people do everything to keep away. There's no need to make a sign saying 'Be awestruck! Saint ahead!'; at the mere sight of his image the body usually springs to attention.

I also used to spring to attention before saints, feeling just as reverent and timid as those who actually believed in their God, if not more so. It would seem that things started to change inside me after my first encounter with a real-life saint, albeit a Buddhist one. By definition, it's impossible to meet a Christian saint in this world; if they're alive, they're not yet a saint, and when they get THERE, we're left HERE.

◾ The Saints or the Living ◾

This meeting took place many years ago, when I was a senator from Buryatia. I don't remember when exactly. I was a senator for nine years – from 2004 till 2013 – and I am still proud of what I did for the development of this region.

Most of my readers surely know nothing about the Republic of Buryatia: it is a federal subject of Russia with a population of one million in an area equal to the size of Germany. It is located in the central south region of Siberia and has 1,200 km of the coastline with Lake Baikal, the world's deepest lake. Ethnic Buryats, the northernmost group of the Mongols, make up 30 per cent of the republic's population. Since prehistoric times, they practice Shamanism and later on got under the influence of Buddhism, like their Mongolian brothers from Mongolia.

One day, one of the members of the republic's government, an ethnic Buryat I knew for many years, called and offered for me to meet a 'real' Buddhist saint from Tibet, a confidant of the Dalai Lama. During the Soviet era, my friend was a communist and an atheist – one couldn't make one's career otherwise – but after the collapse of the USSR, he went back to his roots and became a practising Buddhist.

Of course, I answered that I would absolutely flipping love to, but wondered what was in it for the saint. That's when he started to get flustered and went off on some tangent about the importance of cultural exchange to bring people together. It was only on the strength of our long-standing friendship that we finally got him to admit that the saint's guardians, rather than the saint himself, were counting on some financial assistance in exchange for fervent and incessant prayers for our health and prosperity. It was impossible to get him to clarify what 'some financial assistance' might mean beyond inarticulate mumbling: 'Oh, you know, give however much you can, whatever you can afford.' From previous bad experiences, I knew it would turn out to be very expensive, but it was already too late. I had to prepare myself for an inevitable meeting with a saint and to understand what it means in Buddhism to be a saint. This is what I learned.

A fundamental principle of Buddhism is that everyone can become just as holy and enlightened as all Buddhas, Botthisatvas, and other spiritual leaders. A saint is not made holy by any particular status or inherent pre-eminence, but instead by the ability to overcome his prejudices and abandon stereotypical ways of being (what that actually means remains unclear, but it sounds nice and I like it anyway), as well as fleeting pleasures, illusions, and desires that maul the soul. Saints are absolutely serene and content with their lot. But the main thing about saints is that they have comprehended – or rather acquired – *primeval emptiness*.

The saint came round to my house with his interpreter as he only spoke Tibetan and a couple of words in Russian, despite his frequent visits to Russia, the latest of which was for three months. Initially, I was greatly impressed by the superhuman unflinching silence and stillness that he maintained for one and a half hours, and by his bright blue eyes. He radiated something extraordinary that ordinary people like you and I don't have, as well as this impenetrable spirituality. This meaningful silence seemed to reflect the majesty of his God and I had the distinct sense that even if he wasn't God himself, he wasn't human, either.

However, the more I talked with him, the more acutely I felt a vague and inexplicable disappointment. Now I understand what it was: a bright childhood dream died within me. His first appearance was deceptive; despite the competence and best efforts of his interpreter, he couldn't answer a single one of the questions I posed. My questions reflected off him like light reflects off a mirror.

His eyes didn't see me even when they looked me square in the face. I had the feeling that those eyes weren't looking at the surface, but at what lay beneath. He was absolutely indifferent to the world around him in general and to me in particular. He was prepared to take me however I came: a godly man or a serial killer.

They walked out and left me on tenterhooks, bewildered and unable to say what the hell had just happened. I didn't have the foggiest and didn't even feel like talking about the encounter. At least I didn't regret the cost; you have to pay for your mistakes!

It was a few weeks later over breakfast – I remember this moment very well – that I clearly understood what it was. He was empty. Not primitive, not dumb, but just empty. He was not a bottomless wellspring, but a bottomless abyss. His emptiness was neither good nor bad. It was empty, and one can't discuss or criticise emptiness. There was nothing behind these holy mirrors but black holes. Astronauts are wasting huge amounts of public money searching for black holes in the universe when these holes actually live among us.

This experience left a lasting imprint on my memory and a couple of years later, while working on this book, I realised what primeval emptiness really is. It's actually quite easy to reach a rational understanding of how saints come to be.

Everyone possesses a certain amount of biological energy. Essentially, this energy can be chanelled in three possible directions:

– Towards self-development and creating added value for yourself and for others.

– Towards establishing and maintaining connections with other people, both in private life (with friends, lovers, family, or children) and in public life (by forming interest groups with like-minded people or participating in political parties and movements).

– Towards God or, as Buddhists call it, primeval emptiness.

Religions insist that the sole meaning of Man's birth, life, and death can be found in worshipping and serving God. The best believers, aspiring saints, labour long and hard over the course of decades to expel – or rather to kill – everything that made them human in a desperate attempt to draw near to God and 'see His face'.

The average person finds this almost impossible to execute as it goes against human nature and biological instincts. Only a smattering of individual fanatics have proved able to offer their lives up to God and sever all ties with society, giving up all earthly pleasures including family and children – God absorbs all of it. And they won. Religion succeeded in sucking everything out of them, turning once-living people into empty holes. Their absolute emptiness is what makes them saints. No human can live in a hole like that, only God. Despite the best efforts of religious fanatics, they still don't become gods (there's only room for one God up there) and instead are caught in a lifeless limbo between this world and the next. Formally they are still on earth *among* us, but they are no longer *with* us. They are already with their God. If you look closely you'll notice that all saints, not just Buddhist ones, have a completely absent, dispassionate expression and empty eyes. It's apt to call eyes like that 'heavenly'; the heavens are usually empty if the weather's good. It's not a sign of affected spirituality, but of an empty personality and a lack of zest for life. And a lack of zest for life means a lack of desire.

Sapped of energy, saints become one-dimensional, incapable of creating their own value system. The only thing they can do is stick like glue to pre-existing religious values and become beautiful candy papers. We all know what candy papers are like from when we were little. They are very attractive on the outside, but when you get up close and touch them you discover there's nothing inside – only emptiness, somebody has already eaten the candy!

Can these people perform miracles? Unlikely. Even if miracles exist, to make miracles you need energy, but this is something saints do not have: they lost their human energy and never obtained a divine one. But some naive people want to believe in miracles as children believe in fairy tales – let them be happy with a new toy!

Holiness is a rare accomplishment and there's no denying that it attracts the attention of believers, as well as those who want to become holy. In reality, people of faith are rarely at one with themselves. They cannot master their sinful desires and are tormented by feelings of guilt and sinfulness before God. This is why they are drawn to the holy. Or rather to those who have managed to convince others they are holy.

Believers are attracted to saints for a reason: they hope that saints will help rid them of their sinful passions and ameliorate their chances to reach paradise. They turn to saints for help, in the same way that secular people turn to their bosses at work. Any saint, even an insignificant one, necessarily has some disciples who are attracted to him, just as negative charges attract positive.

The gravitational pull of saints is extremely strong: a saint, being a translucent shell of the human he or she once was, is free of human 'snags' and doesn't repel or reject any-one. A holy hole attracts the thing it's wired to attract, namely other human lives, which immediately collapse into the hole. It's a fact of life: things constantly pour, fall, or climb through holes (especially the holes in pockets).

The image of the saint as a hole could be painted differently. Through religious rituals and prayers, God drains the saint of all his energy. The saint, sapped of his own energy, then sucks it from his disciples; then the saint pours out this energy to God and becomes empty again, meaning he's ready for another portion of human energy from his disciples. Thus, one saint can draw energy from millions of non-saints.

Saints don't offer the slightest bit of help to those who believe in them. We're nothing to the saints and to God, and all our prayers and requests evaporate before them without reply. If it seemed as though a saint heard your plea, it was a mirage; it was just that he couldn't swallow you whole and he spat a bit of you back out. Somebody with nothing can't give anything to anyone else, except for one solid bit of advice: to follow his example and study the Holy Scriptures day and night. The same Holy Scriptures which have already sucked everything out of him and steamrollered his life, and will easily do the same to yours.

Society based on religious community shouldn't expect anything better: the religious fellowship desperately needs more energy for its rituals and so it hunts down new lives that haven't yet been sucked up. The hole expands and gets bigger and bigger while the vitality and creative potential of society gets smaller and smaller, and becomes just as primitive as the majority of its members.

Let's get back to the dog scenario I mentioned. Most people are scared of dogs, but by no means everyone. Dogs in turn are scared of strong and self-assured people, no matter how big and strong they are themselves. If this weren't the case, humans would obey dogs, not the other way round.

The situation with saints is ambiguous. They attract to themselves only weak people tortured by frustrated passions and inferiority complexes. They cannot create their own value and desperately need guiding deities to whom they can offer veneration, worship, and themselves as sacrifices – these deities can be anything from God to saints, dictators, and crime lords. And this only to become fully fledged dummies with no sense of self. Weak people find holiness very appealing, more sublime than anything else.

Weak people are very similar to those free radicals in school chemistry lessons. They are always on the lookout for other weak people so that they can join together in latching onto anything big they can find. It's easy for weak people to get attached – they're hedgehogs without spines or, if you like, spineless hedgehogs. They grow spines later – big and extremely sharp ones in fact. Non-Christians, heretics, dissenters, and outsiders are soon skewered onto these collective prickles and members of the fellowship quickly have to get a handle on the fact that individuality is immorality and will be ruthlessly punished.

Strong and self-sufficient people don't run away from their humanity and therefore don't need saints – strong people are lonely by definition, as they only love themselves and those close to them. They have their own set of rules and demands and they are not even drawn to other strong people. In this respect, they are like hedgehogs and find it difficult even to get close to anyone, let alone nestle beside them. Why would they need lifeless saints? They don't need any kind of saint's *vitae*; they are only concerned with one *vita* – their own – and how to make the best of it. The one reason they might occasionally make use of a saint's image is out of a desire to manipulate other, weaker, people.

■ The Saint Court ■

'Or do you not know that the Lord's people will judge the world?'
(1 Corinthias 6:2)

Personal holiness, which appeared long before the monotheistic religions, is defined in encyclopedias as spiritual perfection, usually in contrast to all that's base and human. It means that saints are singled out and distinguished from everyone else, refusing to rub shoulders with the masses, that is, with you and me.

How did they appear among us? Prehistoric Man believed that the success of his endeavours was directly linked to the sacrifice they brought before their native deity, the guardian of their race – the more valuable it was, the more the giver profited. They would perhaps sacrifice an ordinary sheep and then eat it, or would sacrifice their own children and usually cremate their bodies afterwards. As time went on, there were some votaries willing to offer the greatest sacrifice of all, the most valuable thing they possessed: their very lives. Not literally of course (that happened very rarely), but they devoted and submitted their whole life to their deity, holding nothing back and losing all their human attributes and acquiring 'spiritual' ones instead.

It wasn't that these people were crazy about their god, though there were a fair amount of fanatics and holy fools. They just desperately wanted to stand out. A completely understandable natural urge as much back then as it is today. In exchange for their human life they laid claim to the esteemed status of priest. How could one show that he was more unique than everyone around him? Only by demonstrating that they are indeed different by living a purely spiritual life without passions and natural pleasures. In those days, there was no other way to set yourself apart. A primitive material life was gradually demarcated from a 'higher', purely 'spiritual' life, which was the genesis of a new kind of 'spiritual' religion. Correct 'spiritual' behaviour dressed itself as the manifestation of sublime perfection. This is why a priest, as a spiritual figure, had to remain mystically dispassionate, the best proof of which was the rejection of the greatest and most important pleasure in human existence: sexual gratification. Complete sexual abstinence became symbolic of ideal 'spiritual' behaviour, and despite their generally favourable attitude towards sex, Prehistoric societies started to impose certain restrictions on people who were in contact with the divine, for example when a person approached a sacred object or performed a sacred ritual. Sexual organs were foremost seen as organs of secretion and did not correspond to the rules of ritual purity.

The idea of temperance in sexual activity can be found even in Greek religion, generally tolerant to all human passions. For example, it was necessary to change into clean clothes before approaching a temple or not to have sex after performing rituals or participating in funeral processions. However, the liberal Greeks found a loophole even here: the majority of religious offices demanding a temporary chastity were not lifelong and were given to pre-pubertal children and menopaused women. It is also highly possible that priests' continence is another Greek myth. It is impossible to know for sure whether priests had sex or not.

The concept of holiness – *Hieros* (ερός) – had two contradictory meanings. On the one hand, it encompassed everything related to gods and the territories, religious ceremonies and to priests themselves – holy and sacred things were the opposite of everything. On the other hand, the term was used to mean something forbidden – something horrible and cursed. Both these meanings were carried over into the Latin and now when the French say 'holy' (*sacré*), it can mean any number of things: that they love and admire you or that they hope you burn in hell. But the main point is that the understanding of holiness in Antiquity was different from any other, because for it holiness did not have a moral dimension, and there was no distinction between hopeless sinners and those fit to worship the divine.

Judaism and Islam were not particularly interested in holiness. Judaism considers holiness to be an essential attribute of God. God is holy inasmuch as He is singular and supreme. The Jewish people are holy inasmuch as they distance themselves from material concerns and honour their God. Saturday is holy inasmuch as it is devoted to divine matters, not those of the world. And so it goes on, right to the end of the Torah. The term is applied very cautiously to Man as holiness of any description can only be attained with the help of God. While Man's soul is made in the image and likeness of God, he holds on to his bestial origins without even trying.

Holiness demands serious intellectual and spiritual self-improvement: it means distinguishing oneself from the animals, spirit from flesh, eternal from temporal. Becoming 'different, distinct, set apart'. Once Man has reached the heights of holiness, he is liberated from the dictates of the flesh like God himself. Practically speaking, this means strictly abstaining from idolatry, purging oneself of everything unclean and dishonourable, practicing moderation in sexual relations and, most of all, refusing to take pleasure in sex, if not completely, then at least in part. The latter stipulation makes the path to holiness impossible for the majority of Jews, ardent lovers of sex. Though it's no secret that the majority of clients in Israel's illegal brothels are Orthodox Jews.

There is no canonical interpretation of the word 'holiness' in Islam. In Arabic it translates as 'intimacy, protection', primarily meaning proximity to Allah, the symbol of absolute purity. Anyone who believes in Allah is made to some extent holy since they yearn to draw close to Him and cleanse themselves physically and spiritually. Martyrs of the faith are rewarded with the great favour of Allah, not with sainthood. Islam considers the way Christians venerate their saints to be idolatry. As do I.

Early Christianity enthusiastically adopted the classical understanding of holiness as symbolic of a closeness to the divine and to divine matters, but it turned it on its head. Being deeply concerned with popular approval and knowing full well the strength of human conceit, it proposed to think of *all* members of the new Church as saints, not just its priests. Christians were made saints by virtue of having correctly selected the only 'true' religion on earth and also by rising above the sordid spiritual and material scum of the pagan world.

An excellent approach in terms of mass psychology! If I were in these believers' position, I would burst with our inflated sense of self-importance. But for the first time in human history there was an interstice between religion and society, or rather unlimited loathing, in which any shrewd observer could glimpse the blueprint for future religious wars with their millions of victims, triumphant inquisitions, and burning of heretics and witches at the stake.

In the New Testament, holiness is the greatest moral goal of all believers and is understood as a desire to draw nearer to God and emulate his purity of spirit: 'Be perfect, therefore, as your heavenly Father is perfect.' (Matthew 5:48)

Naturally, it wasn't long before some holy people became holier than others. Everything was just as in George Orwell's immortal phrase: 'All animals are equal, but some animals are more equal than others.' Old Testament prophets and patriarchs came closest to the ideal, as well as Church Fathers and martyrs of the faith. With the unification of disparate Christian congregations into one gigantic religious entity, the number of holy people plummeted. To unify tens of millions of devotees, they didn't need to parachute in hundreds of saints, they only needed a sprinkling of widely revered human demigods, dazzling everyone with their extraordinary merits and celestial grandeur. It became almost as difficult to join the ranks of the saints as it was to ascend to heaven. Evil tongues would say that the pantheon of saints simply superseded the pantheon of classical gods.

The concept of holiness was bound to change with the Church, and its principles were set fast in the seventh and eighth centuries by the Byzantine, Maximus the Confessor, and the Syrian, John Damascene. They understood holiness to be divine energy permeating human nature, running through the flesh during their lifetime and constituting their power after death, such as the way they are depicted in icons. This is why people started to venerate icons and defended the practice against perfectly justified accusations of idolatry. Saints belong to our world only in part: with their divine energy, saints can overcome the friction between the material and the spiritual and undergo divine transformation right here on earth.

It is very profitable for ordinary believers: saints obtain an angelic capacity to guide ordinary Christians and to lobby God on their behalf, as saints are well versed in how best to negotiate. So, believers can appeal to saints to ask for pardon of their sins and grace, which is much simpler. It sounds a lot like what goes on nowadays; in the upper echelons of society, bigwigs have long since done the same, whether as close friends of the king or distant relatives of every president or wheeler-dealer on the planet.

The eleventh century saw Christianity split irrevocably between the Orthodox and Catholic church, which necessarily produced polarised understandings of holiness. This was even more the case five centuries later, when the Catholic Church puked up indigestible Protestantism.

The Orthodox Church bases its concept of holiness on the principles of Maxim the Confessor and John Damascene. Any Christian baptised according to due process is bestowed with the gift of holiness, which only comes to fruition with the help of God as holiness comes from Him alone and leads to the transformation of fallen and always sinful Man. As a result, Man recovers his original, uncorrupted nature and becomes immortal.

It's a wonderful prospect except for one big 'but'. The believer can spend his entire life praying to God and performing rituals glorifying Him, but never receive His grace and become a saint. The huge investment won't have any return: God is hard-nosed and fairly tight-fisted when it comes to helping out, and so, out of millions of hopefuls, only a handful become saints. Those that make the cut become his representatives on earth. Filled with the power of the Holy Spirit, they become powerful and can perform miracles.

The veneration of saints is strictly enforced in the Orthodox Church – they intercede for us in Heaven and they are almost as deserving of worship as God himself.

Despite being a collection of sects, Protestantism is united in claiming that faith in Christ is sufficient for Man's redemption. They reject monasticism and veneration of saints and even icons. This is based on their own cast-iron logic: the veneration of saints takes away from the worthiness of Christ himself as the saviour of mankind by diverting the praise of believers. It is as if the front-row seats are already occupied by several centuries' worth of saints and church elders. Moreover, the veneration of saints contradicts the Holy Scriptures, which say that Man should worship God alone. Finally, Protestants assert with a final 'twist of the knife' that veneration of saints is pointless. Saints are no different from ordinary people: they do not have any supernatural ability to hear our prayers and requests or intercede on the behalf of others and have absolutely no effect on the daily life of believers. You're better off spending time digging up potatoes in your backyard.

The spiritual father of Protestantism, Luther, said that saints were ordinary, albeit very godly people who should be remembered with reverence and respect, but that it was an affront to God to turn to them in prayer. Holiness only finds expression in worldly acts of mercy. Luther writes in his Commentary on the Epistle to the Galatians:

> The scholastics, monks, and others of their ilk fought only against carnal lust and were proud of a victory which they never obtained. In the meanwhile they harbored within their breasts pride, hatred, disdain, self-trust, contempt of the Word of God, disloyalty, blasphemy, and other lusts of the flesh. Against these sins they never fought because they never took them for sins.

All in all, Protestants made a sharp and cheerful about-turn towards the source of Christian teaching, representing nothing less than a revolution in Christianity.

Some new Protestant sects, like Pentecostalism or Charismatic Christianity, denounce asceticism and declare that every churchgoer is holy. How wouldn't he become a saint if the Holy Spirit fills him during the baptism and gives him the supernatural gifts of healing the sick, predicting the future, and speaking foreign languages he never learnt. All believers are saints, having chosen the true religion which bestowed on them miraculous gifts in baptism and cleansed them from sin. This is where contemporary Charismatic Christianity begins to diverge: it denies original sin, beckons all into a rich and happy life at peace with themselves and the world around them, and spices up the intercession with concerts of cool music. It's no coincidence that it's already hundreds of millions of people strong, comprising almost a fifth of all Christians on the planet.

Personally, I don't see anything radically new in this teaching. Christians are 'new', but friends are 'old': demons, miraculous healing, and the 'face' of God. All positive aspects of individual holiness are overshadowed with the statement that, in individual holiness, Man gets no credit, and the glory goes to Jesus Christ alone. Holiness does not mean an absence of sin. Sins still stock up over the course of a lifetime and Man has to repent constantly so that God can cleanse him of all sin.

However, the idea of acquiring the ability to speak in foreign languages is really very appealing. It would be very useful in removing any strains of envy from relatively happy marriages: it would be a handy explanation for the unfamiliar male and female names that spouses pronounce in their sleep at night. It's most probably precisely this that makes enemies of the 'New Christians' so sure it's not the Holy Spirit speaking, but Satan.

The Catholic Church shares the Byzantine-Syrian principles of holiness, but doesn't demand that believers venerate its entire arsenal of saints. Catholic saints are more like models and personifications of moral virtue.

However, Catholic saints have a bigger role to play than the direct intercession we see in Orthodoxy. The Catholic Church entered the era of sophisticated commodity-money relations long before capitalism did (the sale of pardons is but one example), and succeeded in establishing healthy trade relations not only between God and the saints (with the exchange of prayers and holiness), but also between saints and ordinary believers. The thing is that over the course of his career, every saint is lavished with God's favour, and, given his sanctification and guaranteed redemption, he doesn't need any of it. Catholic saints can therefore share their surplus holiness with any ordinary believers that take a shine to them. They exchange this for years of intercession to ensure that the souls of these believers come off in the best possible light on the Day of Judgement.

It is extremely difficult to be recognised as a saint by the Catholic Church. One has to prove not only one's virtuous life, but also one's superhuman nature and ability to produce miracles. There is an impressively pedantic and bureaucratic process for assessing and registering these miracles, and the selection process and demographic of its saints could be seen as a magnificent triumph of democracy. It places the popes alongside mighty emperors, poor, illiterate, rural peasants, and the elderly alongside the young. Whilst old saints are venerated, new saints are canonised in each generation, usually in the region of four to six a year. But some years are more bountiful than others. In 2000, the Pope beatified 120 so-called 'Chinese Martyrs' in one go, and 2007 was something of a world record: for some reason the Vatican remembered the Spanish Civil War and beatified 498 people.

So how do you actually go about becoming a Christian saint and save yourself from sin and death? The success depends on necessary and sufficient conditions, like in maths. I've already covered the necessary condition: God sees fit to offer unlimited assistance to one particular person. There's not much that anyone can do to influence this, so there's nothing to discuss.

The sufficient condition is hinged on the candidate for sainthood convincingly demonstrating his extraordinary virtue by using his divine gift to battle valiantly with sinful desires and passions, especially sexual ones. The accepted authority on questions of holiness, Clement of Alexandria, wrote that it's not so much about desiring less, as the Greeks did, but about refraining from desire all together. Great advice that wouldn't be out of place in Buddhism!

I first became interested in Christian holiness fifteen years ago, after I met a businessman from Lithuania. We were the same age and shared the same opinions on life, having both lived the biggest (but not the best!) part of our lives in the former-USSR; nothing could prevent us from becoming friends. I won't tell you his real name, so let's call him Andrius. Once, we drank a lot and he suddenly started telling me that when he was a child he attended Catechism classes in the Kaunas Catholic Seminary and even wanted to become a priest. However, at some point, he started to doubt the choice of his path. His attitude towards Catholicism started to deteriorate. With time, he lost interest in it and turned to women and money. For some reason, I kept his story in mind and I remembered it when I started to write this book.

■ Saint Anthony's Women ■

Andrius' first encounter with a genuine Christian saint happened during a lesson on patristics. Patristics is the science by which the church proves, beyond doubt, that no matter how intelligent and erudite these guys Socrates, Plato, and Aristotle might have been, our Church Fathers were still more intelligent and more erudite.

This particular lesson was on the sins of woman's flesh. Father Jonas, who had a reputation for extremely nit-picky sermons, had outdone himself on this one. For an hour and a half he held forth on how the sinful and lustful woman's body betrays and desecrates the radiantly innocent man's soul. The Holy Scriptures say it was a woman that first rejected God's law and then lost no time in corrupting the man, who even the Devil hadn't yet managed to corrupt. That's what forced our God, Jesus Christ, to die on the cross as atonement for the sins of mankind.

Andrius understood next to nothing, although he was usually in Father Jonas' good books. It was a bleak and foggy Monday morning, and he wanted nothing more than to sleep after ice-skating for three hours on Sunday. He wasn't in the mood for hearing about female depravity either; he took it as an affront to his mum and older sister. He only tuned in at the point when Father Jonas' voice got dramatically loud and he began his account of the most shining example of a victory in the fight with the flesh: the life and works of the great Christian desert-dwelling hermit, Saint Anthony. Having reached the end of his account, he flourished three coloured prints of some old pictures before the class with the arrogant air of a prophet. Upon seeing them, the bored lads in the front row murmured excitedly and struggled to contain whistles of admiration.

The first picture depicted a busty young woman tied to a cross (so she didn't run off, no doubt) and a bearded old man dressed in rags. There was no question: the old man was mad. Rather than clutching the young and untouched body, which most people so

Félicien Rops, The Temptation of Saint Anthony, 1878.
The fear of Saint Anthony when faced with such female lust is completely understandable.
The woman is so powerful that she succeeded in chasing Christ from the cross.

John Charles Dollman, The Temptation of Saint Anthony, 1897.

rich in years and poor in every other way could all but dream of, he was squirming in the opposite direction, covering his ears with his unnaturally gnarled hands. He was looking away from the appetising body that God had granted him and studying a thick book with strange pictures and incomprehensible captions.

The second picture proved even more interesting. It showed a completely nude young girl amid a troop of apes and what seemed to be hyenas. There was also a kneeling St Anthony, praying in the direction of his cave, paying no attention either to the girl or the animals. Andrius shared the old man's lack of interest in the animals; he'd seen plenty of them at the zoo. But the complete lack of interest in the girl from Anthony felt like complete lunacy to him. She was as gorgeous as the women whose pictures Andrius found in his father's bureau, hidden under thick gardening manuals. She had plenty to admire: she was slim, with a luscious head of hair, firm young breasts, long legs and a pert little behind.

The old man fared better in the third picture. Having evidently grown tired of sitting alone in the suffocating darkness, he had overcome his fear of the naked girls and come out into the open to dance in a ring with the beautiful girl from the second picture and her scantily clad friends. Before doing so, he had tidied himself up a little, trimmed his beard and put on a new robe. It was entirely fitting that the beautiful girl's energetic nature set her apart from the others and led her to mount a cute-looking pig, stark naked. Some might say she had just got tired of dancing, but Andrius thought better of her

Jacques Antoine Vallin, The Temptation of Saint Anthony, 1827.

and imagined that she wanted to cheer up the glum old man after his long stint in the dank, damp darkness of the cave. The joyous news of the old man's recovery had spread throughout the region, and three more girls in the archway on the left were hurrying to join the merry celebrations.

The pictures made a great impression on Andrius, but it wasn't the naked girls that stuck in his mind. Instead, he was tortured by the thought that there was no water for bathing. He never did quite come to terms with this, probably because he dreaded to think how somebody might survive in a cave for years on end without water to wash himself. Like any other boy from a city, his parents had brought him up to shower twice a day, morning and evening, and Andrius couldn't conceive of how somebody could live in a constant state of filth. He had once been pressed up against a homeless man in a packed bus for three whole stops, and the horrifying, stagnant smell of his unwashed body had haunted him for weeks afterwards. For some time, Andrius succeeded in banishing the thought of how this related to Saint Anthony from his mind, but about three weeks after the ill-fated lesson, the Great Hermit's smell suddenly came to him in a dream and he woke up in the most terrible state of panic. He interpreted the dream as a punishment for his sinful thoughts; good boys dream of the Holy Spirit, but he dreamt instead of the Smelly Spirit.

Father Jonas' ladies looked incredibly similar to the girls in glossy magazines, whose photos Andrius regularly tore out and carefully stuck up on the wall opposite his bed when he came home from school each day. He was almost fourteen at the time, when his early adolescence had been swept up in the whirlwind of masturbation that can be expected at that age. After this daily 'self-abasement', he would peel them off, just as carefully, and hide them under his mattress to protect his favourite girlfriends from the wrath of his eternally dissatisfied parents. Being otherwise a good and obedient boy, keeping up this double life left Andrius in a constant fluster. He was torn between feelings of shame and self-loathing in front of all the adults around him, but no amount of self-will and self-reproof could stand in the way of nature's insatiable and overwhelming fervour. Patristics lessons weren't in the least bit helpful in overcoming this terrible habit; in fact, they exacerbated the situation. Andrius' mind began firmly to associate holiness with the naked female body and this added fuel to the fire of his rabid sexuality. In the week following the patristics lesson he

Lovis Corinth, The Temptation of Saint Anthony, 1897.

visited the town library four times, each time asking the librarian for a huge pile of thick illustrated books about saints. The librarian, an elderly grey-haired lady wearing a dress down to her ankles and a limp braid, gushed with admiration for the extraordinary piety of this simple young boy and took great pleasure in clattering about the dusty shelves.

The first two attempts were fruitless. It was only on the fourth occasion that Andrius found what he was looking for. First, he unearthed Father Jonas' second picture – and then, the next bit of the story – the third picture with the dancing and the pig. The Church Fathers had been right to mistrust the girls; as soon as the dancing ended, the holy man was smothered in naked and lustful female flesh. Without a flicker of remorse, Andrius cut it out with a razor he'd set aside for the purpose.

A week later, he found another painting that interested him – Michelangelo's exploration of holiness, *The Torment of Saint Anthony* – even though there were no girls on it and he didn't need his razor anymore. The painting showed a venerable gentleman, our old friend Saint Anthony, hovering in thin air. Demons and various other beasts were cordially helping him into the sky as a mark of respect for the superhuman endurance he had demonstrated, and of gratitude for having inflated the reputation of their beloved Father Devil through the pains he had suffered.

A little later, Andrius struck gold again with a discovery which confirmed that saints are remarkably sexually active even now. This time the saint was female instead – young, heavily made-up, lips parted suggestively. It goes without saying that all these wonderful pictures took their rightful place in the centre of the wall opposite his bed.

Of course, if Andrius had been lucky enough to meet an older confidant to whom he could have bared his soul and confessed everything, he would doubtless have come to appreciate the virtue of sexual abstinence, and his later life could have worked out very differently. Alas, there was nobody to help him. There was no getting anything out of his parents beyond unvoiced irritation and the official line: 'You'll understand when you're older.' Discussing something so profane with Father Jonas was unthinkable.

But he finally decided to ask him whether Saint Anthony got fed up of sitting alone in the dark cave for decades. Father Jonas flapped his arms in irritation and answered that he had had woefully little time to battle with the Devil's incessant temptations, let alone get fed up. He had even had to fight the urge to sleep so as not to let up the relentless prayers that prevented the Devil from infiltrating his cave. Then Andrius mustered all his remaining courage and decided to ask one more question. Wasn't the saint lonely without other people to talk to? It's not even about whether they were ladies, it's just that nobody likes being on their own, do they? Didn't he get the urge to talk to some sweet young lady? Did he have any sensual desires?

On the face of it, it was a praiseworthy question since it came from a place of genuine concern for the holy man, but Father Jonas took it extremely badly. He retreated from Andrius as if he might catch something and, after a lengthy silence, snapped:

'Boy, saints do not need anyone else for company. They are forever and always, night and day, in the company of our Lord Jesus Christ. As regards women, it's about time you learnt that lust separates us from the perfection of Christ. When you're a grown man, you'll be ashamed to have asked something so blasphemous!'

In his four more years at school, Andrius didn't ask Father Jonas anything ever again and never did understand the real reasons for the saint's extremely peculiar behaviour, nor why the Christian church in general, and Father Jonas in particular, liked it so much. Nor did he understand why the Church and Father Jonas so disliked the behaviour of ordinary worldly girls or exactly what it was that these girls had done to offend them. He was challenged with the same questions when he turned twenty and had his first steady girlfriend, but he had nobody to ask: Father Jonas had long since died, completely alone and almost completely destitute, and Andrius' parents were still alive, but barely.

I remembered Andrius' story very well and, when I was writing this book, I started to read about various saints, from the most ancient (emerging straight after Christ's crucifixion) to the medieval. All in all, I much preferred the ancient ones; they had such a strong and genuine belief in God that they didn't even want to live on earth anymore. To convince God of their integrity and devotion, to become perfectly righteous in His sight, they stayed ignorant of the joys of this world. Unworthy and mired in sin, they crippled themselves with fasting, vigils, and prayers. According to the Roman preacher, Symeon the New Theologian, without temptation it would be impossible to live as a saint. Without temptation, a saint quite simply can't fulfil his duty to worship God: 'Whosoever lives a quiet life without temptations shows little zeal for God and does not bless Him with all that they are.' (Hymns)

The spiritual father of all monks, Saint Anthony, was the toughest. At the age of eighteen, when his parents had already passed away, his spirit began to stir. Having first given all his possessions to the poor, he retreated from society into the Egyptian desert for good. Initially he lived in one of the rock-cut tombs and then in some ruins by the Nile, where the deathly struggle against carnal desires and erotic apparitions unravelled. They came at first in the form of a wanton demon – a beautiful woman – and then, when his mind was almost shot, they came in the form of ordinary demons which he usually drove away with the aid of a little bell. Saint Anthony is often depicted beside a pig, that being a symbol of carnality and gluttony, wearing a bell around his neck in a display of solidarity.

In early religious paintings, women were depicted fully-clothed, and horned like the Devil, but from the sixteenth century they began to appear in the nude so as to highlight their sinister role in the seduction of Christian flesh. Saint Anthony's heroic accomplishment is one of those instances, almost unheard of, that the flesh endured complete and utter affliction.

The most famous description of Saint Anthony's fight against diabolical temptations was written by the Greek Church Father, Athanasius of Alexandria. Firstly, the Devil tried to lead Saint Anthony away from discipline, 'whispering to him the remembrance of his wealth, care for his sister, claims of kindred, love of money, love of glory, the various pleasures of the table and the other relaxations of life.' After he failed, he changed tactics: 'The devil, unhappy wight, one night even took upon him the shape of a woman

Michelangelo, The Torment of Saint Anthony, 1487-1488.
As usual, it all began with seductive pretty girls and ended with repulsive demons.

Francisco Goya, Saint Teresa of Ávila, 1830.
You would convert to any faith for such a saint.

and imitated all her acts simply to beguile Antony.' Seeing that 'neither by the spirit of lust nor by blows' did he vanquish Anthony's spirit, he called all the desert's beasts: 'And almost all the hyenas in that desert came forth from their dens and surrounded him; and he was in the midst, while each one threatened to bite.' But Anthony told these villainous beasts: 'If ye have received power against me I am ready to be devoured by you; but if ye were sent against me by demons, stay not, but depart, for I am a servant of Christ.' When Antony said this they fled, 'driven by that word as with a whip'.

I am simply stunned by the huge power of blind faith. In fact, this description is still used in Christian manuals.

I am utterly enthused by Saint Anthony's pedagogical flair too. The most valuable attribute of a good teacher is the absence of envy and the ambition to nurture students to be better than he could ever be. This is exactly what happened: Anthony was personally famed only for his raging battle with devilish temptation, whilst his beloved disciple, Macarius the Great, went one step further and almost rivalled Christ himself. Firstly, to put heathens and heretics alike to shame, he resurrected someone from the dead. Developing quite a taste for it, he forced the dead to speak at will, and even raised one right out of the grave to be sentenced in court.

It's a pity he's no longer with us: with his help, investigators in Christian countries could easily solve all 'shelved' criminal cases.

John Chrysostom felt challenged by Saint Anthony's unprecedented fortitude. True, he only spent four years in the wilderness, but he did devote two of them to standing silently, hardly sleeping, in an attempt to learn the Holy Scriptures by heart. But in some respects he did quite clearly outdo Saint Anthony; in that short space of time he managed to damage his stomach and kidneys permanently, leaving him in severe pain for the rest of his life.

Then came Origen, extreme ascetic, who spent all his time fasting, sleeping on the bare floor, and wearing the same clothes. He probably never washed his body. Then again, why wash yourself when you've got nothing to change into afterwards? Faith was more important than cleanliness and clothing. Otherwise, there is simply no other explanation why women fancied even the likes of Origen. So much so that, tired of battling the temptations they cast about him, he castrated himself.

Saint Augustine, the saint of all Christian Churches, lived with different women for many years. Then, he changed his mind, abandoned his eleven-year-old fiancée, gave away his belongings to the poor and became a monk. This is how he described his younger years in *The Confessions*: 'Thus I polluted the spring of friendship with the filth of concupiscence and I dimmed its luster with the slime of lust.'

Of the later medieval saints, I really liked the humble mystic Francis of Assisi who spent his early years living the high life of a young nobleman but underwent a total transformation at twenty-two. He gave away his entire inheritance and, from being a great lover of women, became a great lover of 'the riches of spiritual poverty', as well as of beggars and lepers. Through lengthy prayers to Him, he managed to get wounds and sores to appear on his body like the wounds of the Redeemer.

Origen castrating himself, illustration from the Roman de la Rose, France, 15ᵗʰ century.

Francis addressed God as if addressing a beloved:

> Let us desire nothing else, let us want nothing else, let nothing else please us and cause us delight except our Creator, Redeemer and Saviour, the only true God, Who is the fullness of good [*Luke 18:19*], all good, every good, the true and supreme good, Who alone is good, merciful, gentle, delightful, and sweet.

He repeatedly declared himself the most unworthy and base of all men, a mere louse: 'I have offended in many ways through my grievous fault, especially because I have not observed the Rule which I have promised to the Lord and I have not said the office as prescribed by the Rule either by reason of my negligence or weakness or because I am ignorant and simple.'

This fervent love for himself made him one of the most popular Catholic saints among millions of other lousy believers. And this despite the fact that he threatened the sinners, who answered the call of the flesh, with the horrors of Hell: 'See, blind ones, deceived by your enemies: by the flesh, the world, and the devil; since it is sweet to the body to work sin and bitter to work to serve God; since all vices and sins come forth and proceed from the heart of man the body weakens, death approaches and so one dies a bitter death. And wheresoever, whensoever, howsoever a man dies in culpable sin without penance and satisfaction, if he can make satisfaction and does not, the devil tears his soul from his body with such anguish and tribulation, that no one can know it, except him who experiences it.'

He was so implacable with the Devil that he invented an original method to fight against him: if he appeared to him again and said unto him 'Thou art damned', he was to say to him these words: 'Open thy mouth!' and by this sign he would clearly know that he was the Devil and not Christ; for no sooner should the words be uttered than he would immediately disappear.

What wonderful advice! At first, I didn't really understand how ordinary people can fight against the Devil if they never saw him nor God, and there are no descriptions of how he looks. Then I remembered one of the stories from *The Decameron* by Boccaccio, where it was told that it was extremely easy to find the Devil, since it is a simple penis. However, it seems to me that a vagina can also pretend to this role.

The story goes as follows: a very rich man had a fair and winsome young daughter by the name of Alibech. She decided to go to the deserts of Thebais in order to see how Christians serve their God. There she met a young hermit, a very devout man, whose name was Rustico, and who, having a mind to make a trial of his own constancy, received her into his cell for the night. He didn't manage to resist the temptations of the flesh and tried to bring her to his pleasures under the guise of serving God.

In the first place, he described to her how great an enemy the Devil was of God. Then, he took off the few garments he had, as did she. He explained that his erect penis was the very Devil they needed to put back in the hell which was in her. And so they did.

Alibech, who had never yet put any Devil in hell, felt some little pain and agreed that 'the Devil must be an ill thing and an enemy in very deed of God'. Later on, the Devil made a very good impression on her and she started to ask Rustico to put it in her hell as often as possible: 'Father mine, I came here to serve God and not to abide idle; let us go put the Devil in hell.' She couldn't really understand 'why the Devil fleeih away from hell; for, and he abode there as willingly as hell receiveth him and holdeth him, he would never come forth therefrom'.

Rustico, who lived on roots and water, could ill avail to answer her calls and what he could do 'was but casting a bean into the lion's mouth'. The girl was unhappy: 'Rustico, and thy Devil be chastened and give thee no more annoy, my hell letteth me not be; wherefore thou wilt do well to aid me with thy Devil in abating the raging of my hell, even as with my hell I have helped thee take the conceit out of thy Devil.'

Is it possible that the hermits' fear of women was also due to the fact that their 'devils' couldn't 'resurrect' when needed?

Another one of Francis' paradoxical ideas was that the closer saints get to God, the more sinful they become. He probably borrowed it from the Christian saint of the fourth century, Abba Dorotheus: I recall how we once spoke of humility, and a noble from the city of Gaza was astonished to hear us say that the nearer one draws to God, the more clearly one sees one's own sinfulness, and thus said, 'how can that be?' And not comprehending, wanted to know the meaning of our words. I said to him: 'Noble sir, tell me, of what estate do you consider yourself in your own city?' He answered, 'I consider myself to be the first and the greatest in my city.' I said to him: 'If you went to Caesarea, how would you consider yourself there?' He answered: 'As the lowliest of all the local nobility.' 'And if,' I said to him again, 'you set out to Antioch, how would you consider yourself there?' 'There,' he answered, 'I would consider myself a plebeian.' 'And if,' I said, 'you went to Constantinople and came nigh unto the king, there who would you consider yourself?' And he answered: 'Almost nobody at all.' Then I said to him: 'This is how it is for saints; the nearer they draw to God, the more clearly they see their own sinfulness.' (*Directions on Spiritual Life*)

A great manipulation of the believers: it is impossible to get rid of sin. So why fight sin if you can never be rid of it anyway?

Whilst reading about famous saints, I found Johannes Nider's treatise on witches with the delightful name *The Anthill*, and Heinrich Kramer and Jacob Sprenger's *Hammer of Witches*, a publication which cost hundreds of thousands of women accused of sexual relations with the Devil their lives. Two descriptions of carnal temptations that tormented holy people drew my attention. The first of these was attributed to Saint Gregory the Dialogist – the one whose fervent prayers brought to an end the plague that killed Pope Pelagius II. He tells of Equitius of Valeria:

> This man, he says, was in his youth greatly troubled by the provocation of the flesh; but the very distress of his temptation made him all the more zealous in his application to prayer. And when he continuously prayed Almighty God for a remedy against this affliction, an Angel appeared to him one night and seemed to make him an eunuch [quite the Christian dream!], and it seemed to him in his vision that all feeling was taken away from his genital organs; and from that time he was such a stranger to temptation as if he had no sex in his body. Behold what benefit there was in that purification; for he was so filled with virtue that, with the help of Almighty God, just as he was before pre-eminent among, so he afterwards became pre-eminent over women. (Kramer and Sprenger, *The Malleus Maleficarum*)

To my mind, the most interesting thing about this story is not the almighty angel's visit, but the fact that after this visit Equitius got unlimited access to young nuns' cloisters, when his life definitely became more interesting. The second description showed me that chastity belts existed not only in chivalric romance, but also in Christian monasteries. It was dedicated to Saint Thomas. His brothers, wishing to tempt him, sent in to him 'a seductive and sumptuously adorned harlot'. But he drove her away with a lighted torch. When he fell asleep after a prayer, two angels appeared to him: 'Behold, at the bidding of God we gird you with a girdle of chastity, which cannot be loosed by any other such temptation; neither can it be acquired by the merits of human virtue, but is given as a gift by God alone.' Thereafter he felt himself endowed with so great a gift of chastity, that from that time he abhorred all the delights of the flesh, so that 'he could not even speak to a woman except under compulsion, but was strong in his perfect chastity'.

I was not really surprised with an angels' visit: after such a long continence, anyone and anything can appear to you. But imagine poor Catholic adolescents who, after reading this story, dream of nothing but a fearsome Christian angel who comes down from heaven to castrate them for the mortal sin of masturbation. These poor people are simply harassed!

Some time later, I found another picture which depicted a very nice girl – again with ample cleavage and a rich head of hair – tempting the Palestinian anchorite Hilarion the Great, one of Saint Anthony's most zealous disciples. Hilarion looked significantly better kempt than Anthony, but at the same time suspiciously effeminate.

I would not hide from you that, at my first encounter with the saints' lifestyle, I was nothing but repulsed. I have passed the last decades of my life alongside a great many dressed and undressed women, scrutinising each in search of their particular transgressions, irredeemable sin and imperfection – in a word, everything which separates them from the so-called saints. But I found nothing. Instead, I saw charm, natural beauty and this sparkling sexuality which has nourished my love for life for many years.

Saints are different. Everyone else lounges by the river on warm, sunny days, while a saint sits in a dark cave without water and stinks. Everyone else eats spit-roasted meat with a quaff of wine. A saint eats stale bread and drinks putrid water. Everyone else gets it on with the ladies. A saint fights his sordid flesh and its temptations: he is even forbidden to masturbate. How can one live such a life?

Dominique Papety, The Temptation of Saint Hilarion, 1843-1844.
Hilarion was tempted by a girl resembling the beautiful and devious Salome who danced for the heinous Herod.

Then, after carefully studying the saints' diet and daily routine, I changed my mind: their lifestyle, more than bizarre from a contemporary point of view, has some advantages.

For example, the Saint Anthony we know well lived for 105 years, of which 70 were spent alone. His brother in deprivation, the first anchorite Paul of Thebes, survived on nothing but bread and dates and set the all-time world record for reclusiveness: 91 years out of his 113. Even though other saints didn't fare quite so well, one can suggest that it was holy people that inspired today's dieticians to extol the benefits of a low-calorie diet.

The question of hygiene in the caverns is not that obvious either. Some researchers affirm that filth is good for health, since a dirty body is more resistant to infections. I am not joking: one can find multiple testimonies in historical books attesting that many oriental and biblical prophets and God's fools lived in the deserts without water, slept under the stars and lived long. Even if they washed themselves, they did it without any soap, which, as it turns out, destroys the protective layer on your skin. Indeed, cleanliness is relative: if the whole family decides one day to stop washing themselves, nobody among them will have any problem. And they will save on their water bills.

So why did Saint Anthony, steeled by 70 years of extreme deprivation, react to the naked female body with such fear, even disdain? Why did all other saints share his hatred? Why does female sexuality separate us from Christ's perfection, as Father Jonas said? After all, isn't the body primarily a symbol of life and the proliferation of the human race, and only incidentally a symbol of sexual temptation?

Saint Anthony and other saints didn't exhibit any personal resentment towards women. It wasn't them who imagined a woman created out of the rib of a man and declared her a second-class entity. It wasn't them who made her the personification of sinful human flesh and accused her of original sin and banished her from paradise, condemning mankind to sickness and mortality.

Saint Anthony simply wanted to be a good saint, and blindly followed the Holy Scriptures. Indeed, this is the holiness which is placed in the very centre of the Christian doctrine, and the aspiration to it is every believer's duty.

Let it be so, the saints' intentions are clear. But how can one explain the incredible resistance of the saints in sexual matters, simply inconceivable for ordinary people?

I found two answers to this question coming from people whose respective attitude towards Christianity is radically different. The first one was suggested by the religious philosopher Saint Thomas Aquinas who once noted that some abstain from the pleasures of the flesh hoping to obtain future glory. The second one was expressed by Nietzsche in *The Antichrist*. He says: 'The histories of saints present the most dubious variety of literature in existence; to examine them by the scientific method, in the entire absence of corroborative documents, seems to me to condemn the whole inquiry from the start – it is simply learned idling'. And concludes: '…the "highest states of mind, held up before mankind by Christianity as of supreme worth, are actually epileptoid in form – the church has granted the name of holy only to lunatics or to gigantic frauds – *in majorem dei honorem*".'

It astonishes me that no one ever asked how Saint Anthony changed during the years of his 'temptations'. Indeed, he managed, alone, to crush his human nature and oppress the desires tearing apart his body. He surely gave a lot for this 'matchless feat' and his mind suffered a great deal. How can one not wonder whether he remained a normal person or became mentally ill?

Alas, we will never know the truth about the state of mind of those saints who lived a couple of thousand years ago. Time and tradition have long ago washed away their personalities and transformed them into legends. They are like dried butterflies in a beautiful frame. However, we can easily evaluate what it means to be a saint today by looking at the modern candidates for holiness.

In theory, there is no discrimination on the basis of occupation or social status during the process of beatification. But in reality 97 per cent of Catholic saints are priests and monks. This is quite logical from the point of view of Church law: once ordained, all members of the clergy have to aspire to holiness, because they live a life of the strictest continence, the life of celibacy.

■ The Hunchbacked, the Lame ■
and the One-Eyed will Never be Saints

Car il n'y a de réellement obscènes que les gens chastes
Only the chaste are truly obscene
Joris-Karl Huysmans, Certains

From its outset, the Catholic Church established a close relationship between faith and the sexual realm. Or rather, there is an inverse relationship, like in communicating vessels: the stronger the faith, the feebler the sex, and vice versa. Man was banished from paradise to earth, and sex was banished from earth to paradise.

Sexual continence, celibacy, concerned the candidates for the priesthood, future mentors of God's folk, who were called to service not by other men, but by the Holy Spirit, an asexual creature one had to imitate in everything.

The problem of sinful sexuality took centre stage in Early Christianity. It was only 306 AD when the synod in the Spanish city of Elvira demanded complete sexual abstinence from its priests and forbade them from having children. The Nicene Council of 325 confirmed this demand. Those who refused were immediately excommunicated from the Church.

Celibacy has never become popular in the Orthodox Church and only monks and some superior hierarchs practised it. Instead of celibacy, the Church demanded from its priests to be strictly monogamous (which is, as you know, almost impossible for an ordinary person), not to remarry nor marry widows and divorcees – they could only marry virgins.

In the Catholic Church, celibacy for bishops was formally proclaimed law in the sixth century in the time of Gregory the Great. I say formally because it wasn't really applied in practice – priests had the hardest time not using their sex organs for their natural

José Benlliure y Gil, The Life of Saint Francis of Assisi.
Fateful sexuality didn't even spare the most infirm.

purposes. The law became effective only in the beginning of the twelfth century when Benedict VIII and Gregory VII categorically forbade the members of the clergy to get married. This was done for rather materialistic reasons – priests' children could have pretended to inherit the Church belongings. It is celibacy which made Christian monasteries so powerful during the Middle Ages: even at those times, money decided everything and was stronger than any prayer.

Lateran Councils of 1123 and 1139 established celibacy for the entire Catholic clergy: We absolutely forbid priests, deacons, or subdeacons to live with concubines and wives, and to cohabit with other women, except those whom the council of Nicaea permitted to dwell with them solely on account of necessity, namely a mother, sister, paternal or maternal aunt, or other such persons, about whom no suspicion could justly arise… marriage contracts between such persons should be made void and the persons ought to undergo penance.

I am not at all convinced that no suspicion could justly arise in relation to mothers, aunts, and sisters, in particular, if Catholic priests are put under these constraints.

The next milestone was the Council of Trent, held between 1545 and 1563 AD. That was when they announced that priests should not be married and must refrain from sex at all times, even if they cease to be part of the clergy. Only the Pope could deliver permission to have sex again.

Moreover, the Canon law prohibited the ordaining of people with certain bodily defects: a missing left eye or right-hand index finger, or being a hunchback, lame or a dwarf.

I can understand the thing about a left eye – it is a canonical one: during the service, the sacred text-prompt is placed on the left, and if you have only a right eye, you can get confused and tell your flock awful absurdities.

One can also understand why not dwarfs: they wouldn't look well at the standard altar, and to create a personalised altar is expensive. Alas, my favourite character in *Game of Thrones*, Tyrion Lannister, could never be ordained.

When it comes to the hunchback, the lame men, and men without a right-hand index finger, I don't have any convincing theories. Personally, I would do the opposite – I would ordain such men in the first place. They are less popular with women than slim men with all their fingers, strong and tender. I'd like to turn now to the many examples the religious tradition has given of the salutary effect of celibacy.

The Catholic Church sees celibacy as an invigorating source, which sustains priests as they withdraw from the material world. It is the reflection of the Kingdom of God, where the resurrected, delivered from original sin, will also be liberated from sexual desire and an obligatory marital relationship.

Celibacy is about increasing willpower and growing as a person, it is an individual holiness and a special gift of God, which allegedly enables priests to relate to their close ones as sexless sons and daughters of God, in need of the love, advice, and support of the Church of Christ, rather than as objects of potential sexual gratification.

In a word, the Catholic Church considered celibacy to be a measure of faith in Christ and the Church.

I see in celibacy something completely different: an inhumane practice of 'spiritual castration', namely abstinence from sexual relations in the case of the presence of a sexual desire – any doctor will tell you that there is nothing more unnatural and abnormal. I am pretty much certain this masochistic idea was a spectacular failure, but I didn't actually hold a candle up to see whether or not the first saints, monks and hermits, gave themselves hand-jobs and if so, how many times a day. In actual fact, deviating from doctrine in this way also has a deep religious purpose: the Christian God loves sinners, not goody-goodies who repent and pray continuously.

The consequences of celibacy are predictable: a completely deformed psyche and sexual deviation. Indeed, you can free yourself of your sexuality only by 'freeing yourself' from life itself. Faith tirelessly reminds us, yelling if it has to, that natural sexuality is the enemy of God, and indulging sexual desires is a crime against Him, and sexual frustration 'explodes' the mind and body, forcing ascetics to focus even more intently on an imagined sex life and fantasise about perverted sexual acts. The contemptible flesh inevitably became the focus of their existence.

Martin Van Maele, illustration from the series "The Great Danse Macabre of the Living", 1905.

The lives of forefathers of monasticism, those innumerable anchorites and stylite hermits of the first centuries of Christianity, attest to the above. In mortifying the sinful flesh by the most forcible means imaginable, they only encouraged the perverted sexual fantasies which tormented the wretched men every minute of their lives, even in their sleep. Just remember the temptations of Saint Anthony! Freud writes in 'On the Universal Tendency to Debasement in the Sphere of Love' that by praising the ascetic monks' feat, 'whose lives were almost entirely occupied with the struggle against libidinal temptation', Christianity tried to destroy sexual love and replace it with the love of God.

It is a pity that Freud did not focus his research on the 'temptations' and the sexual visions of the Christian hermits – there is much more material than in childhood memories and women's sexual deviations. His distinguished protégé Wilhelm Reich maintained that hysteria and perversion flourish more readily in ascetic church circles than in any other social group.

The only way to purge oneself of these fantasies and hide them from others is to accuse somebody else of having them. Accusing pagans of debauchery has been standard practice for almost every Christian theologian in history. Around 300 AD, the newly converted Christian and strict ascetic Arnobius wrote seven tomes, *Against the Pagans*, in which he relishes his own detailed and vivid descriptions of paganism's moral transgressions and debauchery. Most of all I like his description of Pygmalion, king of Cyprus, who loved as a woman an image of Venus. I strongly recommend you to read it – it is much better and healthier than any ordinary porn!

Later, the monasteries became the main centres of debauchery and perversion – this is an indisputable and very well-documented fact. The Church knew about this and even distributed handwritten instruction manuals to monasteries on how to fight sensuality, and instituted cold-water dousing and hard physical labour. These instructions remain relevant to this very day, but you're better off doing intensive exercise rather than hard labour. It did not help at all. This is why in the Soviet army they added bromine to military rations – it was believed that bromine reduced sexual desire and potency.

The framework of the fight against priests' sexuality made all discussions of the legitimacy of celibacy impossible until at least the middle of the eighteenth century. Even then it was not the antihuman nature of celibacy that was discussed, but some of its disadvantages. They discussed the fact that the unmarried priests suffered from a depraved imagination and sinful intentions.

I am sure that the sexual deviations of the Catholic priests have been largely explained above. A significant number of priests, particularly inquisitors, found themselves ensnared by sexual paranoia, with an appetite for sexual sadism in relation to sinners. This was most evident in relation to women, who were forced to strip naked even just for preliminary questioning and precursory water torture. This is well illustrated in Miloš Forman's film *Goya's Ghosts*. You can only imagine the passionate and fervent abandon with which priestly inquisitors masturbated after torturing and punishing the latest sinner.

Has anything changed since then? Only in the sense that the Holy Inquisition is over and the 'treatment' for sinners has got more civilised: confession and repentance. Nietzsche writes about the system of 'priestly medication':

… just ask the doctors dealing with lunatics what always accompanies systematic application of penitential torments, contrition and spasms of redemption. Likewise, study history: everywhere the ascetic priest has prevailed with this treatment of the sick, the sickness has increased in depth and breadth at a terrific speed.

Most probably, when Nietzsche wrote about 'penitential torments', he was thinking about confession, which is optional in the Orthodox Church and compulsory in the Catholic Church which has more than 1.2 billion followers. The 'confession business' is simply huge. Believers have to confess their sins at least once a year, or once a month if possible. Around a hundred years ago, the minimum age for confession was lowered from fourteen to seven, which meant priests were given full authority over really tiny children.

As you'd expect, the sin most often discussed at confession is, and has always been, sex – it's the one that gets to all of us the most. The fact that people had to discuss their sins in order to receive some spurious mercy meant that the priest receiving the confession could dig about in the most minute and intimate details of the confessor's sex life. The Church even went so far as to demand the priests do this in order to expose the sin better. Questions such as 'what position did you have sinful sex in?' and 'did you put his penis in your mouth?' risked arousing the priest beyond belief, prompting him to expose even more obscene and 'dirty' details. The compulsory character of the confession disposed priests to seducing both men and women.

Only a smattering of ascetics managed to stay in the boundaries of normal: they vanquished 'temptations' by purging themselves of their humanity and almost completely transforming their sexuality into religious fever and ecstasy. These winners became known as saints. Those remaining lost the battle and did not manage to crush their human nature. Constant sexual drought filled them with inferiority complexes and hatred towards normal people, making them misanthropic, perverted and, in some cases, maniacs.

■ A Paedophile Celibacy ■

Chassez le naturel, il revient au gallop.
Chase off nature and it will gallop right back.
(*A leopard can't change its spots*) French saying

People with no or few religious convictions find it difficult to appreciate whether celibacy is really an 'invigorating source which sustains priests as they withdraw from the material world' and an action of 'dedicating oneself to humanity'. It's much easier for them to judge the effect of celibacy on the basis of the many articles describing instances of widespread paedophilia in Catholic parishes and schools.

These scandals have been exposed fairly recently, but there's no doubt the situation has been going on far longer and was much worse before: religious paedophilia has proliferated over the centuries and probably emerged the moment universal celibacy was introduced as a Church law.

So why were there not any scandals earlier? Firstly, the Church, and society as a whole, was far less open. Secondly, the Church was much more powerful, and everyone held their

Cornelis Cornelisz van Haarlem, The Monk and the Nun, 1591.
I prefer generous monks of this type to prying ones – nothing human seems strange to me.

tongue – nobody wanted to be burnt at the stake. Thirdly, there was no way journalists could have penetrated the high walls of churches and religious schools. But now churches in developed countries have relented and are no longer completely above suspicion, which has meant an eruption of outrageous scandals in countries across the world.

The first reliable evidence of infractions on celibacy appeared in the eighteenth century after the Archbishop of Paris asked the police to trace the sexual activities of the Catholic priests, whose sins impeded the Church in its fight against Jansenism. In a short time, the police made 970 reports on priests at all levels, who were caught red-handed with prostitutes. This leak didn't really impress public opinion – the priests had long been one of the main characters of pornographic literature.

Another study of the sexual 'weaknesses' of the Catholic clergy – *Petit bréviaire des vices de notre clerg* (*A Small Handbook of the Vices of Our Clergy*) by Louis-Antoine Dessaulles – was published in Quebec at the beginning of the nineteenth century. In the form of a diary, it describes the sins of one hundred priests: sodomy or pederasty. Over the last sixty years, thousands of incidents of sexual abuse involving children, particularly boys, were brought to light. Most victims were aged from eleven to fourteen years old, but in some cases they were only three years old. Around 10,667 accusations were brought against Catholic priests in the US between 1950 and 2002, claiming they had molested minors in their congregation. The reader may have seen *Spotlight*, which shows, according to a journalist from *The Boston Globe*, that there was a whole system in the echelons of power which hid the cases of paedophilia in the Church.

In Ireland in the 90s, a series of documentary films were broadcast about the paedophile priests, *Suffer the Children* (1994, UTV). In 2009 a report was published accusing 46 priests of child sexual abuse from 1975 to 2004. More than 2,000 children could be victims, and there were two times as many boys than girls among them. In 2012 a nun was to appear in a special session of the Irish Circuit court on 87 charges of the sexual abuse of primary school girls.

In September 2010 alone, the public prosecution office in Belgium received 103 complaints of sexual abuse by priests. A commission of the Catholic Church uncovered instances of paedophilia in almost every diocese. Two thirds of the victims were boys, but there were also 100 girls, of whom thirteen committed suicide. The situation was even worse in the 1960s due to the proliferation of boarding schools.

In 2010, the abuse of minors in the Catholic school of Regensburg, in Bavaria, came to light. It is known that from 1945 until the 1990s, 547 boys were sexually abused. This included choirboys from the Regensburger Domspatzen whose director (1964-1994), Georg Ratzinger, was also the brother of the previous Pope Benedict. In the Jesuit Canisius-Kolleg in Berlin, 115 pupils were abused by twelve teachers.

In 2012, in the state of Victoria in Australia, over 600 children fell victim to paedophilic priests and the media reported that 40 of them, abused in childhood, committed suicide. More than 100 priests were sentenced. In 2017, the Royal Commission acknowledged that from 1980 until 2015, there were 4,444 cases of child sexual abuse by 1,880 Catholic prelates. In some religious orders 15 to 40 per cent of its members face charges, and in one of the dioceses there were 170 cases of sexual abuse against children aged from ten to eleven. On 15 February 2017, it was revealed that the Catholic Church of Australia secretly paid 276 million Australian dollars in compensation to the thousands of victims. In June 2017, the third highest-ranking Vatican official – the Australian cardinal George Pell – was charged with sexual assault offenses. The same George Pell who became famous as an inflexible defender of the traditional Catholic values such as celibacy, prohibition of contraception, and same-sex marriage.

In France, it is even better: since 2010, the police received 'only' 157 paedophilia complaints; 9 priests are in jail, 37 have already served their term. In the autumn of 2015, a huge scandal relating to paedophilia in the church unravelled in the diocese of Lyon in France. 'Father' Bernard Preynat had no less than 64 underage victims. The victim support group that formed very soon after insisted that irrefutable evidence of paedophilia was recorded in approximately 30 dioceses. The French Catholic Church even took the genuinely revolutionary measure of thoroughly investigating all its priests for evidence of paedophilia, and not just those that had been accused. The thing was, replacing one priest with another was a very difficult task: in October 2015, the congregation of the Church of the Immaculate Conception was invited to attend the mass celebrating the arrival of its new parish priest. The first mass was the last: the new priest has also been accused of molesting minors.

How symbolic that the incident of paedophilia in Lyon took place in a church called 'The Church of the Immaculate Conception'. The Virgin Mary's holy infallibility clearly didn't help her priests get a handle on sexual temptation! In April 2017, *Le Monde* published a tragicomic story: an abbot from Orleans who was denounced for sexual abuse to the Church authorities was invited to give a speech during a Church conference on the struggle against paedophilia.

There are several possible explanations as to why it was primarily boys who were abused:

– Boys are more accessible than girls, because they sing in choirs, serve as altar boys and other such things. If girls were as accessible, they would have been abused just as much. Gender isn't particularly relevant when it comes to abuse.

– Sex with girls presents priests with a moral dilemma: they might be young, but they're still the same breed that brought mankind to ruin. In the entire history of the female race there's been only one immaculate lady and – alas – she's untouchable.

– Adult priests usually sexually abuse their pupils immediately after confession, which is compulsory for anyone over the age of seven, and thus religion and paedophilic sex become interchangeable in the eyes of future priests.

– The system whereby male teachers educate boys both sexually and spiritually is as old as the world itself; just think of ancient times in China, Japan, Greece, and Egypt.

Paedophilia in the Church became such an obvious and deeply divisive issue that things were taken beyond the jurisdictions of individual states to an international political level. In February 2013, the UN Committee in Geneva publically declared that the Vatican 'has consistently placed the preservation of the reputation of the Church and the protection of the perpetrators above children's best interests', thus letting Catholic priests get away with tens of thousands of acts of child sex abuse and molestation. The Committee demanded the Church disclose all the evidence they had, including the names both of priests who had committed the crimes and of those who had helped to keep them secret.

As you would expect, the Vatican refused to pass on the information it had on about 4,000 individual cases. Defending against general prejudice, it stated that, from 2001 to 2010, 3,000 priests faced charges of sexual assault, some of which were for events which took place fifty years ago. It is almost nothing: 'only' between 1.5 and 5 per cent of the Catholic clergy had been involved in the sexual abuse of children. Not much at all: a mere 23,000 active paedophiles in the whole Catholic Church. Why even discuss that? But if the Church recognises that 5 per cent of its clergy are paedophiles, how horrible must the real numbers be?

Our new Pope Francis deserves some credit. He issued an apology for the 'satanic' moral damage that paedophile priests had inflicted on children and accused them of doing Satan's bidding. Despite this admission, he said that the number of priests who had committed sex crimes was negligible in comparison to the overall number of 'good' priests, and that the Church was doing more than ever to tackle indecent behaviour towards children.

I admit that there are more 'good priests', since the number of paedophilic priests who weren't caught with their pants down is more important than of those who were. There are probably far too many faithful Catholics working for the police. The victims do not really want to worry the old knot and create a scandal: they feel sorry and ashamed for their Church which brought up many generations of their families.

But let's make no pretences that paedophilia is a toxic issue among Catholic priests alone.

In 2013, the New York State Attorney General charged a rabbi in one sitting with five hundred well-documented counts of sexually harassing children, boys and girls alike. Although just this once he should be cut some slack: he chaired the Judaic Committee for the Prevention of Sexual Abuse and was in desperate need of some first-hand experience.

It might also be a good idea to look into what goes on in the day-to-day life of those religious boarding schools called *yeshivas*. We're unlikely to discover endemic paedophilia in Judaism, though: Judaism allowed their rabbis to have some sexual activity, even though limited.

Don't be under any illusions about Orthodox priests either, who think that the above-mentioned evidence has been fabricated to justify an attack on faith. There's been a fair amount of paedophilia in the fold of the Orthodox Church: not long before, in 2006-2007, there was a series of closed criminal proceedings against paedophilic Orthodox priests. The number of incidents reached double figures. A couple of years ago, a protodeacon of the Russian Orthodox Church, A. Kuraev, was dismissed from the board of a theological academy after unearthing evidence of widespread paedophilia in one of the dioceses. In June 2017, the court of the Yakutia Republic arrested a former director of the Orthodox Gymnasium in Sviato-Innokentievsk, a priestmonk Miletiy (Andrey Tkachenko), for the sexual assault of a minor.

However, the scale is nowhere near the same, by virtue of the fact that the majority of clergymen aren't sworn to celibacy.

It would be interesting to find out more about the history of paedophilia in Buddhist monasteries, situated as they generally were in very remote areas and populated exclusively by members of the male sex. It would be particularly interesting in Tibet and Mongolia where up to half of the total male population spent their lives in monasteries. Nobody has kept any records though. Only the more literate and exacting Japanese have left us first-hand accounts of paedophilia. It affected the young attendants of monks, who were as little as five or six years old. They wore silk clothes, powdered their faces, and didn't shave their heads like other monks.

What are our perspectives? There is very little hope that the situation will get much better. The Church will always defend its priests – indeed, can those holy men be guilty of anything? Never in a million years are priests going to admit their guilt, and victims will be silenced by their own sense of shame and loyalty to religious ideals. There is still a torrent of scandals to come from Latin America where the Catholic Church continues to hold huge sway in society, ensuring that the lion's share of sexual offences committed by cult ministers are hushed up. It is already starting.

I don't think the scale of the problem has been exaggerated by the media. If anything, the opposite is probably true.

It is indeed horrible: people who enjoy our complete trust, and who represent the height of spiritual perfection, abuse our children. The most horrible is that the majority of people, even the most forward-thinking and erudite among them, lose all their common sense when it comes to religion and its representatives. It's sometimes as though common sense runs for the hills as soon as anyone utters the word 'religion', just like demons scatter in blind panic at the name of Christ.

My own common sense tells me that paedophilia among priests is not a sad exception, but a norm. A sexual act is a biological and psychological necessity for a human being, whilst long-term abstinence from sex and masturbation is impossible. It's almost the same as not drinking for three days or not going to the toilet for a week. Human nature cannot endure such violence, even if it lasts only for a couple of years – the psychiatrists mention that abstinence destroys people's minds and permanently changes their character, preventing them from ever reaching maturity. That's why future priests, abused by the Church since their childhood, grow up slightly unhinged with some forms of deviant and anti-social behaviour. Then they abuse other people, generally vulnerable children who attract them much more than an almighty, but distant God.

An American psychologist, Lloyd de Mause, gives a good explanation for this in *The Universality of Incest*: 'As an adult, the paedophile must have sex with children in order to maintain the illusion of being loved, while at the same time dominating the children as they themselves once experienced domination.'

This is an objective analysis of the real situation. Instead of this, they try to sell society a false image of the priests' pure and sublime love for children.

Pope Benedict XVI accused the paedophile priests of 'betraying' the Church and wanted to chase the 'demon' out of the Vatican. I categorically disagree with his point of view: it is the Church who betrayed them. They are not to blame but to pity: the Church created inhuman conditions of life and forced sexually normal people to behave like eunuchs. So what should surprise us is not the fact there are pedophile priests, but the fact that there are so few of them.

What can be done to fix this situation? Two things. Firstly, one can prohibit celibacy. Indeed, the regional Catholic Churches complain that there are not enough candidates for priesthood, since many of the young potential candidates have already been spoiled with sexual liberty and do not want to lose it. It is unlikely to happen: the Vatican sees in celibacy a great spiritual significance as well as a powerful means of control over the believers. A priest practising celibacy is available to his superiors 24 hours a day, seven days a week. What wife or girlfriend would allow this?

Secondly, there is a radical way to guarantee the complete sexual abstinence of the priest, preserving his reputation and delivering him from the temptations of the flesh. This method proved its efficiency over centuries and millennia. I should acknowledge that in earlier times, people were significantly more humane in relation to their priests. They knew full well that priests wouldn't be up to high quality intercession if their flesh was being torn apart by sexual desire and so they turned to salutary full or partial castration for help. It is not clear why Christianity, with all its loathing of sexuality, didn't preserve this wise custom.

■ The Joys of Castration ■

Sexual asceticism originated at the dawn of humanity, long before the first monotheistic religions. These restrictions concerned only a small group of priests who either limited their sexual life or hid it from the primitive public. It was necessary to single out those who dedicated their entire life to lobbying spirits and divinities: the community needed a successful hunt, good harvest and victories on the battlefield.

With the development of spiritual practices, the oppression of one's own sexuality broadened and deepened. The most natural things then became sinful, e.g. sexual intercourse and subsequent childbirth. If the sorcerer who preached ritual copulation remained in the material world and was a sorcerer because of his sexual superiority, the priest of the new spiritual type became a priest through the power of manifesting his sexual weakness. The higher social status and the associated material benefits compensated for these spiritual efforts.

However, giving up all sexuality was not easy. Powerful instincts tempted the priests, and prevented them from being a moral example for their flock. It is very likely that the 'spiritual' path was initially chosen by the ones who were the weakest sexually, capable of satisfying themselves with minimal sexual release. The path of religion allowed them to hide their weakness and dominate strong people, who possessed more vital energy.

However, the sexual weakness did not solve the problem: in any area of human activity, leadership is captured by those strong in spirit and in body. They wanted to become priests and feel special, to ascend above all others. But despite their truly superhuman effort, they couldn't crush their sexuality.

The search for the optimal solution lasted for thousands of years. Without any success, even though they tried everything from vigilant control to locking their penis in a special case. Then, the perfect method was found: castration. This horrible mutilation was transformed into a unique privilege: not only did it promote the priest on the social and spiritual level, but it also gave him power to predict the future.

It seems to me that scholars have not attentively studied the phenomenon of castration and its historical significance. Castration was one of the most important legal mechanisms in Ancient society, since it was, along with a death sentence, a basic punishment for disobedience to the ruler. It was also at the core of their ethics. It was the fear of castration which underlaid sexual prohibitions: despite all our sex shops and pornography destined to deliver us from our hidden desires and phobia, sexuality played a much bigger role at the time then it does now. Breaking family law or the rules of decency might easily lead to a sexual death, castration. In Ancient Egypt, they castrated for the rape of a free woman; in India for the liaison between a man from a lower caste with a woman from a higher one; in thirteenth-century England the rape of a young virgin was also punished with death (I wonder how they defined whether a woman was young or not and whether they punished the rape of a spinster). And almost everywhere, especially in Asia Minor and in the East, they castrated criminals and fallen enemies, war prisoners and slaves.

For thousands of years, the castration of young men destined to become eunuchs proliferated. The presence of enormous harems – indeed, no ruler can go without demonstrating the symbol of his sexual and social power – led to a shortage of women; rapacious sexual hunger made men dangerous and one had to hold them away from women. The ban on procreation also possessed great material significance. It solved the problem of property inheritance: all the wealth remained within a small group of fellow eunuchs, also deprived of offspring. The fact known since ancient times should not be forgotten: castrated men live 15-20 years longer than their horny counterparts. They say that old maids also live longer, but it's hard to say if they live better lives.

This practice ceased for a few centuries, but it was revived in the twentieth century: many countries are successfully experimenting in the field of chemical castration of paedophiles. The word 'chemical' doesn't change anything when it comes to the results.

There is no sense in discussing forced castration, so I propose we focus on consented castration. Regarding 'full consent', it is very unlikely. Some scholars argue that the degree of 'voluntariness' has been greatly exaggerated, so the majority of future priests were most likely castrated as children, lest they doubt and suffer. I do not really believe in the voluntary character of castration: despite his will to be 'promoted', the future castrate certainly experienced an enormous degree of animalistic fear in the face of losing the main male organ. In any case, the ritual castration was seen not as a mutilation but as a salutary help. After this there was no further need to prohibit sexual relations and to demand a poor man control himself: without sex organs, the material life made no more sense and the castrate had only a 'spiritual' one. The emergence of castration marked a new turn for human society, one absolutely monstrous and absurd from the perspective of ancient people: those rich in sex somehow become poor in spirit. The reverse is also true: poor in sex were considered to be rich in spirit. What this spirit was is not clear, but it was not human spirit.

Castration was the main reason for the appearance of a new type of religion, so called 'spiritual' religions, which implied a rigid separation between material and spiritual life. The priest gave the deity the most important thing in his possession – his sexual organs – and with this severe sacrifice he certainly proved his exceptional devotion. The priest became a nobody in this earthly life, but gained the hope to become 'everything' in the afterlife, not on earth, but in heaven.

Finally, castration made the priest 'more spiritual' as it protected him from 'baser' sexual intercourse and more. Castration separated him, the neutered and immaculate supreme being, from second-class citizens – women. The priests from certain cults even refused to eat food cooked by a woman, considered unclean by definition.

There is another aspect, a positive one: castration has left a trace not only in the domain of 'spiritual religions', but also in the history of humanity. Ancient Man didn't live for

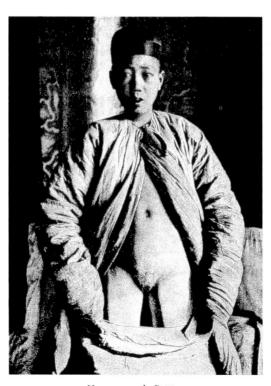

Young eunuch, Beijing.

long, usually dying at the peak of his life, and therefore was extremely sexually active. Castration could reduce the level of sexual energy and shift the attention from 'primitive' sexual practices to the spiritual and intellectual. Become weaker but smarter! In many cultures the words 'eunuch' and 'intellectual' became synonymous. We must thank the Ancient eunuchs: without them, the nameless sexual martyrs, it's highly possible we would not have got to space. Instead, we might be going to the next town in a horse-drawn cart.

Castration has left its traces in many myths and religions. For some reason most of the historians who write about castration mention the overused myth of Uranus emasculated by Cronus, son of Gaia, but rarely mention another well-known myth which describes the castration of two gods at the same time: the myth of the Mother Goddess Cybele and her eternal companion, the great God Attis. This myth, unlike the one with Cronos, had a profound influence on world culture in general and on the formation of the Christian doctrine in particular.

The cult of Cybele is not just another pagan cult. She has more honorary titles than any Generalissimo, even Stalin: the Great Mother of all gods and of all living, which came to us directly from the Neolithic, the oldest of all the great Indo-European goddesses, the main Phrygian goddess. The cult of Cybele penetrated Europe through Asia Minor and entered first the Greek and then the Roman pantheon. The cult of Cybele gradually captured all the major provinces of the Roman Empire: North Africa, Spain, Portugal, and Germany – and even survived the rise of Christianity as the state religion of Rome.

This success is not surprising as Cybele embodies the Majesty of Nature and Fertility; she controls the mountains, rivers and animals. For this reason, she is always portrayed surrounded by wild lions and panthers, which embody natural energy and power. In the Greco-Roman pantheon of gods, she has always stood apart due to her Eastern origins and violent nature (not for nothing her God-partner was the God of wine and revelry, Dionysus); she combines piety and purity on the one hand, and chaos and ecstasy on the other.

The image of Cybele inspired many artists. The most prominent among them belongs to the brush of Rubens and it did not impress me – it's full of lifeless and boring classicism and does not reflect the natural passion inherent in the goddess. I much prefer the Ancient image of Cybele showing her maternal power and the ability to feed all her children.

The image of Attis is very different and, in my opinion, his myth is the most beautiful in all pagan mythology; and the most important since it was this which, despite seeming minor in comparison to the myth of Cybele, provided it with incredible longevity. The myth of Attis took shape in Asia Minor in the mid-thirteenth century BC (in a grim coincidence, a little later than the monotheistic religion of Pharaoh Akhenaten appeared, and almost simultaneously with the emergence of Judaism) and arrived in Greece only in the fourth century.

In the chapter 'Sex Is God's Greatest Enemy', I mentioned that Attis was the grandson of Cybele, but this interpretation of their family ties is not the only one that exists. In some cases, he's her grandson or son and sometimes they are not biologically related. But all versions agree that he was handsome and engaged in a romantic relationship with the old lady Cybele. In some myths the father of Attis, the castrated God Acdestis, was in a homosexual relationship with his son (how a eunuch managed that remains a mystery). For those who want to go further, I give the description of the castration of Acdestis by Arnobius which resembles a fantasy film.

Jupiter assailed Cybele with lewdest desires. But when he could not accomplish what he wanted, he, baffled, spent his lust on a stone. This the rock received and Acdestis is born. In him there had been resistless might and a lust for both sexes, and the council of the gods gave to Liber the task to curb his excesses. With the strongest wine he drugs a spring much used by Acdestis. Once Acdestis is drunk, Liber throws over his foot one end of a halter formed of hair; with the other end he lays hold of his genitals. When the fumes of the wine have worn off, Acdestis starts up furiously and, his foot dragging the noose, with his own strength he robs himself of his sex; there is an immense flow of blood, from which there springs up a pomegranate tree. The fruit of this tree pleases Nana, daughter of Sangarius, and she places some of it in her bosom. By this she becomes pregnant. Her angry father shuts her up and seeks to have her starved to death, but she is kept alive by the mother of the gods until Nana gives birth to a child. Sangarius orders that the newborn be thrown in the forest, but he is saved by a peasant who feeds him with goat's milk and calls him Attis.

The fate of Attis is present in various ways. Some say that King Midas wanted to save the young man from a disgraceful relationship with his father and offered him to marry his daughter. However, Attis was so adored by Cybele that when he was planning to marry, the lustful senile woman became wildly jealous and temporarily deprived all the members of the wedding of their sanity: women began to cut off their breasts, while Attis and the father of the bride castrated themselves. In a slightly different version of this story, it was the father-lover Acdestis who was jealous of Attis. In any case, Attis remained a virgin and died, bleeding in terrible agony, though not on the cross as Jesus did. However, Attis' further destiny was no different from Jesus': a day after his death, Attis resurrected.

Cybele stayed calm, gathered the severed organs, and buried them in the ground, so the violets would grow. This episode enrages Arnobius so much that he comes to hate both heathens and sex organs: Say, again, did the mother of the gods, then, with careful diligence herself gather in her grief the scattered genitals with the shed blood? With her own sacred, her own divine hands, did she touch and lift up the instruments of a disgraceful and indecent office? (*Against the Heathens*)

Then, Arnobius calls to the common sense of the reader who is being told 'fairy tales in the guise of truth'. Personally, I would like to call on the common sense of Arnobius: what is the difference between these fairy tales and Christian fairy tales like the visit of the magi, the Immaculate Conception, the Resurrection, or the Ascension?

In another version of this myth, a quite homophobic one, Attis castrated his father-in-law who sexually molested him (no respect for the daughter bride!), and the bleeding father-in-law in turn castrated Attis.

In the third version, the mighty grandfather of Attis, Zeus, was jealous of Attis and his relationship with Cybele, and in a fit of rage sent a boar to tear Attis into small pieces. After that neither the priests of the cult, nor ordinary believers, would eat pork. From that point on, the castrated and resurrected Attis was followed everywhere by his grand-mother-mother-mistress, Cybele. Imitating her, he became the God of plants, symbolising the death of nature in winter and its resurrection in spring. This is the first ever successful example of sublimation of sexuality, in this case into lush plant life. Later people learned to sublimate sexuality into culture. There is much historical evidence showing that the priests of Attis castrated themselves on the day of his death, 24 March, on the so-called Dies Sanguinis ('Day of Blood'). From that day they no longer considered themselves men: they grew their hair long in preparation, and during the ceremony wore women's suits, pendants, earrings, and put on a lot of makeup. A eunuch who would die on that day would rise the next day, 25 March. This religious ceremony is not just an imitation of a sacred event, but its literal repetition.

During the ceremonial mourning of Attis, priests of Cybele would fall into a wild state, an ecstasy, and to celebrate they flagellated themselves for their sins, and sprinkled the altars and statues of Attis with their blood. Blood, in their belief, gave Attis vitality and contributed to his resurrection. The cult of Cybele in general was very cruel and, according to some historians, at its beginning did not mind human sacrifice.

So how much was the voluntary castration practised? Some historians, like Jacques Marcireau, affirm that castration was practised in such provinces of Asia Minor as Phrygia, Anatolia, Cappadocia, Pontus, and Galatia and also during orgies organised as part of the cult of Bacchus. I doubt that: despite humanity's predisposition to collective madness, it is hard to believe that there could be many people willing to mutilate themselves. What would you say about a person who cut off his head or a healthy leg? That he is mad? And is it normal to cut off your own penis and testicles?

I understand that one should not exaggerate the scale of religious castration in human history and especially during Antiquity, because most people were not affected. Before the appearance of monotheistic religions, most people were not affected by any 'spiritual' practices at all and lived a normal life: they grew up, worked, had children and died. What is sure is that they did not pray all day long.

The rational Greeks did not really engage in the cult of Cybele and Attis, hampered by their well-developed culture and taste: the practice of male castration in the name of some divinity seemed complete nonsense to them.

The Roman lower classes and the barbarians from the outskirts were of quite a different opinion. They liked the drunken bloody ecstasy of worship, which they took for divine inspiration. However, official Rome failed to see the benefits of the wonderful idea of voluntary castration and forbade its citizens from following the cult of Cybele and partaking in its festival. The ban was the result of the Roman fear of infertility (the army does not need eunuch priests, but soldiers), and the generally negative attitude towards feminisation of men, considered a bad example for young people. Everything was under control and therefore the high priests were Senate-appointed Roman citizens, not eunuchs, and they profited from all sexual privileges reserved to the mighty of this world.

The privilege of the joy of castration was left to foreigners and slaves: for its own citizens, Rome at best allowed the sacrifice of a bull, or if the citizen had financial difficulties, a ram. The foolish Roman law believed that any deity would be satisfied with the blood of the sacrificial animal and its testicles – symbols of procreation. Rome's attitude towards religions and cults showed no respect and they were deprived of all governmental support. Roman priests were themselves supposed to pay not only for their own wife, mistresses, and slave concubines, but also for the maintenance of temples and all the necessary servants.

In this respect, the eunuch priests of the Cybele-Attis cult had a huge advantage: not being Roman citizens, holding no rights of inheritance, they didn't have to pay for anyone, did not work, wandered across the huge Empire, and lived only by panhandling. At the end of the fourth century AD, much later than the triumph of Christianity, they still walked the streets of Rome to the sound of drums and wind instruments. In this era, the cult of the great Mother Cybele became very popular among highly educated pagans again, desperately struggling against dull Christianity. The most famous among them was the emperor and theologian Julian, a fervent defender of paganism. He wrote the ardent hymn *To the Mother of the Gods* in which the cult of Cybele is shown as the highest principle of transcendental unity in the world, and Attis, like the God Son in Christianity, plays a mediating role between the heavenly and earthly world. On earth, Attis is represented by the rays of the Sun, which after their physical death human souls walk on up to the sky.

A very beautiful idea, especially since there is no mention of sin and judgement, and heaven lets in everyone without exception. Who knows, if Julian had not been wounded unto death and stayed emperor for at least fifteen years, we would have lived in a completely different culture and religion.

When I was writing this text, I was continuously tormented by one question: why are we all so worried about our sexual abilities, while the priests of Cybele gave up so easily their genitals? Were they primitive idiots? The history and anthropologists showed that Man's intellectual capacities did not improve over the centuries.

No, they were not idiots and there is a rational explanation for their respect for castration:

Attis was immaculately conceived and did not inherit any sexual sin. Moreover, because of his castration he had no time to sleep with his future wife and remained a virgin. But this did not prevent him from rising and becoming immortal, and even becoming god of vegetation which symbolises the triumph of life. It is logical to conclude that if the priests likewise never have sex and even castrate ourselves just to be sure, we too will be resurrected. And if we don't castrate ourselves and start to have sex, then there is no reason to resurrect, since our biological debt is already paid. A bloody self-castration was considered necessary as it became a source of holiness and immortality. I am going into so much detail on the myth of Cybele and Attis, not because I am overcome by some ardent love for mythology. I am not very interested in mythology in itself, and history gave us so many myths that it will take more than a lifetime to get to know all their details.

I am talking about this myth because I truly believe that it is one of the myths which underlie the New Testament. I do not believe in the divine origin of the Christian doctrines and I have always wanted to find their analogues in history. Indeed, the Cybele story has a truly epic scope and deserves to be considered as a forerunner of Christianity. The fact that this cult was vehemently denounced by Christian theologians, especially Tertullian, only confirms my ideas.

The cult of Cybele and Attis and Christianity have too much in common and no honest scholar will believe in its accidental character.

Cybele, like the Judeo-Christian God, permeates all things and is above nature; she created the world and gave life to all living things. She accompanies a person throughout his life cycle: she is present at birth, gives him a soul, watches people while they are still alive, and robs them of life when their time comes.

The virgin gave birth to a demigod Attis who lived as a virgin until his martyr death and miraculous resurrection. The calendar days of the resurrection of Attis and Jesus Christ are about the same. The body and blood of Attis were used in religious ceremonies, like the body and blood of the crucified Christ.

Some scholars believe that the great pagan goddess Cybele was the prototype of the Virgin Mary and that we worship Cybele in our churches. The analogy can be traced to the fact that some images of the Madonna and Child are depicted as black, the colour symbolising the primary matter – the earth. On the first images of the Virgin Mary with a child, they are depicted in black. There are more than three hundred of these black Mothers of God in France, fifty in Spain, and more than thirty in Italy.

Now let's focus on religious practices: the cult priests are fully engaged in spiritual life and constantly travel, they mutilate and flagellate themselves in a way that resembles the Christian ascetic practices and voluntary suffering. The whole flock consist of slaves, foreigners, and professional beggars. The most important thing is that absolutely none of those mentioned engaged in any sex, or wanted anything to do with it. Moreover, a rejection of sex was proclaimed as an indispensable condition of eternal life.

This is a real Gospel of Cybele and Attis! One can easily see in it the roots of the main anti-sexual ideas of Christianity and the notion of holiness: do not the virginity of Attis and the behaviour of his priests resemble the celibacy without which there can be holiness? Most likely, the idea of the cult of Cybele, especially its fascination with the suppression of sex and castration, never fully died. Its embryos were sleeping in the bosom of the mighty Roman Empire, and a few centuries later erupted with new force into the depths of Christian doctrine, inspiring all known textbook myths of the New Testament.

In all fairness, I'd like to note that the anti-sexual character of the cult of Cybele is somewhat broader than the Christian one: God the Father, God the Son, and the majority of priests are not just spiritual eunuchs, but real ones. Not very good for their spirituality: it seems like they just wanted an easy life without the painful temptations of the flesh and debilitating visions of fallen women.

There is another cult which could easily be considered a forerunner of Christianity. I mean the Iranian cult of the sun god Mithras, which coincided with Christianity on almost everything: God the saviour of humanity, whose coming was announced to the shepherds; the belief in the immortal soul and the desire for moral purity and spirituality, recognition of equality in earthly life and the promise of heaven after death, the ritual of baptism using holy water, communion with bread and wine, celebration of the resurrection. Even the birthday of this god is December 25th! This is an actual Christmas! So the problem is not whether these two cults underlie the Christian doctrine, but who we can call the main Christian prophet, the first Christ – Attis or Mithras.

▪ The Eunuchs for the Kingdom ▪ of Heaven's Sake

While we shouldn't exaggerate or underestimate the role of castration: unlike other rites of mutilation, castration has survived through the centuries, because of the way it unites such basic monotheistic ideas as the opposition of body and soul, artificial spirituality and self-abnegation.

Formally, Judaism was against ritual castration, prohibited the appointment of eunuchs (and even men with deformed genitals) to the rank of priests, while castrated animals were not allowed to be sacrificed to God. However, it is impossible to completely separate Judaism from the tradition of castration. Firstly, the rejection of castrated priests in Judaism was probably due to the fact that a eunuch wants nothing and therefore his asexual behaviour is no sacrifice to God. And religion without personal sacrifice is not religion, but a party. Also, the sacrifice of a castrated animal offends God, as such an animal cannot reproduce in heaven and increase the heavenly flock.

Secondly, the question of castration was discussed in Judaism and many respected Jewish philosophers supported the idea. For example, Philo of Alexandria, who was born into a wealthy and very educated family and for his entire life looked for ways to connect classical Greek philosophy with Judaism, came to the conclusion that only castration can help a person achieve spiritual and cultural progress while regaining rational thinking. For Philo the eunuch is the symbol of wisdom, self-sacrifice, the rejection of everything lowly and material and, therefore, an example to follow. On another principle, therefore, it might appear a most desirable thing to be a eunuch, if our soul, by that means escaping vice, might be able also to avoid all knowledge of passion. On which account Joseph, that is to say, the disposition of continence, says to Pleasure, who accosts him with, 'Lie with me, and being a man behave as a man, and enjoy the pleasant things which life can afford.' He, I say, refuses her, saying, 'I shall be sinning against God, who loves virtue, if I become a rotary of pleasure; for this is a wicked action.'

This passage from *The Allegories of the Sacred Laws* clearly shows the main views of Philo: the meaning of human life is not to enjoy life, but to be in the service of God. This is why it is good to be a eunuch: a normal man would not be able to resist the temptation. The same ideas – the amazing power of temptation, the futility of fighting it – are supported by Maimonides in his *Guide for the Perplexed*:

> This is also the case of one whose testicles have a hot and humid temperament and are of a strong constitution and in whom the seminal vessels abundantly generate semen. For it is unlikely that such a man, even if he subjects his soul to the most severe training, should be chaste.

Thus Maimonides admits that chastity is only for biologically weak men, some sort of biological 'garbage'. However, Maimonides limited himself only to hints and did not suggest a method of correcting the sad situation.

Judaism elaborated an elegant solution for the problem of compatibility between the service of God and sexual desires – circumcision.

The Christian Church has been close to the idea of castration for its entire history. But instead of oppressing its priests' sexuality, it wanted to impose restrictions in matters of sexuality to all its flock. With its help, the enemy – lust – can be defeated forever. The main goal is to deal with men, and then women, who are presumed to be weaker and more dependent creatures, will follow with no protest.

In the third and fourth centuries, the heyday of true Christianity, Saint Anthony, Dorotheus of Egypt, and Euthymius the Great were very close to this idea. However, the only Christian hierarch in the history to emasculate himself was the venerable Origen, who didn't allow himself to experience any love other than the divine love of God and declared all carnal love 'demonic'. There was also an early Christian sect of Valesians, who were so enthusiastic about the spiritual significance and potential of castration that they forcibly performed it on any accidental wandering travellers, and even their guests. They accepted the gospel of Matthew not as a spiritual idea, but as a call to action. Everyone remembers a famous passage from the gospel of Matthew, which can hardly be considered a hymn to sensual love – Jesus' answer to the disciples' question of whether marriage is good:

> But he said unto them, "All men cannot receive this saying, save they to whom it is given. For there are some eunuchs who were so born from their mother's womb, and there are some eunuchs who were made eunuchs by men, and there are eunuchs who have made themselves eunuchs for the Kingdom of Heaven's sake. He that is able to receive it, let him receive it. (Matthew 19:11-12)

It is stated very clearly. He who castrates himself is already prepared for the Kingdom of Heaven. Who would refuse such an attractive offer?

The Valesians did not. Their ideology, by the way, set itself apart through rationality and an understanding of everyday human life: young members, not yet castrated, were not allowed to eat meat as eating meat provokes depraved thoughts and desires, and intensifies natural lust. After castration, food restrictions were lifted; it is necessary to compensate for one loss with one pleasure, even if it is less significant!

This idea found its continuation in the world famous Russian sect of Skoptsy (eunuchs), which was founded in the eighteenth century by Kondraty Selivanov. The powerful spiritual movement of Skoptsy quickly spread across the expanses of the vast empire and, for more than the century and a half of its existence, managed to mutilate hundreds of thousands of people. The Skoptsy, unlike religious bureaucrats and graduates of theological academies, were true Christians, both in spirit and in life. They carefully read the Holy Scripture in the part which dealt with the expulsion of Man from paradise. Skoptsy took this well-known story to its very logical conclusion: if people before the Fall did not have sex and were immortal, then they were ethereal and had no genitals. Sexual organs are the consequence of sin, and sin is the consequence of the genitals, which is impossible to understand. This doesn't even matter, like in the case of the chicken and the egg. But it is clear that the destruction of genitalia (castration) will purify Man of sin and return to him the lost paradise and immortality.

A wonderful idea, very close to the ideas of the cult of Attis. Just imagine believing every Gospel word so much! The dream of any totalitarian society!

Another idea of the Skoptsy was that sexuality suppresses the fear of death (as it leads to the birth of children, and creates in children the illusion of immortality). And death (and, most of all, a martyr death) is the essence of the Christian doctrine, representing the blessed path of Christ. It is impossible to vanquish, but voluntary castration can be the way to destroy the greatest enemy of death – sexuality. And deliver yourself the fear of death not through sexual pleasure, but only through prayer to God.

For the full implementation of these ideas, one had to castrate oneself, or as the Skoptsy said 'make oneself white' or 'cut the serpent's head'. This process consisted of several stages, ranging from amputation of the testicles by cauterising them ('baptism by fire', or 'lesser seal') and ending with the full removal of the penis ('tsar's seal'). There were softer techniques, allowing for sexual intercourse without the possibility of conception. To do this, spermatic cords were twisted or punctured.

Women could have more 'seals': they removed the nipples, the breasts, and then the labia and the clitoris. After the operation they were often sewed up ('closed'), very similar to female circumcision in Africa. However, they could still procreate.

Children were also castrated, and victims even paid a lot of money to those willing to castrate. Needless to say, such a strong belief assumed an ascetic life: eunuchs did not eat meat, did not drink wine, did not smoke, did not sing, and generally did not entertain themselves. The official Orthodox Church was treated with the utmost contempt.

The great idea of self-castration in order to save one's soul did not have much of a following in the official Christianity. Moreover, the First Council of Nicaea proclaimed self-castration to be a sin which makes it impossible for a person to be ordained, referring to the rules 21-24 of the Apostolic Canons (a collection of ecclesiastical decrees of the Early Christian Church; their status is close to the Islamic hadiths). Self-castration was widely discussed in the thirteenth century by Byzantine theologians Joannes Zonaras, Alexios Aristenos, and Theodore Balsamon. According to them, if anyone in sound health has castrated himself, he cannot be a priest, because he is an 'assassin of his own self'. But if any have been made eunuchs by barbarians, and should otherwise be found worthy, such men are admitted to the clergy.

Before praising the ardent defenders of the male sex organs, let's ask ourselves a legitimate question: why was there an interest in this subject down the centuries? There can be only

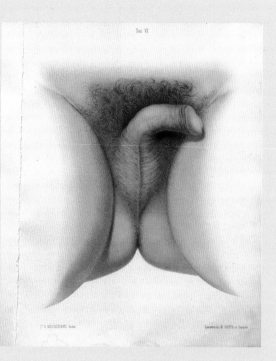

Instruments used for castration: a cobbler's knife,
a gardening tool, a lead pin inserted into the urethra
after removing the genitals, a razor, the end of a scythe.

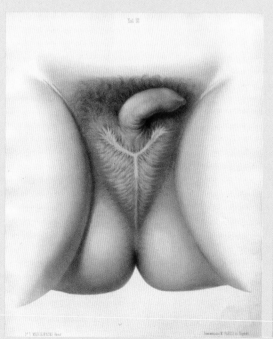

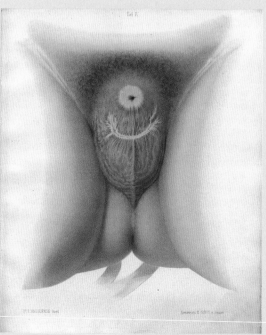

The "little stamp": a scar on the scrotum following
the removal of the testicles.

The "imperial stamp": a scar on what remains
of the scrotum following complete removal.

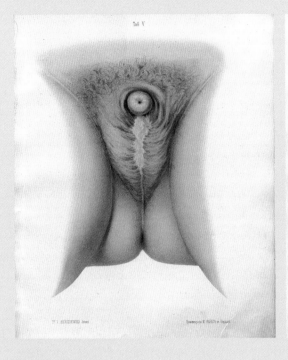

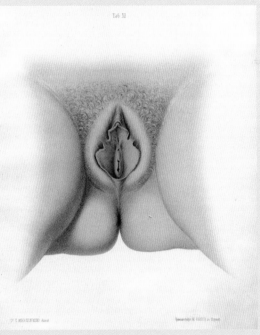

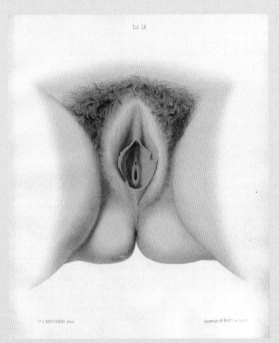

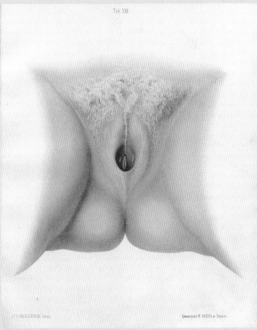

Complete female excision: scars following the removal of parts of the labia majora and minora and the clitoris of a seventy-year-old virgin.

one explanation: there was a strong tendency for self-castration and there were many men wishing to perform it. So why didn't voluntary castration become a mass phenomenon?

I think there are a couple of reasons for that.

The idea itself was relevant only during the initial heyday of new eschatological teachings when the faithful were looking ahead to Christ's Second Coming and the Last Judgement, and there was no point in thinking about offspring. But generation followed generation, and the promised show just wasn't happening. And no good news was arriving from up there. People got tired of waiting and began to look not just up, but around themselves too in order to experience some earthly pleasures.

Moreover, castration is inherently ambiguous. On the one hand, the eunuch, liberated from sexual desire, finds it easier to achieve the required 'spirituality'. Just think of all the time we spend on dating, persuasion, frustration, discussing our love lives with friends; not to mention the treatment of genital diseases.

On the other hand, the Christian doctrine is based on the goodness of permanent suffering, imitating Christ's passion. This is not entirely consistent with the idea of castration as the eunuch suffers only during the short operation, and after its successful completion he is no longer in suffering, but in a stupor due to complete lack of desire. The eunuch has no sexual desire, he is too indifferent to everything, and there is nothing to demand of him. It is much easier to manipulate a person who is in daily agony of the flesh and who can give birth to new martyrs. It is also easy to understand why ordinary people hated the castrates – how else could they treat the traitors of faith who wanted to sneak into paradise without really suffering?

With the advent of monotheism – or rather from the moment when it consumed the whole world – 'spirituality' grabbed most of the population and castrating so many people was impossible. The vast majority of people were not fanatics, loved their flesh, and thought of children, at the very least for mercantile reasons: it is necessary to have somebody nearby in order not to starve to death in old age. The Church did not really insist on this extreme measure as it needed young people for the maintenance and propagation of the doctrine, and protecting the 'spiritual' from the despicable sexually active barbarians.

For these good reasons the Church turned away from physical castration in favour of implementing the spiritual one. Voluntary castration was replaced by hatred towards sex: praise of virginity, mortification of the flesh, celibacy of the clergy. The Church was convinced in the success of this operation: there will be no more sex and as much suffering as possible. John of the Ladder brilliantly expressed this idea: 'Some respect eunuchs by nature as free from the torment of the flesh; and I cherish everyday eunuchs, who use intelligence like a knife, and learned to castrate themselves.'

However, the Church failed! Instead of the priest who would be almost saint, the Church created the sexual abusers of children.

Should one conclude that the Vatican should think seriously about castrating willing priests? They could even perform it on children. With parental consent, of course – we are not medieval barbarians! Moreover, science has developed a more humane and completely painless chemical castration.

This way, the celibacy of the clergy will be guaranteed, paedophilia will disappear and with it the scandals damaging the Church's image. The number of saints will skyrocket.

■ Thou Shalt Have no Other Gods Before Me ■

I emphatically reject any positive appraisal of divine holiness – I am with the Protestants on that one. I don't agree that saints are better than other people and exemplify godliness. Individual saints may well have wonderful traits, but the institution of holiness as a whole has done us no good. Using dubious criteria, unverifiable legends and obsolete references from multitudes that enjoyed more or less equal standing, the institution singled out a pitiful number of demigods. All believers must love them with sublime Christian love, and love them not as people made of flesh and blood, but as untouchable brothers in Christ. The Christian Church continues to recruit these people, justifying it by their dedication to the faith, that beside them everyone else is left unworthy, defective, sinful and all-round guilty.

The concept of divine holiness is made-up and anti-human in its very essence. Human nature is the only holy thing in the world. No social, philosophical or religious system must be allowed to harm the natural course of things. It's impossible for a person to wrench himself from his natural surroundings and alter his biological composition. He'd be better off dead. There is no absolute perfection in nature, only in death, and by imposing an unattainable ideal on normal people religion blights their lives, rendering them guinea pigs for God rather than kings of the natural universe.

By its very nature, holiness is just as much a chimera as the omnipresence of God who keeps an eye on all seven billion of us at the same time, reads every single one of our thoughts, and casts judgement on our behaviour; as much a chimera as the immortality of the soul and the possibility of a life beyond the grave. Nietzsche beautifully describes it by saying that the Christian religion 'had to devise for itself a new concept of "perfection", a pale, sickly, idiotically ecstatic state of existence, so-called "holiness" – a holiness that is itself merely a series of symptoms of an impoverished, enervated and incurably disordered body!'

It can be surprising at first sight that the Church Fathers, who usually would vehemently defend every word of the Scripture, let the concept of holiness exist, despite its evident transgression of the second commandment. However, it is easy to understand why it happened and who profited from it. The Church needs it to manipulate believers. Faced with the unattainable grandeur of the saints, they are bound to feel like an absolute nobody, hence they develop an inferiority complex and turn to the Holy Spirit to overcome it.

You shouldn't think that I am an angry atheist and that I attack the beloved children of the Church, the saints, for this reason. I am not an atheist and I did not write this chapter to defile the notion of holiness – the pinnacle of moral behaviour – that prevailed in Christian civilisation for 2,000 years, and that looks over us from a multitude of icons and paintings in the form of a nice-looking and elegantly dressed old man. I didn't want to disappoint those who hold dear this notion and are ready to sacrifice their life for it. However, it is clear that most people recall that saints exist only on special occasions, as a wonderful Spanish proverb says, '*Charco pasado, santo olvidado*'.

I wanted to depict holiness in her pyjamas with no make-up on and prove that it's much more dangerous than appearances would have you believe, and could easily bring society to ruin. It has already happened: just remember the pretty rapid decline of the Roman Empire after it accepted Christianity and its saints as the official religion. Priority then was given to venerating the saints and fighting heretical gentiles and the defense of the empire and its principles took a back seat. Then, for many centuries, holiness was painted on the banners of religious armies, and millions of men, women, and children were killed in its name.

And if we don't watch out, the same thing could happen again. Even a healthy nation can collapse into the holy hole. We're referring here to a union of independent and proud-hearted individuals willing to defend their values and their way of life, as well as the pleasure they take in it. The traditional institution of holiness has no place in a civilised secular democratic society that stands for the principle of equality. Saints are bad for our society, and political saints are even worse since their holiness rapidly transforms into immunity and opportunity to commit any crimes.

However, holiness can be damaging to an individual too. All my readers will no doubt be familiar with the well-known lines from the poet John Donne, an English priest, which Ernest Hemmingway uses as an epigraph to one of his most famous novels: 'Therefore, send not to know for whom the bell tolls: it tolls for thee.'

If I were to paraphrase this wonderful line, resounding like scripture, I could say that as soon as you open your mouth to express indignation at any religious saint, the funeral bells begin to toll for thee. Wouldn't it be better to worship the work of the exceptional people who created Apple, Google, and Facebook, who, in the space of ten or fifteen years, succeeded in dramatically changing the lives of billions?

But the idea of holiness in and of itself, like anything, has a positive side to it. I think there is an inherent gift of individual holiness within every human. I am even prepared to agree with the Orthodox Church that the gift of holiness is evident from birth and can be honed through the efforts of the individual, independently of God. If God exists at all then he certainly doesn't exist outside of Man, but within him. There's nothing to be found on the outside anyway, there is only one God, implacable and violent – that of Death.

Every one of us is sufficient unto himself and worthy of respect, and every one of us is God. Some are bigger Gods than others. That's what makes every one of us holy in the most general sense of the word. Or we are the Devil. If all of us are considered equal and worthy, then there's not really any difference. I personally like to consider every person to be holy without the ability to speak foreign languages, without mass hysteria (climaxing in nervous breakdowns), and without any kind of God. My notion of holiness is somehow more humane and moderate.

We all recognise the sanctity of human life, right? So why don't we consider every human to be holy, without exceptions and prerequisites? Then there wouldn't be any need for people to search out shortfalls in each other and play themselves off against each other; and if you wanted to see a real-life saint, you would just have to look in the mirror.

CHAPTER VIII

The Crusade
against Onanism

Onanism, or masturbation, is known by all, a universal human need, a pleasure available to everyone. Due to its ubiquitous nature and the incomparable thrill it brings, masturbation has long been a vivid symbol of peace and friendship between peoples.

Onanism is a natural and healthy manifestation of the instinct of procreation. It is almost as strong as the instinct of self-preservation: only the desire to survive can overcome the desire to have sex. It is no different from other physiological needs such as drinking, eating, urinating or defecating. For young men masturbation is an excellent means to get rid of the unused liquid in their reproductive gland. It helps girls to satisfy the desires typical of their age, without having sex with random strangers and putting themselves at risk of getting pregnant. For adults of both genders it is the only way to release sexual tension in the absence of a good sexual partner, or by making their sex life more fulfilling by cheating; instead they simply explore their fantasies during the act of masturbation. For the elderly it is a nice way to keep their sex organs in good shape since, as with all muscles, they need to stay active.

Far from everyone has regular sex. Some people don't need it because of their age or for many other reasons like sickness, imprisonment or seclusion – indeed, anything can happen! However, it has nothing to do with onanism. Everyone masturbates. Those who have never masturbated are most probably mentally or physically ill. Or, if they are still healthy, they will get sick very soon. They might even become maniacs because their own sexual dissatisfaction will lead to violence against another person's sexuality. Therefore, one should wish for masturbation to flourish, rather than be extirpated: it has saved many from grave diseases, neuroses and committing sex crimes.

If it were all so clear, why would I even write this chapter? My goal is actually to show how the prohibition of masturbation, supported first by monotheistic religions and then in the eighteenth century by secular society, has poisoned many millions (or even billions) of ordinary lives.

■ Sperm Rivers ■

Biologists write that masturbation is an everyday occurrence in the animal world. Masturbation has been seen in elephants, whales, bears, lions, sheep, deer, polecats, weasels, and of course our dearest cats and dogs. In order to have an orgasm, animals use their paws and pads, their mouth and tongue, as well as exterior objects. Almost all birds masturbate – from tropical parrots to penguins in Antarctica. I said 'almost' just to be scientifically exact – indeed, ornithologists have not examined every bird on earth – and also to make a concession to our dear moralists. The latter would probably want to make an exception for white swans, the symbol of monogamy. I am also ready to exclude insects from this list – I have not found anything pertaining to their masturbatory abilities – and amoeba with infusoria. Indeed, those organisms are studied in primary school and one should probably avoid drawing children's attention to this aspect of nature.

Our ape ancestors have treated it with no less respect than copulation over millions of years. Therefore, the history of self-satisfaction began in the crowns of mighty trees. Indeed, the first objective of primates' and men's sexual activity is pleasure, not reproduction: they help themselves with their hands, and sometimes they swallow their semen and rub their clitoris. As in human society, male apes love masturbating in the presence of females. The former often engage in mutual masturbation and create small gay communities of both genders.

The act of masturbation long predates any word used to describe it. It existed long before the appearance of culture, idols, gods, and the upright walking human. Some time ago, I read about a stunning discovery: the echographia made by different scientists have shown that a human foetus begins to masturbate manually and orally in the 26th week of pregnancy; the erection of the male foetus and arousal of the female prove this. I won't write about infant masturbation – it is already a well-known fact.

Primitive men had no one to explain to them that masturbation is a mortal sin before God and very harmful to the health, so prehistoric men, women, and children indulged in masturbation anywhere and without shame. This is demonstrated by prehistoric cave paintings in all parts of the Ancient world, created long before the official advent of Man according to major religions, or perhaps, as the latter would claim, maliciously placed there along with the bones of mammoths to tempt weak believers.

For primitive men semen was a symbol of life and its force. The sacred cults of the phallus and vagina, symbolising nature's fertility, were combined with the cult of male and female masturbation, the magic symbol of creation. For example, many pagan rites included masturbation on the newly sown field in order to increase the harvest. In some tribes young boys performed oral sex on young men and swallowed their sperm in order to become stronger and to reach maturity sooner, while women wore jewellery in the form of phalluses of various sizes and materials and probably used them to masturbate. Those places that have no traces of masturbation are the places where Ancient men did not live.

Statuette representing a scene of masturbation, Jama-Coaque culture, 500 BC.

All known Ancient civilisations treated male and female masturbation quite positively. Some philosophical and religious movements (e.g. Taoism) even argued that masturbation contributes to achieving greater spirituality.

One of the main Sumerian gods – Enki, the Master of Universe and Faith – not only made the first man, Adam, from clay but also helped him to survive: by masturbating, Enki filled rivers and canals with his sperm. As for men, the Sumerians believed that solitary or mutual masturbation increased sexual power. In Ancient Egypt masturbation was considered to be a magic act of creation. By masturbating and inseminating himself, Atum-Ra created two gods – Shu and Tefnut – as well as the world itself and all men, including the whole population of Sudan (I am not sure that this would please the contemporary Muslim Sudanese!). The god of fertility, Min, can be also called the god of masturbation: he is often depicted holding his penis erect in his left hand and a flail in his upward facing right hand. It is interesting to note that Ancient Romans believed that one had to masturbate with the left hand. The frequency of divine masturbation was connected with the tide and the low-tide of the Nile – the foundation of life of any Egyptian – and that is why, in honour of Min, the pharaohs sometimes masturbated on this life-giving river. Ordinary Egyptians made some efforts too. During the annual festival of the growing season men happily masturbated each other.

Tourists taking photos of statues of masturbating Sumerian and Egyptian gods must be quite embarrassed by the lack of decency of the Ancient men, who had not known the One God's rigid morals. But they are wrong: this rite is very useful for bonding and creating common values. It is a pity it sank into oblivion!

Ancient Greeks paid less attention to the sacred meaning of masturbation than to its accompanying pleasure and utility. It was considered to be a normal substitute for copulation and was promoted as a reliable remedy to sexual dissatisfaction in the absence of a partner and love. Struggling against masturbation was unthinkable, as was the prohibition of all other bodily pleasures. In medical books at the time, masturbation occupied less space than sweating and chewing. Indeed, why talk about a common and evident

The Egyptian god Min.

practice? Even Hippocrates, a tireless fighter against the negative effects of sexual excesses, remained indifferent to the practice of masturbation. Foucault notes in *History of Sexuality* that even if masturbation was sometimes mentioned in the medical writing of that era, it arose 'in a positive form: an act of natural elimination, which has the value both of a philosophical lesson and a necessary remedy'. Diogenes, who preached against excess, encouraged masturbation for depending entirely on our own desire and being good for our health. Diogenes masturbated in public, arguing that satisfying a natural need cannot be indecent. When scolded for masturbating in public, he said 'I wish it were as easy to banish hunger by rubbing my belly.' According to John Chrysostom, Diogenes had another amazing idea: he believed that if the Ancient heroes had masturbated, it would have been possible to avoid the bloody Trojan war, because Menelaus would have easily forgotten his kidnapped wife, the beautiful Helen.

In Ancient Rome masturbation was also seen as a harmless natural pleasure which reduced stress. Otherwise, there would not have been this graffito in Pompeii: '*Multa mihi curae cum [pr]esserit artus has ego mancinas, stagna refusa, dabo*' ('When my worries oppress my body, with my left hand I release my pent-up fluids'). I'll take this opportunity to tell a popular joke on the subject: 'From the diary of a first-year student. Monday. Did it with the right hand, as usual. It was simply amazing! Tuesday. Tried with my left hand. A little off, not enough thrill. Wednesday. First came to know a woman. A pitiful semblance of the left hand!'

There was another expression designating masturbation – 'to sing a wedding song with your hand'. A prominent Greek physician of the second century, Galen, prescribed masturbation since long abstinence and an excess of semen would lead to the deterioration of physical and mental health.

To be fair, I should note the opposite trend. Or maybe not the opposite, but a balancing one.

On the one hand, the Chinese encouraged sexual intimacy with many people, which they believed to lead to longer life; on the other, they criticised male masturbation as leading to a loss of semen, life force, and psychological stability. Women's masturbation was not criticised, however: they had nothing to lose through masturbation and could do whatever they wanted.

Hinduism condemned excessive masturbation because it led to a loss of semen, which led to a loss of the strength, energy and stamina so badly needed by warriors. An addiction to fleeting pleasures also endangers moral progress. Copulation with a 'wrong' woman was also condemned because it made Man lose his individuality and led to the birth of bad progeny. This eugenic idea is topical even today: parents might decide a woman is unfit for their son.

The Greeks and the Romans debated the nature of semen and encouraged its preservation by avoiding excessive masturbation. Aristotle believed that semen was the residue derived from blood when at the optimal temperature. The Stoics argued that Aristotle had simplified the process, and that semen consisted not only of blood, but also of other products of the body. Galen later advanced a 'two-seed' theory: male and female seeds fuse

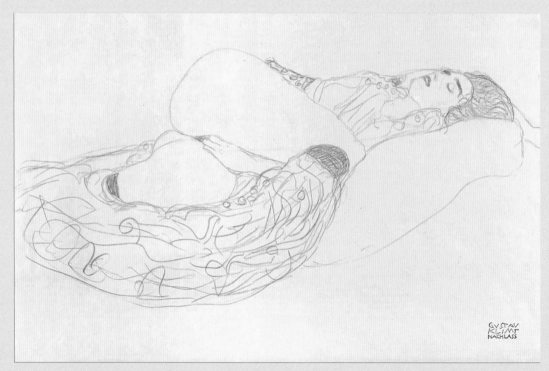

Gustav Klimt, Nude, 1914.

together to form a new life (pure genius, it is almost our contemporary genetic theory). Hesiod, Hippocrates and Galen connected sexual activity with health and taught that an excessive loss of semen impoverished and weakened men. Man is hot and dry, but he becomes a woman – a cold, moist and secreting being.

The Romans found other, more socially inspired, reasons for blaming excessive masturbation, which impressed me much more than the medical ones. Such as masturbation is a sign of a weak character and absence of self-control; it deprives men of their virility and their life spirit. It is also a sign of sexual weakness: a Roman citizen had to be a real 'macho' and put his dick in someone, no matter who – man or woman. Besides that, if men masturbate too much, women will have fewer babies. If there are no more new citizens, who will support the State and fight its wars?

In any case, no Ancient civilisation ever considered masturbation to be a sin. It has always been a natural sexual practice filled with a lot of positive meaning, and responsible for many important social functions. In this context, it is important to note one fact: though they ascribed importance to semen, neither the Greeks nor the Romans associated the 'loss of semen' with a 'lost child's life', even a potential one. For them it was pure nonsense: nature has provided males with such an amount of semen that it would be enough for inseminating not only 'their' females, who do not require a renewed insemination during pregnancy, but also of many random women.

The fate of masturbation took a sinister turn only when it met the first true monotheistic religion – Judaism. Judaism turned the concept of 'spilling the semen' upside down: it ceased to have anything to do with health, life force or danger of feminisation. Judaism abruptly passed from medicine to God, declaring that masturbation did not serve any of God's purposes because its only objective was to obtain 'illicit and immoral pleasure'. It is interesting to note that seventeen centuries later the discourse on masturbation will be turned upside down once again, from God to medicine.

To be honest, Judaism's negative attitude towards semen was formed in Ancient times when this religion was only starting and the Old Testament had not yet been written. The Ancient Hebrews, as well as many other tribes, believed that spilling sperm could summon evil spirits. After the first men were banished from paradise and lost immortality, Adam didn't touch Eve for religious reasons for 130 years. He had to masturbate and discovered that this summoned evil spirits. Male spirits, provoked by the presence of the lustful Eve, impregnated her and female spirits were inseminated with Adam himself. It is no surprise that we, their descendants, are no good. The transformation of the Old Testament into the Absolute Truth created an even more negative attitude towards masturbation. Mentioned only in three lines of the biblical text, it was then seen as treason and an affront to God and it quickly transformed from simple leisure into the worst enemy of doctrine, and a mortal sin. Any release of sperm without the possibility to procreate was prohibited: semen should only go into a vagina. Those who broke that rule were punished.

The only thing I don't understand is why the Jewish God was so angry. Indeed, if He really created Man in His own image, He must want to masturbate too, as did all the

pagan gods! If so, there is nothing bad in masturbation. If God doesn't want to masturbate, it means that He has done his work poorly and there is no sense in affirming that
Man has been created in God's image.

◼ Two Romeos and One Juliet ◼

In the popular mind, the history of masturbation has been preserved in a distorted
and cropped version – unfortunately, the faithful have stopped reading original sources.
It is believed that the simple Palestinian man Onan wanted to find a little sexual pleasure
in his mostly dull country life, but the kind and almighty Creator was in a very lousy
mood that day and reacted to Onan's desire by killing him as quickly and as mercilessly
as he would an annoying fly. So the first act of onanism for Onan was the last one too.

This version of events does not correspond to the biblical reality. What may come as
a surprise to most readers is that Onan never masturbated, because he was married and
masturbating was not necessary for him. He was punished with death for coitus interruptus, which has very little to do with masturbation: 'And Onan knew that the seed should

Arent de Gelder, Tamar and Judah, 1667.
Judah, the father, was the cause of dread throughout his whole biblical family;
not only amongst his sons Er, Onan and Shelah, but also Tamar, his sons' wife.

not be his; and it came to pass, when he went in unto his brother's wife, that he spilled it on the ground, lest he should give seed to his brother. And the thing which he did displeased the Lord; therefore He slew him also.' (Genesis 38:9-10)

I would just note that from the point of view of Judaism, the smiting of Onan seems perfectly justified. Releasing the seed away from the vagina of his wife, Onan deliberately and wilfully violated two divine laws, which in the biblical wording are presented with exquisite precision.

Firstly, God commanded His people in the beginning to: 'be fruitful, and multiply, and replenish the earth' (Genesis 1:28), and fulfilling this commandment is possible only by spilling one's seed inside the woman.

Secondly, Onan didn't 'give seed to his brother' because he knew that 'the seed would not be his'. Understanding this requires a little explanation, which the worst students in the most run-down yeshiva in the world could give. According to Jewish law, if a child-less man dies or disappears, his younger brother or other relative must marry his widow. Indeed, it would be too cruel to leave her to die of hunger! The new husband must also do everything possible to help her have children. But there is a hitch. According to Jewish law, the first-born male child receives the name not of the biological father, but of the deceased relative.

What really happened in the family of Onan? To answer this question, I turned to the full version in the Bible.

Judah found a wife, Tamar, for his firstborn son, whose name was Er, but the marriage didn't last long. For some reason Er 'was wicked in the sight of the Lord; and the Lord slew him'. Then Judah ordered the second brother, Onan, to marry Tamar and 'raise up seed to thy brother'. Onan didn't obey and was also killed by God. Then, using a formal excuse of Shelah's minority, who was supposed to become Tamar's next husband according to the law, Judah sent this double widow to her father's house. This is when the real biblical thriller starts.

Episode 1: After the death of his wife, Judah goes to Timnah to check his sheep. Once Tamar learns of this, she removes her widow's garments, covers herself with a veil, and sits on the road where Judah is going to pass.

Episode 2: The plan works out perfectly: Judah believes her to be a harlot and wants to have sex with her, promising to give her 'a kid from the flock'. As a professional harlot, Tamar asks him to give her something as a guarantee for future payment. Judah gives her his signets and bracelets. They then have sex.

Episode 3: Judah inspects his flock and sends her the 'kid from the flock' he has promised. But no one can find her.

Episode 4: Three months later, it becomes evident that Tamar, widow of Er and Onan and bride of Shelah, is pregnant. Judah is infuriated and demands to burn her alive (I didn't know that the Hebrews were so bloodthirsty!). But while she is being dragged to the place of execution, she shows her bracelets and signets to the crowd and says that she is pregnant by the man who owns them.

Episode 5: Judah recognises his possessions. He also recognises that she has done well: 'She hath been more righteous than I, because I gave her not to Shelah my son.' He no longer seeks her death. Tamar gives birth to twins. The end. We can see the almighty Creator was in a dreadful mood, not only on the day of the murder of Onan, but on one of the previous days when He, for no apparent reason (at least in the biblical text we are not told), smote Er, the older brother of Onan. After the untimely death of his two eldest sons, Judah did not trust his creator and began to fear for the fate of his only remaining son, almost certain that after marrying Tamar, Shelah would repeat the fate of his older brothers and perish at the hands of God. Most likely, God disliked his family from the beginning and for this reason Judah thought he could lose all his children.

But that's not the end. Further development of the story strayed from the correct monotheistic path towards the depraved ways of despicable Greco-Roman paganism. Judah was a passionate man (and his wife died, so he didn't have sex for a long time), so he really wanted to have sex with Tamar, whom he did not recognise in a new dress. Or, as you might suspect, pretended not to know. It is possible that he wanted to have sex with her for quite some time, even though she was his sons' wife. In the end they still slept together and she and Judah had a child, which freed Er from the obligation of marrying Tamar, and saved his life.

The first thing that catches the eye is the complete lack of explanations about why God killed Onan's older brother Er. His death was quite unusual: he didn't die from sickness, or from a lightning strike or a bite from a Palestinian scorpion. It was God in person who killed him. Of course, God has every right to kill whomever He wants. He doesn't need reasons to do this. Moreover, He does not have to report to anybody about the motives of His actions. Yet, an understanding of His motives would be very useful in making a judgement about God: this is a perfect example of the same theodicy we discussed at length in the chapter 'The Sovereign of Evil'. In addition, today a murder is a crime and in those days murder was almost an everyday business. Why was Er 'wicked in the sight of the Lord'? Maybe he also 'poured out seed on the ground' and thereby did not comply with the commandment 'be fruitful and multiply'? In this case God killed him justly.

Secondly, the biblical story, even though quite short, gives us enough information to put forward several plausible theories about Onan. He might have been a jealous and selfish man who could not imagine that those children who are born from his seed, so much like him, would be considered the children of another man, even his own brother. So, Onan did not want Tamar to become pregnant and his decision not to pour out his seed into her was completely conscious, for which he paid.

One can assume that Onan didn't really like Tamar. She probably seemed too old to him. Unfortunately, taking another, younger wife, was out of the question: the shepherd salary of Onan would not support two wives. For this reason, Onan decided to deceive. The same laws of Judaism that forced him to marry Tamar allowed him to divorce her in the case of proven infertility and to take another wife. It's very simple: Onan does not pour out his seed into Tamar, Tamar does not give birth within a couple of years, then someone younger and hotter appears on the horizon with whom he can pour out his seed whenever he wants and have children only for himself. But that didn't work. God, who, as everyone knows, is omniscient, saw Onan's intent and smote him right away.

The rabbis have many diverging explanations for this story, but they cannot doubt any word of the Scripture. They can discuss what has *not* been said, for thousands years if they want to. It is interesting to note that none of their explanations accused Onan of masturbation. They all agree that he was punished with death for breaking the Levitical law. Let me start with the first explanation found in Midrash. I even prefer it to my explanations since it gives an answer to the questions I asked myself: Isn't it strange that both brothers, young and God-fearing Jews, so easily violated an important divine commandment? Is there any compelling reason that pushed them towards such a terrible crime?

Here is what Midrash says: through the efforts of Judah the father, Er received the righteous, very beautiful and quite fertile Tamar. Indeed, she conceived after only one copulation with Judah. And did not conceive with Er. Why? Er was in such awe of her body that he didn't want to get her pregnant, and ruin her figure with childbirth and breastfeeding. For this reason, he first committed the sin of 'outpouring of semen on the ground' and became the first *onanist* in biblical history or, rather, 'erist'. (I suspect that the word 'onanism' caught on only because of its greater euphony.) In any case, Er was the first to break the divine covenant to 'be fruitful and multiply', and for this crime was executed by God.

Alas, the tragic example of Er was not a lesson to his younger brother Onan. He too wanted to preserve the beauty of Tamar and could not bring himself to put his seed directly into her, and repeat the sad fate of his older brother. In this regard, the fears of Judah over the fate of his younger son Shelah are understandable and justified: 'Lest perhaps he die also, as his brethren did.' Judah also appreciated the body of Tamar (no wonder he had unearthly passion and desired her so much later!), knew the romantic characters of his sons, and was sure that if Shelah grew up and married Tamar, he too would 'pour out [the seed] on the ground' and God would kill him.

Personally, I find that God can also be understood. It's not even the fact that the brothers didn't want to spill seed where they should. What made the brothers criminals represented an open challenge to God personally: they prefer the beauty of mortal earthly woman to the immortal divine commandments. Does not such a crime deserve immediate death?

Other rabbis believed that this story was not about mad love, but about sexual preferences of the brothers: they violated the sacred commandment 'to be fruitful and multiply' by having exclusively anal sex with Tamar. In principle, Judaism allows anal sex, but if a woman is capable of getting pregnant, one needs to take the penis out of the anus and put it in the vagina just before ejaculation (I can only imagine the horror of contemporary gynaecologists after reading this!). According to Philo, the main crime of Onan for which he was justly killed by God consisted in 'going beyond all bounds in love of self and love of pleasure'. It comes as a surprise that my friends and I are still alive!

And me again. The story of Onan is not an insignificant story with one's teenage son. In light of all the above versions, the story of Onan and, most importantly, onanism

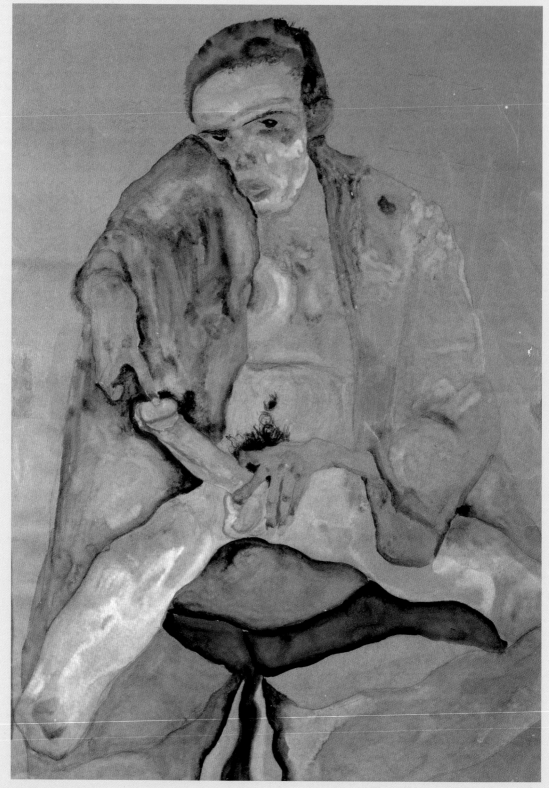

Egon Schiele, Eros, 1911.

itself, became truly historically significant and acquire universal scope. It becomes a phenomenon on a truly cosmic scale in terms of distribution and its significance to human life. Judge for yourself.

The first fallen woman, Eve, tempted Adam to transgress divine law. We all remember how this seduction ended.

The second fallen woman, Tamar, seduced not one man, but two, to violate divine laws. As a result, humanity was subjected to eternal damnation – the mortal sin of masturbation.

Two romantic Jews, Er and Onan, showed us the highest example of love, an example of passionate love towards a woman; in comparison the story of Romeo and Juliet looks like a run-down provincial affair. Both brothers slept with their wife every day after sweating in the fields harvesting their crops and relieving themselves in the same cesspool, but still loved her so much that both even refused the irresistible biological need to have children by her. Refused with a fatal risk to their own lives and died for her sake! Where else have you ever seen such love?

But there is a silver lining. Onan's death was not in vain. By sacrificing himself, he received all the laurels of sexual fame and will forever remain one of the most famous characters not only in the Old Testament, but in the whole of human history, leaving the unfortunate Greek Herostratus with a shameful glory and the eternal torments of impotent envy. In truth, the idea of a Herostratus was, from the very beginning, doomed to fail as a piece of media. Onan always lives with us, since early adolescence, and is always ready to lend us his sweaty lewd hand. We never forget about his existence and after a serious quarrel with one's husband or boyfriend, we are ready to repeat his great feat, risking our own salvation in the process.

■ Hands Full of Blood ■

In order to understand Judaism's attitude towards masturbation, one needs a short introduction into the history of its transformation from a patriarchal ideology into the religion of the masses. So here it is, the brief history of Judaism (writing this, I remembered Stalin's most famous book, *History of the All-Union Communist Party: Short Course*; indeed, I spent the greatest, but not the most pleasant, part of my life in the USSR).

Moses received two Laws at Mount Sinai – the Written Torah, known as the Old Testament in Christianity, and the Oral Law (the redaction of which is called Mishnah), which has been transmitted without being written down for more than 1,500 years. In the beginning of the first century AD, due to the bad political situation, it was decided it should be written down. It was done in the beginning of the third century by Judah the Prince (*Yehudah HaNasi* or *Judah HaNasi*, also known as Rabbenu HaQadosh). After its codification, the Oral Torah lost all its flexibility and became just another sacred book, which could be discussed, commented on and explained, but never doubted.

However, it is clear that both during the codification of Mishnah and after it, the rabbis debated with one another. Two commentaries on the Mishnah – the Gemara – appeared in the centres of Judaism, Palestine and Babylon. Each of these Gemara with their respective Mishnah formed two versions of the Talmud at the end of the fourth century: a Jerusalem version and a Palestinian version. Everything which, for some reason, was not included in those two versions of the Talmud – legends and parables – was later gathered in the Baraita. The Jewish laws concerning religious, civil and family life were gathered into the Halakha, based on the Written Torah, the Talmud and the Baraita. The latter two with their clear rules of behaviour are more important to a simple Jew than abstract matters treated in the Torah. In the sixteenth century, the Code of Jewish Law (Shulchan Aruch) was redacted in order to simplify the life of ordinary believers.

I presented you this brief history of Judaism for just one reason. I want to show you that the most important principles of Judaism concerning the sex life, were established not by many generations of unknown rabbis, but a couple of famous rabbinic sages (Tannaim) who lived in the first centuries AD, the era of the final codification of Mishnah. Among them was Meir, who explained to the people the rules for a sex life; Tarfon and Eliezer ben Hurcanus Eliezer ha-Gadol (Eliezer the Great), who declared war on illicit sexual excitement; and Rabbi Ishmael 'Ba'al HaBaraita' (Ishmael ben Elisha) who promoted early marriage. The opinions of those Tannaim represent real Judaism, before it was influenced by a hostile environment and life in the diaspora.

The significance of these people in the history of Judaism can only be compared to the Church Fathers of the Early Christian Church, such as Tertullian, Clement of Alexandria, Athanasius the Great or Gregory of Nyssa, whom I have already cited in this book.

The Amoraim succeeded the Tannaim. As their name suggests, their role was limited to a supporting one because all their ideas were based on the principles of the sages of the first centuries AD and they did nothing but comment on Mishnah codified by the Tannaim. What else could they do when everything was written down and became untouchable? However, there were a couple of bright personalities among them: the rabbis Yannai, R. Johanan, Assi II, and Safra. They are the renowned experts on masturbation, minimum age for copulation and female puberty. However, this movement disappeared by 350 AD, so I have no clue who redacted the most important text of Judaism, the Babylonian Talmud, two hundred years later.

That's it. Now we can examine Judaism's arduous relationship with masturbation.

Judaism revealed to us the terrible story of Onan and it is clear that Judaism never appreciated masturbation. And not only masturbation, everything praised by the sacred books was adored and everything they condemned could never recover from it and immediately became a hideous crime. In fact, anything one could find in the book, even if it was there because of a scribe's mistake, could be considered a crime. There was a special logic in it, a religious one: a Jew who commits even a small sin, a crime against God's Law, actually makes the first step on the road to disobedience and shows his inclination towards sin. He will inevitably sin again. Indeed, after an insignificant sin comes a greater one – one just has to start, 'He who will steal an egg will steal an ox'. One who yields to a 'small' diabolical temptation – for example by praying less than required – will most certainly betray his God and his brothers in faith. Indeed, the Book of Isaiah (1:14-16) says that if a man does not cease to do evil, e.g. break any of God's commandments, God will hide His eyes from him and will not hear his prayers, no matter how much he prays. Such a person's hands 'are full of blood', as if he committed a murder and were caught *in flagrante delicto*. However, it is quite surprising to read that, according to Isaiah, the 'new moons' and the 'appointed feasts' are the examples of this bloody evil. It is the same with masturbation: even though it has never been the most important sin, it interferes all the time in the battle for the purity of faith.

Being a serious, systematic and ritualistic religion, Judaism starts examining the question of masturbation from afar, namely by stating that reproduction is a key duty towards God: 'Then God blessed Noah and his sons, saying to them, "Be fruitful and increase in number and fill the earth."' This commandment, as well as all other commandments of the Book, cannot be broken in any case. It is forbidden even to abstain from sex which is equal to breaking God's order to reproduce. Judaism is convinced that reproduction is not a human affair and that there are not two but three participants in it: a man who gives his seed – a future skeleton, nails and organs of the embryo; a woman who gives her ovules which become the blood of the embryo; and the most important participant – God – who gives soul to the embryo. Not only humans need children: male seed bears in it the future generations of God's servants and thus spilling the seed is a big step in the chain of disobedience to God. It is a bloody murder, a murder of potential lives.

Despite Judaism's quivering attitude towards reproduction and its approval of a free sex life in marriage, the situation is not that simple. The Torah's understanding of male seed leaves much to be desired. How can one explain why it is necessary to get rid of semen traces? Indeed, according to Judaism, both semen after intercourse and semen from nocturnal emissions desecrate men:

> When a man has an emission of semen, he must bathe his whole body with water, and he will be unclean till evening. Any clothing or leather that has semen on it must be washed with water, and it will be unclean till evening. When a man has sexual relations with a woman and there is an emission of semen, both of them must bathe with water, and they will be unclean till evening. (Leviticus, 15)

The Talmud teaches what measures must be taken in order to avoid nocturnal emissions. It is not very difficult: before going to bed, or after waking up during the night, one has to read out loud a couple of psalms and ask God for help against this desecration. If God does not help and there is an emission of semen, one has to wash himself and ask God for mercy.

What does Judaism say about masturbation? An onanist is a person who 'causes children to flow in the wadis', who 'slay the children in the valleys under the clefts of the rocks'. In Arab and Hebrew *wadi* means a valley that has a river that is usually dry, except when it has rained. I saw those wadi in the Negev, in Israel, in Egypt and Jordan, but the most beautiful ones are situated in Oman. Thanks to science, we know now that every time a man discharges semen in vain, approximately one hundred million spermatozoids die.

Each of them could have become a child. Indeed, it is way worse than an abortion that kills a maximum of two embryos. I imagined a man with a penis in his hands full of blood. One hundred million small children fly out of his penis crying for help and are washed away in the cloudy flow.

This behaviour must be severely repressed and it certainly deserves a death sentence. This is why the death of Onan was just. Not only masturbation, but any sexual act, if it doesn't end with ejaculation in a woman's vagina, is a crime.

In this context, masturbation is worse than adultery. Any sexual act, even an illicit and severely condemned one, can lead to procreation, while masturbation is useless in this sense. Thus it makes sense that Judaism doesn't differentiate between male masturbation, premature withdrawal and foreplay without intercourse. Masturbation is even more dangerous than the rejected sexual intercourse. Even though the result is the same, i.e. the useless loss of semen, during masturbation this loss doesn't happen for natural reasons, but occurs as a result of sinful imagination. And a sinner can think about anything, even having sex with demons.

The Talmud did not ignore the nervous system. The wise book states that 'the brain of those who masturbate dries up'. Now I finally understand why boys have such bad grades at school!

That's it. Now we have all elements to explain the rabbi's aversion to masturbation.

First, the Tannaim. Ishmael forbids masturbation not only with hands but also with feet: 'Thou shalt not practise masturbation either with hand or with foot.' Eliezer accuses onanists of 'committing adultery with their hand', while Eliazar and Jose ben Halafta warn that onanists will not enter the World to Come.

The Amoraim agree with the Tannaim: Jonathan, Assi, Ammi, and Isaac remind that before God those who discharge their semen in vain are no better than those who spill the blood of the innocent or adore idols. Such a man definitely deserves immediate death, the fate of Onan. Maimonides shared this point of view and Shulchan Aruch states that onanists will be ostracised:

> It is forbidden to release semen for no purpose and this iniquity is more serious than all the sins in the Torah. Those that masturbate and release semen for no purpose, it's not enough for them that this is a serious prohibition but that those who do it are ostracised and about them it is said: "your hands are full of blood" and it's as if they have killed. (Chapter 151)

However, it is much more important to do everything to prevent this crime rather than denounce it in vain. The rabbis are convinced that the most effective method against masturbation is suppression of illicit sexual excitement. Indeed, before getting pleasure from masturbation and 'spilling seed in vain', a potential onanist must get excited. According to religion, the 'smallest' sin starts here and it is at this moment that everything must be done in order to prevent future crimes against the faith. Moreover, it is not important whether a person had an intention to get excited or he got excited spontaneously – the result is the same.

First of all, one needs to eat exclusively kosher food and pray a lot because it will help to avoid sinful sexual fantasies. Jose ben Halafta and Rabbi Ammi say that excitement built around sinful thoughts has awful consequences: such a person, a traitor (*avaryen*), will never enter the Kingdom of Heaven, because he will inevitably yield to sinful temptations (*yetzer ha ra*). His fall will never stop and in the end he will adore the idols. The Talmud clearly states (BT Nidah 13a-b) that if a man is incapable of controlling his desire to have an orgasm, he will not resist idolatry, ritually impure food or sports. That is not all: a man inclined to frequent masturbation loses interest in his wife and forgets about his duties towards the community.

I agree with these conclusions, but I see the problem from the opposite point of view. A man starts to masturbate frequently when he is fed up with his wife and his obligations towards the community, such as going to the synagogue, studying the Torah and praying for many hours.

Besides that, to avoid temptation, boys and men should not touch their penis and never approach it with their hands. The Mishnah and the Talmud (Nidah 2:1, Niddah 13a, 13 b) are very clear: 'Every hand that "checks" [the genitals] frequently – if by a woman, it is praiseworthy, but if by a man it should be cut off.' Tarphon goes even further and demands some drastic solutions like cutting a man's hands to the navel. Here is an excerpt from this discussion in the Babylonian Talmud:

> If his hand touched the membrum let his hand be cut off upon his belly. It is better to be without a hand than to end up "descending into the pit of destruction". "But", they said to him, "would not his belly be split?" "It is preferable," he replied, "that his belly shall be split rather than that he should go down into the pit of destruction." They said to R. Tarfon, "If a thorn stuck in his belly, should he not remove it?" "No," he replied. (Niddah 13a-b)

I visited a couple of yeshivas and I was very interested in whether students followed this prohibition or not. It was hard to believe that their hands were not aware of the road to the most popular destination among teenagers. Anyway, their pants were large, but their hands were not cut off and I saw with my own eyes how they used these sinful hands to touch the thick books filled with the sacred commentaries. Modern Judaism, however, can give a more humane and socially acceptable interpretation of the rules regarding the touching of one's penis: it is not necessary to wash your hands again.

In Judaism, there are two interpretations of whether it is allowed and commendable for a woman to touch her sex organs. The first one states that a woman must frequently touch her sex organs in order to be aware when she menstruates because menstruation imposes on her some ritual limitations – Nidah, or seclusion. The second one (BT Nidah 13a) affirms that women can touch their sex organs because, unlike men, women do not feel anything when they touch themselves.

I have never heard anything so stupid! It seems that the Hebrew women were different from ours and they had no idea that women are naturally more sensual than men and that they can have far more orgasms. However, I noted the only positive thing in the arduous relationship between Judaism and masturbation – female masturbation. Neither the Torah nor the Talmud says anything about it.

Most probably, women's sins or apostasy did not really interest God and He did not care about their prayers. Hebrews' blind faith in their own superiority and the infallibility of the Talmud allowed women to retain this little sinful pleasure. It is also possible that women are allowed to masturbate, because they cannot spill their ovules and kill potential lives. Jewish women are lucky!

Jewish men are anything but. According to tradition, they have to wear very large trousers (so that their sex organs never touch the cloth and get excited), sleep only on the side, and never touch the penis while urinating: this is how the Hebrews were taught to urinate. The question of how to urinate properly became so important that there is a big discussion around it in the Talmud.

Eliezer affirmed that a person who holds his penis during urination puts the world in danger of the flood. It is a clear allusion to the story of Noah's Ark and the worldwide flood God sent to humanity to punish it for its sins. Hearing this, the astonished disciples feared that urine could splatter the feet of a man and then people would think that his organs were damaged. In this case, some people could doubt that he is the father of his children and think that the latter are bastards. However, the rabbi is firm in his ideas: it is better to let people think that your children are bastards for your entire life than be a sinner for a small time. There is only one concession: one can climb to a roof and urinate on the ground so that it doesn't splash.

As any Amorai faithful to the tradition, Abaye agreed with the Tannaim. He said that it would be nice to have a roof to urinate from, but if there was none, one had to reconcile oneself with the idea that the urine would get everywhere. It is better than to betray God!

The disciples' fears were quite well-founded – indeed, it is quite difficult to urinate without holding a penis and avoid splash-back. It is so difficult that the Amorai Nachman bar Yaakov tried to soften the absolute prohibition of Eliezer by proposing to let at least married men hold their penises while urinating: 'If a man was married, this is permitted.' I believe that this concession can be explained by two circumstances: firstly, a belief that a sexually satisfied married man would not get excited during urination and, secondly, a desire to spare a religious man from daily family drama. Just imagine the reaction of a wife when she discovers that the bathroom floor and her husband's clothes are soaked with urine! Another rabbi proposed an alternative way: to point the urine flow in the right direction by holding the testicles. Some very reasonable advice from a very reasonable rabbi! In fact, it really does solve the problem of 'not holding the penis'. But what should one do if there is an urgent need to examine one's penis – an injury, a pimple, or an infection, for example, gonorrhea. It happens to all men. Abaye brilliantly solves this problem: one has to use a piece of driftwood, some broken pottery, or a thick tissue. But only thick – one has to be sure to feel nothing while touching his penis.

Despite all this great advice, the rabbis were perfectly conscious that men would touch themselves no matter what they said or prohibited. For this reason, the only effective method of making men follow the divine commandments consisted not in struggling against illicit sexual excitement, but in transforming it from an illicit one to a licit one. It can be done only through religious marriage.

◾ A Three-Year-Old Wife ◾

A marital relationship in Judaism is a two-stage process consisting of a betrothal (*kiddushin*), when a couple lives separately, and a marriage (*nisuin*), when husband and wife form a real family. The betrothal can also be considered a legal marriage because a couple can have regular intercourse. The betrothal can be annulled only if one of the future spouses dies or if one of them starts the divorcing process (*get*).

If we consider the conditions of marital relationships in Judaism from our contemporary point of view, it seems perfectly fine. Such a marriage corresponds perfectly to the traditions of the contemporary democratic ideal. The Gemara and later the Shulhan Aruch state that a father, the main figure in the patriarchal society, can arrange betrothal for his daughter only with her full consent: 'A woman can only become engaged by her will. One who engages a woman against her will, she is not engaged.' And, in general, it can be done only when she attains maturity or is close to it. The Talmud explains that a betrothal is celebrated in three cases: a bride has been bought, a contract has been concluded, or a couple has had intercourse. One of these conditions suffices to make the betrothal legal.

As for the legal age of maturity, there has been a curious discussion between the rabbis on this subject. The 'main' rabbi, Judah the Prince, believed that a woman attained maturity when her pubis was almost entirely covered with pubic hair, while the Amorai Safra (Yevamot 12b) believed that it was useless to wait for so long and defined the age of maturity as the time when a girl had her first two pubic hairs (Niddah 52a). Usually it happened when a girl was thirteen and a boy fourteen years old. I'd like to note that nowadays girls can start having pubic hair at the age of eight or nine, much earlier than back then. Moreover, a pubescent young woman could not be betrothed to a small boy or an old man. The reason for this was not her indifference or bad feelings towards her future husband, but the belief that she would be sexually unsatisfied in such a marriage and would commit adultery: 'Marriage to an old man or a minor leaves the woman unsatisfied and is apt to lead to licentiousness.' (Sanhedrin 76b)

A woman was also considered mature if she managed to conceive and give birth to a child before having any pubic hair. The fact of giving birth to a child automatically made her mature and a full member of the community. She could henceforth divorce (if the rabbis gave their permission) and had some incumbent duties, for example studying the Torah. This way of attaining maturity through giving birth to a child has never been contested by any rabbi. A child was more important than pubic hair. I would contest it: the fact that young women gave birth before attaining physical and psychological maturity is rather gruesome to my mind.

If we examine the conditions of marital relationships in Judaism in a more profound manner, say by returning to the era of the 'founding fathers', the era of the redactors of the Mishnah, our understanding of marriage customs will radically change. As paradoxical as it may seem, in the fundamental Talmudic sources marriage and sexual intercourse (it is prohibited to abstain from sex!) are not discussed in light of sexual or psychological maturity. The Baraita stipulates unequivocally that God commanded the arrangement of child marriage. An early marriage was preferable and desirable, and usual on important religious grounds; it actually has three important advantages.

First of all, any potential sinful sexual excitement is under total control in an early marriage. Once a child experiences sexual desire, he or she has someone to satisfy it with.

Secondly, only this kind of marriage satisfies the Torah's demand to start children's religious education as early as possible. Ishmael ben Elisha says: 'The Scripture tells us, "Thou shalt teach them to thy sons and to thy sons' sons; and how may one live to teach his sons' sons unless one marries early?"'(Deuteronomy 4:9; Yerushalmi Kiddushin, ch. 1, page 61a; Bavli Kiddushin 29b) The earlier children get married, the earlier they have their own children, the earlier those children will have children, etc. Imagine a girl having children when she was ten or eleven. When she is twenty-one or twenty-two she can be a grandmother; when she is thirty-two she can be a great-grandmother and so on. Her husband, a rabbi, will be able to teach the Torah to three or even five generations by the time he is only sixty years old!

In order to explain the third advantage of an early marriage, I have to make a clarification because the rules of betrothal and divorce radically change in the case of an early marriage. A young woman has the right to take a decision concerning the betrothal (whether to consent to a marriage or not) and to accept the gifts (*kiddushin*) only when she attains maturity, when she becomes a *bogeret* (Niddah 44a-b, 47a), and this regardless of her father's will. But when she is still a minor, *ketanah*, according to the Halakha rules, it is only her father who can decide whether to marry her off or not and he is the only one to have the right to take money, the gifts, or *kiddushin* on her behalf (Niddah 44a-b). He can also annul the betrothal and marry her to anyone else at any moment, receiving the *kiddushin* once again. (Niddah 47a, Ketoubot 46b) Let's be indulgent and believe that he would do all this following her demands.

If a *ketanah* does not have a father, her mother or her brothers can marry her off, but in this case the minor wife not only has some sexual obligations, but also the miraculous right granted by God called *mi'un* (denial, refusal) and can annul her marriage herself at any moment. She can declare her aversion to her husband and leave him without starting the *get*. (Yevamot 107a) She can also leave him without any explanation, guided only by the desire, as Maimonides says, to get a better *kiddushin* from another man. (Yevamot 108a; Maimonides, 'Yad,' Gerushin, xi. 3; Shulḥan 'Aruk, Eben ha-'Ezer, 155, 3) Alas, the right of refusal, *mi'un*, does not last long, only until a girl gets her first two pubic hairs. Judah the Prince was kind to the *ketanah* and proposed to extend this right until the time when 'black hair predominates'. I wonder whether the *ketanah* tried to prolong their privileges and shaved these unfortunate hairs.

Now we can pass to the most interesting aspect of marriage customs in Judaism described in the Babylonian Talmud, and I won't deny it was what motivated me to study the sexual and marital relationship in Judaism in the first place. What is the minimum age for a girl to be recognised as a *ketanah*, be betrothed by her father, and be obliged to have intercourse with her husband? If you are not an inveterate Talmudist, you will never guess. So I won't torture you and will give you an answer right away: she must be three years and one day old!

Meir, the most important Palestinian sage, who is cited by the Niddah (44b), Yevamot and Ketoubot of the Babylonian Talmud, states that a girl aged three and one day can be betrothed by intercourse: 'A girl of the age of three years and one day may be betrothed by intercourse.' (Niddah 44b) The Talmud says that some rabbis disagreed with Meir and believed that a girl of two years and one day can be betrothed by intercourse or, as Johanan thought, a girl of two years and thirty days ('Thirty days of a year are counted as the full year). However, the authority of Meir made it possible to wait until an appropriate age before regularly having sex:

> An objection was raised: A girl of the age of three years and even one of the age of two years and one day may be betrothed by intercourse; so R. Meir. But the Sages say: Only one who is three years and one day old.

One hundred years after Meir, the rabbi Yosef defines this idea taken from the Mishnah's Niddah 44b more precisely by emphasising that a girl aged three years and one day, betrothed by her father, must be betrothed by full intercourse. It cannot be different and as I have already mentioned, abstinence is prohibited:

> Come and hear a resolution from a Mishna: A girl who is three years and one day old whose father arranged her betrothal is betrothed with intercourse, as the legal status of intercourse with her is that of full-fledged intercourse.

All rabbis of that time agree that early marriages help to avoid the awful sin of 'spilling the semen'. Everyone agrees that sexual immaturity of a girl finishes when she is three years old. Look what is happening here: Judaism strictly prohibits lustful fantasies, touching the penis with hands, touching it with pants, 'spilling the semen' outside of a vagina, intercourse with an infertile woman, but it does not prohibit and in fact promotes intercourse with a three-year-old girl. Take also into account that at this time puberty came later and a girl aged twelve looked like one of eight. However, the rabbis do not even doubt whether it is acceptable to have intercourse with a child. When I realised the horror of this, I felt that I was losing my mind: even if we ignore moral conventions, I cannot imagine how it is possible to have full-fledged intercourse with a three-year-old.

Can you imagine this? I also remembered that betrothal with an 'old man' was prohibited and a question popped into my head: if she is three years old, and he has already attained maturity (thirteen years old), is he considered to be 'old'? I do not have answers to these questions, but the rabbis of the first centuries most probably did: intercourse with a three-year-old is analysed in detail, including in the Levitical laws. In the case of her husband's untimely death, his brother must engage in intercourse with her and make her his wife, as said Yosef: 'And in a case where the childless husband of a girl who is three years and one day old dies, if his brother, the *yavam*, engages in intercourse with her, he acquires her as his wife.'

In the Babylonian Talmud, there is only one discussion concerning the intercourse with underage girls, and more specifically concerning their pregnancy and childbirth: in this discussion also arises a new aspect to the question of 'spilling the seed'. For a girl aged from three to eleven, there is no problem: she is unlikely to get pregnant, even if she has some pubic hair, so there is no need to use any birth control. If a girl is aged twelve or more, there is also no problem: she is ready to get pregnant and give birth to a child. The only dangerous period is when a girl is aged eleven to twelve: she can get pregnant, but it is highly improbable that she can give birth. She is far too physically undeveloped and there is a great risk that she would die during childbirth. Moreover, it is forbidden to use the pull-out method because it means breaking the most important divine commandment. It goes without saying that for true monotheism every word of the Book is far more important than a human life!

Therefore, in the Babylonian Talmud, the rabbis discuss exclusively one question: is it acceptable from a religious point of view to put a contraceptive sponge in the vagina of an eleven- or twelve-year-old girl? Indeed, this sponge is an analogue of withdrawal and 'spilling the seed'. It is a great dilemma: Is it acceptable to use contraception for a short period of time, less than a year, in order to reduce the risk of death? Is a couple obliged to observe the commandment and take the risk that a wife and a child might die during the labour?

This is what Meir says:

> Who is [considered] a minor? It is a girl from the age of eleven years and one day until the age of twelve years and one day. If she was younger than this or older than this, she may go ahead and have intercourse in her usual manner.

It seems to me that a non-kosher contraceptive sponge was not very popular among the rabbis of that time. Most of them are against it: one should not mourn the potential victims of early pregnancy. If a pregnant girl is destined to die, then she dies. One should implore God – He, the Almighty, knows better. He will certainly take care of all the innocent and save who needs to be saved! The divine Law must be respected, no one should betray the religion. The following citation from Meir shows that he prefers the Holy Book to the salutary sponge: '…and Heaven will have mercy upon her and prevent any mishap, since it is stated: "The Lord preserves the simple (Psalms 116:2)."' (Yevamot 12 b)

While writing this, I remember the phrase I cited in the chapter *The Sovereign of Evil*, 'Kill them all, God will know his own', allegedly spoken by Papal legate and Cistercian abbot Arnaud Amalric prior to the massacre at Béziers, the first major military action of the Albigensian Crusade. I think that the analogy is quite convincing.

I believe that the problem of the sponge proves that early and very early marriages were quite popular back in the time. Although I am horrified to call intercourse with a three- to eleven-year-old girl an early marriage or lawful conduct respecting the divine commandments. I want to call it by the name it deserves – disgusting legitimised pedophilia, which cannot be understood by any normal person. In the best-case scenario, it can be explained by saying that religious ideas have completely destroyed rabbis' morals and intelligence. In the worst-case scenario, it is very bad: they were probably aware of the horror of such actions, but were pleased not only to continue doing it, but also to recommend others to follow their example. As everyone knows, everything not forbidden by the Holy Book is allowed!

I decided not to tell you about contemporary Judaism's position on the question of birth control in marriage. What can it change? One has to tell the whole story without omitting any unpleasant part of it. Hence it is not possible to omit anything written on this subject in the Mishnah, the Talmud and the Baraita, transformed into a petrified relic many centuries ago. As far as I am aware, no one has ever dared to modify the Talmud or, even worse, to abolish its principles. That is why I am interested to know whether the yeshiva students learn about three-year-old wives and what they think about them. I hope they do not envy them.

Let me remark that nowadays there are many rabbis who are opposed to any form of birth control and do not permit its use in any circumstance. It is highly probable that if secular society had not introduced the notion of the sexual inviolability of children, and had not defined a legal minimum age to marry, which corresponds not to the appearance of some pubic hair but to the social maturity of a person, religious communities would have continued to marry off children. Probably not three-year-olds, but, let's say, starting with eleven- or twelve-year-olds as was practised a couple of decades ago in Jewish communities in Yemen and Morocco. The reason is the same: the fear of the uncontrolled sexuality of youth. There is another good example of the same dynamics – the fierce fight of American justice against the Mormons concerning the minimum age of the bride and the number of wives allowed.

In conclusion, I would like to apologise to my readers who won't be able to listen with awe to the rabbis' discourses about the wonderful principles of the Jewish family and rules of sex life and contraception therein. You will remember another family, the one where a girl can be married off at the age of three and one day. You will also remember the rabbis, the fathers, the mothers who were searching for the first two small hairs on the pubis of a child.

What else should I have done after discovering and systematising these religious rules? Let me be honest with you – I never expected a monotheistic religion to be that absurd. A great number of people, one generation after another, spend all their time and energy studying very old texts written and redacted by some very strange people. And they feature one insane idea after another! Should we not refuse to take seriously all other ideas of this religion? Or, at least, carefully examine them for the signs of madness known to all psychiatrists.

■ If Your Hand Seduces You, Cut It Off ■

Once Christianity hatched from Judaism, the situation became even worse for masturbation. The Christian tradition in the field of masturbation developed as a young, strong, and vibrant offshoot from the powerful but slightly mossy stump of Judaism.

It was not an escape into sexual freedom, quite the contrary. In full compliance with the new doctrine, the emphasis was not placed on disobedience and the futile waste of seed, but instead it emphasised the sinfulness of receiving forbidden pleasure connected with passions and fantasies. It started, as always, with the weak: women immediately lost their historic privilege of masturbation; the responsibility to behave according to religion was now placed on everyone. At least they did not impose anything on small girls, even though it was highly recommended to young girls to marry early to preserve their health and virginity. Yet no one ever talked about three-year-olds!

In fairness, I must say that both Judaism and Christianity do not consider female masturbation to be a serious crime, though the opinions on it diverge. For example, a thirteenth-century Christian philosopher, Albert the Great, strongly recommended pubescent girls to rub their clitoris themselves or to ask a midwife to do it in order to get rid of bad liquids accumulating in their innocent bodies. It was also supposed to help them to struggle against temptations with greater success. However, this advice didn't last long and already in the seventeenth century the majority of Christians believed that female masturbation led to an exaggerated growth of the clitoris, beard growth, and repulsive lesbian desires.

There is no better evidence of the extremely negative attitude of primitive and medieval Christianity towards sexuality than its condemnation of not only male masturbation, but also uncontrolled nocturnal emissions, and the inability of the Church to cope with the latter enduring to this day. Nocturnal emission is a sin, but a pardonable one. Do you know who were exempt from this rule? That's right, the young priests. Indeed, is it humanly possible for a priest not to ejaculate while listening to the confessions of young sinners? Or during the torture of naked young witches?

After many centuries of hesitation and deliberation, the second exception was made for an unintentional ejaculation without pleasure. For the readers who do not understand what I am writing about and how this could even happen (indeed, I did not understand at first, before I studied religion), let me explain. This is a forgivable sin where the absence of erection by a spouse bars him from performing his conjugal duty, and so he must arouse himself or ask for his wife's help (only with her hand, not mouth!). Pure sacrifice, without any intention to derive pleasure from the offence, and preferably hatred towards it. Then, a small part of either original sin or his fatal sinful nature spills from the man. We need to pray more and God will forgive us, but deliberate 'spilling', a deliberate desire to experience pleasure, is an unforgivable sin, a clear insult to God, barring the road to paradise, and the first step to hell.

In order to 'spill the seed' one needs to use the hand and it is quite understandable that, as well as in Judaism, this 'hand full of blood' (Isaiah 1:14-16) was condemned:

> If your hand causes you to stumble, cut it off. It is better for you to enter life maimed than with two hands to go into hell, where the fire never goes out. And if your foot causes you to stumble, cut it off. It is better for you to enter life crippled than to have two feet and be thrown into hell. And if your eye causes you to stumble, pluck it out. It is better for you to enter the kingdom

of God with one eye than to have two eyes and be thrown into hell, where 'the worms that eat them do not die, and the fire is not quenched'. (Mark 9:42-48)

The basis of the Christian attitude towards masturbation is in the words of Apostle Paul from the First Epistle to the Corinthians:

> Know ye not that the unrighteous shall not inherit the Kingdom of God? Be not deceived: Neither fornicators, nor idolaters, nor adulterers, nor the effeminate, nor abusers of themselves with mankind… (1 Corinthians, 6:9)

> Do you not know that your bodies are temples of the Holy Spirit, who is in you, whom you have received from God? You are not your own; twenty you were bought at a price. Therefore, honour God with your bodies. (1 Corinthians, 6:19-20)

Please note that the terrible sin of Sodom, the sin of effeminacy (masturbation), holds a place of honour in the list of sins immediately behind adultery and before homosexuality, and it is the first step to paedophilia, bestiality, and even necrophilia. This proximity is easily explained by the fact that homosexuality and masturbation are directly related to pleasure, but bear no relation to fertility. Clement of Alexandria repeats the idea found in Judaism according to which it is unacceptable to spill the seed outside of a woman, and he adds that such an act 'offends nature and common sense'. He must have considered nocturnal emissions to be unnatural. One thousand years later, Thomas Aquinas reinforced the thesis of the offence against nature and advanced an idea that 'a male seed obtains its force from the stars which God uses to rule over the world' (it is quite bold to accuse stars of masturbation!). It comes as no surprise that Thomas considered masturbation to be the -most important sin of the flesh. The human body is the resting place of the Holy Spirit and does not belong to Man, but to God. The body was given to Man to serve God, not to receive pleasure. God explained to Man everything he could do with His property; therefore, masturbation is an illegal use of another's property, which has long been punishable by law. That is why masturbation is a mortal sin against the God-given body. It is deadly not because of its effects on health, as one might think at first glance, but because it is the reason behind spiritual death – the Holy Spirit wouldn't live in such a disgraced body! The practice of masturbation puts a person into the category of God's enemies. Instead of using his hands for some good purpose, like building another temple, a man uses these very hands to kill God directly and knowingly in his own soul, at any time that suits him.

Just imagine how scary this sounded to a man of that era who strongly believed in the Last Judgement and the Kingdom of Heaven. He probably believed it even more than the communists believed in the bright future of all mankind!

Many Christian theologians who followed the sages of Judaism consider masturbation a graver sin than adultery, and the biggest sexual offence before God. Unlike Judaism, they explained this seemingly absurd point of view not only by the fact that it makes it impossible to conceive. They believed that sexual intercourse could still be justified by the fact of being seduced; but the crime of masturbation has no mitigating circumstances, and it must be prohibited to all Christians, either married or single.

In fact, masturbation undermines the status of the Christian family. The Church exposes a person to the harsh experience of family life and imposes on him the obligation to perform conjugal duties. Masturbation, being a solitary pleasure, is an attempt to shy away from one's experience and duties. It is associated with particularly vivid fantasies, which have nothing to do either with God or one's spouse. And it is extremely easy to run away from one's duties, even in a familial setting, since there will always be some bathroom unavailable to the other spouse.

The Church has invented a special term for the mortal sin of withdrawal and mutual masturbation, '*fraude conjugale*' (adultery in marriage). I was naïve to think that one could cheat his spouse only by having sex with another person!

Nowadays Christian religion is less attractive and strong than it used to be in the Middle Ages, but the idea that masturbation makes you God's enemy is still quite popular among the conservative Catholic and Orthodox believers. Masturbation has always been and remains a disgusting sin committed in the presence of God and Mary. Sexual fantasies are also highly criticised and some Catholics believe masturbation to be a kind of rape of another person; they say that when women are used in sexual fantasies, they are sexually abused, even if they are untouched and do not know about it. It is quite an interesting point of view if you believe fantasies to be a sin. However, if, like me, you do not believe it to be some sort of fornication, you will recognise that they bring a little bit of beauty and charm to our dull everyday life.

The *New Catholic Encyclopaedia*, a very respected source in the Catholic world, shares these ideas. It recognises that 'the sexual instinct is one of man's strongest instincts and the pleasure connected with its activation is one of the keenest of sensual pleasures'. And – I simply cannot believe it – it says that 'many normal persons may at times choose this form of self-gratification', but also that 'deliberate choice is always a mortal sin'. It repeats that a person who chooses self-gratification will inevitably commit other awful sins and become God's enemy.

Is it possible that all people I know are God's enemies? I was horrified when I realised that I did not know anyone who did not masturbate. Crippled with my studies of mathematics and physics, I could only come to one conclusion: the 'normality' of a person is an 'affront to God' and a 'mortal sin'.

The Mormons, who declare themselves the inheritors of Abraham, also engaged in the fight against masturbation. They proposed quite original methods to struggle against this ungodly practice: never sleep alone, sleep dressed, sing uplifting anthems if aroused and, the most interesting, 'imagine as you bathe in a tub/barrel of worms, scorpions, spiders, centipedes, and think about what can be eaten by them in the time that you masturbate'. One has to have a very good imagination, as powerful as that of an onanist's. I strongly believe that by fighting against masturbation and mutual masturbation, the Christian religious worldview works against its own interests: it could be the Church's best friend, not its worst enemy. Masturbation reduces overall excitability and suppresses desire, easing the unbearable anguish of human lust, preventing infidelity, and preserving the inviolability of the Christian family. Moreover, masturbation is difficult to control, much harder than adultery. Even the all-seeing Big Brother ruins his eyes, nervously trying to capture hundreds of millions of acts of masturbation at the same time.

Islam is the most tolerant towards masturbation. There is no outright condemnation of masturbation in the Quran and all judgements about it are based on subsequent interpretations of the following well-known Sutras of the Quran:

> And they who guard their private parts except from their wives or those their right hands possess, for indeed, they will not be blamed. But whoever seeks beyond that, then those are the transgressors. (Quran 23:5-7)

This is why most of the *ulema*, the wise men, consider that masturbation is forbidden (*haram*) as it represents lust and may contribute to excessive incitement of desire and indulgence in lust.

However, some influential Islamic scholars considered the seed a natural secretion of the human body, no different from all the others and saw no reason to ban masturbation. They said that if you prohibit masturbation you have to prevent bloodletting. Indeed, the Quran does not directly prohibit it, so even if there is no virtue or merit in self-gratification, it does not invalidate the fast or the hajj.

The adherents of one of the most influential Sunni schools, the Hanafi, believe that the above verses of the Koran apply only to adultery and if a person is faced with a choice between adultery and masturbation, masturbation becomes permissible. However, they made a crafty clause stating that the permission applies only to liberation from lust, not satisfaction of it. Personally, I do not see the difference, as I always feel satisfaction upon release from lust.

It is time to make some brief conclusions. Fierce condemnation of masturbation by monotheistic religions, especially Christianity, most clearly reveals the negative attitude of the monotheistic doctrine towards sexuality.

I can understand the desire to limit sexual practices: sex plays an essential role in the relationship between people and is extremely important for society in general, which needs the stability of the family as the fundamental building block and a guarantee of the purity of its descendants. That is why one can understand the condemnation of adultery: it is not good to violate this oath in public. At the same time, it is even better not to make any oaths that you simply cannot respect. But hatred of masturbation, a symbol of human nature, can only be explained by hatred of Man himself, as to prohibit masturbation is to deny life itself. It represents the apotheosis of religions' desire to dominate and humiliate Man by making him feel guilty and sinful in the eyes of God. Monotheistic religions bear the entire responsibility for the consequences of the taboo of masturbation, which have caused psychological problems and hysteria for entire generations. However, from monotheism's point of view, there are many reasons to hate self-gratification.

Masturbation is anthropocentric: one does not need God or a partner for it. It is a strictly personal choice which represents the highest degree of love of oneself, and self-love is equivalent to a blatant disregard for God.

The sin of self-gratification is associated with loneliness, which is an unacceptable state for any religious doctrine, where the notion of community is central. It is loneliness which reinforces temptations and weakens faith. That is why, when religion condemns self-gratification, it also condemns loneliness. Hermits are no exception to this rule since they are always under God's eye.

Masturbation quickly and effectively removes nervous and physiological stress; this does not allow for the development of religious ecstasy and undermines the desire to read the Holy Book. After orgasm, people only want to sleep. Thus the influence of the Church on children, adolescents, and unmarried young people is lost at the most important age for indoctrination. In short, how to inspire people with the idea of spiritual transformation when they are much more attracted to the idea of sticking their hands between their legs?

Now I will tell you something which may seem extremely paradoxical after all the wrathful religious pathos thus far: religion's condemnation of masturbation, as fierce as it may seem, did not inflict anything terrible on humanity. One could continue self-gratification: Christianity and Judaism vehemently condemned masturbation in word, but not in action. The religious texts considered self-gratification to be a mortal sin, but only one of many other sins. Until the end of the seventeenth century, the clergy saw in masturbation something quite harmless and did not pay much attention to it, even during confession. It goes without saying that the medical community was far more interested in sexually transmitted diseases.

Until the end of the eighteenth century, the term *onanism* did not even exist, though by this time the biblical image of Onan had existed for nearly three thousand years. Adult masturbation was considered a minor sin and child masturbation was generally condoned. There were more important things: heretics, witches, pagans, and basic sinful adults. The children were told 'no' and scolded, but they were not subjected to violence. Sometimes they were even encouraged: in the sixteenth century a distinguished physician, Fallopius, discoverer of the fallopian tubes and the inventor of the condom made of linen, recommended parents to 'diligently increase the penis of their son by letting him touch it'. The explanation is very simple: the prohibition of any sexual practices, particularly masturbation, is very beneficial to any religion. For example, the formal prohibition of masturbation became a boon for the Christian Church, a brilliant marketing ploy – all men masturbate, they all feel guilty, and all come to Church to repent. Manipulation, pure and simple.

Fortunately, for both people and religion, in the foreseeable future this will end: I am confident that before the Abrahamic religions people masturbated and they will continue doing so after they disappear. Everyone without exception: adolescents, bachelors, married men, widows and, of course, rabbis and priests – they do it even more than anyone else! To prove it, I can cite the opinion of the doctors of the eighteenth and nineteenth centuries, the era of the fierce struggle against masturbation, who believed that the clergy could not recover from the disease of masturbation.

So, if you need advice from a self-gratification expert, ask a priest and go and confess to him: you will never find a more experienced consultant. I suspect that the Church perfectly knows its priests as the worst sinners of all: it will always think that a priest yielded to temptation and got more pleasure from masturbation than prayer.

The peaceful cohabitation of the Church, society, and masturbation finished at the end of the eighteenth and start of the nineteenth century. The medical world and secular society unexpectedly declared war on masturbation. Unfortunately, secular society turned out to be dumber than the Church, and the marketing ploy by religion was adopted by bourgeois society at face value. Medicine secularised onanism and added the idea that loss of precious liquid was not a simple moral crime, but also a threat to the health of a person and to the survival of society as a whole.

■ A 'Cynical Spasm': ■
Medics' and Philosophers' War against Masturbation

The term *onanism* first appeared in an anonymous pamphlet published in England in the early eighteenth century (according to different sources, in 1710, 1712, 1715 or 1716) called *Onania, or the Heinous Sin of Self-Pollution, And All Its Frightful Consequences, In Both Sexes, Considered: With Spiritual and Physical Advice To Those Who Have Already Injured Themselves By This Abominable Practice*. It threatened amateur masturbators with stunting, giving birth to feeble children, and God's curse. The author of the pamphlet is still not known: some say it was the Danish theologian, Balthazar Bekker, others think it was the British surgeon, John Marten. One can hardly believe in Dr Marten's purity of purpose: the medicines to treat this terrible crime were displayed on the same shelf as the book. In 1809 Dr Marc-Antoine Petit published *Onan, ou le tombeau du Mont-Cindre. Fait historique.* In the 1860s, the Christian philosopher Jean-Philippe Dutoit-Mambrini published a book threatening those who committed the sin of self-gratification with eternity in hell.

Alas, most of the prophets are forgotten by the ungrateful: all those works fiercely denouncing masturbation were consigned to oblivion and only one book entered history – the passionate and uncompromising *Onanism* by Swiss doctor Samuel Auguste Tissot, published in 1760. Almost immediately it became a huge bestseller. It accused masturbation, for a long time a grim phenomenon in human life, of much more serious issues than all the religious books put together. Tissot said, with a fervour worthy not of a doctor but of a legendary preacher like Savonarola, that 'this terrible habit led to the death of more young people than all diseases put together'.

Was Tissot religious or was his fervour due exclusively to his medical ideas? It is hard to say, but it is not important. It will be enough to cite some of his most shocking statements. For example, he stated that onanism was the sin of sins which caused more moral, physical and intellectual harm than all other sexual sins put together. Moreover, he decared:

> Onanism is much more dangerous than excessive copulation with women. Those who believe in divine Providence affirm that the harm caused by this evil comes from a special will of God to punish it.

Nevertheless, Tissot's work had a huge impact on his contemporaries and it was reprinted sixty-three times, never contested, and only re-edited.

By the mid-nineteenth century, ideas about the huge dangers of masturbation were accepted both in the medical community and society; by the end of the century, masturbation was declared an epidemic that had infected a large part of humanity. Most encyclopaediae and medical dictionaries agreed with Tissot that masturbation was 'the surest and the shortest way to death'. No one in Europe had any further doubt that masturbation was responsible for psychological deviations and physiological diseases, that it was disgusting and immoral by its own nature: all maniacs and homosexuals certainly began their journey with masturbation.

The obsession with the issue of masturbation quickly gained such momentum that it began to resemble the collective madness of the witch hunt, with only one difference: the devil of masturbation was always present as it was firmly settled in between a person's legs. The Catalan doctor Pedro Felipe Monlau's hate was even more expressive. In his *Higiene*

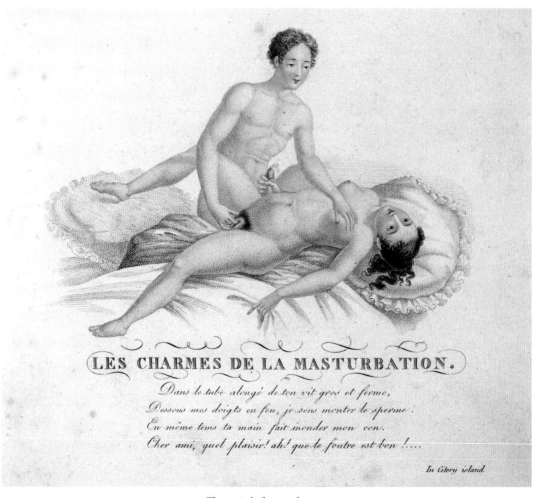

The appeal of masturbation.

del matrimonio, he stated that masturbation is a 'disease without pain, a disgusting and harmful vice which leads to the destruction of the body and fall of the soul'. In another work, *Higiene privada*, he denounced masturbation in the following terms: 'Onanism is a brutal and cynical spasm, a prostitution of oneself by oneself which leads, as any vile action, to remorse and sadness, and does the same harm as excessive copulation.'

It goes without saying that such a course of events was not a moralist's or doctor's whim which spread throughout society. It was a predictable consequence of the victory of the bourgeoisie over the aristocracy. I, however, do not think that the struggle with masturbation gained popularity in aristocratic and creative environments: independence of mind and self-love bred since early childhood are not viable media for mass hysteria. In the case of the bourgeoisie, it is all clear and I understand its fears and reasons for hating masturbation.

The bourgeoisie of the seventeenth to nineteenth centuries condemned the morals of the aristocracy and tried to be seen not only as a class possessing wealth, but also as the champion of virtue and puritan moral values (even if they visited brothels regularly). The bourgeois fear of the aristocrats' unbridled sexuality is well-grounded: their children were building their careers and married much later than their ancestors. For this reason, they were at a higher risk of moral corruption and sexually transmitted diseases. Masturbation is even worse. It is a sign of complete moral corruption which leads to exhaustion, the loss of vital forces, and human dignity. One should not waste one's sperm and emotions, as well as money; one has to use these resources rationally, preserving them for future procreation, and not wasting them while searching for pleasures. From this point of view, young men should not only learn to avoid masturbation, but also to practice a pull-out method during intercourse. They should also avoid having sex too often: once per month is more than enough! Foreplay outside of the marital bed must be avoided too because it provokes excessive excitement in men and vaginal lubrication in women, which is a sort of 'nocturnal emission'. Moreover, masturbation is dangerous for bourgeois society as a whole: it elevates the risk of its degradation and the loss of domination of the superior white business class over the working class.

The bourgeoisie joined in Tissot's condemnation of female masturbation – probably for the first time in the history! Tissot affirmed that female onanists were more lustful, emancipated, and had a kind of a butch spirit. They possess all the characteristics of mutants: they grow taller, their arms and legs get thicker, their voice is gruff, their clitoris gets bigger and starts to resemble a penis. However, male onanists are also mutants: they lose their virility and become effeminate.

Many philosophers of that time shared Tissot's point of view and considered masturbation to be a crime against oneself, nature and society. However, those 'thought leaders' ideas were more profound and global.

In the *Encyclopedia*, one of the key works of the Enlightenment written by Denis Diderot, masturbation and even nocturnal pollutions are condemned in the most virulent terms. According to the work, there are two types of pollutions depending on the morality of a person. The author says: 'All agree that it is a sin against nature. The rabbis put it on the same list as homicides; And St Paul says that those who fall into this crime will not enter the kingdom of God. I. Cor. Vj. Ten'.

According to the *Encyclopedia*, pollutions can be involuntary or voluntary. The first 'serves rather to maintain health by the necessary excretion of superfluous humour' and 'is familiar to the persons of both sexes who live in a too rigorous continence'; it 'make[s] them taste pleasures they deprive themselves of because of their virtue or even cruelty'. The second is 'a vicious disposition of the members or the brain, and which rightly deserve the frightful definition of disease'. The sick men experienced 'in the region of the prostate and urethra sensations similar to those he would experience if these bodies were poked with red-hot iron'. At the end of the article the author makes the following conclusion: 'nature always finds a punishment, so a person can atone for his sins against its laws, and that it acknowledged the cruelty of the punishment with the crime.'

To me it sounds like another monotheistic religion: one should not wait for the Last Judgement anymore, its time has already come here on earth!

Why did the philosophers become interested in this problem and even elevate it to an ontological level? Why were they opposed to masturbation? I will discuss it only to show that even the greatest minds can be mistaken. There is no other reason to talk about it: in our age all these philosophical and medical arguments have disappeared into thin air.

Kant, a philosopher-moralist and product of protestant puritanism, ruthlessly stigmatised self-gratification and profoundly despised those who practised it. It is quite strange to hear about this from a person who had never been married and was rumored to have died a virgin. He considered masturbation to be a double sin in relation to oneself.

Firstly, God the Creator defined function and predestined every being and every action. It presupposes a distinction between a sexual subject and object which is annulled in masturbation. This is the reason why masturbation is fundamentally immoral: the subject uses himself merely as a means for the gratification of an animal drive.

Secondly, a masturbating subject creates a fictional object of desire between himself and his body, which is created exclusively by his imagination and does not correspond to natural necessity. As a result, the entire body suffers and the normal process of sexual excitement is distorted, which makes the pleasure unnatural.

Moreover, a sexual act of self-pleasure does not have any value because it damages the concept of a social individual and is directly connected with the problem of suicide: both self-pleasure and suicide violate our duty to preserve the species.

Like Kant, Rousseau links self-pleasure to death. Masturbation means having sex with oneself, which represents a dangerous replacement of a real object of sexual desire by an imaginary one. Any replacement of this kind is an assault on the natural diversity of life. Besides that, masturbation is a perversity of a child's body, which needs to learn *the other* and not the self. Imagination replaces natural sexual desire, provokes the development of obsessions, and allows one to control sexual satisfaction while disregarding a woman's desire. In his most famous book, *Émile*, he condemns the onanist in the following terms:

The memory of things we have observed, the ideas we have acquired, follow us into retirement and people it, against our will, with images more seductive than the things themselves, and these make solitude as fatal to those who bring such ideas with them as it is wholesome for those who have never left it. (…).It would be very dangerous if instinct taught your pupil to divert these senses and to supplement the occasions for satisfying them. If once he acquires this dangerous supplement he is lost.

Rousseau, who 'suffered' himself from onanism his entire life, makes a very original conclusion. Even though no one can avoid masturbating, it does not cease to be a blatant filth which can make you lose any sexual attraction to people of the opposite sex. It is way better to have sex with prostitutes: debauchery is one thousand times better than self-pleasure.

Even Voltaire, a fervent defender of individual liberties, was opposed to masturbation: 'However, onanism has nothing to do with Socratic love, it is rather a very disordered effect of self-love.' (Philosophical Dictionary) Yet it is hard to see why 'disordered' self-love is so bad, and why it is worse than 'Socratic' love.

In the ideological context of that time, one can easily understand Rousseau's and Kant's confidence that the main threat of masturbation consisted of the absence of object. Through the sacrament of marriage God gives us only one partner. Secular society agrees with it. But the onanists do not: their imagination forms not a representation of a real person, but a polymorphic image of a person in general as an object of sexual desire. They must stop this sick relationship with their own bodies. Gender domination is present in any healthy society: boys should desire girls and not their hands, and girls should play the role of a passive object of men's imagination.

I certainly understand the anger of philosophers and I can even summarise their ideas in a more contemporary manner: masturbation fucks a person! So what? Why would we owe anything to anyone, but ourselves? Why cannot we desire both girls and our hands' gentle touch? What is bad about self-love? Indeed, both Leviticus (19:18) and the Gospels exhort to 'love your neighbour as yourself', which means that you have to love yourself first! How is it possible to love and give pleasure to your neighbour before loving yourself and understanding your own desires? I am convinced that contemporary philosophers would agree with me on this, and that it is the reason for their strong interest in insane medical methods which struggled against masturbation in the eighteenth and nineteenth centuries.

For example, commenting on the movement against masturbation, Michel Foucault writes that a masturbating child enters the discourse in a twofold manner: first, with an old image of a sinner, and second with a new image of a sick person who must be healed through surveillance and punishment. The universal secret which is known to everyone, but never discussed, becomes an issue not only for an onanist and his confessor, but for the entire social environment of the former: his brothers and sisters, his parents, teachers and doctors. This secret was the real reason for almost all diseases.

Though many doctors of the eighteenth and nineteenth centuries and even of the begin-ning of the twentieth century (the Swiss doctor Tissot, the French Lallemand, Lafond,

Fournier, the Germans Fürbringer and Rohleder) wrote about awful diseases caused by masturbation and gave many spectacular examples of it, their works lacked system and coherence. I will try to fill that gap. Their ideas on masturbation are like clones; it is pretty easy to me to resume them in an impersonal manner. I suggest you do not simply read, but imagine implementing their absurd ideas in your life. Indeed, it would be way too arrogant to believe that people who lived just two centuries ago were foolish and that their sexual life was radically different from ours.

Let me start with this extraordinary idea according to which sperm is not one of the bodily fluids that needs to be released when in excess. Sperm was believed to be formed by blood and to accumulate in the corresponding reservoirs in order to attain perfection and transform into blood again. It plays the role of the 'divine' stimulation of all other physiological functions of the organism. In this context, the excessive loss of sperm is a real crime against oneself since it reduces or even suppresses the mechanism of its transformation back into blood. It is the source of all physiological and psychological diseases of an onanist.

Furthermore, frequent orgasms make the body lose vital force that it desperately needs. The onanist cannot compensate for what he is spending and this is why one can recognise him by pallor and depletion. Moreover, the onanist usually masturbates standing or sitting down and he gets much more tired than a lover who lays on his partner's body (it is a hymn to the 'missionary position' so much appreciated by Christianity). During such intercourse, one also benefits from intensive mutual sweating. That is why a tired onanist deprived of a life-giving sweat does not experience pleasure, exaltation, or delirium proper to natural intercourse. I agree with this argument and propose to allow my children to do anything they want in bed; as long as they use protection of course. It comes as no surprise that onanism leads to premature ageing, loss of freshness and beauty, swelling, bags under the eyes, acne, itch, and early baldness. This process has particularly negative effects on young women who can transform from beauties into hags in the space of a year or two.

The numerous opponents of masturbation also wrote that it was the cause of fever and pain in different parts of the body. The list of diseases caused by it include the circulatory, respiratory (cough, tuberculosis, nosebleed), digestive (bad breath, loss of appetite, nausea, vomiting, diarrhoea, incontinence), and reproductive (impotence, infertility, penis skin orders), as well as eye infections and even blindness.

Onanism's negative influence on the nervous system was also discussed. As ejaculation is accompanied with a spasm, cramp, or convulsion, psychiatrists affirmed that excessive ejaculation can lead to insomnia, epileptic fits, hysteria, or even paralysis.

According to the authors of medical treatises of the era, partial or complete memory loss was equally possible. Diderot says that such a loss is preferable because it can help those criminals to forget the reason for their awful state of health. It was also said to lead to the decline of mental abilities and learning capacities (Tissot's example of the twelve-year-old boy who could barely speak and was completely illiterate was largely cited), and in the worst-case scenario to premature dementia, imbecility, and madness.

There is more to it: extreme forms of masturbation were said to cause a very dangerous pathology called spermatorrhea, an uncontrollable and continuing ejaculation without any sexual desire, erection, or pleasure resulting in an emission of mucus resembling snail slime. Spermatorrhea causes great damage to the onanist's body and mind, especially to his reproductive organs which become depleted and cease to function normally. The first description of a patient suffering from this disease was given by Tissot, but the French surgeon Claude François Lallemand is considered to be the 'father' of this theory and his works were particularly popular in England and America. According to him, each man only had 5,400 ejaculations so it was necessary to preserve this valuable resource, the loss of which could cause the degradation of the next generations. The good news was that it was possible to recover from this disease, but not everyone could – nothing could help the priests who experienced regular pollutions and doctors who worked with females suffering from erotomania.

The medical madness was unchained: all possible diseases were then said to be caused by masturbation, which transformed into a pathology and a retarded death sentence. Once he understands how masturbation harms his health and will kill him, even an avid onanist immediately feels remorse and starts thinking about suicide. Just as Kant said. In a word, he transforms into a living corpse (if it were true, all my friends and I would have died many years ago).

I have no doubt that doctors, moralists, and educational institutions of that time have done much more to defeat onanism than all Abrahamic religions put together. They have done much more harm, too: their medical articles, books, encyclopediae and dictionaries managed to instil fear of masturbation in the entire population of Europe, Great Britain, and America. It actually does not matter whether Tissot and all his disciples believed what they preached, whether they were honest and well-meaning doctors, paranoiacs, or manipulative pathological liars exaggerating the negative effects of onanism in search of glory and honour. In any case, the campaign against masturbation was mired in lies and falsification; it was the first global medical fib in history. Nowadays it seems obvious. But back then people felt that it was necessary to do everything possible to eradicate this harmful practice. And they did it by outlawing it and fighting it using medical, administrative, and educational terror.

Medicine started with the statement that children's sexuality is contrary to human nature. This was very close to an attack on the single manifestation of infantile sexuality – masturbation. All children were considered potential sex offenders and they were under total control: they could never be alone, neither day nor night, either at home or in educational institutions. They were supposed to sleep only in separate beds and with lights on; in boarding schools beds should not come into contact in order to avoid any sexual games. Even more widely used were psychological methods of intimidation: doctors and parents threatened boys and girls with horrible diseases. They scared the child with a total loss of the penis, or threatened to cut off his genitals with a knife or scissors: sperm preservation became parents' most important duty.

Images of young women suffering the consequences of masturbation accompanied by descriptions of the resulting illnesses (mental debility, hunched back, swollen neck). Dr Rozier, Secret Habits or Illnesses Caused by Female Masturbation, Paris, Audin, 1830.
How could you not fight the urge to masturbate if it results in such problems?

Secret Habits or Illnesses Caused by Female Masturbation
by Dr Rozier, Paris, Audin, 1830.
The fight against masturbation was led with the help of huge lies:
just look at the supposed consequences of it!

The taboo of children's masturbation brought with it a wide variety of ways to treat the dreaded disease, as a bland regime for both sexes. There was an interdiction to ride a horse or a bicycle and a direction for girls to climb trees with crossed legs. In the nineteeth and twentieth centuries, multiple patents for devices against masturbation were granted in the USA and in England. In mild cases, they confined themselves to simple measures, which nevertheless prevented the touching of the genitals with the hands: sewed-up pockets in the pants, and underpants with buttons in the back were used, while hands were bandaged at night. Enemas with cold water also helped, tying hands to the headboard and using hospital type straitjackets. The design of school desks did not allow one to cross one's legs.

In more severe cases, one applied plaster bandages, thick cotton paper bandages with a hole for urination and menstruation, burning plasters, wire mesh, or metal belts (very reminiscent of the medieval chastity belts) and small cages to one's body. Such devices were supposed to be worn either constantly or during the night and were usually locked. You can only imagine the smell! Parents also dressed the child's hands with metal trowel gloves and the penis with a spikey tube. The German professor Hermann Rohleder offered many original designs for such devices in his *Onanism* published in 1911 and in which he was constantly citing his French and German predecessors.

All this happened not in the distant and wild Middle Ages, but at the end of the nineteenth century – a period of rapid scientific and technological revolution: the advent of internal combustion engines, powerful electric generators, cars, the first aeroplanes, telephone, radio, organic chemistry of plastics, and cinema.

Over time doctors realised that the most important thing for children was the prevention of sexual arousal. The very existence of the genitals was to be associated with pain. Any erection in boys and sexual arousal in girls should have been accompanied by extremely painful sensations. After long attempts they managed to develop some effective methods, which do credit to human ingenuity:

The use of burning bandages on the genitals – it is better for a child to suffer constantly than to masturbate! This method was particularly efficient for girls.

The use of a ring with internal spikes. In case of any erections, even during sleep, they dug into the trunk of the penis and caused incredible pain. Later, shock was used to curb erection (it is quite possible that electricity was invented for this). Spineless parents replaced the shock with a sound signal from a Milton device. Imagine the noise on our streets if such a device were ubiquitous! Louder than an aircraft taking off or a Formula 1 race.

Locking of the foreskin with a pin or through infibulation (stitching) in the front, leaving a small hole for urination. Sewn foreskin limits the length of the penis, and the swelling of the member during erection caused unbearable pain. Such a radical method is only effective in cases of multiple relapse. A shocking version of this method was the infibulation of the foreskin around the edges. The foreskin was pulled forward and slashed across the front with a thick needle. After the appearance of scar tissue, which became dense and hard, a thick silver thread was passed through it, which prevented contact of the foreskin with the penis and caused extreme pain when trying to move the foreskin

Martin Van Maele, illustration from the series "The Great Danse Macabre of the Living", 1905.
Parents, fear not if your children start doing the same – it's completely normal!

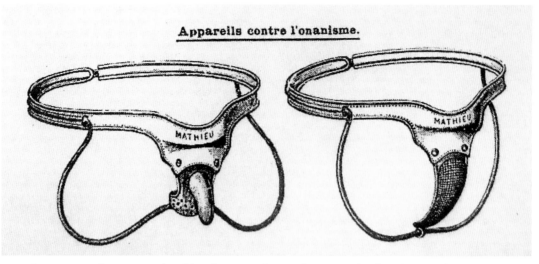

Instruments used to prevent girls and boys from masturbating. Illustration taken from the work of Jean Stengers and Anne Van Neck entitled "Masturbation: The History of a Great Terror".

relative to the glans. Another version of this method consisted in sewing the emission rings into the gland. Very convenient – masturbation and masochism at the same time. Treatment should not stop before the infibulation of the female organ or sewing the labia with silver strings leaving a hole of no bigger than the diameter of a little finger – only in this case, a girl could not touch her clitoris. In the worst case, a clitoris needed to be cut;

Cauterisation of the penis with acid and placing leeches on it – this experience, after even one treatment, would discourage touching one's penis for a long time. No need for the wide Jewish pants. Society and science did not forget about helping poor girls, victims of masturbation. Cauterisation of the clitoris with a hot iron or electricity was recommended for them.

Placing burning solutions and long needles into the urethra then burning it with hot wires. This is an innovative yet incomprehensible way of dealing with the issue. It turned out that apparently many masturbators get their main pleasure from stimulation of the urethra. I am clearly not adept at onanism!

What was the result of this terrible hazing by doctors and moralists of children and teenagers? As one should have expected, nothing. The 'criminal' sexual excitement never ceased to grow naturally during puberty. The crusade against masturbation which lasted for over a century and a half has become the best example of human stupidity, weakness in the face of chimeras, and meaningless rebellion against human nature.

Onanism did not give up; it actually won the war declared against it. It flourished everywhere: at home, in boarding schools, in summer camps, in front of the parents, teachers and tutors. I am ready to believe that doctors and moralists 'saved' a few boys – indeed, boys need to be alone and be able to use their hands in order to masturbate. Dealing with girls, however, was a real challenge: even if there were no holes or gapes

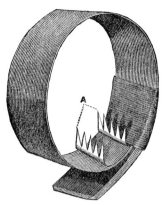

Toothed Urethral Ring.

Pollution ring.

in the devices protecting their genitals, it could not prevent them from doing it because they could simply use their leg muscles to obtain the desired result.

The complete fiasco of the movement against children and adolescent masturbation became evident to all honest doctors in the middle of the nineteenth century. They came up with a new brilliant idea: instead of fighting the healthy sexuality of a young body, one should tire it out with sports, so that the body cannot have any more 'dirty' desires, besides sleeping. The Ancient maxim 'In a healthy mind a healthy body' was transformed into 'In an exhausted body an exhausted mind'. Besides, it is pretty easy to manipulate an exhausted mind.

To be honest, the idea of repressing sexual desires with physical exercise seems quite reasonable: I remember having been told the same thing back at school. And I would love to collect data about masturbation among professional athletes. But not too popular ones: they have too many fans to even think about masturbation.

France was the first European country to implement this idea. Claude François Lallemand, who discovered spermatorrhea and was the first one to suggest circumcision as a method of healing it, recognises in his *Des pertes séminales involontaires* (*Involuntary Losses of Semen*; 1836-1842) that energetic young men, even brought up in bourgeois families with strong religious morals, could not resist their flesh and inevitably fall victim to unbridled masturbation and sexual delirium. In order to avoid this dangerous situation, young men should do diverse and tough exercises on a regular basis. No surveillance, even a very well-organised one, can replace them: 'Therefore, there must be a gym, a sports teacher, and sport competitions prizes in every school and educational institution.' Lallemand provides a very convincing argument as to why physical exhaustion is useful in the fight against masturbation of the young bourgeois risking the loss of virility specific to the dominant class:

Why is not a child of a poor man, dirty, malnourished and ill-garbed, crushed with an excessive amount of work? The reason is that this very exhaustion preserves him from bad habits. Why does a child of a wealthy man, who was taken good care of, often fail in their physical, intellectual and moral development?

In a word, the virtuous bourgeois parents had a dream: once their children improve their physical health thanks to sports they will immediately stop masturbating. And not only masturbating, but also having dangerous sex at an early age, which can bring only sexually transmitted diseases and trouble with young maidens. Two decades later, the French doctor Emile Jozan went even further: in his work *On a Frequent and Little-Known Cause of Premature Exhaustion* published in 1864, he urged parents and mentors to harbour no illusions:

Do not hold any chimerical illusions! The success is in maintaining good health; it is not in maintaining the impossible state of innocence and absolute purity… Do not count on education, morality or threats! The hideous spectre of onanism is moving forward. Nothing can stop it but disease and death!

And he shows us the only way to succeed:

One should proceed by diversion: it is the body which must be exhausted by physical exercise in order to control the mind; it is in the muscular system that all excessive life energy should be directed through regular exercise. It is in the gym that all criminal desires and bad thoughts disappear.

He finishes with an appeal worthy of a record in history: 'Let's restore the Antique gymnasia and glorify the Olympic crown!' (This was said decades before Coubertin!)

The leading doctors' opinions must have been heard in the highest echelons of power because the state decided to intervene. In February 1869, the minister of education Victor Jean Duruy issued a decree reforming the education system. It introduced new curricula focusing on philosophy and languages and obliged all educational institutions to install a gym and made school sports compulsory for boys.

Don't worry, girls weren't forgotten: they were also told to do a lot of exercise in order to struggle against masturbation. Cycling and horse riding were highly recommended, though long before those sports were accused of provoking women to sin! One should not be surprised, it has happened a lot throughout history.

I would like to think that there is a global paradox: the fight against the despised and hated onanism, which is responsible for so much suffering and victimisation, was not useless. It brought us back mass sports and the Olympics!

By the beginning of the twentieth century, the movement against onanism faded away in France. In Great Britain and the US it was not the case at all: huge resources and sustained efforts were made to struggle against this terrible disease. I am talking about the Boy Scouts movement which was joined by around 100,000 people when it was founded in 1907. This movement was literally obsessed with onanism. It believed it threatened the very survival of the Anglo-Saxon race, a bigger threat than sexually transmitted diseases

Mihaly Zichy, Boy Masturbating in a Toilet, 1911.
Masturbation in our great-grandparents' time.

or illegitimate children. For them masturbation was caused not by natural sexuality, but by eating too good food (one should eat like the Spartans or the Japanese), by looking at pornographic images, and listening to 'dirty stories' boys would tell each other. The mentors deluded themselves into thinking that it would be enough to explain to the boy scouts onanism's sinful nature and the harm it does to the health (weakness, nervousness, timidity, and dementia), and to make them do intensive exercise: they would put an end to this awful habit once and for all and would patiently wait for their future wife. What a marvellous solution to the problem!

The Boys Scouts movement also left us extensive literature on masturbation. It presented it as the biggest threat to the health and the psyche of a young boy. The movement has some very serious arguments against it. Sexual fluids which were given to men by God are good since they produce virility and force, but its conscious loss is very bad. However, the adolescents' premature sexual drive can be overcome by intensive physical activities and games. The mentors were so stupid that they did not officially acknowledge the existence of nocturnal emissions until 1943.

What conclusion can we make from this fight against onanism in secular Western society? Only one: the verbal crusade of Christianity against masturbation transformed into a real crusade of medicine against adolescent sexuality, which was marked by an impressive campaign of repression against hundreds of thousands of young bodies. Its terrifying results can still be seen, but now they affect not hundreds of thousands of mutilated kids, but hundreds of millions of children and adults.

▪ The Triumph of the Onanist ▪

At the end of the nineteenth and beginning of the twentieth centuries, the struggle against masturbation faded into the background, as if it had not been raging just a few decades ago. I cannot explain the sudden loss of interest in something that was believed to be the main cause of all human misery.

God continued to play the role of the omniscient Big Brother and religious preachers did not disappear. The thick Holy Book could still be found everywhere, in every home and hotel, and it continued to tell the story of the horrible sin of self-gratification. Doctors would receive the same training and have the same degrees from the same universities, they would treat the same patients, and there were just as many philosophers and moralists as before. But the high and thick wall the Europeans and the Americans had built in order to protect themselves from the worst enemy of humanity suddenly started to collapse. Perhaps it was bourgeois society, who got so rich that, after getting rid of the aristocracy, they wanted to try out their loose morals.

Doctors might have opened their eyes and sobered up from their crusading dream. Then came the terrible hangover. They realised that the onanism warriors led by Tissot had falsified the scientific data in order to provoke neurosis, and poison the life of adolescents by imposing strict interdictions, violence, and guilt. Such sobering up – the return to reality – has

Félicien Rops, Saint Teresa.

happened to all of us. However, there is something good in disappointment. Evil tongues say that it was the study of methods in the struggle against masturbation that led Sigmund Freud to invent psychoanalysis.

At the end of the nineteenth century doctors discovered that female hysteria (which does not really exist – it was doctors who were hysterical) was caused not by masturbation or sexual fantasies, but by the absence of sexual release due to the prohibition of onanism, or a life without sufficient sex.

Instead of devices preventing masturbation and orgasms, doctors proposed the opposite method: to make women have an orgasm right in the examining room using a vibrator. They say that it became the sixth most-bought electronic device after the light bulb, sewing machine, fan, electric kettle, and toaster. I was not surprised that the vibrator was invented so long ago: it should actually have been invented before all other electronic devices, considering the importance of sexuality in our lives. In the end, what doctors had seen as the reason for deadly diseases became the cure.

Many men, whose virility was 'restored' with the devices limiting masturbation when they were children, needed help as adults: the 'victory' over masturbation frequently led to complete impotency which could be cured only with electricity. Not the best method for the patient's psychological stability!

In 1924, the Larousse dictionary stated that adolescent masturbation was no reason for concern and, starting in the second half of the twentieth century, masturbation became acceptable. Every child discovers that touching their genitals gives pleasant sensations and so touches them. Nature does not leave any choice, and neither prayers nor exhortations can have any effect. Sexologists and psychoanalysts started talking about masturbation as a necessary stage in the sexual development of adolescents of both sexes, and as absolutely harmless for society in general and a person's future family life in particular. They even suggest that masturbation is extremely important for girls because the capacity of an adult woman to reach an orgasm might depend on whether she masturbated as a child. Parents should worry when their children do not masturbate, which is a symptom of a somatic illness or a psychological deviation. Not masturbating as an adult is even more unlikely, because masturbation helps lonely people to dilute their loneliness with bright fantasies, to release unbearable tension, and not to lose their minds. It goes without saying that the Church does not agree with such conclusions, and continues to denounce self-gratification with the same hatred.

And what about all those secular personalities who supported barbaric repressions against masturbating children? What about Kant, Rousseau, and even Voltaire? What about other eminent medical and moral voices? How could they all be mistaken?

It is absolutely possible! We have seen that the 'secular' crusade against masturbation may have been the most aggressive and tragic one. Everyone makes mistakes.

Surprisingly enough, some American doctors still share the Church and Tissot's point of view. I disagree with their negative view of masturbation, but I would not affirm that it is extremely good for health; everything can harm one's health, even walking or jogging. It is possible that there are cases of nervous and physical depletion and even of

Egon Schiele, Woman in Red, standing, 1913.

loss of interest towards the opposite sex caused by masturbation. There are exceptions to everything.

In preparing to write this chapter I reviewed dozens of books, articles, and research papers on sociology, sexology, and school education, searching for statistical materials on masturbation. It was worthless; I found no reliable statistics, and not because I was bad at looking. People don't want to admit to something so very personal, even to very close friends. Obtaining reliable data would be possible only with methods of neuroleptic programming, 'truth serums', the CIA, the KGB, and the Holy Inquisition. The authors of existing statistics mainly rewrite the numbers from one another without any verification through experience.

We know that by 1948, 99 per cent of 8-12 year old boys masturbated (this percentage seems somewhat inflated even to my modern and liberal mind). There is nothing about girls. However, it is known that in 1953 only 40 per cent of women masturbated before first real sex and in 1990 it was 70 per cent. There can be two reasons for this colossal difference: a) In less than 40 years, women have changed their sexual culture; b) There is less social pressure and women became more open.

It is much simpler to deal with contemporary data. According to the *Sexual Context in France* (Insem, INED, 2006), 90 per cent of men and 60 per cent of women masturbate on a regular basis (and here is gender inequality once again!). The anthropologist Philippe Brenot published a set of new data in 2013 (*A New Praise of Masturbation*): 87 per cent of men and 68 per cent of women masturbate. I actually like the title of his book!

According to common European statistics, 85 per cent to 96 per cent of adult men masturbate. And the most recent data from the USA of September 2016: practically all Americans, the pioneers of the total prohibition of masturbation, do it. 95 per cent of men, both married and single, do it on average 15 times a month and 81 per cent of masturbating women are more family-oriented: single ladies masturbate even more often than single men – 16 times a month – and married women only 8 times! I recommend paying attention not only to numbers, but also to qualitative data: 20 per cent of masturbating men and 30 per cent of masturbating women say that masturbation brings more pleasure than intercourse. Swedish families seem much more solid: only 10 per cent of men and 29 per cent of women share that point of view.

The fact that single people masturbate is not very interesting in contrast to married couples masturbating. This is the kind of information we have to share with high school students and young couples at the beginning of their relationships. We should not teach them all this romantic nonsense which exists only in classic literature, but a good technique of self-pleasuring. If men cannot make use of anything other than primitive movements with a right or left hand – it is so boring being a man! – women keep pace with technological progress. They have left behind candles, cucumbers, bananas, and showers; they even use smart-vibrators and ultrasonic magnetic devices.

After collecting all this data I grew so tired of the various figures and endless contradictions that I was left with no other choice but to provide you with my own statistics, researched only through my life experience, the experiences of my friends, acquaintances, and a little common sense. This statistic is very simple and convincing: all people masturbate, except the very young, very old, very sick, and perhaps the armless.

The Surgeon General of the USA, Dr Minnie Joycelyn Elders, proclaimed from the podium of the United Nations in 1994 that 'masturbation is part of human sexuality and perhaps it should be taught'. Later she affirmed: 'We know that more than 70 to 80 per cent of women masturbate and 90 per cent of men masturbate, and the rest lie.' She was fired by President Clinton for this dangerous opinion offensive to the Church. She was fired exactly one year ago before the President started practising rejected oral intercourse with Monica Lewinsky. However, Dr Elders' feat was not forgotten and the sex-positive retailer Good Vibrations declared International Masturbation Day in her honour. This wonderful event is still celebrated, especially in the Czech Republic, where many thousands of amateurs of group masturbation from all over the world gather on the Old Town Square in Prague. They say that group masturbation brings them an 'amazing feeling of unity and brotherhood', particularly in ejaculating on each other's faces. It is a pity that I am too old to participate in such events.

The US does not keep up with the Czech Republic: the festival of masturbation is not held in the capital, but in the middle of nowhere. However, there is Healthy Friction (Masturbation Vacation) at the annual Burning Man festival, famous all around the world. Men are invited to show their penises and share some masturbation tips.

So can I finally breathe a sigh of relief? Is it all good now? People always masturbated before they were formally prohibited to do so first by God's law for two thousand years and then by doctors and moralists. But are we now back the way we were? Does no one torture him- or herself or their children?

No, the situation is not perfect. Remaining mostly in the past, the paranoid struggle against masturbation has left us with a terrible legacy: its most 'effective' and barbaric method – circumcision of the foreskin that still mutilates millions of boys. The idea of preventing masturbation led to tolerance of the mass circumcision of boys and male babies in Western culture, depriving them forever of the full sexual life destined for them by nature. Not only boys suffered: for decades girls were mutilated too, but they prefer to forget about it.

The idea of the removal of the foreskin and amputation of the clitoris and labia minora as an extreme, but very efficient method against masturbation, appeared in the nineteenth century. The *Medical and Chirugical Dictionary* published in 1877 advises without hesitation the circumcision of the foreskin and infibulation for both sexes. Rohleder, whom I have cited above, recommends the amputation of the clitoris as an extreme method. How wonderful it is that the struggle against 'chronic masturbation in girls and women' is not popular anymore. Otherwise, all our girls and women would have neither clitoris nor labia minora!

The greatest successes in the struggle against masturbation were made in the USA where Lallemand's theory of spermatorrhea was extremely popular. The consequences of this disease were widely discussed in American society. As evidence, they cited the fact that the recognised genius Newton, throughout his entire life, did not waste a drop of semen and that the writer Balzac complained that after a night of wet dreams he couldn't write for a whole day. (I am somehow the opposite: I can neither live nor write without sexual release. I am clearly not going to be a great writer.) I see another explanation, plausible enough in the rapidly growing economy of capitalism and furious competition. The owners of enterprises could not fail to notice that after masturbation the workers were more relaxed and unable to move quickly, which had a negative impact on productivity. This convenient pseudoscientific concept helped to transform sexual energy into productive energy and the male seed into money.

Inspired by the awareness of their historical mission and the big wads of money, doctors eventually came to the brilliant conclusion that the main source of spermatorrhea, and thus the main enemy of society, was the body part that causes a feeling of irritation and criminal erection. The foreskin is a mistake of nature which is no use to a man. The same foreskin which Jews circumcised for many centuries as a sign of their covenant with God. However, in Christian America one had to proceed to circumcision not because of some strange 'covenant', but exclusively to improve male health by reducing the sensitivity of the penis. Many Protestant priests supported this idea because circumcision would decrease sexual pleasure and make men less inclined to have extramarital sex. Simply genius: if there is less sensitivity, there is less pleasure, less sexual desire, fewer sexual 'excesses', the family is more solid!

This solution was warmly supported by a swathe of eminent doctors of Jewish origin, in whom the thousand-year tradition of living without a foreskin instilled a strong aversion to the foreskins of others. It was a clear conflict of interest. Their main argument consisted of the clearly false claim that Jewish boys circumcised shortly after birth never masturbate. The circumcision must be done in the correct way – one has to cut off as much skin as possible so that the potential onanist could not move it when aroused. If a boy's parents were negligent enough not to circumcise him and the boy touches his penis all the time, it must be cut off.

Women got their due too as they personified enhanced sexuality and absolute evil, and communication with them inevitably led to unhealthy ejaculation. It was believed that sexual intercourse with a frigid wife was much less harmful as the man lost much less sperm (sounds like the truth: with lack of novelty the body becomes more economical). A clitoridectomy was recommended for masturbating girls who could become harlots in the future.

This simple surgery allowed girls to partake fully of all the benefits of male circumcision and get better marks at school. Very logical advice, by the way; it is even easier to masturbate an uncircumcised clitoris than an uncircumcised penis.

In this struggle for life and death, special activity was shown by the inventor and doctor, John Kellogg, an ardent supporter of sexual abstinence and the vegetarian diet, which helped to sustain abstinence. He called masturbation 'a vicious devil', which depleted the physical, mental, and moral health of the individual, and he accused it of 31 diseases, including alcoholism, rheumatism, diseases of the genitourinary system, and even cancer of the uterus: 'In my opinion, neither plague, nor war, nor smallpox, nor similar diseases have not led to results so disastrous to the human race as the habit of onanism; it is a destructive force in human society, constantly undermining the health of the nation.'

Kellogg claimed that the victim of masturbation is literally 'dying by his own hand' and so in saving them any methods are to be used, especially the stitching of the foreskin, circumcision,

Auguste Rodin, Reclining Woman with Open Legs and Hands on her Gentials, 1900.
For Rodin, the masturbating woman embodied the principle of life and liberated instinct.

electric shock, applying burning acid to the clitorises of young girls and, if this does not help, a full removal of the clitoris. All this should have been done without anaesthesia in order to make a child stronger and make him remember the horrors of sexuality. Along the way he invented the well-known breakfast cereal, which was supposed to reduce sexual drive and diminish the desire to masturbate (they say that Dr Graham invented the Graham Cracker for the same reasons). However, some argue that he made more money from books against masturbation than he did from Cornflakes. It is possible that we overestimate the power of his religious zeal in the fight against masturbation and underestimate the purely commercial interest: avid masturbators ate badly in the morning, especially when having Cornflakes.

However, the most astonishing statement in English medical literature can be found in the *British Medical Journal* (1935). Its author, Dr R. W. Cockshut, full of love towards morality and hatred towards nature, believed universal circumcision to be not only a very efficient method against masturbation, but also a necessary social action because the loss of sensitivity of our sex organs corresponds to the sacred principles of our civilisation:

> I suggest that all male children should be circumcised. This is "against nature", but that is exactly the reason why it should be done. Nature intends that the adolescent male shall copulate as often and as promiscuously as possible, and to that end covers the sensitive glans so that it shall be ever ready to receive stimuli. Civilisation, on the contrary, requires chastity, and the glans of the circumcised rapidly assume a leathery texture less sensitive than skin. Thus the adolescent has his attention drawn to his penis much less often. I am convinced that masturbation is much less common in the circumcised. With these considerations in view it does not seem apt to argue that "God knows best how to make little boys".

I have not managed to find any serious evidence proving that circumcision impedes masturbation. Circumcised boys and men masturbate as much as uncircumcised ones, but with less pleasure. Mass 'hygienic' circumcision, which started in the USA in the second half of the nineteenth century, is still practised nowadays. The word 'hygienic' was likely added so that parents of non-Jewish or non-Muslim origin would not flee in fear. One had to present circumcision as a secular norm which had nothing to do with religious rules. However, religious circumcision is not very popular in the US: according to the data I have found, there are only 3 million male Jews and 1.5 million male Muslims.

The result was catastrophic. Hundreds of millions of boys had their genitals mutilated. Every year 1.3 million newborn boys are circumcised, which represents roughly 70 per cent of all newborns. There are 110 million circumcised men out of 160 million in America. The biblical chimera of the mortal sin of masturbation was dormant for almost three thousand years, when it suddenly rose from the ashes in secular society and started mutilating innocent children. And this despite the fact that in contemporary America masturbation has transformed from a reprehensible habit into a dear, almost sacred ritual.

American and European girls were lucky: only several thousand girls were subjected to clitoridectomy, mainly in England and America. This medical procedure, recommended by nineteenth-century doctors as an efficient method against masturbation, has never been accepted and is condemned by most countries. Nowadays it is called FGM (Female Genital

South Korean Army.
All the soldiers have to be circumcised.

North Korean Army.
These soldiers have a bit more luck – they've kept their bodies intact
and will do so at least until the possible reunification of the two Koreas.

Mutilation) and this phenomenon, quite widespread in the Northern and Central Africa, is fought by multiple humanitarian organisations. I also participate in this struggle and made a quiet contribution to it in two Western regions of Ethiopia. My charitable foundation, *Espoir*, is also very active in the regions of Somalia and Afar.

Contemporary Islamic scholars and doctors are trying to 'educate' the youth with the same arguments as the European doctors of the seventeenth to nineteenth centuries. As for boys, masturbation leads to weakness, dystrophy, eyesight deterioration, tuberculosis, bad memory, anguish, and suicidal thoughts. And, of course, impotency and disintegration of their future families due to their wives' adulterous behaviour. It can be even worse for girls. In the case of chronic masturbation, they risk a lot: having a saggy chest which secretes some awful white fluid, the thickening of the labia minora and the inflammation of the sex organs, bleeding, and difficulties during intercourse.

The disease for men and women can be 'healed' quite easily: one has to consume less spicy food, meat, tea and coffee, and to sleep on the back or on the belly. However, the best way is still to get rid of the foreskin and the clitoris whose natural secretions provoke desire. The most rigorous Islamic moralists recommend vehemently the obligatory excision of the clitoris and labia minora for all women – no object, no temptation!

There are more than 1 billion circumcised men in the world, including more than 400 million who are circumcised for no religious reason, and approximatively 200 million women who have undergone female genital mutilation. To my mind, this phenomenon cannot be ignored and I will write more about it in my next book.

In the end I cannot resist giving you an example illustrating one of the most important issues of contemporary global politics. I am talking about the growing tensions on the Korean peninsula, where two dissembling Korean states have been at war for more than 64 years.

You will be right to ask what this geopolitical issue has to do with the crusade against masturbation that I have been discussing in this final chapter. As paradoxical as it may seem – a lot – because it shows how a difference in socio-political systems can divide the same people.

Before the Korean War of 1950, Korean men had heard of neither the illness of masturbation nor circumcision. During this war, the American army occupied the Southern part of the country and by the time it left, most Korean men miraculously lost their foreskin: the data suggests that in South Korea 70 per cent to 90 per cent of the 25 million male population have been circumcised. And if we do not count very old men, 100 per cent of the male population is circumcised. It is probable that this sacrifice was a sign of gratitude towards America and its army, which saved the country from communism. Nevertheless, there are two armies opposing each other – a capitalist circumcised one and a communist uncircumcised one. It would be very helpful during a future war with its inevitable casualties: it will be quite easy to understand to which camp the corpse belonged.

This is how the fight against masturbation experienced yet another metamorphosis: it entered the geopolitical level in the twenty-first century in a different part of the world. How do you like this grimace of history?

Epilogue

I would like to believe that most of you took pleasure in reading this book. Those who did not, I thank you for your patience and indulgence. I did not want to impose my values on you, nor change the world. Any sober-minded person understands that the world is impossible to change. All I wanted is to share my views on our world, based exclusively on the laws of nature and common sense. As you already know, I do not accept any other criteria. This is why I made an attempt to separate the wheat from the tares, as the Gospel puts it, and examined all traditional ideals and values.

However, the Gospel says that the wheat is what God gives to us and what can be found only outside of Man, while the tares, including temptation, sin and false teachings, come from the Devil and are proper to human beings. I see things quite differently: my wheat is the biological nature of Man acquired through evolution, while the tares are all those chimeras I described here. I absolutely disagree that the tares are Man incapable of becoming a higher creature.

My only desire while I was writing this book was that it would help my reader, living in today's hectic world, with its constant lack of time, to better understand what to believe and what not to believe.

This is even more topical nowadays than it used to be. Though we live in the twenty-first century, the tares, ripened before the harvest, are as powerful as ever. Superstition, intolerance and religious extremism are increasing everywhere. They are so omnipresent that I sometimes feel the need to cry, three centuries after Voltaire, 'Crush the infamy'.

However, as loud as I might cry, in the foreseeable future, humans are unlikely to follow chimerical ideals to the extent that they become the centre of the universe. The centuries-old traditions entail a relaxing stability, simplify everyday life, and make life easier. There is no doubt that an independent life is more difficult, for it requires daily independent decision-making. The 'wheat' and 'tares' have lived, do live, and will continue to live together as one big happy family.

I am very concerned about our children's faith. Classics of psychoanalysis have fully and clearly explained that childhood is the foundation of a personality and, for the rest of our days, it remains the mirror of our nature. In this regard it is simply impossible not to notice that children are the only unconditionally happy people on earth. Their natural egoism allows them to live only in the present, here and now, free from any ideals, any invented or embellished past or bright future. Small children don't feel any guilt or sin, and do not want to accept the existence of many strange and illogical taboos. They haven't yet devoted their little life to anyone: parents, Church, society or future spouse. They keep it to themselves. This is why children are more perspicacious than adults, often ask 'inconvenient' questions and sometimes generate brilliant ideas.

Their ostensible happiness is often explained by a lack of adult worries and problems in their life. I think the real reason is that they are free from dangerous illusions. School starts the intensive process of indoctrination with the higher wisdom of the Sacred Books. It exhorts them to curb their young flesh in order to learn the value of sacred marriage and the sin of divorce. And the children's eyesight fades. One cannot deny that children growing up in deeply religious families are much less carefree, that they play less and are not as happy as others. You can see their already grown-up eyes, revealing the power of the Chimera. This scary monster is not from a fairy tale, but from impending adulthood.

The Chimera of the golden age explains that in the beginning of time, before Man was expelled from paradise, all people were sinless, immortal, and lived happily ever after. Today we live among a huge number of unforgivable sins, and therefore suffer from loneliness, get sick and die like flies. But there is hope: once we overcome the sin, we will become immortal once again.

The Chimera of idealistic romance and the sanctity of marriage has deeply embedded itself in most of us from early childhood. It says that men and women are creatures from different planets, that marriage is made in heaven, and is therefore indissoluble, that human sexuality is by its nature monogamous and that true love dies only in the grave. The result was not long in coming: daily hypocrisy, constant cheating, thriving family violence, and the anguish of divorce. The Chimera of the bright future – the apotheosis of human stupidity – was extremely popular in the twentieth century all over the world. It has somehow faded away after killing more than one hundred million people. All nations believe that a bright future will happen one day, and that for now Man has to wait and believe that the worse life is now, the better it will be for his descendants. In the world yet to come.

Alas, chimeric marketing will inevitably fail. And not because we sin, have little faith, live unrighteous lives, but because the Illusion cannot become a reality. None of these chimeras has ever existed; they don't now and they never will. There has been no golden age, no eternal life, there is no hope for a bright future, and love is only true when it is doomed to end.

Chimeras make us play a dangerous game with our own destinies. We must all ask ourselves a simple question: what do monotheism's promises give to us and what do they take? I do not doubt that the intensity of emotions provoked by God are capable of consoling in the most desperate situation and of preparing for the most difficult, one's death. It is obvious that religion is a powerful painkiller or tranquiliser. Who would accept leaving this delusional hope and reconcile with the idea that it all ends with worms in one's grave? As I said in my introduction: if the probability of eternal life was not 50 but just 5 per cent, I would be the first to burn this book. I would immediately go to the church and never leave it again. Moreover, I am ready to admit that monotheism can be a unifying force which forms the moral ideals for those who are not capable of doing so themselves.

But the dark side of faith is more significant than its positive side. One has to pay for it with one's freedom. One has to give up so much for eternal life, without any proof that it exists. In order to maintain its power, religion destroys the harmony of human nature and divides it into two incompatible parts – body and soul. It makes Man refuse much of his natural pleasure and replace it with useless adoration of God. It makes Man a zombie by inculcating in him that his mind is weak and that he is sinful. It makes him fear not to be 'saved' and receive a punishment instead of resurrection, according to the notion of Good and Evil religion imposes. These notions are in general radically different from the ones nature has given to Man. Religion is the most powerful drug and it never ceases to push Man towards the edge and to demand him to exchange his only life for an illusion of the eternal one.

There will be no reward in this life. Monotheistic religions consider secular ethics to be imperfect and transient. However, it is impossible to build universal ethics with these religions, since each of them has its own god and is intolerant to other beliefs. Why else did religions fight heresies and each other for millennia and why do they continue to do so? They have only a couple of things in common: their doctrine of the fundamental littleness of Man compared to God. Man's only merit can be his obedience.

Moreover, these religions thrive to expand from the private sphere and conquer the public one and penetrate the state itself. A spiritual life – the act of creation of new values for oneself and other people – becomes an illusion in monotheistic religions. The result of this religious life based exclusively on the Revelation, which blurs the natural human values comprehensible to our mind and senses, is not spiritual perfection, but a denial of one's own essence. In reality there is only the imperfect, problematic, painful, and at the same time delightful present where there is human life. We will have no other life, and no one is able to give it to us.

Our Western civilisation is most affected with Christianity, which has formed the core of our values and has been the main force in the formation of our mentality and lifestyle. It has weakened. Jesus Christ did not come back and did not give any sense to our lives. He left us alone with evil, sin, suffering and death. Christianity has been fought by the anticlericalism of the French Revolution. It became less aggressive thanks to the separation of the state and church and the common school movement. However, it is far from being dead (Nietzsche was wrong!) and it still has an influence on our politics and culture. We cannot forget Christianity so quickly, which is still present in our holidays, births, weddings, and funerals. The symbol of death and agony, the crucified Jesus, is still the media star number one. It will flourish again at any opportunity, and will demand money from the state, justifying its needs by the proliferation of sin and the necessity to build new churches. It will most certainly try to reintroduce religious education at public schools. The secular state will only finance its future executioner. I am always surprised to see that people who seem to defend the principles of the secular state still have the genetic memory of atheism being a sin. Thus, they feel it indispensable to exhort us to respect 'religious values'.

I never felt this way. I have long been indifferent to any concepts of the divine: my family has never had its god and I never liked any others. However, when I was working on this book, I discovered the idea of God the Creator which is different from the monotheistic one.

My God the Creator does not affirm that He created Man in His image and gave him an immortal soul. He never insisted on the littleness of Man. On the contrary, He has always respected human intellect. It means that humanity is doing just fine – there is no need to aspire to return to the golden age or spend one's life suffering in wait for the Last Judgement. He has never passed the divine commandments to anybody. He is one for all nations and accepts anyone who believes in Him. His existence does not have any influence on our life: He does not see us, does not listen to us, does not read our minds, He never promised us eternal life. And the most important is that it is useless to pray to Him since He cannot help. This God is the centre of light and warmth. He is the fire. Man aspires to Him in order to get warm and inspired, and not to repent his sins. Man aspires to Him as small children want to be near their parents, gods in human form.

I am not alone in my understanding of the divine: it has always existed, at least in Christianity. Only a very naïve person would think that Christ's teaching and the Christian doctrine formed by St Paul, which sees in Man only a sinner, are equal.

There was a powerful movement of Gnosticism which believed our world to be created not by God, but by the evil Demiurge. God, who exists outside of this world and does not show any interest in human deeds, personifies the Good and Spirit. Man has a limitless freedom of will and is responsible for all of his actions. He should not aspire to unite with God because he fears a non-existent punishment after death. He should do it voluntarily. The Gnostics were tolerant of all people, whether they believed in Christ or not, for sin is not the property of an individual, but an inherent characteristic of the material world and humanity as a whole. There was no place for saints in Gnosticism.

The true Christians, the Cathars, were decimated during the Second Crusade. They chanted love and denied any possibility of revenge, murder, or war. They helped each other, recognised the civil and religious rights of women. They rejected the notion of original sin, the expiatory sacrifice of Christ, the icons and the cult of the saints.

The philosopher and theologian Pelagius has yet another Christianity to offer. Man is created free, good and capable of creating its own ethics and he does not need any asceticism. The original sin has happened once and it cannot be inherited by future generations. It is not the cause of illness, death and evil. If one is obliged to sin, it cannot be considered as a sin. All other sins can be vanquished independently, thanks to our free will: it is Man who sins and it is only him who can save himself.

Other theologians consider this 'alternative' Christianity to be the only true one. Who knows, probably if it had won the ideology war, we would have lived in a different world where the terrifying God would have become what it is supposed to be – just an idol, an absolutely useless painted piece of wood and a hardcover book distributed in the hundreds of millions of copies. However, it lost, and it was the most radical doctrine that won. We live in a world where glorification of death, asceticism and oppression of sexuality have reigned for more than two thousand years. Extremism feels well when the reason is persecuted.

What do I wish for my readers? Nothing special and unattainable.

Stop poisoning your life with useless thoughts about good and bad in human beings. Man is what he is and he is neither good nor bad. He cannot be changed. Forget about your original sinful nature: you have committed no original sin. You will still get sick and die but you will certainly live better with original sin.

Love yourself and live in harmony with your body and its natural instincts. No one can love you more, and give you more, than you yourself. Satisfy all your desires without thinking about religious dogma and the pressure of public morality. The many restrictions of the penal code are enough. Be proud of your natural instincts.

Get rid of everything that prevents you from loving yourself and enjoying life: close all religious books, delete all religious channels, stop idealising other people and listening to their opinion. Do not blindly believe what is written, and doubt everything, including this book.

Do not read the society pages and gossip about the sex lives of politicians and stars. Everyone has the right and even the responsibility to live the way they want and can. It is much healthier to read books on delicious and healthy food. Do not fear to express your opinion even if you have more enemies than allies.

This is when the true miracle will happen. You will finally dedicate your life not to chimeras, but to yourself. You will stop waiting for the bright future and do everything you can to make your life better. You will be happy and share your happiness with others. With everyone you truly love.

In short, I wish you to live without chimeras and not live a lie.

Bibliography

in order of appearance

■ Chapter I ■
Reason or Chimeras

le Bon, Gustave, *The Psychology of the Peoples* (New York, 1898)

Plato, *Plato in Twelve Volumes*, Vol. 12 translated by Harold N. Fowler, Cambridge, MA, Harvard University Press; London, William Heinemann Ltd. 1921, 152a

Epicurus, *Letter to Menoeceus*, translated by Robert Drew Hicks (CreateSpace Independent Publishing Platform, 2016)

Seneca, Lucius Annaeus, *Moral letters to Lucilius*, translated by Richard Mott Gummere, J C Rolfe (Createspace Independent Publishing Platform, 2016)

Aurelius, Marcus, *Meditations*, translated by Maxwell Staniforth (London, Penguin, 2005 [1964])

Plato, Theaetetus and Sophist, ed. Christopher Rowe (Cambridge, Cambridge University Press, 2015)

Seneca, Lucius Annaeus, *The Works, Of blessed life,* tr. Thomas Lodge, 1620.

Freud, Sigmund, *The Future of an Illusion,* trans. and ed. James Strachey (London, Norton & Company, Incorporated, W. W., 1961)

Judaeus, Philo, *The Works of Philo Judaeus: Volume I*, translated by Charles Duke Yonge (Ontario, Andesite Press, 2017)

Maimonides, Moses, *The Guide for the Perplexed,* translated by Shlomo Pines (Chicago, University of Chicago Press, 1963)

Gersonides, Levi, *Perush' al ha-Torah (Commentary on the Pentateuch),* Vol. I-VI, eds. Baruch Brenner and Eli Fraiman (Maale Adumim, Maaliot, 1992-2008).

Halevi, Yehudah, *Kitab al Khazari,* translated by Hartwig Hirschfeld (London, George Routledge & Sons, Ltd., 1905)

Kellner, Menahem, "R. Isaac bar Sheshet's Responsum Concerning the Study of Greek Philosophy", *Tradition* 14 (1975): 110–18.

Martyr, Justin, *On the Resurrection and Addresses to the Greeks* (Ohio, Beloved Publishing LLC, 2015)

Tatian the Assyrian, *Address To The Greeks*, translated by J. E. Ryland, in *The Ante-Nicene Fathers.* Vol. II, eds. Alexander Roberts, Sir James Donaldson (Massachusetts, Hendrickson Publishers, 1999)

Tertullian, *The Sacred Writings of...Tertullian,* Vol. II, translated by Peter Holmes, Sidney Thelwall.

The Ante-Nicene Fathers: Vol. III – Latin Christianity, ed. by rev. Alexander Roberts, Sir James Donaldson & Arthur Cleveland Coxe (New York, 2007)

of Nyssa, Gregory, *Gregory of Nyssa Against Eunomius* (London, Aeterna Press, 2016 [1892])

Chrysostom, John, *Homilies of St John Chrysostom on the Epistles of St Paul the Apostle to Timothy, Titus, and Philemon*, translated by the members of the English church (Oxford, J.H. Parker, 1843)

Hitchens, Christopher, *God is not great* (London, Atlantic Books, 2007)

of Clairvaux, Saint Bernard, *Commentary on the Song of Songs*, retrieved from https://archive.org/stream/StBernardsCommentaryOnTheSongOfSongs/StBernardOnTheSongOfSongsall_djvu.txt (Etext arranged by Darrell Wright, 2008)

Aquinas, St Thomas, *Summa Theologica Volume I – Part I*, translated by St Thomas Aquinas (New York, 2007)

Dawkins, Richard, *The God Delusion* (London, Bantam Books, 2006)

Spinoza, Baruch, *Tractatus theologico – politicus*, translated by Samuel Shirley: new introduction 1998 by Seymour Feldman (Indianapolis, Hackett Publishing Company, 1998)

Lewis, Charles, *The Problem of Pain*, (Québec, 2016 [1940]) (possibly HarperCollins)

Nietzsche, Friedrich, *The Antichrist*, translated by Henry Louis Mencken (Newport Beach, The Noontide Press, 1997)

Hammond, Robert, *The Philosophy Of Alfarabi And Its Influence On Medieval Thought* (New York, Book Press, 1947)

Al 'Arabi, Ibn, *Meccan Revelations,* 2 vols. (New York, Pir Press, 2002–2004)

Al-Ghazali, *The Book of Knowledge*, translated by Nabih Amin Faris

Thiessen, Matthew, *Contesting Conversion. Genealogy, Circumcision & Identity in Ancient Judaism & Christianity* (New York, Oxford University Press, 2011)

Theophilus, *Theophilus of Antioch,* translated by the rev. Marcus Dods (London, Aeterna Press, 2016)

Russell, Bertrand, *Why I Am Not a Christian* (Lulu Press, Inc., 2016 [1927])

■ Chapter II ■
The Sovereign of Evil

Chrysostom, John, *Commentary on the Sages: Commentary on Job* (St John Crysostom: Commentaries on the Sages), translated by Robert Charles Hill (Brookline, Massachusetts, Holy Cross Orthodox Press, 2006)

Luther, Martin, *The Bondage of the Will,* translated by J.I. Packer, O.R. Johnston (Michigan, Revell, 1990)

Leibniz, Gottfried Wilhelm, *Theodicy: Essays on the Goodness of God the Freedom of Man and the Origin of Evil* (CreateSpace Independent Publishing Platform, 2015)

Kant, Immanuel, "On the miscarriage of all philosophical trials in theodicy" *in* Religion within the Boundaries of Mere Reason And Other Writings, translated and edited by Allen Wood, George di Giovanni (Cambridge, Cambridge University Press, 1998)

Van Inwagen, Peter, "The Argument from Evil" *in* Joel Feinberg, Russ Shafer-Landau, *Reason and Responsibility: Readings in Some Basic Problems of Philosophy* (Boston, Cengage Learning, 2015)

Adams, Marilyn McCord, *Christ and Horrors: The Coherence of Christology* (Cambridge, Cambridge University Press, 2006)

Neusner, Jacob, *Understanding Jewish Theology. Classical Issues and Modern Perspectives* (New York, Classics in Judaic Studies, Global Publications, Binghamton University, 2001)

Tauber, Ezriel, *Darkness Before Dawn, The Holocaust And Growth Through Suffering* (Shalheves, 1992)

Grodzinsky, Rabbi Chaim Ozer, *Achiezer,* vol. III (Vilna, 1939)

Miller, Avigdor HaKohen, *A divine Madness: Rabbi Avigdor Miller's Defense of Hashem in the Matter of the Holocaust* (New York, Simchas Hachaim Pubishing, 2013)

Berkovits, Eliezer, *Faith After the Holocaust* (New York, KTAV Publishing House, 1973), p. 89.

Cohen, Arthur Allen, *The Tremendum: A Theological Interpretation of the Holocaust* (New York, Crossroad Publishing, 1981)

Fackenheim, Emil, *The Jewish Return into History: Reflections in the Age of Auschwitz and a New Jerusalem* (New York, Schocken Books, 1978)

Maybaum, Ignaz, *The Face of God After Auschwitz* (Amsterdam, Polak & Van Gennep1965)

Greenberg, Irving, *The Third Great Cycle in Jewish History* (New York, National Jewish Resource Centre, 1981)

Rubenstein, Richard L., 'The State of Jewish Belief: A Symposium,' *Commentary*, August 1966 (Vol. 42:2)

Rubenstein, Richard L., *After Auschwitz: History, Theology, and Contemporary Judaism* (Baltimore, John Hopkins University Press, 1992)

Wiesel, Elie, *All Rivers Run to the Sea: Memoirs,* translated by Marion Wiesel (New York, Alfred A. Knopf, 1995)

■ Chapter III ■
Hello Death, Our First Step Towards Heaven

Graham, A.C., tr. *The Book of Lieh-tzŭ: A Classic of Tao* (New York, Colombia University Press, 1960).

Rousseau, Jean-Jacques, *Julie,* or *The New Heloise* Julie, or the New Heloise: Letters of Two Lovers Who Live in a Small Town · at the Foot of the Alps (Hanover and London, University Press of New England,1997)

Kant, Immanuel, *Anthropology from a Pragmatic Point of View*, translated by Robert B. Louden (Cambridge, Cambridge University Press, 2006)

Nietzsche, Friedrich, *The Gay Science. With a Prelude in German Rhymes and an Appendix of Songs* translated by Adrian del Caro (Cambridge, Cambridge University Press, 2001)

Camus, Albert, *The Myth of Sisyphus,* translated by Justin O'Brien (London, Penguin Classics, 2013 [1942]

Eliade, Mircea, *Occultism, Witchcraft, and Cultural Fashions: Essays in Comparative Religion* (Chicago, University of Chicago Press, 1976)

Rousseau, Jean-Jacques, *Julie,* or *The New Heloise* Julie, or the New Heloise: Letters of Two Lovers Who Live in a Small Town at the Foot of the Alps (Hanover and London, University Press of New England, 1997)

Freud, Sigmund, *Reflections on War and Death,* translated by A. A. Brill (Auckland, The Floating Press, 2014 [1915])

Freud, Sigmund, *Totem and Taboo. Resemblances between the Mental Lives of Savages and Neurotics,* translated by A. A. Brill (e-artnow, 2016)

Epicurus, *Letter to Menoeceus*, translated by Robert Drew Hicks (CreateSpace Independent Publishing Platform, 2016)

Seneca, Lucius Annaeus, *Moral letters to Lucilius*, translated by Richard Mott Gummere, J.C. Rolfe (Createspace Independent Publishing Platform, 2016)

Aurelius, Marcus, *Meditations*, translated by Maxwell Staniforth (London, Penguin Classics, 2005 [1964])

Toland, John, *Letters to Serena* (B. Lintot, 1704)

Goodhart, Sandor, 'From the Sacred to the Holy: René Girard; Emmanuel Levinas, and Substitution' In *The Prophetic Law: Essays in Judaism, Girardianism, Literary Reading, and the Ethical* (Michigan State University Press, East Lansing, 2014)

Kaplan, Rabbi Aryeh, *Mir bil sozdan dlya menya [The World was Created for Me]* (Jerusalem, Shamir Publishing, 1987)

Taliqani, Mahmud, Mutahhari, Murtaza, Shariati, Ali, Abedi, Mehdi, Legenhausen, Gary, *Jihad and Shahadat: Struggle and Martyrdom in Islam* (Institute for Researc and Islamic Studies, Houston, 1986)

Celsus, *On the True Doctrine: A Discourse Against the Christians*, translated by R. Joseph Hoffman (Oxford University Press, New York, 1987)

Minucius Felix, Marcus, *Ancient Christian Writers. The Octavius of Marcus Minucius Felix* translated by G. W. Clarke (Paulist Press, New York, 1974)

Nietzsche, Friedrich, *The Antichrist*, translated by Henry Louis Mencken (Noontide Press, Newport Beach, 1997)

Kierkegaard, Søren, *Sickness Unto Death*, translated by Alastair Hannay (Penguin Classics, London, 1989)

Climacus, John, *Ladder of divine Ascent,* translated by Archimandrite Lazarus Moore (Faber & Faber, New York, 1959)

À Kempis, Thomas, *The Imitation of Christ* (Mercer University Press, Macon, 2007)

Berdyaev, Nicholas, *The Destiny of Man: An Experiment of Paradoxical Ethics* (Zovremennye Zapiski, Paris, 1931)

of Assisi, Saint Francis, 'The First Version of the Letter to the Faithful' in *Francis and Clare: The Complete Works* (Paulist Press, Mahwah, 1982)

Grigg, Russel, *Why Did God Impose the Death Penalty for Sin*, https://creation.com/why-did-god-impose-the-death-penalty-for-sin.

Dickens, Charles, *Pictures from Italy* (Penguin Classics, London, 1998)

Philostratus, Eunapius, *Lives of the Sophists. Eunapius: Lives of the Philosophers and Sophists,* translated by Wilmer C. Wright (Loeb Classical Library, Cambridge, 1921)

Duby, Georges, *Age of Cathedrals: Art and Society, 980–1420,* translated by Eleanor Levieux, Barbara Thompson (University of Chicago Press, Chicago, 1983)

Huizinga, Johan, *The Waning of the Middle Ages* (Benediction Classics, Oxford, 2010)

Eco, Umberto, *Inventing the Enemy,* translated Richard Dixon (Houghton Mifflin Harcourt, Boston, 2012)

Montaigne, Michel de, *The Complete Essays,* translation M. A. Screech (Penguin Classics, London, 1991)

406

■ Chapter IV ■
The Unbearable Joy of Suffering

Kundera, Milan, *The Unbearable Lightness of Being,* translated by Michael Henry Heim (London, Faber & Faber, 1984)

Nietzsche, Friedrich, *The Gay Science. With a Prelude in German Rhymes and an Appendix of Songs* translated by Adrian del Caro (Cambridge University Press, Cambridge, 2001)

Freud, Sigmund, *Totem and Taboo. Resemblances between the Mental Lives of Savages and Neurotics,* translated by A. A. Brill (e-artnow, 2016)

Guthrie, William Keith Chambers, *The Sophists* (Cambridge University Press, Cambridge, 1971)

Aristotle, *Nicomachean Ethics,* translated by W. D. Ross (Batoche Books, Kitchener, 1999)

Epicurus, *Letter to Menoeceus,* translated by Robert Drew Hicks (CreateSpace Independent Publishing Platform, 2016)

Seneca, Lucius Annaeus, *Moral letters to Lucilius,* translated by Richard Mott Gummere, J C Rolfe (Createspace Independent Publishing Platform, 2016)

Freud, Sigmund, *The Future of an Illusion,* translated and edited James Strachey (Hogarth Press, London, 1961)

Eliade, Mircea, *The Myth of the Eternal Return: Or, Cosmos and History,* translated by Williard R. Task (Princeton University Press, Princeton, 1992)

'Nasreddin Hodja Stories', compiled and retold in English by Lale Eskicioglu http://www.readliterature.com/hodjastories.htm

Luther, Martin, 'Sermon at Coburg on Cross and Suffering' [1530], *Works*, American Edition, vol. 51, translated by John W. Doberstein (Fortress Press, Philadelphia, 1959)

Scupoli, Lorenzo, of the Holy Mountain, Nicodemus, *Unseen Warfare: The Spiritual Combat and Path to Paradise of Lorenzo Scupoli* (St Vladimir's Seminary Press, New York,1978)

Nietzsche, Friedrich, *On the Genealogy of Morality*, translated by Carol Diethe (Cambridge University Press, Cambridge, 1994)

Rotterdam, Erasmus, *The Manual of the Christian Knight* (London, 1533 [1513]; reprinted by Methuen and Co, London, 1905

Lewis, Charles, *The Problem of Pain* (Québec, 2016 [1940])

Nazianzen, Gregory, *Select Orations of Saint Gregory Nazianzen* translated by Charles Gordon Browne (Aeterna Press, London, 2012)

Levering, Matthew, *The Theology of Augustine: An Introductory Guide to His Most Important Works* (Baker Academic, Minneapolis, 2013)

Theophan the Recluse, Correspondence, in Russian, Lepta Kniga, Moscow, 2007.

of Nazianzus, Gregory, *Carmen Lugubre 45,* translated by P. Gilbert in P. Gilbert 'On God and Man' (Crestwood, New York, 1994)

Saint Cyprian, *Treatises* (Fathers of the Church, New York, 1958)

Bertram, James Glass, *Flagellation & the flagellants; a history of the rod in all countries,*1824-1892 (William Reeves, London, 1877), retrieved from https://archive.org/stream/B20442336/B20442336_djvu.txt (accessed 11/01/18)

Delumeau, Jean, *Sin and Fear: The emergence of a Western Guilt Culture 13th-18th centuries*, translated by Eric Nicholson (St Martin's Press, New York, 1990)

Sysoev, Daniel, 'Christ's martyr next door', pravda.ru 23/03/2011

Nietzsche, Friedrich, *Thus Spoke Zarathustra* (Bill Chapko, 2010)

Osho, *The Psychology of the Esoteric* (Diamond Books, New Delhi, 2004)

'Dhammacakkappavattana Sutta' (The Wheel of Law) translated by Soma Thera (BPS Online Edition, 2010), retrieved from http://www.londonbuddhistvihara.org/Dhammacakkapavattanasutta.pdf

Nietzsche, Friedrich, *The Antichrist*, translated by Henry Louis Mencken, (Noontide Press, Newport Beach, 1997

Berdyaev, Nicholas, *The Destiny of Man: An Experiment of Paradoxical Ethics* (Paris, 1931)

Berdyaev, Nicolas, *Spirit and Reality* translated by George Reavey (London, 1939)

Berdyaev, Nicholas, *The Destiny of Man: An Experiment of Paradoxical Ethics* (Sovremennye Zapiski, Paris, 1931)

'The Rhino Horn: A Teaching for the Hemit-minded' *in Sutta Nipāta* translated by Laurence Khantipalo Mills (SuttaCentral, 2015)

Al-Bukhari, Muhammed Ibn Ismaiel, *The Translation of the Meanings of Sahih Al-Bukhari*: *Arabic-English (English and Arabic Edition)* translated by Muhammad M. Khan (Dar-us-Salam Publications, Houston, 1997)

Sahih al-Bukhari, Book 75, Hadith 8 https://sunnah.com/bukhari/75

The Gardens of the Righteous', hadith 1323 http://bewley.virtualave.net/riyad7.html (accessed 16/08/16)

■ Chapter V ■
The Great Battle Against Pleasure

Blake, William, *The Marriage of Heaven and Hell* (Dover Publications, New York, 1994)

Maslow, Abraham Harold, *Motivation and Personality* (Penguin Classics, New York, 1987[1954])

Epicurus, *Letter to Menoeceus,* translated by Robert Drew Hicks (CreateSpace Independent Publishing Platform, 2016)

Chrysostom, John, *Homilies of St John Chrysostom on the Epistles of St Paul the Apostle to Timothy, Titus, and Philemon,* translated by the members of the English church (J. Parker, Oxford, 1843)

of the Cross, Saint John, *Ascent of Mount Carmel,* translated by David Lewis (Cosimo Inc, New York, 2007)

Kierkegaard, Søren, *Sickness Unto Death,* translated by Alastair Hannay (Pearson, London, 1989)

the Syrian, Isaac, *The Ascetical Homilies of St Isaac,* translated by the Holy Transfiguration Monastery (Holy Transfiguration Monastery, Boston, 1984)

Antonius, *The Lives of Simeon Stylites* translated by Robert Doran (Cistercian Publications, Kalamazoo, 1992)

Saint Cyprian, *Treatises* (Fathers of the Church, New York, 1958)

of Alexandria, Clement, *Christ the Educator,* translated by Simon P. Wood (Catholic University of America, Washington, 1954)

Tertullian, *On the Apparel of Women* (Codex Spiritualis Press, Conneticut, 2012)

Cyprian of Carthage, 'On the Public Shows' in *The Sacred Writings of Saint Cyprian* (Jazzybee Verlag, Altenmunster, 2012)

Chrysostom, John, *Homilies on the Gospel of St Matthew,* translated by George Prevost (Gorgias Press, Piscataway, 2010)

of Alexandria, Clement, *Christ the Educator,* translated by Simon P. Wood (Fathers of the Church Inc., 1954)

Saint John of Kronstadt, *Complete Works,* in Russian, Moscow, 1894

Marx, Karl, Engels, Friedrich, *The Communist Manifesto* (Penguin Classics, London, 2002)

John XXIII, Mater et Magistra, May 15, 1961, http://w2.vatican.va/content/john-xxiii/en/encyclicals/documents/hf_j-xxiii_enc_15051961_mater.html.

Climacus, John, *The Ladder of divine Ascent (The Classics of Western Spirituality),* translated by Colm Luibheid, Norman Russell (Paulist Press, New York, 1982)

Osho, *The Psychology of the Esoteric* (Diamond Books, New Delhi, 2004)

'Dhammacakkappavattana Sutta' (The Wheel of Law) translated by Soma Thera (BPS Online Edition, 2010), retrieved from http://www.londonbuddhistvihara.org/Dhammacakkapavattanasutta.pdf

The Middle Length Discourses of the Buddha: A Translation of the Majjhima Nikaya (New York, 2005)

Maimonides, Moses, *The Guide for the Perplexed,* translated by Shlomo Pines (University of Chicago Press, Chicago, 1963)

Al-Ghazali, *Wonders of the Heart,* translated by Walter James Skellie (Islamic Book Trust, Malaysia, 2007)

Nietzsche, Friedrich, *The Geneology of Morals* (Oxford University Press, Oxford, 1996)

■ **Chapter VI** ■
Sex is God's Greatest Enemy

Montaigne, Michel de, *The Complete Essays,* translated by M. A. Screech (Penguin Classics, London, 1991)

Herodotus, *The Histories,* translated by Tom Holland (Penguin Classics, London, 2013)

Mircea Eliade, *Patterns in Comparative Religion,* translated by Rosemary Sheed (Sheed and Ward, New York, 1958)

Montaigne, Michel de, *The Complete Essays,* translated by M. A. Screech (Penguin Classics, London, 1991)

Frazer, James George, *Folklore in the Old Testament Studies in Comparative Religion Legend and Law* (Kessinger Publishing, Whitefish, 2010)

of Hippo, Saint Augustine, *The City of God,* translated by Marcus Dods (Random House, New York, 1950)

Ganzfried, Solomon, *Code of Jewish law = (Kitzur schulchan aruch): a compilation of Jewish laws and customs* translated by Hyman E. Goldin (Hebrew Publishing, New York, 1928)

of Alexandria, Philo, 'On the Migration of Abraham' in *The Works of Philo,* translated by C. D. Yonge, retrieved from http://www.friendsofsabbath.org/Further_Research/e-books/PHILO.pdf

Maimonides, Mose, 'Chapter 7' in *Mishneh Torah: Hilchot Yesodei HaTorah*, retrieved from http://www.chabad.org/kabbalah/article_cdo/aid/380357/jewish/Becoming-a-Prophet.htm

Freud, Sigmund, *Moses and Monotheism* (Martino Fine Books, Eastford, 2010)

Nefzawi, Sheik, *The Perfumed Garden* (Kessinger Publishing, Whitefish, 2010)

Al-Ghazali, *Book on the Etiquette of Marriage,* translated by Madelain Farah, retrieved from https://www.ghazali.org/works/marriage.htm

al-Albaani, Sheikh Muhammad Naasirudden, *The Etiquettes of Marriage and Wedding*, retrieved from https://islamhouse.com/fr/books/1275/

Saint Augustine, *On Marriage and Concupiscence* (CreateSpace Independent Publishing Platform, 2015)

of Hippo, Saint Augustine, *The City of God*, translated by Marcus Dods (The Modern Library, Random House, New York, 1950)

Chrysostom, John, *Homilies on the Gospel of St Matthew,* translated by George Prevost (Gorgias Press, Piscataway, 2010)

Chrysostom, John, *On Virginity,* translated by Sally Reiger Shore in *On Virginity, Against Remarriage,* p. 1-128 (Edwin Mellen Press, New York, 1983)

von Nettesheim, Agrippa Heinrich Cornelius, *The Glory of Women: or, a Treatise declaring the excellency and preheminence of Women above Men,* translated by Edward Fleetwood (Robert Ibbiston, London, 1652)

Saint Augustine, *On Marriage and Concupiscence* (CreateSpace Independent Publishing Platform, 2015)

of Alexandria, Clement, *Christ the Educator,* translated by Simon P. Wood (Fathers of the Church Inc., 1954)

Zalkind, Aron, *The Twelve Commandments of Revolutionary Sex*, (The Sverdlov Communist University Press, Moscow, 1924)

Orwell, George, *1984* (Penguin, London, 2004)

Reich, William, *The Mass Psychology of Fascism* (Farrar, Strauss & Giroux, New York, 1970)

Assisi, Francis, *The Little Flowers of Saint Francis of Assisi,* translated by Dom Roger Hudleston (Heritage Press, New York, 1965)

Kramer, Heinrich Godfrey, *Malleus Maleficarum, Or: The Hammer of Witches,* translated by Montague Summers, (readaclassic.com, 2011)

Nietzsche, Friedrich, *The Antichrist,* translated by Henry Louis Mencken (Noontide Press, Newport Beach, 1997)

Huysmans, Joris-Karl, *Ecrits sur l'art : L'Art moderne ; Certains ; Trois primitifs* (Editions Flammarion, Paris, 2008)

First Lateran Council 1123 A.D., *Canons,* 'No. 7' and 'No. 21', retrieved from http://www. papalencyclicals.net/Councils/ecum09.htm

Strachey, James (ed.), *The Standard Edition of the Complete Psychological Works of Sigmund Freud* (London, 1953-1974)

Nietzsche, Friedrich, *On the Genealogy of Morality,* translated by Carol Diethe (Cambridge University Press, Cambridge, 1994)

De Mause, Lloyd, 'The Universality of Incest', *The Journal of Psychohistory,* Vol. 19, №2 (Lloyd de Mause, 1991)

Arnobius, *The Sacred Writings of Arnobius* (Jazzybee Verlag, Altenmunster, 2012)

Maimonides, Moses, *The Guide for the Perplexed,* translated by Shlomo Pines (University of Chicago Press, Chicago, 1963)

■ Chapter VIII ■
The Crusade Against Onanism

Anonymous, *Onania; or The Heinous Sin of Self-Pollution, And All Its Frightful Consequences, In Both Sexes* (H. Cooke, London, 1718)

Petit, M. A., *Onan, ou le tombeau du Mont-Cindre* (Chez les Principaux Libraires, Lyon, 1809)

Tissot, Samuel, *L'Onanisme, Essai sur les maladies produites par la masturbation* (Paris, 1760, Garnier Freres, [1905])

Monlau, Pedro Felipe, *Higiene del Matrimonio&El libro de los casados (Imprenta y Estereotipia de M. Rivadeneyra, Madrid, 1858)*

Monlau, Pedro Felipe, *Elementos de higiene privada* (Imprenta y Estereotipia de M. Rivadeneyra, Barcelona, 1846)

Rousseau, Jean-Jacques, *Émile, ou de l'éducation* (Paris, 1762, Classiques Garnier, [1999])

Lallemand, François, *Des pertes séminales involontaires* [*Involuntary loss of semen*] (Bechet Jeune, Paris, 1836-1842)

Jozan, Emile, *D'une cause fréquente et peu connue d'épuisement prématuré: traité des pertes séminales, à l'usage des gens du monde, contenant les causes, les symptômes, la marche et le traite- ment de cette grave maladie* [*On a Frequent and Little-Known Cause of Premature Exhaustion*] (J. Masson, Paris, 1864)

Cockshut R. W., 'Circumcision', *British Medical Journal,* vol. 2, 1935

Acknowledgements

I would like to thank all those close to me who have been by my side throughout the years I spent writing this, I can only imagine how difficult it must have been for them to have their husband, father, or friend there in person but unavailable to them because he was immersed in research, writing, or both.

A huge thank you must go to those who helped me to gather all the material and who discussed my ideas and interpretations with me. Every one of them demonstrated patience in the face of my stubbornness and provided me with excellent advice that I naturally did not always follow.

I would also like to thank my editors: you wrestled with many things and through you the book was all the better for it. Nevertheless, I am also grateful to you for respecting my style of thinking and opinions. I personally wrote every line of this work and remain fully responsible for it.

Photo credits

1.1 De Agostini Picture Library / G. Nimatallah / Bridgeman Images; 1.2 Duccio di Buoninsegna, (c.1278-1318) / National Gallery, London, UK / Bridgeman Images; 1.3 Tarker / Bridgeman Images; 1.4 Reni, Guido (1575-1642) / Galleria Borghese, Rome, Lazio, Italy / Bridgeman Images; 1.5 Gozzoli, Benozzo di Lese di Sandro (1420-97) / Metropolitan Museum of Art, New York, USA / Bridgeman Images; 1.6 Rembrandt Harmensz. van Rijn (1606-69) / State Hermitage Museum, St Petersburg, Russia / Bridgeman Images

2.1 Bonnat, Leon Joseph Florentin (1833-1922) / Musée Bonnat, Bayonne, France / Bridgeman Images; 2.2 Jenny Matthews / Alamy Stock Photo; 2.3 somjai ledlod / Shutterstock.com; 2.4 REUTERS/Navesh Chitrakar; 2.5 Tallandier / Bridgeman Images; 2.6 Cott Nero E II pt2 f.20v / British Library, London, UK / © British Library Board. All Rights Reserved / Bridgeman Images; 2.7 Buyenlarge Archive/UIG / Bridgeman Images; 2.8 Universal History Archive/UIG / Bridgeman Images

3.1 British Library, London, UK / © British Library Board. All Rights Reserved / Bridgeman Images; 3.2 Tarker / Bridgeman Images; 3.3 Liron-Afuta / Shutterstock.com; 3.4 Creative Commons; 3.5 trabantos / Shutterstock.com; 3.6 Caravaggio, Michelangelo Merisi da (1571-1610) / Galleria Borghese, Rome, Lazio, Italy / Bridgeman Images ; 3.7 akg-images / Paul Koudounaris; 3.8 Marie-Lan Nguyen; 3.9 f.321v-322r / Metropolitan Museum of Art, New York, USA / Bridgeman Images; 3.10 f.321v-322r / Metropolitan Museum of Art, New York, USA / Bridgeman Images; 3.11 Albrecht Kauw, 1649 (watatercolour), Manuel, Niklaus (c.1484-1530) / Bernisches Historisches Museum, Bern, Switzerland / De Agostini Picture Library / A. Dagli Orti / Bridgeman Images ; 3.12 akg-images / Paul Koudounaris; 3.13 INTERFOTO / Alamy Stock Photo

4.1 Memling, Hans (c.1433-94) / Muzeum Narodowe, Gdansk, Poland / Bridgeman Images; 4.2 Bosch, Hieronymus (c.1450-1516) / Museum voor Schone Kunsten, Ghent, Belgium / © Lukas – Art in Flanders VZW / Bridgeman Images; 4.3 Grunewald, Matthias (Mathis Nithart Gothart) (c.1480-1528) / Musee d'Unterlinden, Colmar, France / Bridgeman Images; 4.4 Grunewald, Matthias (Mathis Nithart Gothart) (c.1480-1528) / Musee d'Unterlinden, Colmar, France / Bridgeman Images; 4.5 Grunewald, Matthias (Mathis Nithart Gothart) (c.1480-1528) / Musee d'Unterlinden, Colmar, France / Bridgeman Images; 4.6 Gregorio B. Dantes Jr./Pacific Press / Alamy Stock; 4.7 REUTERS/Fayaz Kabli; 4.8 Majority World/ UIG / Bridgeman Images

5.1 Giovanni di Paolo di Grazia (1403-82) / Fogg Art Museum, Harvard Art Museums, USA / Gift of Sir Joseph Duveen / Bridgeman Images; 5.2 Botticelli, Sandro (Alessandro di Mariano di Vanni Filipepi) (1444/5-1510) / Galleria degli Uffizi, Florence, Tuscany, Italy / Bridgeman Images ; 5.3 William-Adolphe Bouguereau (1825-1905) / Art Collection 2 / Alamy Stock Photo; 5.4 Jan Styka – Saint Peter / Art Collection 3 / Alamy Stock Photo; 5.5 Russian School, (16th century) / Kremlin Museums, Moscow, Russia / Bridgeman Images; 5.6 REUTERS/ Ronen Zvulun; 5.7 Vatican Museums and Galleries, Vatican City / Photo © Anatoly Pronin / Bridgeman Images; 5.8 Murillo, Bartolome Esteban (1618-82) / Private Collection / Photo © Christie's Images / Bridgeman Images

6.1 Cranach, Lucas, the Elder (1472-1553) / Alte Pinakothek, Munich, Germany / Bridgeman Images ; 6.2 Archaeological Museum of Heraklion, Crete, Greece / Bridgeman Images; 6.3 Grunewald, Matthias (Mathis Nithart Gothart) (c.1480-1528) / Musée de l'oeuvre de Notre-Dame, Strasbourg, France / Bridgeman Images; 6.4 Masaccio, Tommaso (1401-28) / Brancacci Chapel, Santa Maria del Carmine, Florence, Italy / Bridgeman Images; 6.5 Gian Lorenzo Bernini (1598-1680) Santa Maria della Vittoria, Rome, Italy / De Agostini Picture Library / G. Nimatallah / Bridgeman Images; 6.6 Louvre, Paris, France / Peter Willi / Bridgeman Images; 6.7 Ikonen-Museum, Recklinghausen, Germany / Bridgeman Images; 6.8 Fouquet, Jean (c.1420-80) / Koninklijk Museum voor Schone Kunsten, Antwerp, Belgium / © Lukas – Art in Flanders VZW / Bridgeman Images; 6.9 Martin Van Maele La Grande Danse macabre des vifs 24 / Paul Fearn / Alamy Stock Photo; 6.10 Martin Van Maele La Grande Danse macabre des vifs 15 / Paul Fearn / Alamy Stock Photo; 6.11 Basilica of Sainte-Marie-Madeleine, Vézelay, France / Photo © Bednorz Images / Bridgeman Images

7.1 Félicien Rops / Archivart / Alamy Stock Photo; 7.2 Dollman, John Charles (1851-1934) / Art Gallery of New South Wales, Sydney, Australia / Gift of Captain Guy Dollman 1935 / Bridgeman Images; 7.3 Vallin, Jacques Antoine (1760-p.1831) (circle of) / Musee d'Art Thomas Henry, Cherbourg, France / Bridgeman Images; 7.4 Lovis Corinth / Artepics / Alamy Stock Photo; 7.5 Buonarroti, Michelangelo (1475-1564) / Kimbell Art Museum, Fort Worth, Texas, USA / Bridgeman Images; 7.6 Goya y Lucientes, Francisco Jose de (1746-1828) (attr. to) / Chateau de Villandry, Indre-Et-Loire, France / Bridgeman Images; 7.7 The Bodleian Library, University of Oxford, MS. Douce 195 [fol.24r]; 7.8 Papety, Dominique Louis (1815-49) / Wallace Collection, London, UK / Bridgeman Images; 7.9 José Benlliure y Gil (1858-1937); 7.10 Martin Van Maele La Grande Danse macabre des vifs 06 / Paul Fearn / Alamy Stock Photo; 7.11 Cornelis Cornelisz van Haarlem / Peter Horree / Alamy Stock Photo; 7.12 K. Chimin Wong and Wu Lien-teh, History of Chinese Medicine, 2nd edition, Shanghai, 1936 / Pictures from History / Bridgeman Images; 7.13-20 Skoptsy / E. Pelikan, *Sudebno-medizinskie issledovaniya skopchestva*, St Petersburg / 1872

8.1 EdgarLOwen.com; 8.2 De Agostini Picture Library / G. Dagli Orti / Bridgeman Images

8.3 Klimt, Gustav (1862-1918) / Heritage Image Partnership Ltd / Alamy Stock Photo; 8.4 Gelder, Aert de /ART Collection / Alamy Stock Photo; 8.5 Schiele, Egon (1890-1918) / Private Collection / Bridgeman Images; 8.6 Wellcome Collection; 8.7-10 Des habitudes secrètes ou des maladies produites par l'onanisme chez les femmes par M. le docteur Rozier, Paris, Audin, 1829, source: BIU Santé Paris ; 8.11 Martin Van Maele, La Grande Danse macabre des vifs 21 / Paul Fearn / Alamy Stock Photo; 8.12 Paul Fearn / Alamy Stock Photo; 8.13 J.L. Milton «Pathology… Spermatorrhoea»: urethral ring' / Wellcome Collection; 8.14 Zichy, Mihaly von (1827-1906) / Private Collection / The Stapleton Collection / Bridgeman Images; 8.15 Félicien Rops / Art Collection 2 / Alamy Stock Photo; 8.16 Egon Schiele / akg-images; 8.17 Rodin Auguste. 1840-1917 / akg-images; 8.18 Yeongsik Im / Shutterstock.com; 8.19 Astrelok / Shutterstock.com

Cover: Artepicks Alamy Stock Photo / Bridgeman / Prisma Archivo

Contents

Find the complete bibliography and more about the author
on the website of the book

Printed in Italy by LEGO S.p.A., Vicenza
May 2018